WAR, COMMERCE, AND
INTERNATIONAL LAW

WAR, COMMERCE, AND INTERNATIONAL LAW

JAMES THUO GATHII

UNIVERSITY PRESS

Oxford University Press, Inc., publishes works that further Oxford University's objective of excellence in research, scholarship, and education.

Oxford New York
Auckland Cape Town Dar es Salaam Hong Kong Karachi Kuala Lumpur Madrid
Melbourne Mexico City Nairobi New Delhi Shanghai Taipei Toronto

With offices in
Argentina Austria Brazil Chile Czech Republic France Greece Guatemala Hungary
Italy Japan Poland Portugal Singapore South Korea Switzerland Thailand
Turkey Ukraine Vietnam

Copyright © 2010 by James Thuo Gathii

Published by Oxford University Press, Inc.
198 Madison Avenue, New York, New York 10016

Oxford is a registered trademark of Oxford University Press
Oxford University Press is a registered trademark of Oxford University Press, Inc.

All rights reserved. No part of this publication may be reproduced, stored in a retrieval system, or transmitted, in any form or by any means, electronic, mechanical, photocopying, recording, or otherwise, without the prior permission of Oxford University Press, Inc.

___

Library of Congress Cataloging-in-Publication Data
Gathii, James Thuo.
  War, commerce, and international law / James Thuo Gathii.
    p. cm.
  Includes bibliographical references and index.
  ISBN 978-0-19-534102-7 (hardback: alk. paper)
  1. War (International law)—Economic aspects. 2. War—Economic aspects.
  I. Title.
  KZ6385.G38 2010
  343'.087–dc22   2009030620

___

1 2 3 4 5 6 7 8 9
Printed in the United States of America on acid-free paper

Note to Readers
This publication is designed to provide accurate and authoritative information in regard to the subject matter covered. It is based upon sources believed to be accurate and reliable and is intended to be current as of the time it was written. It is sold with the understanding that the publisher is not engaged in rendering legal, accounting, or other professional services. If legal advice or other expert assistance is required, the services of a competent professional person should be sought. Also, to confirm that the information has not been affected or changed by recent developments, traditional legal research techniques should be used, including checking primary sources where appropriate.

(Based on the Declaration of Principles jointly adopted by a Committee of the American Bar Association and a Committee of Publishers and Associations.)

You may order this or any other Oxford University Press publication by visiting the Oxford University Press website at www.oup.com

CONTENTS

Acknowledgments ix
Introduction xiii

CHAPTER 1. FOUR RELATIONSHIPS BETWEEN WAR AND COMMERCE 1

   I. Introduction 1
   II. The Relationship Between Confiscation and Commerce 2
      A. Confiscation Trumps Commerce 2
      B. Commerce Trumps Confiscation 14
      C. Balancing between Commerce and Confiscation 20
      D. The Exceptional Circumstances Doctrine 28
   III. Conclusions 40

CHAPTER 2. THE EFFECT OF CONQUEST ON PRIVATE PROPERTY AND CONTRACT RIGHTS 43

   I. Introduction 43
   II. The Prohibition of Confiscation of Private Property Under Classical Customary International Law 46
      A. Rationales Underlying the Exemption of Property and Contract Rights from Extinction upon Conquest 47
      B. Unevenness and Inconsistency in the Application of the Traditional Canon Proscribing Extinction of Private Property Rights and Contracts 51
   III. Hegemonic Erosion of a Customary International Law Canon over Non-European "Property" 58
      A. *West Rand Central Gold Mining Company v. The King*: Conquest Does Not Limit the Prerogative

of the Crown to Extinguish Corporate Private Property 59
B. *Daniel F. Strother v. John B. C. Lucas*: Native American Land Claims Do Not Survive Conquest 61

IV. Conclusions 69

CHAPTER 3. THE EFFECT OF OCCUPATION ON PRIVATE PROPERTY AND CONTRACT RIGHTS 71

I. The Iraqi Occupation 76
  A. Private Property under Occupation: The Applicable Law and Available Remedies 77
  B. Private Property Claims of Iraqis 81
  C. Private Property Claims of Iraqi Women 82

II. Transforming Occupied Iraq 85
  A. The Applicable Rules 85
  B. The Iraqi Conquest and Occupation Reforms 88

III. The Effect of Conquest and Occupation on Iraqi Private and Economic Rights in a Comparative Context and Remedial Options 93
  A. Comparing and Contrasting De-Fascistization, De-Baathification, De-Nazification, and the Liquidation of Japanese Zaibatsu 93

IV. Conclusions 100

CHAPTER 4. THE CREATIVE TENSION BETWEEN COMMERCIAL FREEDOM AND BELLIGERENT RIGHTS 105

I. Introduction 105

II. The United States' Military Weaknesses and Economic Dependence in the Late-Eighteenth Century 107

III. International Legal Responses to U.S. Military and Economic Weaknesses 115

    A. The Early Justice Marshall: Defending Virginian Debtors Against British Creditors 115

    B. Marshall's Government Experience: Development of International Legal Jurisprudence Grounded in the Policy of Neutrality 119

    C. The Later Marshall: Using the Court to Solidify the Commercial Rights of Non-Belligerents and Neutrals During Wartime 121

  IV. A Different Rule for United States–Native American Economic Relations 137

  V. Conclusions 143

CHAPTER 5. WAR, INVESTMENT, AND INTERNATIONAL LAW 145

  I. Introduction 145

  II. The Relevance of War in Shaping Rules of International Economic Governance 146

  III. The Calvo Clause and its Progeny 157

  IV. African and Asian Challenges to International Economic Law and Governance 158

  V. State Responsibility for War Destruction in Investment Disputes 168

  VI. From Forcible Interventions to Coercive and Unequal Economic Relations 185

  VII. Conclusions 188

CHAPTER 6. SLIPPAGES OF THE PUBLIC AND PRIVATE IN RESOURCE WARS 191

  I. Introduction 191

  II. Genealogical Antecedents to Today's Resource Wars 200

       A. Antecedent One: Mercantile Companies with Special Reference to King Leopold's International African Association 200

       B. Antecedent Two: The Acquisition of Swazi Territory by the British and the *Sobhuza II* Case 207

  III. Resource Conflicts and Slippages of The Public and Private Distinction in International Law 211

  IV. Conclusions 220

CHAPTER 7. COMMERCIALIZING WARS 223

    I. Introduction 223

   II. Commercializing War and Deferring Accountability 225

  III. International Law and Mercenaries 230

  IV. The Accountability of Economic Actors in War 237

   V. The Limits of Self-Regulation for Private Military and Security Companies 242

  VI. Emerging Rules and Norms to Regulate Private Security Companies 247

 VII. Conclusions 252

Index 257

ACKNOWLEDGMENTS

This book would not have been written without the help of so many people. First, I would like thank my immediate family: my wife, Caroline and our two sons, Michael and Ethan, who provided enormous and loving support to me in so many ways. While this book was written over a number of years, it crystallized during my sabbatical in the 2007–2008 academic year. I am grateful to Dean Thomas Guernsey at Albany Law School for providing that opportunity. In particular I want to thank Professor David Kennedy, who provided outstanding support and guidance since I worked under his supervision for my doctoral work at Harvard Law School. His own work influenced my ideas in this book and my other work.

Many friends who I met there and elsewhere including Antony Anghie, Bhupinder Chimni, Makau Wa Mutua, Willy Mutunga, Obiora Okafor, Nathaniel Berman, Balakrishnan Rajagopal, Karin Mickelson, Celestine Nyamu-Musembi, Joel Ngugi, Sylvia Kangara, Vasuki Nesiah, Robert Wai, Kerry Rittich, Penelope Andrews, Dianne Otto, Mary O'Connell, William Alford, Ruth Okediji, Athena Mutua, Ruth Gordon, Ikechi Mbeoji, Obi Aginam, Robert Chu, Siba Grovogui, Branwen Gruffydd Jones, Patricia Kameri-Mbote, Joe Kieyah and Ibironke Odumosu contributed in one way or another to the work in this book. These friends, over a number of years, provided opportunities for me to explore (and shape) my ideas with them at workshops, conferences, or over a drink or meal. I was particularly inspired by the work of Antony Anghie, whose important book, *Imperialism, Sovereignty and the Making of International Law, 2005*, made a new contribution to our understanding of the colonial origins of international law. I must, of course mention that this book also owes a debt of gratitude to the work of many of the members of the Third World Approaches to International Law network (many of whom were already mentioned). I cannot forget my colleagues at Albany Law School, including Timothy Lytton, Stephen Gottlieb, Peter Halewood, Donna Young, Maria Grahn-Farley, Anthony Farley, Stephen Clark, and Alicia Ouellette with whom I had numerous discussions as this book progressed. I would also like to thank the School of Law at the University of Nairobi, which hosted me during my sabbatical while I completed this book, for providing an especially conducive atmosphere for reflection. The University of Illinois Law School also provided further room for active reflection on the book project by inviting me to teach a short course on war, commerce, and international law while on sabbatical. Over the years, while I wrote this book, I benefited from very useful research assistance from the following: James Leary, Elaine Haonian, Robert Gregor, Maryam Kougholi, Abena Asante, Patrick Sorsby, Adam Herbst, Kohei Higo, Tania Magoon, Raji Zeidan, Joshua Boone, Joseph Rogers and Guinevere Seaward. The reference librarians at Albany Law School, Mary Wood and Robert Emery, provided invaluable assistance in accessing everything I needed to complete this project, and I thank them for their professionalism. Thanks too to Linda Murray and Evette Dejesus, my legal assistants, for providing important order and support as I wrote the book. At Oxford University Press, I thank Chris Collins, my editor, and his assistant, Jessica Picone, for their patience and very helpful assistance. I also thank Erica Woods Tucker for overseeing the production of this book so effortlessly and to my dear brother, Stephen Gathii, for his help and support particularly for ideas for the book cover.

Parts of this book were previously published in different form: "Foreign and Other Economic Rights Upon Conquest and Under Occupation: Iraq in Comparative and Historical Context," 25 University of Pennsylvania Journal of International Economic Law, 491(2004); "Commerce, Conquest and Wartime Confiscation" 31 Brooklyn Journal of International Law, 709 (2006); and "The American Origins of Liberal and Illiberal Regimes of International Economic Governance in the Marshall Court," 54 Buffalo Law Review 765 (2006); "How American Support for Freedom of Commerce Legitimized King Leopold's Territorial Ambitions in the Congo," in Trade as the Guarantor of Peace, Liberty and Security? Critical, Historical and Empirical Perspectives (ASIL Studies in Transnational Legal Policy), 97, Padideh Alai, Tomer Broude & Colin B. Picker, (eds.) (2006); "War, Investment, and International Law," 11 International Community Law Review 353 (2009). To these journals,

I am grateful for providing me with the first stub at exploring the ideas that I examine at fuller length in this book.

Last but not least, I thank my parents, Joseph and Theresiah Gathii, for their unfailing love and support over the years. I dedicate this book to them.

INTRODUCTION

Modern international law has repudiated war between States except in the exceptional instances of self-defense and collective authorization by the UN Security Council. In addition, since the early twentieth century, pillage, plunder, and confiscation of private property and contract rights have been prohibited during wartime. This is equally true in the context of occupation.[1]

However, these prohibitions are less the rule than the exception in the wars and conflicts that continue to characterize the first part of the twenty-first century. In addition, these rules are seldom applied with uniformity from war to war or from one occupation to another. Sometimes, security concerns are cited as requiring destruction or seizure of private property and contracts, even if they are not tainted with an enemy status.

Thus, the relationship between war and commerce invariably involves relationships of power between militarily powerful and less powerful States; between occupying and occupied States; between private military companies and weak and poor States; between countries in the center and on the periphery of the world system; and lately, between lawless bandits and a myriad of other non-State actors, on the one hand, and States and alliances of States, on the other.[2] For the

---

1. The same could be said in the context of conquest, but conquest is no longer permissible under international law. *But see,* Eugene Kontorovich, *International Responses to Territorial Conquest,* 102 AM. SOC'Y INT'L L. PROC. (2009) (examining five episodes of territorial conquest in the post-World War II era and arguing there are at least 12 to 18 cases of forcible conquest since the UN Charter came into force).

2. The underlying tension that I address in this book between powerful and less (weak, poor) powerful countries is not aimed at suggesting that these two groups of States are homogeneous among themselves and totally different between themselves. For example, a less powerful State in the center periphery system may nevertheless be powerful relative to its constituent groups. Similarly, the exercise of power by a State is seldom unilateral and unchallenged both within and without it. My strong versus weak State axis is informed by the secular absolutism of the external relations of a State that has

most part, international law provides rules to justify the primacy of a belligerent's right to defend its security interests as it does to defend the rights of a neutral to engage in safe commerce during war.

To explore the relationship between commerce and international law this book addresses the following questions. In what respects are commerce and war two sides of the same coin?; in what respects do they depend on or complete each other? Can the two exist in contradiction? In essence, I am interested in the changing definitions of war and commerce in international law; their historical connections; their changing applications and interpretations in different places at the same time and at different times; as well as their functional linkages and slippages. The materials studied in this book show that commerce and war do not necessarily "exclude each other, but rather they frequently blur with and into each other."[3] Within such a relationship, war and commerce appear less as sharp antidotes to each other. Rather, they appear to depend on and complete each other. Thus in the resource wars of the contemporary period, the commercial benefits that go to the various actors involved predispose them to continuing rather than stopping resource-extraction wars. In short, the relationship between war and commerce is not fixed and unchanging. Thus when rules of international law seek to separate the two with a view to giving commerce safe passage from and during war, such compartmentalization is often tenuous.[4]

The study of the fluid relationship between war and commerce lays the backdrop against which I trace the extent to which the legacy of colonial disempowerment has continued into the era of decolonization. Indeed, although the doctrines and rules of international law relating

---

arisen in modern international law recently articulated by ANTHONY CARTY, PHILOSOPHY OF INTERNATIONAL LAW (2007).

3. See GIORGIO AGAMBEN, STATE OF EXCEPTION 23 (Trans. K. Attell, 2005).

4. In Chapter 1, I summarize four relationships between war and commerce that emerge in this book: war trumps commerce (where belligerents justify their confiscation of enemy property as the spoils of war or as justified on security grounds); commerce trumps war (where rules permit the continuation of commerce during wartime); a balance between war and commerce (embodied in rules such as those relating to neutrality), and the extraordinary circumstances doctrine under which a powerful belligerent justifies conquest or confiscation of the property or territory based on the perceived backwardness of a people.

to war and commerce and the historical record covered do inhere fairness between all States, particularly because of the modern guarantees of sovereign equality and self-determination, I am able to show that at various times these rules and doctrines nevertheless simultaneously carry forward within them the legacy of imperial and colonial conquests.

This analysis of continuity and discontinuity involves investigating how rules of international law relating to war and commerce are crafted, applied, and adjudicated from several perspectives and in a variety of contexts, including those involving conquest, occupation, resource wars, and the regulation of private military companies. This analysis is conducted by examining not only the rules themselves, but also the choices made between alternative meanings ascribed to a particular rule in its application in one context as opposed to another.[5] In so doing, I discuss the choices made in crafting rules relating to war and commerce one way as opposed to another or applying and adjudicating these rules in a manner that precludes equally legitimate conclusions that may, for example, be consistent with the interests of militarily less powerful countries. Thus, in this book I have sought to consistently expose these outcomes rather than merely focus on the content of the rules and doctrines of international law relating to war and commerce.

The materials covered in the book roughly fall into three historical periods. In the pre-1850 period, the United States is the periphery while the center of the international system in Europe. We thus see in the diplomatic history and in the emerging jurisprudence of the U.S. Supreme Court in this period, moral condemnations of the interference of its commercial ventures by the naval powers that Great Britain, Germany, and France were. While in this period, the United States was declaring that advances in the morality and conscience of nations gave commerce safe passage over the rights of belligerents to interfere with it, the United States was also declaring that discovery and conquest gave it good title to Native American territory.

---

5. The kind of bias I am interested in is therefore not that the origin of these rules is European or from the United States. In addition, I am not making the claim that bias is merely traceable to the fact that "the big countries seldom play by the rules."

Similarly, the pre-1850 period is the era of ascendance of natural law in the law of nations. Hugo Grotius argued that natural law justified the slavery of prisoners of war because it was a milder punishment than the previous practice of killing them. Natural law thus justified one inhumanity because it was superior to another. Indeed, the pre-1850 period is one in which the right to conquer and the results from conquest could be as much justified as they would have been rejected under the law of nations. This was, after all, international law's natural law period where distinctions between law and morality and between the public and private spheres had yet to be sharply separated in international law. Positivists who followed the natural law tradition foregrounded sovereign consent as the basis of obligation in international law and began the process of its systematic codification.

In the second period, from the mid-nineteenth to about the mid-twentieth century, positivism contributed to the consolidation of the separation of public authority and private right and rearranging the rules and doctrines of international law accordingly. For example, the Berlin Conference of 1875 covered in Chapter 6 sought to extend the most liberal rules of free commerce as an antidote to the illegitimate slave trade; the Hague Peace conferences resulted in a series of important rules including those proscribing confiscation of private property during wartime and prohibiting the use of force in the collection of State debt—a theme that I address in Chapter 5.

Period three began with the post-World War II period of a move to self-determination for all peoples and the accompanying United Nations guarantees of the equality of all States, as well as the prohibition of the use of force in international relations. It was also the golden era of international institutions with the birth of the United Nations and the Bretton Woods institutions—with their aspiration of the universal membership of all States and of the functional separation of their respective political and economic mandates. It was also the period when the center of the international system was indisputably the United States.

Moving forward to this early period of the twenty-first century, this post-World War II order witnessed renewed challenges to its State centeredness. It was a period in which the role of private actors and commercial interests in contemporary warfare—the privatization of warfare and the role of mercenaries gained unprecedented ascendance.

Conventional warfare between States is therefore no longer the only or always the most significant type of conflict on the international scene. Weak and poor States, in particular, no longer have a monopoly of the use of violence, if they ever had any. This period is in some ways therefore reminiscent of the period before 1850, where the distinction between public and private uses of violence had not crystallized as it eventually did in twentieth-century European and American history.[6]

This book, however, is less about these historical periods; rather, a primary aim of this book is to investigate how the rules of international law relating to war and commerce show the differences between doctrinal and legal arrangements, and their applications in the center and periphery of the world system in each of these periods particularly in relations between militarily powerful and weak States. It is also a study of the normative relativity of the kind of soft law and self-regulatory regimes that have powerfully emerged in the context of resource wars and the regulation of private military companies covered in Chapters 6 and 7 respectively.

Looking at these three historical epochs, I see less a history of continuity or progress in which commercial and trade relations are freed from the vagaries of war than a messy story in which the relationships between law and morality, on the one hand, and violence on the other, produced and continue to produce new rules, soft norms, and doctrines of international law as well as replaying old rules, norms, and doctrines. These three periods therefore represent changing ideas about the relationship between public power and private right that challenge the claim that international law today stands undoubtedly "forward of subjugation, in independence and equality."[7]

This book shows that it is not infrequent that in times of strength, States favor not being bound by restraints of international law to make war and confiscate or destroy the property of their enemies, whereas in times of weakness they rely on it to argue against instances of plunder, pillage, and confiscation of private property by powerful States. Stronger States do not necessarily repudiate this modern regime of prohibitions in such cases. Instead, they rely on traditional

---

6. See Chapter 2 for the full discussion.

7. David Kennedy, *Remarks by David Kennedy: On Panel on International Law and Religion*, 82 AM. SOC'Y INT'L L. PROC. 200 (1988).

doctrines that embrace the absolutist rule by which a successful belligerent has a right to confiscate the property of a defeated belligerent. Under extreme interpretations of this doctrine, successful war justifies the taking of the private property of a defeated belligerent government and its supporters particularly in wars between European and non-European peoples.

As a young nation in the late-eighteenth and early-nineteenth centuries, the United States often deferred to the naval and military superiority of the British and French. Concurrently, the U.S. Supreme Court enunciated the most liberal rules announcing the prohibition of interference of its commerce from being subject to confiscation, sequestration and attacks by countries that had superior naval abilities. The Court was also instrumental in developing concepts of neutrality in commerce well in advance of the Hague Peace Conferences of the early twentieth century. Thus as I show in Chapter 4, military weakness was a crucial factor in predisposing the United States to favor strong anticonfiscation rules and rules of neutrality during wartime as a way of safeguarding its interests as an independent commercial nation in the wars between other countries in that period.

By examining the jurisprudence of the Marshall court, I show the controversies that surrounded prize law required judicial innovation, because they presented issues without clear answers under the pre-1850 law of nations or in the precedents of the court at the time. For example, it was unclear if recaptured neutrals were liable for salvage or whether a neutral had the right to condemn or confiscate the goods of a neutral if carried in a hostile vessel—questions that touched on the interests and sensitivities of citizens from the militarily more powerful European States in relation to the United States. The Court more often than not decided such cases in favor of the most liberal rules that permitted the continuation of commerce in the face of war—notwithstanding the fact that those cases would equally have been decided in favor of belligerent rights with the consequence of frustrating free commerce by confiscating and sequestrating the cargo of neutrals and those from militarily weak States.

Similarly, Chapter 5 shows how Venezuela, a militarily weak State, in the early part of the twentieth century strongly advocated against collection of State debts through forcible means, a principle that also came to be recognized in Hague Peace Conferences. The Drago doctrine, named after the Venezuelan Foreign Minister at the time, was enshrined in the codification of the laws of war in the Hague Peace conference of 1907. Thus, military strength and weakness with regard to the early United States and Venezuela in the early-twentieth century played a role in the articulation and development of rules surrounding commerce and war.

What is also remarkable is that, although international weakness of the early United States was consistent with supporting strong anticonfiscation and antidepredation rules, at home, the United States supported conquest as a justification for taking the lands of Native Americans without compensation. Similarly, weak and poor countries at the international level today often exhibit this dual sensibility—support for strong anticonfiscation rules internationally and disregard for such rules at home in dealing with local populations and peoples in the context of war and rebellion. This is exhibited by the example of the Sri Lankan government's military offensive against the Tamil Tigers, which resulted in damage to the property of a foreign investor discussed in Chapter 5. The foreign investor then successfully sued the Sri Lankan government for war damage under a bilateral investment treaty. The liability of the Sri Lankan government for war destruction while exercising a right to defend its national security also illustrates the asymmetric differences in the entitlements protecting the rights of foreign investors, on the one hand, and the prerogatives of poor States hosting those investors to protect their national security interests, on the other.

A similar, although not perfectly analogous, example is the U.S. support for strong anticonfiscation rules in its commercial relations with European States of the late-eighteenth and early-nineteenth centuries at a time when the U.S. Supreme Court was declaring war was necessary to deal with Native Americans, because regular commercial contact could not be established with them. These two foregoing examples show that the relationship between war and commerce cannot easily be categorized into epochs where commerce prevails over war or vice versa.

Even now, in the early part of the twenty-first century, the U.S. support for freedom of commerce particularly for its business and commercial interests occurs simultaneously with restrictions on commerce insofar as it is inconsistent with its national security interests.⁸ What brings these two examples together is the relationship of a militarily powerful State on the one side and a militarily weaker one on the other—in the late eighteenth to early nineteenth century, the same relationship between a militarily weak United States on the one hand, and the naval powers that the Netherlands, Great Britain, France, and Germany were, on the other hand. In addition, between the United States, on the one hand, the Native Indian populations that had been militarily defeated in the course of building the United States, on the other.

I offer one other example showing differential applications of the rules prohibiting interference with the private property. The protection of the private property of Italians and Germans during the Allied occupation after World War II, for example, stands in sharp contrast with the widespread disregard of these rules in non-Western societies, such as Japan, after the World War II, for example, and more recently in Iraq following the U.S.-British–led war that began in early 2003.⁹ The confiscation of Jewish property by the German Nazi government also demonstrates how racist arguments justified the disregard not only of private property rights, but also of the lives and dignity of a people.

The foregoing example has similarities with the justifications used to justify the seizure of Native American territory by the Marshall court alluded to earlier. The occupation of Iraq in 2003 and accompanying de-Baathification, which involved taking the property of the Baathists, and the justifications for assuming title over Native American Indian territory were not simply based on the absolute power of the U.S.-led coalition. Rather, in both instances the presumed backwardness of the Indians and the Iraqi Baathists respectively, as well as the proclaimed superiority of the values of the early American republic and the U.S. British led occupying coalition played into the equation. As I argue in Chapter 1, there is a genealogical similarity in the racially charged jurisprudence with respect to

---

8. See, e.g., Marjorie Florestal, *Terror on the High Seas and the Trade and Development Implications of US National Security Measures*, 72 BROOK. L. REV. 385 (2007) (discussing the adverse economic and development outcomes of security measures aimed at reducing the risk of terrorists from using shipping containers arriving in the United States to attack the United States).

9. See Chapter 3 for the full discussion.

INTRODUCTION xxi

non-Christians and non-Europeans in the encounter between metropolitan policy and local colonial encounter.[10] In this book, I show that the extraterritorial expansion of metropolitan authority in the context of war and commerce produced predictable routines for ordering relations between powerful and less powerful States and entities, between public and private power as well as between peoples from vastly different cultural and racial backgrounds.

The key to my analysis in this book is therefore to identify the extent to which the legacy of colonial disempowerment has continued into the era of decolonization in the relationship between war and commerce in international law. I show that, although the doctrines and rules of international law relating to war and commerce and the historical record covered inhere fairness between all States, the application, interpretation, and adjudication of these rules and doctrines in a variety of contexts nevertheless simultaneously carry forward within them the legacy of imperialism or colonial conquest.

Although international law carries within it this legacy of imperialism and colonial conquest, its guarantees of the equality of all States and of the human rights of all individuals continue to offer hope for poor and weak States and individuals everywhere. This is equally true in the war and commerce context. Indeed, as I argue in Chapter 7, although current definitions of mercenaries in international law do not explicitly prohibit mercenaries motivated by ideological or religious reasons or the prospect of getting paid with natural resources, it would be foolhardy to argue that mercenaries motivated for unprohibited reasons are therefore automatically unregulated. This would effectively acquiesce to the permissibility of mercenarism inconsistently with the prohibition of the use of force especially given that this prohibition is recognized both as *jus cogens* norm[11] as well as

---

10. On this, I borrow from ANTONY ANGHIE, IMPERIALISM, SOVEREIGNTY AND THE MAKING OF INTERNATIONAL LAW 2005.

11. *Case Concerning Military and Paramilitary Activities in and Against Nicaragua*, [1986] I.C.J. Rep. 14, at 100, *available at* http://www.icj-cij.org (follow "Cases" hyperlink; then follow "List of All Cases" hyperlink; then follow "More..." hyperlink under "1984: Military and Paramilitary Activities in and against Nicaragua (Nicaragua *v.* United States of America)"; then follow "Judgments" hyperlink).

a cornerstone principle of the UN charter.[12] In addition, mercenaries still pose the threat of deposing governments in weak States, which is inconsistent with current antimercenarism international law rules, or providing arms to rebel groups that pose a threat to governments that reign terror on citizens. The payment of mercenaries or private security and military companies by governments with natural or mineral resources is also inconsistent with both the letter and spirit of the international legal norms on permanent sovereignty over natural resources, and the principles relating to the right to development. In short, although I have focused on exposing the legacy of imperialism and colonialism in the context of war and commerce, I firmly believe that the liberal guarantees of international law have much to offer to counter these inegalitarian tendencies. Exposing the tendency in international law toward inegalitarian consequences in the war and commerce context is, in my view, a useful step toward moving in a positive direction.

---

12. *Case Concerning Armed Activities on the Territory of the Congo*, [2005] I.C.J. Rep. 1, ¶ 148, *available at* http://icj-cij.org (follow "Cases" hyperlink; then follow "List of All Cases" hyperlink; then follow "More . . . " hyperlink under "1999: Armed Activities on the Territory of the Congo (Democratic Republic of the Congo *v.* Uganda)"; then follow "Judgments" hyperlink).

1. FOUR RELATIONSHIPS BETWEEN WAR AND COMMERCE

> All the Advantage procured by Conquest is to secure what we possess ourselves, or to gain the Possessions of others, that is, the produce of their Country, and the Acquisitions of their Labor and Industry; and if these can be obtained by fair Means, and by their own Consent, sure it must be more eligible than to exhort them by Force.
>
> This is certainly more easily and effectually done by a well regulated Commerce, than by Arms.[1]

I. INTRODUCTION

In this chapter, I explore the relationship between commerce, conquest, and the confiscation of private property in the context of war. I do this by examining illustrative case law and other materials. In doing so, I make two primary arguments. My first argument is that the relationship between conquest and confiscation, on the one hand, and commerce, on the other, is not fixed or even stable but rather occupies a continuum between at least two extremes: on one end, the absolute power of a sovereign belligerent to confiscate enemy private property upon conquest, and on the other, the policy of allowing commerce safe passage during times of war. Given this relationship, my second argument is that it is inaccurate to portray the eighteenth and nineteenth centuries as periods during which the absolute power of confiscation prevailed, and the twentieth century as a period in which a rule prohibiting confiscation of private property during wartime held sway.[2]

---

1. 3 CATO'S LETTERS: ESSAYS ON LIBERTY, CIVIL AND RELIGIOUS 179 (John Trenchard & Thomas Gordon eds., Da Capo Press 1971) (1755).

2. This narrative of progress, from the dark nineteenth century as a time of confiscation to today's more acceptable rules proscribing confiscation during wartime, is recently exemplified by the Eritrean Ethiopian Claims

I proceed by discussing the four manifestations of the relationship between confiscation and commerce. These manifestations include the following: confiscation trumps commerce; commerce trumps confiscation; balancing between commerce and confiscation where neither trumps the other; and finally, the doctrine of exceptional circumstances under which warfare between lawful belligerents and actors, who are thought of as existing outside the law, are regarded as beyond legal regulation.

II. THE RELATIONSHIP BETWEEN CONFISCATION AND COMMERCE

A. Confiscation Trumps Commerce

The inherent power of confiscation during wartime is traceable to absolutist notions of sovereignty.[3] Proceeding from such views of the

---

Commission. In this dispute, between the State of Eritrea and the Federal Democratic Republic of Ethiopia, the Commission noted in part that:

[U]ntil the nineteenth century, no distinction was drawn between the private and public property of the enemy, and both were subject to expropriation by a belligerent. However, attitudes changed; as early as 1794, the Jay's Treaty bound the United States and the United Kingdom not to confiscate the other's nationals' property even in wartime. This attitude came to prevail; the 1907 Hague Regulations reflect a determination to have war affect private citizens and their property as little as possible.

Eritrean Ethiopia Claims Commission, Partial Claims Award, Civilians Claims, Eritrea's Claims 15, 16, 23 & 27–32, 125 (Dec. 17, 2004), *available at* http://pca-cpa.org/ENGLISH/RPC/EECC/ER%20Partial%20Award%20Dec%2004.pdf. To be fair, the Commission does acknowledge in a later paragraph that these prohibitions are accompanied by a "competing body of belligerent rights to freeze or otherwise control or restrict the resources of enemy nationals so as to deny them to the enemy State." *Id.* at ¶ 127.

3. Thus in *Ware v. Hylton*, Justice Chase quoting *Bynkershoek Q. I.P. de rebus bellicis* states "[s]ince it is a condition of war, that enemies, by every right, may be plundered, and seized upon, it is reasonable that whatever effects of the enemy are found with us who are his enemy, should change their master, and be confiscated, or go into the treasury." 3 U.S. (2 Dall.) 199, 226 (1796). To further illustrate the absoluteness of the claims of confiscation, the Confederate government passed retaliatory legislation permitting it to confiscate the property of Northerners when Congress passed legislation

power of the State, domestic courts have affirmed confiscations as an exercise of a war power, as opposed to a municipal power,[4] suggesting that war powers are more expansive than the more limited municipal powers. Other justifications for the authority to confiscate private property during wartime include the military necessity doctrine,[5] executive orders claiming expansive authority in the conduct of war,[6] as well as the kind of broad powers exemplified by the United States' International Economic Emergency Powers Act[7] and the expansive powers to freeze assets it confers on the Office of Foreign Assets Control.[8]

Several American Civil War cases demonstrate the far-reaching claims of the absoluteness of the rights of belligerents to confiscate private property. In *American Insurance Co. v. 356 Bales of Cotton*, the

---

permitting the confiscation of enemy property during the Civil War. *See* JOHN SYRETT, THE CIVIL WAR CONFISCATION ACTS—FAILING TO RECONSTRUCT THE SOUTH 6 (2005).

4. *Miller v. United States*, 78 U.S. (11 Wall.) 268, 304–05 (1870). Here, the Court held that the restrictions of the Fifth (prohibiting deprivation of private property without due process of law) or Sixth (presentment or indictment by jury) Amendments did not preclude the confiscations because Congress has the power to declare war, which includes "the power to prosecute it by all means and in any manner in which war may be legitimately prosecuted." *Id*.

5. *See* Wayne McCormack, *Emergency Powers and Terrorism*, 185 MIL. L. REV. 69, 75–79 (2005) (discussing military necessity as a justification for property seizure and destruction).

6. In *Paradissiotis v. United States*, the Federal Circuit held that the United States did not effect an unlawful taking of property when it refused to permit a person determined to be an agent of the Libyan government to exercise stock options included among assets that were frozen by executive order. 304 F.3d 1271 (Fed. Cir. 2002).

7. In *Dames & Moore v. Regan*, Justice Rehnquist noted that "[t]he language of IEEPA [referring to 50 U.S.C. § 1702(a)(1)(B) in particular] is sweeping and unqualified. It provides broadly that the President may void or nullify the 'exercising [by *any* person of] *any* right, power or privilege with respect to . . . any property in which any foreign country has any interest,'" 453 U.S. 654, 671 (1981) (quoting *Chas. T. Main Int'l v. Khuzestan Water & Power Auth.*, 651 F.2d 800, 806–07 (1st Cir. 1981)) (emphasis in original).

8. On the role of the Office of Foreign Assets Control, *see* Jill M. Troxel, *Office of Foreign Assets Control Regulations: Making Attorneys Choose between Compliance and the Attorney-Client Privilege*, 24 REV. LITIG. 637, 652–54 (2005).

United States Supreme Court reaffirmed the absolute power granted to the government to confiscate property without compensation.[9] In some Civil War cases, Congress's power to pass legislation authorizing the confiscation of private property, even in cases where it was held by noncombatants, was justified as arising under the power of Congress to "make regulations [sic] concerning captures on land and water."[10]

During the Civil War period, Courts generally upheld broad powers of the Union government and army to confiscate cotton owned by southerners, even though the Confiscation Acts were vague and unclear.[11] One case affirms the legitimacy of wartime confiscation of cotton as being "not for booty of war, but to cripple the enemy."[12] Thus in *Miller v. United States*, Justice Strong noted that:

> The whole doctrine of confiscation is built upon the foundation that [*property*] *is* an instrument of coercion, which, by depriving an enemy of property within reach of his power . . . impairs his ability to resist the confiscating government, while at the same time it furnishes to that government means for carrying on the war.[13]

Although the courts affirmed confiscation in broad terms, the Lincoln administration only grudgingly supported confiscation.[14] Some Union army officers, by contrast, argued that the Confiscation Acts empowered them to confiscate slaves as they continued to be

---

9. *Am. Ins. Co. v. 356 Bales of Cotton*, 26 U.S. 511, 542 (1828).

10. *Haycraft v. United States*, 89 U.S. (22 Wall.) 81, 94 (1874) (quoting U.S. CONST. art. I, § 8, cl. 11).

11. SYRETT, *supra* note 3, at 155. Some scholars have suggested that civil war confiscation cases had a direct bearing on the emergence of laissez-faire constitutionalism and the emergence of a particularly strong right to private property, Daniel Hamilton, *A New Right to Property: Civil War Confiscation in the Reconstruction Supreme Court*, 29 J. SUP. CT. HIST. 254, 255 (2004).

12. *Haycraft*, 89 U.S. (22 Wall.) at 94.

13. *Miller*, 78 U.S. (11 Wall.) at 306 (emphasis added). In *American Manufacturers Mutual Insurance Co.*, the court held that there was no compensation available for property destroyed as part of the fortunes of war. *Am. Mfrs. Ins. Co. v. United States*, 197 Ct. Cl. 99 (1972).

14. SYRETT, *supra* note 3, at 186.

described as property.[15] The Second Confiscation Act[16] referred to slaves as property,[17] consistent with the racist *Dred Scott* view that blacks could never attain citizenship in the United States.[18]

The enhanced authority of belligerents in cases such as *Miller v. United States* was invoked in the post-World War II case, *United States v. Caltex*, in which the court held that military necessity justified the U.S. military's destruction of terminal facilities after the attack on Pearl Harbor, and that such destruction was necessary to prevent the use of the facilities by the enemy.[19] In 2003, the Court of Federal Claims in *El Shifa v. United States* affirmed such broad powers when it held that the President's designation of "war-making property" was judicially unreviewable, and as such, the mistaken bombing of private property abroad was not subject to compensation under the Fifth Amendment of the U.S. Constitution.[20]

This strong rule of confiscation also manifests itself under contemporary international law. United Nations Security Council Resolution 1373 of 2001, passed only a few days after the terrorist attacks on the United States on September 11, 2001, authorized States to freeze, and in effect to confiscate the financial assets and other private property belonging to individuals and entities linked to terrorism.[21]

---

15. *Id.* at 22 ("Slaves remained property in descriptions of confiscation but became people in reference to their rights after the fighting, however.").

16. *An Act to Suppress Insurrection, to Punish Treason and Rebellion, to Seize and Confiscate the Property of Rebels, and for Other Purposes.* 37 Cong. Ch. 195, 12 Stat. 589 (July 17, 1862).

17. SYRETT, *supra* note 3, at 24.

18. PAUL FINKELMAN, DRED SCOTT V. SANDFORD: A BRIEF HISTORY WITH DOCUMENTS 4 (1997).

19. *United States v. Caltex*, 344 U.S. 149, 154–55 (1952).

20. *El-Shifa Pharm. Indus. Co. v. United States*, 55 Fed. Cl. 751, 771–72 (2003). The Court in *El-Shifa* considered a claim resulting from destruction of Sudanese property by the United States in retaliation for terrorist attacks on the American embassies in Kenya and Tanzania. *Id.* at 753–54. For further analysis, see Nathaniel Segal, Note, *After El-Shifa: The Extraterritorial Availability of the Takings Clause*, 13 CARDOZO J. INT'L & COMP. L. 293 (2005).

21. S.C. Res. 1373, U.N. Doc. S/RES/1373 (Sept. 28, 2001). Paragraph 1(c) of Resolution 1373 obliges States to:
> Freeze without delay funds and other financial assets or economic resources of persons who commit, or attempt to commit, terrorist acts or participate in or facilitate the commission of terrorist acts; of entities

The Security Council also established the Counter-Terrorism Committee to monitor the implementation of this resolution.[22] At the September 2005 UN World Summit, a resolution was adopted expanding the work of the Counter-Terrorism Committee to include incitement to commit acts of terrorism.[23] The resolution, however, called on States to comply with rules of international human rights in complying with their enhanced obligations to combat terrorism.[24] The expansive authority the Security Council assumed in combating terrorism has fundamentally shifted its role, from dealing with crisis on a case-by-case basis, to legislating entirely new rules of international law.[25] Given the unrepresentative nature of the Security Council, where no African, Arab, or Latin American country occupies a permanent seat with veto authority, these new rules may very well represent the will of a tiny minority of the States in the world today.[26]

---

owned or controlled directly or indirectly by such persons; and of persons and entities acting on behalf of, or at the direction of such persons and entities, including funds derived or generated from property owned or controlled directly or indirectly by such persons and associated persons and entities.

S.C. Res. 1373, ¶ 1(c), U.N. Doc. S/RES/1373 (Sept. 28, 2001). *See also* Jose Alvarez, *Hegemonic International Law Revisited*, 97 Am. J. Int'l L. 873, 874–76 (2003) (discussing the implications of the Counter-Terrorism Committee's ability to impose financial sanctions).

22. The Security Council describes the Counter-Terrorism Committee as follows:

The Committee, comprising all 15 Council members, was tasked with monitoring implementation of resolution 1373 (2001), which requested countries to implement a number of measures intended to enhance their legal and institutional ability to counter terrorist activities at home, in their regions and around the world.

Security Council Counter-Terrorism Committee: About Us, *available at* http://www.un.org/sc/ctc/aboutus.html (last visited Feb. 1, 2009).

23. S.C. Res. 1624, ¶ 1, U.N. Doc. S/RES/1624 (Sept. 14, 2005).

24. *Id.* at ¶ 4.

25. *See* Paul C. Szasz, *The Security Council Starts Legislating*, 96 Am. J. Int'l L. 901, 902–05 (2002) (discussing Security Council Resolution 1373 and the Security Council's increasing willingness to make demands on States).

26. I pursue this theme much more fully in my article, *Assessing Claims of a New Doctrine of Pre-emptive War Under the Doctrine of Sources*, 43 Osgoode Hall L.J. 67 (2005).

The work of the Security Council's Sanctions Committee (established in accordance with resolution 1267), initially established in 1999 to monitor sanctions against the Taliban regime and extended to cover individuals linked to the Al Qaeda organization in 2000[27] is authorized to freeze an individual or entity's financial assets if they are associated with Al Qaeda, Osama Bin Laden, or such other individuals or entities listed by these committees.[28] States are now obliged to bring their laws and practices into conformity with these Security Council mandates even though the process of blacklisting and delisting individuals and entities as a step toward the freezing of their financial assets still raises questions of its compatibility with protections of international human rights law including due process and fair hearing rights.[29] As a result of these concerns, in 2002, the

---

27. S. C. Res. 1333, ¶ 8(c), U.N. Doc. S/RES/1333 (Dec. 19, 2000) and reaffirmed in S.C. Res. 1390, ¶ 2, S/Res/1390 (Jan. 16, 2002). See also S.C. Res. 1267, ¶ 6, U.N. Doc. S/RES/1267 (Oct. 15, 1999); For a description of post-September 11, 2001, international reaction to terrorist financing, see Ilias Bantekas, *The International Law of Terrorist Financing*, 97 AM. J. INT'L L. 315 (2003) and regarding the human rights issues surrounding the Implementation of this international law of terrorist financing, see Andrew Hudson, *Not a Great Asset: The UN Security Council's Counter-Terrorism Regime: Violating Human Rights*, 25 BERKELEY J. INT'L L. 203 (2007). See Alvarez, supra note 21, at 876–77.

28. For a discussion of this and related counter-terrorism committees, see Eric Rosand, *The UN-Led Multilateral Institutional Response to Jihadist Terrorism: Is A Global Counterterrorism Body Needed?*, 11 J. CONFLICT & SECURITY L. 399 (2006).

29. In Judgment of the European Court of Justice (ECJ) in Joined Cases C-402/05 P and C-415/05 P, *Yassin Abdullah Kadi & Al Barakaat International Foundation v. Council of the European Union and Commission of the European Communities*, at ¶¶ 280–327, 345, & 370 (September 3, 2008), available at http://curia.europa.eu/ (follow "en" hyperlink; then follow search "Case no C-415/05"; then follow "C-415/05 P" hyperlink alongside "Judgment") found it had jurisdiction to review the lawfulness of a measure giving effect to a UN Security Council Resolution. The ECJ held that the European Union's regulation implementing the Security Council's 1267 Sanctions Committee's authority to freeze the funds and other assets of listed persons infringed the rights to be heard and to effective judicial review as they involved no procedure for communicating evidence justifying the listing of the appellants. The ECJ also held that the freezing of the appellants assets was an unjustified restriction on their property. *But see*, Swiss Federal Supreme Court case in

United Nations agreed to potentially consider appeals of more than 200 individuals whose assets had been frozen, and whom the Security Council's Sanctions Committee had listed as having suspected links to terrorism.[30]

Another instance illustrating the absolute policy of confiscation arose following the 2003 war and subsequent occupation in Iraq by the United States. The de-Baathification of that country became one of the most important occupation objectives.[31] It involved the dissolution of not just the Baath party, but a whole continuum of entities affiliated with Saddam Hussein, including defense, security, information, and intelligence organs of government and the entire structure of the Iraqi military, including paramilitary units.[32] All the property and assets of the now defunct Baath party were seized and transferred to the U.S. appointed and controlled Coalition Provisional Authority

---

Nada v. State Secretariat for Economic Affairs, Budesgericht [BGer] [Federal Court], Nov. 14, 2007, 133 Entscheidungen des Schweizerischen Bundesgerichts [BGE] II 450–67 (Switzerland) (coming to the conclusion that Swiss Federal Council's decision pursuant to a decree to add Mr. Nada to be listed pursuant to the Security Council's 1267 Committee mandate, which resulted in the freezing of his assets and banned him from traveling was required by Security Council decisions and that the guarantees Mr. Nada claimed were violated did not conflict with jus cogens norms, which would have given the Court jurisdiction to annul the Swiss decree). For further discussion, *see* Gráinne de Búrca, *The European Court of Justice and the International Legal Order After Kadi*, forthcoming 51 HARV. INT'L L.J. (2009).

30. *UN Eases Tough Stance Frozen Assets*, 8/16/02 MX (Austl.) at 15, *available at* 2002 WLNR 6240311.

31. The Preamble to the first order of the Coalition Provisional Authority on de-Baathification notes in part:

[T]hat the Iraqi people have suffered large scale human rights abuses and depravations over many years at the hands of the Ba'ath Party . . .

[And] the grave concern of Iraqi society regarding the threat posed by the continuation of Ba'ath Party networks and personnel in the administration of Iraq, and the intimidation of the people of Iraq by Ba'ath Party officials.

Coalitional Provisional Authority Order No. 1: Implementation of De-Ba'athification of Iraqi Society, Preamble (May 16, 2003), *available at* http://www.cpa-iraq.org/regulations (on file with the *Brooklyn Journal of International Law*).

32. Coalitional Provisional Authority Order No. 2: Dissolution of Entities, Annex (May 23, 2003), *available at* http://www.cpa-iraq.org/regulations.

"for the benefit of the people of Iraq."[33] Individuals in possession or control of Baath party property were required to turn it over to the Coalition.[34] An Iraqi Property Claims Commission was authorized to return seized private property.[35] The Iraqi De-Baathification Council was charged with locating Baathist officials, the assets of the party and its officials, with a view to eliminating the party and its potential

---

33. Coalitional Provisional Authority Order No. 4: Management of Property and Assets of the Iraqi Baath Party, § 3(1) (May 25, 2003), *rescinded by* Coalitional Provisional Authority Order No. 100, § 4: Transition of Laws, Regulations, Orders, and Directives Issued by the Coalition Provisional Authority (June 28, 2004), *available at* http://www.cpa-iraq.org/regulations.
34. *Id.* at § 3(3), *rescinded by* Coalitional Provisional Authority Order No. 100, § 4: Transition of Laws, Regulations, Orders, and Directives Issued by the Coalition Provisional Authority (June 28, 2004), *available at* http://www.cpa-iraq.org/regulations. Similarly, "Iraq owns all buildings, non-relocatable structures, and assemblies connected to the soil that exist on agreed facilities and areas, including those that are used, constructed, altered or improved by the United States Forces ... [u]pon their withdrawal, the United States Forces shall return to the Government of Iraq all the facilities and areas provided for the use of combat forces of the United States." Operation Iraqi Freedom, Agreement between the United States of America and the Republic of Iraq on the Withdrawal of United States Forces from Iraq and the Organization of Their Activities during Their Temporary Presence in Iraq, Article 5, ¶¶ 1–2 (Nov. 17, 2008), *available at* http://www.mnf-iraq.com/images/CGs_Messages/security_agreement.pdf.
35. Coalitional Provisional Authority Regulation No. 8: Delegation of Authority Regarding an Iraq Property Claims Commission (Jan. 14, 2004), *amended by* Coalitional Provisional Authority Regulation No. 12: Iraq Property Claims Commission (June 24, 2005), *available at* http://www.cpa-iraq.org/regulations. The Iraq Property Rights Commission (IPCC) and the Iraq Property Rights Reconciliation Facility (IPRF) were both developed, in part, to collect and resolve real property claims. However, the IPCC is a quasi-judicial agency under the direction of the Governing Council, whereas the IPRF acts more like an executive agency under the direction of the Administrator; Coalitional Provisional Authority Order No. 4: Management of Property and Assets of the Iraqi Baath Party (May 25, 2003), *rescinded by* Coalitional Provisional Authority Order No. 100, § 4: Transition of Laws, Regulations, Orders, and Directives Issued by the Coalition Provisional Authority (June 28, 2004), *available at* http://www.cpa-iraq.org/regulations. The Iraqi Property Claims Commission was carried over by the elected Iraqi Government in Section 136 of the October 2005 Iraqi Constitution.

to intimidate the population.[36] The October 2005 Iraqi Constitution continued the work of the Iraqi Property Claims Commission[37] and the High Commission for De-Baathification,[38] prohibited the Saddamist Baath party's participation in Iraqi politics.[39]

The power of confiscation or the freezing of assets advanced in each of the foregoing instances was justified as a response to a danger and as a means of defeating the enemy with whom the danger was associated. In the context of the U.S. Civil War, courts even justified the power of confiscation where those involved were not belligerents on the premise, by focusing on the mere possibility that if their cotton fell into the hands of the Confederate army, it could be used to support the rebellion against the Union. In addition, the power to confiscate has been claimed in a variety of historical epochs. As noted above, in the contemporary international scene, new institutions such as the Security Council's Counter-Terrorism Committee has powers to freeze the financial assets of individuals and entities associated with identified terrorist groups or individuals. This continuity undermines claims that a successful belligerent's authority to confiscate enemy private property has receded into historical memory. Although there is certainly continuity in the power of confiscation or at least seizure of property and financial assets during wartime from the pre–self-determination era into the present, there have been instances of discontinuity in some exercises of the extreme

---

36. Coalition Provisional Authority Order No. 5: Establishment of the Iraqi De-Baathification Council, § 3 (May 25, 2003), *rescinded by* Coalitional Provisional Authority Memorandum No. 7, § 3: Delegation of Authority Under De-Baathification Order No. 1 (Nov. 4, 2003), *available at* http://www.cpa-iraq.org/regulations.

37. Iraq Const. § 136 (Oct. 2005).

38. *Id.* at § 135.

39. *Id.* at § 7, which in full provides that "[a]ny entity or program that adopts, incites, facilitates, glorifies, promotes, or justifies racism or terrorism or accusations of being an infidel (takfir) or ethnic cleansing, especially the Saddamist Baath in Iraq and its symbols, under any name whatsoever, shall be prohibited. Such entities may not be part of political pluralism in Iraq." Notably, § 135(5) provides that mere membership in the Baath Party is not a sufficient reasons for referral to court and that Baath members equality before the law unless they are covered by the provisions of De-Baathification High Commission and the directives issued thereunder.

authority of belligerents. One example is that unlike in the medieval era of international law, the taking of prisoners of war as slaves is no longer permissible. Let us look briefly at this example.

Seventeenth-century international law jurist, Hugo Grotius, argued that "persons captured in a war that is public become slaves."[40] Thus, although for Grotius slavery was contrary to the law of nature, he argued that it was not in "conflict with natural justice that slavery should have its origin in a human act" such as a convention or a crime.[41] Alan Watson has persuasively argued that this contradiction between the practice of enslaving captives of war and the claim that slavery was contrary to natural law is best understood from the premise that, for jurists such as Grotius, natural law had no moral dimension.[42] Grotius understood the practice of slavery as justified by a natural law that was immutable or natural—he did not regard it as "improper or blameworthy."[43] Thus for Grotius, even those captured in enemy territory during war were subject to seizure as slaves even if such captives had not done "any impious deeds."[44] Indeed, not only did the captives become slaves of such prisoners of war, but also their descendants.[45] Trading in slaves was therefore permissible in this Grotian framework—a view compatible with his unwavering support for freedom of trade and navigation.[46]

The powers over slaves are expansive for Grotius. For him, "there is nothing which a master is not permitted to do with his slave. There is

---

40. HUGO GROTIUS, THE LAW OF WAR AND PEACE, BOOK III 690 (1964).
41. *Id.* It is notable that Grotius also endorsed this idea of natural slavery, *see* HUGO GROTIUS, DE JURE PRAEDAE COMENTARIUS 61–62 (Gwladys L. Williams & Walter H. Zeydel trans., 1950).
42. ALAN WATSON, SLAVE LAW IN THE AMERICAS 117 (1989). This is a contested view. In fact, anti-slavery courts of the eighteenth century frequently invoked natural law to justify the immorality and illegality of slavery, *see* Jenny S. Martinez, *Anti-Slavery Courts and the Dawn of International Human Rights Law*, 117 YALE L.J. (2007).
43. *Id.*
44. GROTIUS, WAR AND PEACE, *supra* note 40.
45. *Id.* at 691.
46. One of the best treatments of this is Ileana Porras, *Constructing International Law in the East Indian Seas: Property, Sovereignty, Commerce and War in Hugo Grotius' De Iure Praedae—The Law of Prize and Booty, or "On How to Distinguish Merchants from Pirates,"* 31 BROOK. J. INT'L L. 741 (2006).

no suffering which may not be inflicted with impunity upon such slaves, no action which may not be ordered, or forced by torture, to do, in any way whatsoever; even brutality on the part of masters towards persons of servile status is unpunishable except in so far as municipal law sets a limits and a penalty for brutality."[47] For Grotius, slavery was permissible, even if cruel, because the alternative was harsh. The sale of prisoners of war as slaves, according to Grotius, was a practice that "had many advantages" than the slaying of these captives by the commanders who captured them.[48] In this sense, Grotius concluded that the practice of nations was to classify prisoners of war as booty—slaves were thus in the "same category as things."[49] These slaves had no right to liberty since they had lawfully become slaves.[50] Cornelius van Bynkershoek had similarly justified slavery as preferable to the obsolete practice of massacring prisoners of war, and a legitimate power of a conqueror over the life and death over captives of war.[51]

Grotius' justification of the power of a belligerent to take slaves coincided with the ascendance of natural law in the pre-1850 period and its admixture of morality, politics, and law. Grotius offered a framework that could at once justify the most extreme powers of a belligerent balanced against considerations that seemed reasonable, although consistent with the prerogatives of the powerful countries of his time. In essence, unlike modern lawyers of international law who begin by acknowledging the ban on the use of force in relations between States, Grotius explained the practice of the States of his time from the view that war was justified by "considerations of power, not of justice."[52] However, Grotius' points out that the taking of prisoners of war as slaves, as opposed to killing, was the State practice

---

47. HUGO GROTIUS, WAR AND PEACE, *supra* note 40.
48. *Id.*
49. *Id.* at 692–93. Grotius then quotes Gaius for the proposition that "Also what is captured from the enemy becomes at once, by the law of nations, the property of the captors, to the extent indeed that even free men are led off in slavery," *id.* at 693.
50. HUGO GROTIUS, DE JURE BELLI AC PACIS: BOOK II §§ 11–12 (1625).
51. CORNELIS VAN BYNKERSHOEK, QUAESTIONES JURIS PUBLICI 1.3 (1737).
52. Benedict Kingsbury & Adam Roberts, *Introduction: Grotian Thought in International Relations*, *in* HUGO GROTIUS AND INTERNATIONAL RELATIONS 17 (Benedict Kingsbury & Adam Roberts eds., 1990).

of the time that showed that he [Grotius] did not fully intend to "overshadow all other considerations of justice and prudence."[53] In this sense, Grotius was a medieval jurist of international law for whom the source of obligation of the law of nations did not necessarily come from the consent of States. For Grotius, the source of law was "manifest in nature but discerned by human reason."[54] Unlike the positivists who were soon to follow, Grotius' medieval international law was a mishmash of morality and law.[55]

The transatlantic slavery and its attendant brutalities followed in the heels of Grotius' justification of the taking of slaves precisely at the time when the ideals of the Enlightenment were increasing in Europe.[56] The economic imperatives that led to the rise of the transatlantic trade in slavery can hardly be distinguished from the imperatives that informed Grotius' support for freedom of trade and navigation. Whereas Grotius' preindustrial endorsement of slavery may not have explicitly endorsed the slavery of non-European peoples, the transatlantic slave trade involving slaves from Africa to the New World of the Americas including the Caribbean by European merchants that emerged with the rise of industrial capitalism was entirely consistent with the economic and imperial imperatives of European States and the plantation owners of the new world, and it was in no small part possible in light of the freedom of trade and navigation on the part of both States and individuals that Grotius had so vigorously defended.[57]

---

53. *Id.* at 23.

54. *Id.* at 30. Grotius also referred sources of law in divine law as well as to laws made by man.

55. David Kennedy, *Primitive Legal Scholarship*, 27 HARV. INT'L L.J. 9 (1986).

56. DAVID BRION DAVIS, THE PROBLEM OF SLAVERY IN WESTERN CULTURE 14 (1966).

57. *See, e.g.*, ERIC WILLIAMS, CAPITALISM AND SLAVERY (1964); J. D. Hargreaves, *A Critique of Eric Williams, Capitalism and Slavery*, in THE TRANSATLANTIC SLAVE TRADE FROM WEST AFRICA (Center for African Studies, University of Edinburgh 1965). *See also* Kingsbury & Roberts, *Introduction: Grotian Thought in International Relations*, in GROTIUS AND INTERNATIONAL RELATIONS, *supra* note 52, at 46 (arguing that Grotius' view of slavery "does not appear to stem from his consideration of issues concerning relations between Europeans and non-Europeans or Christians and non-Christians.").

Finally, just as the slavery example shows, it is important to note that it is not always true that the absolute power to confiscate is always opposed to the ends of commerce. Rather, the question might more appropriately be whose commerce is affected and what or who is being traded in such commerce, because confiscation may well only divert the gains of commerce from one party to another. For example, in *Young v. United States*, the Supreme Court upheld the confiscation of cotton found within confederate territory, as well as the decision of the Union army to sell it and as such to divert the benefit of trade and commerce away from the Confederacy, in favor of the Union.[58] This example illustrates that it is possible to simultaneously weaken the enemy by confiscating private property, in accordance with the absolutist rule, while continuing in commerce and trade at the same time. In this scenario, rather than destroying private property, the absolutist rule seeks to divert the gains of trade and commerce from the enemy belligerent to the defeated belligerent.

B. Commerce Trumps Confiscation

A second relationship between commerce and confiscation during wartime is that commerce trumps confiscation. According to Justice Marshall in *United States v. Percheman*, property rights are not abolished with a change in sovereign power. According to Marshall:

> The modern usage of nations, which has become law, would be violated; that sense of justice and of right, which is acknowledged and felt by the whole civilized world, would be outraged; if private property should generally be confiscated and private rights annulled, on a change in the sovereignty of the country. The people change their allegiance . . . but their relations to each other, and their rights of property remain undisturbed.[59]

---

58. *Young v. United States*, 97 U.S. 39, 61 (1877) (noting "the national government acted with double power upon the strength of the enemy: first, by depriving them of the means of supplying the demand for their products; and, second, by lessening the demand").

59. *United States v. Percheman*, 32 U.S. (7 Pet.) 51, 51 (1833). The government's position in the case is captured by the following quote:

> What, indeed, can be more clearly entitled to rank among things favourable [sic] than engagements between nations securing the private property of faithful subjects, honestly acquired under a government which is on the

This view is also reflected in British cases of the same period.[60] Perhaps in overstating the significance of commerce during war, Chief Justice Marshall in *Brown v. United States* noted that the "practice of forbearing to seize and confiscate debts and credits [is] universally received"[61] and that this "modern rule . . . appears to be totally incompatible with the idea, that war does of itself vest the property in the belligerent government."[62] Attitudes about the positive role of commerce in society are strongly correlated with the rejection of any

---

eve of relinquishing their allegiance, and confided to the pledged protection of that country which is about to receive them as citizens? *Id.* at 68.

60. See *In re* Rush, 1922 WL 15910 (CA), [1923] 1 Ch. 56 (Younger, L.J., concurring) ("Lord Birkenhead, in *Fried Krupp Aktiengesellschaft v. Orconera Iron Ore Co.*(1), in 1919 observed: 'It is a familiar principle of English law that the outbreak of war effects no confiscation or forfeiture of enemy property.'" (quoting (1919) 88 L.J.R. (Ch.) 304, 309)). Somewhat analogously, in *Commercial Bank of Kuwait v. Rifidian Bank and Central Bank of Iraq*, the United States Court of Appeals for the Second Circuit held that a default occasioned by war, economic sanctions and the freezing of its assets making it impossible to obtain foreign currency to repay its debts did not preclude it from finding that Iraq had willfully defaulted, 15 F.3d 238, 242–43 (2d Cir. 1994).

61. *Brown v. United States*, 12 U.S. 110, 123 (1814).

62. *Id.* at 125. In a more forthright statement of the principle, Justice Marshall observed that the "proposition that a declaration of war does not, in itself, enact a confiscation of the property of the enemy within the territory of the belligerent, is believed to be entirely free from doubt." *Id.* at 127. However, Justice Marshall conceded that war gives a sovereign the "full right to take the persons and confiscate the property of the enemy[,]" but that this "rigid rule" had been moderated by "the humane and wise policy of modern times." *Id.* at 122–23. By contrast, Justice Story dissented, arguing that, although mere declaration of war did not ipso facto operate as a confiscation of the property of enemy aliens, such property is liable to confiscation "at the discretion of the sovereign power having the conduct and execution of the war" and that the law of nations "is resorted to merely as a limitation of this discretion, not as conferring the authority to exercise it." *Id.* at 154 (Story, J., dissenting). Although Justice Marshall appeared to have suggested that the modern rule prohibited confiscation under the law of nations and limited the sovereign power to confiscate enemy property, *id.* in *United States v. Percheman*, he affirmed the rule against confiscation under the law of nations unambiguously, 32 U.S. 51 (7 Pet.) (1833).

claims of restricting commerce, such as through the public power of confiscation of private property without compensation.

Thus, French philosopher Montesquieu argued that the influence of commerce and industry "polishes and softens barbaric ways."[63] Alexander Hamilton also observed that some individuals believe that the "natural effect of commerce is to lead to peace."[64] One of the most important justifications accounting for the preeminence of commerce over a belligerent's right to confiscation is the salience of private property rights over competing claims of confiscation made by sovereigns. For example, Alexander Hamilton supported the prohibition against confiscation contained in the Jay's Treaty in the strongest terms stating, in part that:

> [N]o powers of language at my command can express the abhorrence I feel at the idea of violating the property of individuals, which, in an authorized intercourse, in time of peace, has been confided to the faith of our Government and laws, on account of controversies between nation and nation.[65]

The rise of individualism associated with the Enlightenment that had influenced the American and French revolutions,[66] and the Spanish Constitution of 1812,[67] are closely associated with the importance placed on protecting the inalienable rights to individual property

---

63. *See* Albert O. Hirschman, *Rival Interpretations of Market Society: Civilizing, Destructive, or Feeble?*, 20 J. ECON. LITERATURE 1463, 1464 (1982) (quoting CHARLES MONTESQUIEU, DE L'ESPRIT DES LOIS 81 (1961) (1748)).

64. Although Hamilton, himself, disagreed with this notion. *See* THE FEDERALIST No. 6, at 33–36 (Alexander Hamilton) (E. H. Scott ed., 1898).

65. Otto C. Sommerich, *A Brief Against Confiscation*, 11 LAW & CONTEMP. PROBS. 152, 156 (1946) (quoting 4 HAMILTON'S WORKS 343 (Lodge ed., 1885)).

66. *See* G. Richard Jansen, The Provenance of Liberty and the Evolution of Political Thinking in the United States (Feb. 1, 2003) (unpublished manuscript) *available at* http://lamar.colostate.edu/~grjan/provenanceliberty.html. The merchant and bourgeoisie classes were strong driving forces behind the French Revolution in 1789. *Id.*

67. The Spanish Constitution of 1812 was based, in large part, on the Jacobian Constitution of 1793. KARL MARX, REVOLUTIONARY SPAIN 62–63 (1854) IN XII WORKS OF MARXISM-LENINISM: REVOLUTION IN SPAIN (International Publishers 1939).

from tyrannical governments.⁶⁸ The Lockean views of property ownership were argued to derive right from the labor of the individual rather than from a grant from the sovereign.⁶⁹ As such, some of the framers of the United States Constitution argued that, when individuals were deprived of certain inalienable rights, such as the right to property,⁷⁰ they were entitled to revolt against such abuses of their inalienable rights.⁷¹

In international humanitarian law, this attitude is reflected in the prohibition of destruction or seizure of enemy property "unless . . . imperatively demanded by the necessities of war" found in Article 23(g) of the 1907 Hague Regulations,⁷² as well as Article 33 of Geneva Convention Relative to the Protection of Civilians in Time

---

68. Jansen, *supra* note 44. The French National Assembly, in its Declaration of the Rights of Man and the Citizen, written by the Marquis de Lafayette, assisted by Thomas Jefferson, included property as a natural and inalienable right of man. *Id.*

69. JOHN LOCKE, *Second Treatise on Government*, *in* TWO TREATISES OF GOVERNMENT 285, 303–20 (Peter Laslett ed., Cambridge Univ. Press 1988) (1690).

70. Jefferson, during the Revolution wrote of the right of people to recognize a new government when the existing government fails to protect those rights. *See* Christian G. Fritz, *Recovering the Lost Worlds of America's Written Constitution*, 68 ALB. L. REV. 261, 264 (2005) ("In the Declaration of Independence, Thomas Jefferson considered the people 'endowed by their Creator with certain unalienable Rights,' including the right to alter or to abolish governments destructive of the legitimate ends of government. These words are often associated with Locke's justification for the right of revolution." (footnotes omitted)). The Fifth Amendment of the United States Constitution provides that "no person shall be . . . be deprived of . . . property, without due process of law; nor shall private property be taken for public use without just compensation." U.S. CONST. amend. V. *See generally* J. FRANKLIN JAMESON, THE AMERICAN REVOLUTION CONSIDERED AS A SOCIAL MOVEMENT 27–46 (Beacon Press 1964) (1926) (discussing how the ownership system of land influenced the American Revolution).

71. David C. Williams, *The Militia Movement and Second Amendment Revolution: Conjuring with the People*, 81 CORNELL L. REV. 879, 886 (1996). The framers were highly skeptical of a powerful centralized government and favored an inherent right of the citizenry to revolt when deprived of certain inalienable rights. *Id.*

72. Convention Respecting the Laws and Customs of War on Land art. 23, Oct. 18, 1907, 36 Stat. 2277, 1 Bevans 631 [hereinafter Hague Regulations].

of War (IV), which prohibits pillage and reprisals against protected persons' property.[73] With respect to occupied territory, Article 53 of the Geneva Convention Relative to the Protection of Civilians in Time of War (IV) prohibits destruction of private property except where "rendered absolutely necessary by military operations,"[74] whereas Article 46 of the Hague Regulations prohibits confiscation,[75] and Article 47[76] forbids pillaging by military authorities in occupied territory. The international law rule that outlaws interference with private property during war is now supplemented by the customary international law rule that territory cannot be lawfully acquired through the use of force.[77] I discuss these rules more fully in Chapter 2, which compares and contrasts the application of these rules in the occupations of Germany, Italy, and Japan following World War II and that of Iraq following the 2003 American and British–led war.

The strong support of private property rights against belligerent confiscation found similar expression in the post-World War II period, when a jurist noted that the norm against confiscation of private property was an important precondition for the United Nations to build durable peace.[78] Perhaps building on this view, Article 8(2)(a)(iv) of the Statute of the International Criminal Court, which entered into force on July 1, 2002, makes it a war crime to engage in "extensive

---

73. Geneva Convention Relative to the Protection of Civilians in Time of War art. 33, Aug. 12, 1949, 6 U.S.T. 3516, 75 U.N.T.S. 287.

74. *Id.* at art. 53.

75. Hague Regulations, *supra* note 44, at art. 46.

76. *Id.* at art. 47. Notably in the 1970s, the U.S. State Department took the position that Israel's occupation of the Gulf of Suez did not authorize it to violate the concessionary rights granted by Egypt to an American corporation, as these rights were protected under the law of belligerent occupation. Memorandum of Law, Monroe Leigh, United States Department of State, Israel's Right to Develop New Oil Fields in Sinai and the Gulf of Suez (Oct. 1, 1976), *reprinted in* 16 I.L.M. 733, 750–53 (1977).

77. *See* Declaration on Principles of International Law Concerning Friendly Relations and Co-operation Among States in Accordance with the Charter of the United Nations, Annex, G.A. Res. 2625, ¶ 1, U.N. GAOR, 25th Sess., Supp. No. 18, U.N. Doc. A/8018 (Oct. 24, 1970).

78. John Dickinson, *Enemy-Owned Property: Restitution or Confiscation?*, 22 FOREIGN AFF. 126, 141 (1943).

destruction and appropriation of property, not justified by military necessity and carried out unlawfully and unwantonly."

In *Congo v. Uganda*, decided by the International Court of Justice (ICJ) in December 2005, the Court found against Uganda for violating rules proscribing the looting, plundering, and exploitation of the natural resources of the Democratic Republic of the Congo.[79] Similarly, in December 2005, the Eritrea Ethiopia Claims Commission found Ethiopia liable for failing to compensate Eritrean civilians, whose trucks and buses it had requisitioned contrary to international law rules requiring full compensation for wartime confiscations.[80]

The reinforcement of the primacy of private property over the rights of belligerents to confiscate it in the foregoing rules and cases is belied by other rules and cases that continue to justify the confiscation of private property. I outlined a variety of such rules and cases above. Professor Joseph Singer has, for example, shown how, notwithstanding the extremely strong support for private property rights in the United States, courts have simultaneously justified the uncompensated taking of Native American property.[81] On the international level, Chapter 3 demonstrates the differential application of the rules prohibiting interference with the private property of Italians and Germans during post-World War II Allied occupation, which stands in sharp contrast with the widespread disregard of these rules in the non-Western societies of Japan after the World War II, and Iraq following the U.S.-led war.[82] In short, there is a tension

---

79. Armed Activities on the Territory of the Congo (*Dem. Rep. Congo v. Uganda*), 2005 I.C.J. 7, 75–79 (Dec. 19). The Court found that Uganda had failed to live up to its obligation of vigilance as an occupying power as required by Article 43 of the Hague Regulations of 1907 by failing to stop the "looting, plundering and exploitation" of the natural resources of the Congolese territory it occupied. *Id.* at 79.

80. Eritrea-Ethiopia Claims Commission, Partial Award, Loss of Property in Ethiopia Owned by Non-Residents, Eritrea's Claim 24, ¶¶ 15–26 (Dec. 19, 2005), *available at* http://pca-cpa.org/ENGLISH/RPC/EECC/FINAL%20ER%20CLAIM%2024.pdf; *see also* Partial Claims Award, Civilians Claims 15, 16, 23, & 27–32, *supra* note 2, ¶¶ 123–52.

81. Joseph William Singer, *Sovereignty and Property*, 86 Nw. U. L. Rev. 1, 1–5 (1991) (and discussing other cases in which Indian nations received equivalent as opposed to just compensation).

82. See Chapter 3.

between the right to private property and a sovereign's claim to broad ranging power. As Franz Neumann observed, regarding the opposition between sovereignty and the rule of law—if we were to imagine the limitation of the sovereign right to confiscate as limited by the rule of law—whenever a reconciliation between the two is sought "insoluble contradictions" arise.[83]

C. Balancing between Commerce and Confiscation

Courts and jurists invented a number of doctrines between the two irreconcilable views of the absolute right of confiscation during wartime, on the one hand, and the freedom of commerce during wartime, on the other. Thus the third manifestation of the relationship between commerce and confiscation during wartime that I address here is a continuum between these two otherwise opposing ideas. I will briefly outline them here. I have more fully elaborated this continuum in Chapter 4.

In the United States, the balancing between the rights to confiscate and to engage in commerce during war found its clearest expression when the United States was less powerful as an economic and military state, relative to Britain and France, and also at a time when countries

---

83. FRANZ NEUMANN, THE RULE OF LAW: POLITICAL THEORY AND THE LEGAL SYSTEM IN MODERN SOCIETY 4 (1986). Justice Marshall recognized this dilemma in *Brown*, where he noted:

> [W]ar gives to the sovereign full right to take the persons and confiscate the property of the enemy wherever found. . . . The mitigations of this rigid rule, which the humane and wise policy of modern times has introduced into practice, will more or less affect the exercise of this right, but cannot impair the right itself. That remains undiminished, and when the sovereign authority shall chuse [sic] to bring it into operation, the judicial department must give effect to its will.

Brown, 12 U.S. at 122–23. In this case, Justice Marshall however concluded that the modern rule was that in the absence of congressional authorization to confiscate enemy property upon the declaration of war, there was no automatic power of confiscation. *Id.* at 126–27. In *The Nereide*, Justice Marshall, speaking of two conflicting rules of neutrality of commerce, one allowing a neutral to carry enemy property without confiscation, and another to the contrary, noted: "If reason can furnish no evidence of the indissolubility of the two maxims, the supporters of that proposition will certainly derive no aid from the history of their progress from the first attempts at their introduction to the present moment." 13 U.S. 388, 420 (1815).

such as the Netherlands had superior naval capabilities in safeguarding their commerce. To illustrate this balancing, I will also examine confiscation cases arising from the American Civil War, particularly those which arose in relation to congressional limitations on the Union government's power to confiscate the assets of Southerners.

The first doctrine I will examine is that of suspension and restoration. One of the best cases illustrating this doctrine is *Hanger v. Abbott*, a Civil War case in which the United States Supreme Court held that debts and executed contracts that existed prior to the Civil War, and that played no part in undertaking the war, even though confiscated, remained suspended during the war and revived only with the restoration of peace.[84] By contrast, under the rule in this case, executory contracts are dissolved on the premise that "all trading, negotiation, communication, and intercourse between the citizens of one of the belligerents with those of the other" ceased with the declaration of war.[85] The doctrine of suspension, enunciated in *Hanger v. Abbott*, is a sharp departure from cases such as *Miller v. United States* in which the Supreme Court held that the mere presence of property within enemy territory rendered the property of those present therein subject to capture and confiscation.[86]

Closely related to the doctrine of suspension is the view of the Supreme Court in *Haycraft v. United States*.[87] In this case, an insurgent's cotton had been confiscated and sold by the Union government during the Civil War. The insurgent then sought amnesty and pardon, as provided by statute, in order to be entitled to recover the proceeds of the sale of his or her property.[88] Under the statute, pardon and amnesty had the effect of restoring the property rights of the

---

84. *Hanger v. Abbott*, 73 U.S. 532, 536 (1867). The court also noted that this rule was justified by the fact that a creditor had no ability to sue for the debt during the war because the courts where the debtor was located were closed or inaccessible. Thus, the law of nations results in the suspension of the debt during the pendency of the war. The court also noted that the statute of limitation stops running with declaration of the war, and with the return to peace, the statute of limitation starts to run. *Id.* at 539–40.

85. *Id.* at 535. By contrast, executed contracts such as a preexisting debt are not dissolved but suspended. *Id.* at 536.

86. *Miller*, 78 U.S. (11 Wall.) at 306; see *id.* at 317–18 (Field, J., dissenting).

87. *Haycraft*, 89 U.S. (22 Wall.) 81.

88. *Id.* at 95–96. See also *United States v. Klein*, 80 U.S. 128, 128–29 (1871).

insurgent or enemy whose property had been confiscated. In *Klein v. United States*, the Supreme Court held that, under the 1863 Captured and Abandoned Property Act, those who had not given aid or comfort to the rebellion, and whose property had nonetheless been seized or confiscated, were not divested of their ownership in the captured property.[89]

The United States was even more circumspect in exercising a right to confiscation in its international relations during the late eighteenth and early nineteenth century. Thomas Jefferson reflected this caution in 1793 when he summed up U.S. policy on confiscation of a belligerent's private property saying that: "the making of reprisal on a nation is a very serious thing. Remonstrance [and] refusal of satisfaction ought to precede; [and] when reprisal follows it is considered as an act of war."[90] Thus, while the United States, in its initial years as a nation, recognized the right of a belligerent to confiscate the goods of its enemy, it wished to remain neutral in the ongoing conflicts between Britain and France, and took no position on either side in an attempt to "cultivate the arts of peace."[91] In *Findlay v. The William*, a Pennsylvania court therefore observed that it was "difficult for a *neutral nation*, with the best dispositions, so to conduct itself as not to displease one or the other of belligerent parties, heated with the rage

---

89. *Klein*, 80 U.S. at 139 (citing *United States v. Padelfield*, 76 U.S. 531, 541 (1869)) (holding in part that: "(1) That the cotton of the petitioner was, by the general policy of the government, exempt from capture after the National forces took possession of Savannah. (2) That this policy was *subject to modification* by the government, or by the commanding general, in the exercise of his military discretion. (3) That the right of possession in private property is not changed, in general, by capture of the place where it happens to be, except upon actual seizure in obedience to the orders of the commanding general.") (emphasis added). Another doctrine demonstrating the absolute power of confiscation had moderating doctrines is the rule permitting transactions that are the result of necessity between an alien enemy and a citizen. See *Hallet v. Jenks* 7 U.S. 210 (1805).

90. THOMAS JEFFERSON, *Opinion on "The Little Sarah," in* 7 THE WORKS OF THOMAS JEFFERSON 332, 335 (Paul Leicester Ford ed., Putnam's Sons 1904).

91. *Findlay v. The William*, 9 F. Cas. 57, 61 (D. Pa. 1793). *Findlay* held, inter alia, that as a neutral nation, the United States does not have the right to affect the confiscation practices of another sovereign but can forbid the sale of confiscated goods on American soil. *Id.* at 59.

of war, and jealous of even common acts of justice or friendship on its part."⁹²

The doctrine of neutrality and the caution expressed in establishing the legality of confiscations of foreign States announced in *Findlay* can best be understood against the background of the then new government's desire to forge peaceful relations with foreign nations. As a relatively new nation, the United States lacked the military resources to wage war with superpowers of the period, such as England and France, as well as Spain and Holland.⁹³ Further complicating political matters, the general population had a great distrust and contempt for the creation of a standing military, fearing that a permanent military would become little more than a resource for political patronage jobs, among other concerns.⁹⁴ As a result, early lawmakers were both practically and politically estopped from adopting a policy of confiscation of the property of the citizens of more powerful nations. Instead of fighting British and French confiscation of American cargo with force,⁹⁵ United States diplomats attempted to use access to

---

92. *Id.* at 59 (emphasis added).

93. BENSON J. LOSSING, THE PICTORIAL FIELD-BOOK OF THE WAR OF 1812, at 154 (Harper and Brothers 1869). Lossing notes that a French decree of December 17, 1807, promulgated in response to British decrees in turn sparked similar decrees from Spain and Holland. As a result, the commerce of the United States was "swept from the ocean" within a few months, even though it had been conducted "in strict accordance with the acknowledged laws of civilized nations." *Id.* As a result, Lossing notes that the United States was "utterly unable, by any power it then possessed, to resist the robbers upon the great highway of nations [and] the independence of the republic had no actual record. It had been theoretically declared on parchment a quarter of a century before, but the nation and its interests were now as much subservient to British orders in council and French imperial decrees as when George the Third sent governors to the colonies of which it was composed." *Id.*

94. *Id.* at 167–69. Lossing also notes that "notwithstanding the many [depredations] upon American commerce and the increasing menace of the belligerents of Europe, very little had been done to increase the efficiency of the navy of the United States since its reduction at the close of the war with the Barbary States." *Id.*

95. 3 HISTORY OF NEW YORK STATE 1523–1927, at 1072 (James Sullivan et al. eds., 1927). By 1792, Northeastern merchants were already complaining of British confiscation of American cargo. *Id.*

American ports as leverage in their treaties with England.[96] This infuriated the French, who feeling betrayed by the nation they had assisted in overthrowing the British, embarked on a campaign of seizure of American goods on the high seas.[97]

Following the defeat of Thomas Jefferson by John Adams in the 1796 presidential election, France commissioned its war vessels to seize certain U.S. ships.[98] In January of the following year, France's Executive Directory issued a proclamation, whereby any ship containing any item of English manufacture was subject to seizure.[99] This led to the United States' first quasi-war. In retaliation to French privateering,[100] Congress authorized the capture of French military vessels,[101] and the seizure of French cargo.[102] Although the Congressional Acts gave American vessels the right to seize French property,

---

96. Gregory E. Fehlings, *America's First Limited War*, NAVAL WAR C. REV. (Summer 2000), *available at* http://www.nwc.navy.mil/press/Review/2000/summer/art4-Su0.htm (last visited Mar. 23, 2006). In 1794, the United States and Britain entered into Jay's Treaty, which authorized British privateers' use of American ports in their conflicts against France. *Id.*

97. *Id.*

98. *See* Decree of the Executive Directory Concerning the Navigation of Neutral Vessels, Loaded with Merchandise Belonging to Enemies of the Republic, and the Judgments on the Trials Relative to the Validity of Maritime Prizes, 12 Ventose *an* 5 (Mar. 2, 1797), Duv. & Boc. 358 (1825). In reaction to Adams' defeat of Jefferson, the Directory (France) commissioned its war ships and privateers to seize all U.S. flagged vessels with insufficient cargo inventories or carrying contraband. *See* ALEXANDER DECONDE, THE QUASI-WAR 36–73 (1966).

99. *See* Law which Determines the Character of Vessels from their Cargo, Especially Those Loaded with English Merchandise, 29 Nivose *an* 6 (January 18, 1798), Duv. & Boc. 214 (1825).

100. *See Talbot v. Seeman*, 5 U.S. (1 Cranch) 1, 6 (1801).

101. An Act to Authorize the Defence of the Merchant Vessels of the United States Against French Depredations, ch. 60, §§ 1–2, 5th Cong., 2d Sess., *in* 1 THE PUBLIC STATUTES AT LARGE OF THE UNITED STATES OF AMERICA 572–73 (Richard Peters ed., Little & Brown 1845) (1798) [hereinafter PUBLIC STATUTES].

102. An Act to Further Suspend the Commercial Intercourse between the United States and France, and the Dependencies Thereof, ch. 2, § 6, 5th Cong., 3d Sess., *in* PUBLIC STATUTES, *supra* note 79, at 615–16 (1799).

the laws were not unfettered[103] and contained a number of restrictions regarding the nature of property to be confiscated.[104] One act provided that aliens of hostile nations could depart the United States with their property intact.[105]

The United States' legislated seizure of its enemy's private property provided the Supreme Court with an opportunity to define early American judicial attitudes toward the law of nations. In the 1801 opinion of *Talbot v. Seeman*, Chief Justice Marshall, writing for the Court, upheld the constitutionality of the 1798 and 1799 Congressional Acts designed to safeguard U.S. commerce from armed foreign vessels,[106] but limited the scope of the Acts' application, and provided some criticism of the doctrine of confiscation.[107] In *The Nereide*, Marshall articulated the principle that war does not confer the right to confiscate the goods of a friend,[108] and that property belonging to a neutral nation, found on a belligerent ship, was not belligerent in nature and thus, not subject to confiscation.[109] According to Marshall,

---

103. *See* Fehlings, *supra* note 74. Congress specifically withheld the right to prey on unarmed French vessels in fear of an all-out war between the French and the United States. The United States' reluctance to authorize seizure of unarmed French vessels was less a product of enlightened thinking and more the product of America's fear of an all-out war and possible French invasion. *Id.*

104. *See* An Act to Further Suspend the Commercial Intercourse between the United States and France, and the Dependencies Thereof, ch. 2, § 6, 5th Cong., 3d Sess., *in* PUBLIC STATUTES, *supra* note 79, at 615–16 (1799).

105. *Id.* at 615; *see* JAMES KENT, 1 COMMENTARIES ON AMERICAN LAW 132 (Univ. of Chicago Press 1826).

106. *See Talbot*, 5 U.S. at 9, 31.

107. *Id.* at 41. Marshall wrote that a violation of the law of nations by one belligerent did not justify a subsequent retributive violation by the other belligerent. Marshall added that remonstrance was the appropriate initial course of action for an aggrieved nation but conceded that once all remonstrative options had been exhausted, use of hostilities was in conformity with the law of nations. *Id.*

108. *The Nereide*, 13 U.S. at 418–19. Marshall attributed recent variations to this principle to nations acting in their own self-interest, deeming a non-belligerent's right to avoid confiscation as a "simple and natural principle of public law." *Id.* at 419.

109. *Id.* at 419–20.

it was "harsh indeed to condemn neutral property, in a case in which it was clearly proved to be neutral."[110]

American efforts at retaliation showed little success, and by 1800, French military vessels and privateers had seized more than 2000 American ships.[111] Throughout the next decade, the French government continued to issue decrees and proclamations authorizing the seizure of American vessels and property.[112] This provided ample opportunity for Jefferson's political opponents to criticize his policy.[113]

The increasing number of English confiscations of American vessels on the high seas further complicated U.S. policy on confiscation and commerce.[114] With Congressional Acts authorizing the United States to seize belligerent property having little to no effect on French and British privateering, President Jefferson offered a new policy approach, whereby the United States would cut economic ties with countries confiscating the private property of its citizens.[115]

---

110. *Id.* at 417.

111. *See* Fehlings, *supra* note 74. In 1797, Secretary of State Pickering reported to Congress that during the previous 11 months, the French had captured 316 merchant ships. *Id.*

112. The Berlin Decree of November 21, 1806, declared the British Isles closed to commerce and authorized the seizure of both packages sent to England and letters written in the English language. Nov. 21, 1806, Duv. & Boc. 66 (1826). The Milan Decree, issued by Napoleon on December 17, 1807 authorized seizure of any ship and all cargo traveling from or to an English port. Dec. 17, 1807, Duv. & Boc. 223 (1826). The Bayonne Decree, issued on April 23, 1808, authorized the immediate seizure of all American vessels found in France. Lossing, *supra* note 71, at 170. The Rambouillet Decree, issued on March 23, 1810, Duv. & Boc. 69 (1826), in response to the Non-Intercourse Act, ch. 24, 2 Stat. 528 (1809), provided that any American ship traveling in French controlled territory or any ship carrying an American or American goods was subject to seizure.

113. Lossing, *supra* note 71, at 168. Lossing quoted a Jefferson critic who noted that his policy was "wasteful imbecility." *Id.*

114. Lossing, *supra* note 71, at 158. The attack on the American vessel the Chesapeake by the British was heavily criticized across the board within the United States. *Id.*

115. *See generally* L. M. Sears, Jefferson and the Embargo (1927) (exploring Jefferson's perspective on the use of embargo and its role in the law of nations). The first attempt was the Nonimportation Act of 1806, ch. 29, 2 Stat. 379, forbidding the importation of specified British goods in order

The effects of this policy shift did little to thwart privateering.[116] In 1810, America's resumption of trade led France to repeal many of their decrees authorizing confiscation of American goods.[117] England's refusal to follow suit, and their continued plundering of American goods led President Madison to ask Congress for a declaration of war, and the War of 1812 ensued.

Following the 1812 war, U.S. policy regarding a sovereign's confiscatory rights continued to shift from the absolute to the limited. Some scholars have attributed this shift to the expansion of voting rights during the 1820s and 1830s.[118] The argument in support of this shift is that, with a larger populace able to express their preferences through the ballot box, politicians began paying more attention to the right of individual ownership of personal property. More importantly, the

---

to force England to relax its rulings on cargoes and sailors. The act was suspended, and replaced by the Embargo Act of 1807, ch. 5, 2 Stat. 451, which forbade all international trade to and from American ports. Britain and France stood firm, and not enough pressure could be brought to bear. In March of 1809, the embargo was superseded by the Non-Intercourse Act, ch. 24, 2 Stat. 528. This allowed resumption of all commercial intercourse except with Britain and France, but failed to bring pressure on the belligerents. In 1810, it was replaced by Macon's Bill No. 2, ch. 39, 2 Stat. 605, which provided for trade with both Britain and France so long as they timely revoked their restrictions on American shipping; the President was empowered to forbid commerce with either Britain or France if they failed to revoke their offensive measures.

116. SEARS, *supra* note 93, at 124–42. Jefferson's acts had little impact on the seizure of American cargo but irritated Northeast merchants, who expressed their concern in the ballot box and in the press. However, Sears suggests that ultimately Northeast merchants adapted to the embargo as it spurred the development of domestic manufacturing in the North. Although Southerners tended to support the embargo, it actually harmed them as the embargo did not encourage the development of manufacturing in the South. *See id.* at 125–28, 145–51.

117. In a letter dated August 5, 1810, the Duke of Cadore, speaking on behalf of Napoleon declared the Berlin and Milan decrees repealed, effective November 1, 1810. LOSSING, *supra* note 71, at 178–79.

118. *See* Jansen, *supra* note 44 ("During the 1820's and 1830's suffrage became wider and property and freehold requirements for voting gradually were abandoned. More offices at state and local levels [also] became elective rather than appointive in nature.").

courts, and Marshall in particular, established that it was within the judicial power to chastise those sovereigns abusing the right to seize the property of belligerents. Although many of the Court's decisions during this time period left the ultimate decision on matters of confiscation in the hands of the legislative branch, the Court was quick to limit acts of confiscation performed outside the realm of war.[119]

In sum, doctrines balancing the right of confiscation and of private property, in part, was a reflection that early U.S. leaders lacked the military strength and economic leverage required for the application of the sovereign's absolute power to seize private property during times of conflict. As a result, early American exercise of its confiscatory power was used as a retributive last resort when all other methods of diplomacy had been exhausted. However, even as American military strength grew throughout the early nineteenth century, the Supreme Court, and specifically, Justice Marshall, sought to limit the sovereign's confiscatory power, and consistently held that the decision to confiscate lay in the hands of elected officials rather than with the courts.[120] The foregoing cases and analysis demonstrate judicial creativity in managing the tension between the absolute powers of confiscation, on the one hand, and giving commerce a definite freedom during wartime, on the other. By inventing a variety of doctrines, courts deemphasized sharp distinctions between the power to confiscate and the right to engage in commerce during wartime.

D. The Exceptional Circumstances Doctrine

The exceptional circumstances doctrine is the fourth and final doctrine on the relationship between commerce and conquest during war that I will explore here and more fully elaborate on in Section III of Chapter 2. Unlike any of the foregoing doctrines, it is founded on

---

119. *Percheman*, 32 U.S. (7 Pet.) at 86–87. In *Percheman*, private landowners used the United States for enforcement of the 1819 Treaty regarding Spanish cessation of Florida. Specifically, the treaty guaranteed landowners continued possession of all property owned prior to the change in sovereignty. Justice Marshall, writing for the court, held that a change in sovereignty does not affect the right of private individuals to possess and enjoy their property. *Id.*

120. *Id.* at 89–90. In fact, Marshall labelled the practice of confiscation unjust and morally outrageous. *Id.* at 86–87.

extremely broad and troublesome claims of authority. For example, although Justice Marshall strongly argued in favor of limiting the power of confiscation without congressional grants of approval, he nevertheless argued that conquest[121] and discovery[122] give conquerors a legitimate title to the territory of Native Americans. Hence, in exactly the same time period that he was urging limitations on the power of confiscation, he was endorsing the acquisition of titles to territory by conquest and discovery. He also favored the incorporation of conquered peoples into American society.[123] However, he specially singled out what he referred to as Indian "tribes" for nonincorporation, because in his view they were "fierce savages, whose occupation was war, and whose subsistence was drawn chiefly from the forest."[124] Marshall argued that it was impossible to "govern them as a distinct people" and because of their fierceness, it was necessary to enforce European claims to the land occupied by these Indians "by the sword."[125] War then, rather than incorporation, was the solution

---

121. In *Johnson v. M'Intosh*, Marshall held that, "[c]onquest gives a title which the Courts of the conqueror cannot deny, whatever the private and speculative opinions of individuals may be, respecting the original justice of the claim which has been successfully asserted." 21 U.S. 543, 587 (1823).

122. According to Marshall:
However extravagant the pretension of converting the discovery of an inhabited country into conquest may appear; if the principle has been asserted in the first instance, and afterwards sustained; if a country has been acquired and held under it; if the property of the great mass of the community originates in it, it becomes the law of the land, and cannot be questioned.
Id. at 591.
In affirming this further Marshall notes:
This opinion conforms precisely to the principle which has been supposed to be recognised [sic] by all European governments, from the first settlement of America. The absolute ultimate title has been considered as acquired by discovery, subject only to the Indian title of occupancy, which title the discoverers possessed the exclusive right of acquiring. Such a right is no more incompatible with a seisin in fee, than a lease for years, and might as effectually bar an ejectment.
Id. at 592. *See also id*. at 595.

123. *Id*. at 589.
124. *Id*. at 590.
125. *Id*. Marshall claimed that the Indians were incapable of legally owning the land and that they merely possessed it and as such could not pass on valid

for the subjugation of the Native Americans. Marshall endorsed this subjugation by arguing that "European policy, numbers, and skill, prevailed" over Indian aggression.[126]

As Marshall's holding in *Johnson v. M'Intosh* illustrates, under this exceptional circumstances doctrine, the power of confiscating or assuming title over Indian territory arises, not simply out of a belligerent's absolute power, but rather out of the presumed backwardness of those whose territory or property was subject to seizure, as well as by virtue of the proclaimed superiority of Europeans over these peoples. Similar to Marshall's unqualified support of the effect of conquest on Indian territory and the arrogance of European conquest, a British court in the early twentieth century upheld the refusal of the British government to compensate a South African company whose gold had been seized. The court, recalling an earlier case, observed that "where the King of England conquers a country . . . by saving the lives of the people conquered [he] *gains a right and property in such people*, in consequence of which *he may impose upon them what laws he pleases.*"[127]

This basis of this doctrine in the common law finds expression in the landmark 1602 *Calvin's Case*, where Lord Coke noted:

> And upon this ground there is a diversity between a conquest of a kingdom of a Christian King, and the conquest of a kingdom of an infidel; for if a King come to a Christian kingdom by conquest, seeing that he hath *vitæ et necis potestatem*, he may at his pleasure alter and change the laws of that kingdom: but until be doth make an alteration of those laws the ancient laws of that kingdom remain. But if a Christian King should conquer a kingdom of an infidel, and bring them under his subjection, there *ipso facto* the laws of the infidel are abrogated, for that they be not only against Christianity, but against the law of God and of nature, contained in the decalogue.[128]

Similarly, Alexander the Great extolled the idea that conquerors dictate the law to the conquered, and the conquered are expected to

---

title to the white population. Marshall claimed that the Indians were merely the ancient inhabitants of the land. *Id.* at 591.

126. *Id.* at 590.

127. *W. Rand Cent. Gold Mining Co. v. R.*, 2 K.B. 391, 406 (1905) (emphasis added).

128. *Calvin v. Smith*, 7 Coke Rep. 1a, 77 Eng. Rep. 377, 397–98 (K.B. 1608).

abide by that law.[129] Even during the Roman Empire, it was "an indubitable right of war, for the conqueror to impose whatever terms he pleased upon the conquered."[130] There is clearly a lineage of Western thought exemplified in *Calvin's Case*, designating non-Christian and non-European peoples not only as infidels, but as perpetual enemies with whom their conquerors could have no peace.[131] Some scholars have argued that the prejudice against nonbelievers in *Calvin's Case* was a throwback to a very medieval time, and that this dictum was also quite contrary to the "commercial interests of a country which was beginning to conduct a prosperous trade with infidels."[132]

It is certainly true that the prejudice against nonbelievers is medieval.[133] It is also important to note that this prejudice was sometimes expressed in subtle, although still Eurocentric, ways in the process of justifying European conquest and acquisition of non-European territory and resources.[134] For example, in a groundbreaking analysis of

---

129. HUGO GROTIUS, THE RIGHTS OF WAR AND PEACE 348 (A. C. Campbell trans., M. Walter Dunne Publisher 1901) (1625), *available at* http://oll.libertyfund.org:81/Texts/Grotius0110/LawOfWarPeace/0138_Bk.pdf.

130. *Id.*

131. *Calvin*, 77 Eng. Rep. at 397; *see* 8 WILLIAM HOLDSWORTH, A HISTORY OF ENGLISH LAW 409 (2d ed., Little, Brown, and Company 1937) (1903).

132. 8 HOLDSWORTH, *supra* note 110, at 409. The *writ de haeretico comburendo*, an English writ dating back to 1401, permitted the execution of a heretic. BLACK'S LAW DICTIONARY 435–36 (7th ed. 1999).

133. Today international law recognizes freedom of religion in Article 18 of the International Covenant on Civil and Political Rights. International Covenant on Civil and Political Rights, art. 18, *adopted and opened for signature* Dec. 16, 1966, 6 I.L.M. 368, 999 U.N.T.S. 171.

134. *See, e.g.*, Robert A. Williams, *The Algebra of Federal Indian Law: The Hard Trial of Decolonizing and Americanizing the White Man's Indian Jurisprudence*, 1986 WIS. L. REV. 219, 244–245 (1986). Williams notes that:

Eurocentrically-defined reason's mediating function, represented conceptually in the law of God and nature, was used to determine the status and rights of all individuals according to universal normative criteria. Those who could presumptively comport their conduct according to these universalized norms, such as European Christians at peace with the King, were granted rights consistent with their status. Those who presumptively could not, such as infidels, were not even entitled to inclusion within the hierarchy of statuses accorded to individuals in Coke's English common law jurisprudence.

Id.

the writings of Vitoria, the sixteenth-century international legal jurist credited with being one of the founders of international law, Antony Anghie shows that, whereas Vitoria exhibited an apparently progressive approach to dealing with the Indians by arguing in favor of incorporating them within the universal law of *jus gentium*, he soon thereafter began to argue that their incorporation into this universal law laid a basis to justify the imposition of Spanish discipline on them.[135] Vitoria argued that because Indians were resisting the right of the Spanish to sojourn on their territory, the Spanish were entitled to use forcible means to enforce this right.[136] In addition, Vitoria argued that the humanitarian limitations of waging war did not apply to Indians. In Vitoria's words:

> And so when a war is at that pass that the indiscriminate spoliation of all enemy-subjects alike and the seizure of all their goods are justifiable, then it is also justifiable to carry all enemy-subjects off into captivity, whether they be guilty or guiltless. And inasmuch as war with pagans is of this type, seeing that it is perpetual and that they can never make amends for the wrongs and damages they have wrought, it is indubitably lawful to carry off both the children and women of the Saracens into captivity and slavery.[137]

Vitoria's writings here sound eerily similar to Lord Coke's dictum in *Calvin's Case*.[138] Like Lord Coke, Vitoria justified as lawful the killing of the Indians in the course of the war, noting that this is "especially the case against the unbeliever, from whom it is useless ever to hope for a just peace on any terms."[139] Thus, according to Vitoria, war and the destruction of all the Indians who bore arms against the invading Spanish conquerors was the only remedy available to the Spaniards.[140]

---

135. Antony Anghie, *Francisco de Vitoria and the Colonial Origins of International Law*, 5 Soc. & Legal Stud. 321, 327–31 (1996).
136. *Id.* at 328.
137. *Id.* at 330.
138. *Calvin*, 77 Eng. Rep. at 398.
139. Anghie, *supra* note 113, at 330.
140. *Id.* at 328. Under Eurocentric jurisprudence, conquest was thought necessary to "'bring the Infidels and Savages' . . . to human Civility, and to a settled and quiet Government.'" Williams, *supra* note 108, at 246 (quoting S. Commanger, Documents of American History 8 (1968)).

What is remarkable about Justice Marshall, Vitoria, and Lord Coke's dictum in *Calvin's Case* is the genealogical similarity in their racially charged jurisprudence with respect to non-Christian and non-European peoples. One could surmise that such similar jurisprudential moves arise in the encounter between metropolitan policy and local colonial conflict.[141] As Laura Benton has argued, the extraterritorial expansion of metropolitan authority in the periphery produced predictable "routines for incorporating groups with separate legal identities in production and trade and for accommodating (or changing) culturally diverse ways of viewing the regulation and exchange of property."[142] Thus, widely repeated conflicts between people from vastly different cultural and racial backgrounds reproduce similar solutions and rules for ordering relations between them.[143] The solution under English law for ordering these relations was "Christian subjugation and remediation."[144] Ordering these relations was then ultimately a question of power.[145]

In my view, the haphazard[146] and massive transformation of the Iraqi economy by the U.S.-led occupation paralleled the expansive and extraordinary powers of subjugating non-European peoples as

---

141. For further discussion, see LAUREN BENTON, LAW AND COLONIAL CULTURES: LEGAL REGIMES IN WORLD HISTORY, 1400–1900 at 4–5 (2002), which has heavily influenced my work.

142. *Id.* at 5.

143. *See generally* ANTONY ANGHIE, IMPERIALISM, SOVEREIGNTY AND THE MAKING OF INTERNATIONAL LAW (2005) (arguing that sovereignty doctrine emerged through the encounter with cultural difference).

144. Williams, *supra* note 112, at 247.

145. *See* Judith Resnik, *Dependent Sovereigns: Indian Tribes, States, and the Federal Courts*, 56 U. CHI. L. REV. 671, 675 (1989) (arguing that the issues of power and sovereignty "dominate the scholarship of 'federal courts' jurisprudence").

146. For an acknowledgement of the haphazard nature of this transformation by a senior U.S. administrator in Iraq, see L. PAUL BREMER III & MALCOLM MCCONNELL, MY YEAR IN IRAQ: THE STRUGGLE TO BUILD A FUTURE OF HOPE (2006). *See also* GEORGE PACKER, THE ASSASSINS' GATE: AMERICA IN IRAQ (2005). For a view that the market reforms were not embraced by the U.S. military but only by its civilian administrators, see Laura Dickinson, Outsourcing War and Peace (forthcoming 2009, Yale University Press).

claimed by Vitoria, Lord Coke, and Justice Marshall.[147] The 2003 Anglo-American war against Iraq was primarily premised on finding weapons of mass destruction to preempt their use in future terrorist attacks.[148] However, the goal of finding weapons of mass destruction amounted to naught.[149] For this reason, other justifications given by the Bush and Blair administrations for going to Iraq need to be taken seriously. According to Colin Powell, then Secretary of State, the U.S.-led coalition was waging war to "liberate the Iraqi people"[150] from Saddam Hussein's tyrannical dictatorship, including his torture chambers. Fully aware that the war against Saddam Hussein would be widely regarded as the conquest of a militarily weaker and oil-rich country, former President Bush argued that the United States exercises its "power without conquest" and that it sacrifices "for the liberty of strangers."[151] Thus, according to President Bush:

> America is a nation with a mission, and that mission comes from our most basic beliefs. We have no desire to dominate, no ambitions of empire. Our aim is a democratic peace—a peace founded upon the dignity

---

147. See Ash U. Bali, *Justice Under Occupation: Rule of Law and the Ethics of Nation-Building in Iraq*, 30 YALE J. INT'L L. 431, 440–45 (2005) (criticizing the United States' desire to establish a market economy in post-Saddam Iraq as in conflict with its obligations as an occupying power). See generally Henry H. Perritt, Jr., *Iraq and the Future of United States Foreign Policy: Failures of Legitimacy*, 31 SYRACUSE J. INT'L L. & COM. 149 (2004) (evaluating and critiquing the United States political trusteeship of Iraq). See also James Thuo Gathii, *Foreign and Other Economic Rights Upon Conquest and Under Conquest and Under Occupation: Iraq in Comparative and Historical Context*, 25 U. PA. J. INT'L ECON. L. 491, 534–43 (2004) (discussing the international rules governing an occupying power).

148. Robert F. Turner, *Operation Iraqi Freedom: Legal and Policy Considerations*, 27 HARV. J.L. & PUB. POL'Y 765, 778 (2004).

149. Robert Cryer & A. P. Simester, *Iraq and the Use of Force: Do the Side-Effects Justify the Means?*, 7 THEORETICAL INQUIRIES IN L. 9, 10 (2006). "In post-Saddam Iraq, after more than a year of searching, the coalition failed to find any evidence of WMD in Iraq." Id.

150. Colin L. Powell, Secretary of State, United States of America, Remarks at Briefing on the State Department's 2002 Country Reports on Human Rights Practices (Mar. 31, 2003), available at http://www.state.gov/secretary/former/powell/remarks/2003/19218.htm (last visited Mar. 23, 2006).

151. George W. Bush, President, United States of America, State of the Union Address (Jan. 28, 2003), available at http://www.whitehouse.gov/news/releases/2003/01/20030128–23.html (last visited Mar. 23, 2006).

and rights of every man and woman. America acts in this cause with friends and allies at our side, yet we understand our special calling: This great republic will lead the cause of freedom.[152]

Clearly then, spreading freedom and other humanitarian goals clothe the geopolitical ambitions of conquering States today as did the mission to spread the benefits of civilization during the times of Spanish conquest of the New World, as seen by jurists like Vitoria. Similar to the jurisprudence of Justice Marshall with regard to Native Americans, or of Lord Coke with regard to the Irish in *Calvin's Case*, the cause of freedom that justified the 2003 war against Iraq is an expression of military power laced with the desire to subjugate so-called "primitive" peoples.[153]

The mission of bringing freedom to Iraq and to the Middle East is no less informed by a view that presupposes the superiority and inevitability of the values of liberty and freedom as Western norms to be spread around the globe with forcible means if need be.[154] This parallels Vitoria's sixteenth century views that the Spanish were free to wage war against the Indians if they resisted the right of the Spanish to sojourn in the New World.[155] Just as Vitoria recognized the humanity of the Indians, the Bush administration similarly acknowledges the humanity of the Iraqis and the peoples of the Middle East,[156]

---

152. George W. Bush, President, United States of America, State of the Union Address (Jan. 20, 2004), *available at* http://www.whitehouse.gov/news/releases/2004/01/20040120-7.html (last visited Mar. 23, 2006).

153. For an excellent exposition of this theme in the context of human rights, see Makau Mutua, *Savages, Victims, and Saviors: The Metaphor of Human Rights*, 42 HARV. INT'L L.J. 201 (2001).

154. Jacinta O'Hagan, *Conflict, Convergence or Co-existence? The Relevance of Culture in Reframing World Order*, 9 TRANSNAT'L L. & CONTEMP. PROBS. 537, 565 (1999) (describing a "clash of civilizations" analysis where Western universalism "projects Western evolved norms and values" including the use of force as a means to achieve that end).

155. *See supra* notes 117–18.

156. Thus, according to President Bush, "Our desire is to help Iraqi citizens find the blessings of liberty within their own culture and their own traditions." *See* Press Release, White House, President Signs Iraq Resolution (Oct.16, 2002), http://www.whitehouse.gov/news/releases/2002/10/20021016-1.html (last visited Mar. 23, 2006).

but it nevertheless justifies the use of force to spread the benefits of freedom to them.[157]

Lurking[158] behind these humanitarian justifications is the fact that the United States and the United Kingdom were unable to procure Security Council consent to use force against Iraq or even to build a broad based coalition in the war effort.[159] Thus, it is legitimate to ask whether the reasons given for the invasion were pretexts for seeking control of one of the richest oil sources in the world today, or whether it was to demonstrate the unparalleled military might of the United States to other so-called rogue States.

The U.S.-led coalition also assumed broad powers in the governance of occupied Iraq. After the coalition single-handedly appointed Civilian Governor Paul Bremer without any apparent consultation with the then U.S.-appointed Iraqi Governing Council,[160] Bremer issued a series of wide-ranging orders authorizing, among other things: foreign investors to own up to 100 percent interest in Iraqi companies (without profit-repatriation conditions) in virtually all sectors of the economy,[161] while leaving the oil industry in the hands

---

157. According to President Bush, "[p]art of the war on terror is to promote freedom in the Middle East." *See* Press Release, White House, President Discusses Energy, Iraq and Middle East (Aug. 19, 2003), http://www.whitehouse.gov/news/releases/2003/08/20030819.html (last visited Mar. 23, 2006).

158. The remainder of this section is largely based on and is a further exploration of a section of my previous article, *Foreign and Other Economic Rights Upon Conquest and Under Occupation: Iraq in Comparative and Historical Context*, 25 U. PA. J. INT'L ECON. L. 491, 536–43 (2004).

159. *See France Warns of "Illegitimate" War*, CNN, Feb. 26, 2003, http://www.cnn.com/2003/WORLD/meast/02/26/sprj.irq.france.warn/index.html (last visited Mar. 1, 2006). Countries argued that a U.S.-led force to overthrow Saddam Hussein without UN approval was an illegitimate use of force. They urged the United States to refrain from launching a unilateral invasion against Iraq, believing that international approval in the form of a Security Council Resolution should be obtained before any military attack was made. *See id.*

160. *See* Dmitry Kirsanov, *Paul Bremer Appointed Chief of Civilian Authorities in Iraq*, ITAR-TASS NEWS AGENCY, May 2, 2003.

161. Coalitional Provisional Authority Order No. 39: Foreign Investment (Sept. 19, 2003), *available at* http://www.cpa-iraq.org/regulations. Some commentators have suggested that this Order is highly troublesome because it conflicts with the Iraqi Constitution. *See* Thomas Catan, *Iraq Business Deals*

of a professional management team who would be independent from political control;[162] the appointment of a former Shell Oil Company CEO to be chair of an advisory committee to oversee the rehabilitation of Iraq's oil industry;[163] a flat tax;[164] a U.S.-Middle East free trade area;[165] the privatization of the police force;[166] formation of a stock market with electronic trading;[167] and the establishment of modern income tax, banking, and commercial law systems under the direction of U.S. contractors.[168]

A secret plan dubbed "Moving the Iraqi Economy from Recovery to Sustainable Growth," drafted, in part by U.S. Treasury Department officials, was written as a blueprint for reorganizing the Iraqi economy

---

May Be Invalid, Law Experts Warn, FIN. TIMES, Oct. 29, 2003, at 14. An article published by the conservative Heritage Foundation has called for widespread privatization of publicly held Iraqi assets. Ariel Cohen & Gerald P. O'Driscoll, Jr., *The Road to Economic Prosperity for a Post-Saddam Iraq*, HERITAGE FOUND, Mar. 5, 2003, http://www.heritage.org/Research/MiddleEast/loader.cfm?url=/commonspot/security/getfile.cfm&PageID=37452.

162. *See* Chip Cummins, *State-Run Oil Company is Being Weighed for Iraq*, WALL ST. J., Jan. 7, 2004, at A1 (noting the opinion of the occupation advisors that the oil industry should be state-owned).

163. *See* Neela Banerjee, *A Retired Shell Executive Seen as Likely Head of Production*, N.Y. TIMES, Apr. 2, 2003, at B12 (noting that the former chief executive of Shell Oil is expected to be the leading candidate to oversee Iraqi oil production).

164. Coalitional Provisional Authority Order No. 37: Tax Strategy for 2003 (Sept. 19, 2003), *available at* http://www.cpa-iraq.org/regulations. The flat rate tax is apparently down from 45 percent under Saddam Hussein. Dana Milbank & Walter Pincus, *U.S. Administrator Imposes Flat Tax System on Iraq*, WASH. POST, Nov. 2, 2003, at A09.

165. *See* Jess Bravin & Chip Cummins, *U.S. Offers Concessions to U.N. in Bid to Lift Sanctions on Iraq*, WALL ST. J., May 9, 2003, at A1.

166. *See* Andrew Higgins, *As It Wields Power, U.S. Outsources Law and Order Work*, WALL ST. J., Feb. 2, 2004, at A1.

167. *See* Neil King, Jr., *Bush Officials Draft Broad Plan for Free-Market Economy in Iraq*, WALL ST. J., May 1, 2003, at A1. Private American contractors will be primarily responsible for establishing the proposed Iraqi electronic stock market. *Id.*

168. *See id.* at A8; *see also* Bob Sherwood, *Legal Reconstruction: Investors Want Reassurance Over Iraq's Framework of Commercial Law*, FIN. TIMES, Nov. 3, 2003, at 14.

along a free market model.[169] Two primary premises of the privatization effort underpinning this effort were that Western-based firms are capable of making Iraq's assets and resources more productive, and that private ownership at a time when there is no stable government in the country is preferable to public ownership of assets.[170] In addition, these reforms were predicated on the view that a future Iraqi government organized around a model of free market democracy would unlikely become dictatorial or inclined to develop weapons of mass destruction, as did the Saddam Hussein regime.[171] These reforms were widely criticized for being thinly veiled plans to give multinational corporations access to Iraqi assets.[172]

The exercise of these expansive powers to transform Iraq into a free market economy incorporating controversial elements, such as a flat tax, have been justified as falling within the scope of the Coalition Provisional Authority's (CPA) mandate of promoting "the welfare of the Iraqi people through the effective administration of the territory"[173] and assisting in the "economic reconstruction and the conditions for sustainable development."[174] The powers exercised by the CPA in signing privatization contracts lacked legitimacy among a broad range of Iraqis[175] and may potentially be subject to reversal by a post-occupation

---

169. King, *supra* note 145, at A1, A8.

170. For similar views justifying a role for the private sector in post-war reconstruction, see Allan Gerson, *Peace Building: The Private Sector's Role*, 95 AM. J. INT'L. L. 102 (2001).

171. *See generally id.* (discussing the international community's recognition of the importance of private-sector involvement in unstable areas).

172. *E.g.*, Sara Flounders, *Why Best-Laid Plans Can Go Astray: The Corporate Looting of Iraq*, WORKERS WORLD (N.Y.), July 24, 2003, at 6–7, available at http://workers.org/pdf/2003/ww072403.pdf; *The Rape of Iraq*, WORLD SOCIALIST WEB SITE, May 9, 2003, http://www.wsws.org/articles/2003/may2003/iraq-m09_prn.shtml (last visited Feb. 23, 2006).

173. S.C. Res. 1483, ¶ 4, U.N. Doc. S/RES/1483 (May 22, 2003).

174. *Id.* ¶ 8(e).

175. *See* Cummins, *supra* note 140 at A1. *See also* ANDREW NEWTON & MALAIKA CULVERWELL, ROYAL INSTITUTE OF INTERNATIONAL AFFAIRS, SUSTAINABLE DEVELOPMENT PROGRAMME, LEGITIMACY RISKS AND PEACE-BUILDING OPPORTUNITIES: SCOPING THE ISSUES FOR BUSINESSES IN POST-WAR IRAQ 1, (stating that "business must earn legitimacy if it is to approach successfully the opportunities arising from the need to reconstruct Iraq"), *available at* http://www.chathamhouse.org.uk/viewdocument.php?documented=3953.

Iraqi regime exercising its internationally recognized sovereignty over its natural and other resources.[176] Further, justifying a broad mandate on the premise that it is consistent with the welfare of the Iraqi people is very reminiscent of the "sacred trust of civilization," under which European countries justified their mission of colonial rule and administration.[177]

Thus, in addition to the broad-ranging measures confiscating the property of Baathists discussed earlier in this chapter, the massive transformation of the Iraqi economy, without the consent of the Iraqi people, based on the presumed superiority of the free market model of economic governance and constitutional democracy, the occupation forces exercised extremely broad powers to transform the Iraqi economy into something of an idyllic bastion of the free markets.[178] Even the U.S. economy is not governed by market norms as extensively as the U.S. reforms under then occupied Iraq suggest. For example, the conservative economic idea of a flat tax imposed in Iraq has found

---

176. Paragraph 7 of General Assembly Resolution 1803 provides that the "[v]iolation of the rights of peoples and nations to sovereignty over their natural wealth and resources is contrary to the spirit and principles of the Charter of the United Nations and hinders the development of international cooperation and the maintenance of peace." G.A. Res. 1803, ¶ 7, U.N. GAOR, 17th Sess., Supp. No. 17, U.N. Doc. A/5217 (Dec. 14, 1962). Paragraph 1 of General Assembly Resolution 1803 provides that "[t]he right of peoples and nations to permanent sovereignty over their natural wealth and resources must be exercised in the interest of their national development and of the well-being of the people of the State concerned." *Id.* ¶ 1. The Preamble of Security Council Resolution 1483, in addition, provides that "the right of the Iraqi people freely to determine their own political future and control their own natural resources." S.C. Res. 1483, ¶ 4, U.N. Doc. S/RES/1483 (May 22, 2003); note that U.N. Security Council Resolution 1511, adopted on October 16, 2003, underscored "that the sovereignty of Iraq resides in the State of Iraq," and reaffirmed "the right of the Iraqi people freely to determine their own political future and control their own natural resources." S.C. Res. 1511, pmbl., ¶ 2, U.N. Doc. S/RES/1511(Oct. 16, 2003).

177. *See* James Thuo Gathii, *Geographical Hegelianism in Territorial Disputes Involving Non-European Land Relations: An Analysis of the Case Concerning Kasikili/Sedudu Island (Botswana/Namibia)*, 15 LEIDEN J. INT'L L. 581 (2002) (discussing the role of racism in the European colonization of African nations).

178. *See* Duncan Kennedy, *Shock and Awe Meets Market Shock: The Dangerous Mix of Economic and Military Goals in Iraq*, BOSTON REV., Oct.–Nov. 2003, http://www.bostonreview.net/BR28.5/kennedy.html.

little attraction in the United States. Furthermore, the claims of the unassailable superiority of the occupation's goal of achieving of both human and economic freedom was undermined by the torture of Iraqis,[179] as well as massive economic corruption.[180]

III. CONCLUSIONS

Since the end of the nineteenth century, commerce has often been thought of as an antidote to war and wartime confiscation. In this

---

179. *See generally* REPORT OF THE INTERNATIONAL COMMITTEE OF THE RED CROSS (ICRC) ON THE TREATMENT BY THE COALITION FORCES OF PRISONERS OF WAR AND OTHER PROTECTED PERSONS BY THE GENEVA CONVENTIONS IN IRAQ DURING ARREST, INTERNMENT AND INTERROGATION (2004) *available at* http://download.repubblica.it/pdf/rapporto_crocerossa.pdf (discussing incidents of torture of Iraqi detainees by U.S. forces in Iraq prior to the revelations of the Abu Ghraib torture scandal). HUMAN RIGHTS WATCH, THE NEW IRAQ? TORTURE AND ILL TREATMENT OF DETAINEES IN IRAQI CUSTODY 2 (2005) (demonstrating that human rights violations continue at the hands of Iraqi police and an inability to confirm that U.S. torture violations are not continuing), http://www.hrw.org/reports/2005/iraq0105/iraq0105.pdf. It is also noteworthy that the President has resisted congressional legislation to prohibit torture of overseas detainees. *See Bush Urged to Specify U.S. Policy on Torture*, L.A. TIMES, Jan. 20, 2006, at A18; Editorial, *Vice President for Torture*, WASH. POST, Oct. 26, 2005, at A18.

180. Michael Hirsh, *Follow the Money*, NEWSWEEK, Apr. 4, 2005, at 34 (discussing the fraudulent actions of Custer Battles, a military contractor in Iraq contracted by the U.S. government). Custer Battles overcharged occupation authorities and therefore increased its profits by claiming inflated costs. When the fraud was exposed by whistle-blowers who brought an action against the contractor, the Bush administration refused to participate and attempted to retrieve the money that essentially the government was defrauded of. The Justice Department has never responded to requests by the presiding judge of the case to join the lawsuit. In a surprising response, the government says that the CPA is not an arm of the U.S. government. *Id. See also* CHRISTIAN AID, BRIEFING PAPER FOR THE MADRID CONFERENCE ON IRAQ, IRAQ: THE MISSING BILLIONS: TRANSITION AND TRANSPARENCY IN POST-WAR IRAQ 5 (2003) *available at* http://www.christian-aid.org.uk/indepth/310iraqoil/iraqoil.pdf; Adam Davidson & Mark Schapiro, *Spoils of War* (NPR Marketplace radio broadcast Apr. 20–23, 2004) *available at* http://marketplace.publicradio.org/features/iraq/index.html (last visited Mar. 23, 2006).

chapter, I have demonstrated that the relationship between war and the confiscation of private property is more complicated. The view that either commerce or wartime confiscation supersede each other has to be seen against a series of legal doctrines, such as neutrality and suspension. In addition, the continued vitality of the exceptional circumstances doctrine, under which belligerents have claimed inherent authority to override commerce, undermines the view that commerce has prevailed over wartime confiscations. The massive transformations of the Iraqi economy and society have been justified on the basis of such exceptional powers. It is therefore plausible to argue that it is not so much that commerce has prevailed over the barbarity of wartime confiscations, but that at various historical moments, powerful countries employ the ascendant ideas of liberty and freedom as a means of prevailing over culturally and politically different but militarily weaker societies.[181] My argument then has been that these projects of liberty and freedom, as promoted and supported by the most powerful countries, contain and sometimes conceal the raw power of wartime confiscation. Wartime confiscation is therefore not an aberration of the contemporary international legal order, but rather a constitutive component of it—albeit one that no country wants to claim adherence.

A major upshot of the analysis in this chapter is that conquest ultimately involves the domination of a militarily weaker society by a militarily stronger society. The power of confiscation in early U.S. history in relation to more economically and militarily powerful States of the period was therefore carefully hedged by the Marshall court. By contrast, in the contemporary period of unchallenged military superiority, the U.S. federal judiciary has acquiesced to the expansive claims of Executive authority to conduct the war and its military policy abroad with little, if any, checks in the context of destruction of private property.[182] Similarly, the United Nations

---

181. See Obiora Okafor, *Newness, Imperialism, and International Legal Reform in Our Time: A TWAIL Perspective*, 43 OSGOODE HALL L.J. 171 (2005).

182. However, in the context of availability of habeas for detainees captured by the United States and held abroad, the Supreme Court reversed the Bush administration at least twice for declining to extend habeas. See *Rasul v. Bush*, 542 U.S. 466 (2004) (over-ruled by statute see *Rasul v. Myers*, 512 F.3d 644 (2008)); and *Boumediene v. Bush*, 553 U.S. ___, 128 S. Ct.

Security Council has, through the Counter-Terrorism Committee, expanded its authority to legislate and in particular, to empower States to freeze, block, and confiscate assets of individuals or groups with ties to terrorism. However, the expansion of the power to confiscate in the context of conquest has not been unambiguous. There continue to be efforts to check the unbridled exercise of these powers through the human rights guarantees of the United Nations system, as well as through limiting the power of belligerents to use force inconsistently with international legal prohibitions. Curbing the excesses of war, not to mention wartime confiscations, as well as the accompanying racial and cultural arrogance of powerful northern States, continues to be an important imperative in the twenty-first century as it was in prior periods.

2229, (2008). For a critical appraisal, see Ernesto Hernandez-Lopez, *Boumediene v. Bush* and Guantánamo, Cuba: Does the "Empire Strike Back"?, 61 SMU L. Rev. 117 (2009).

2. THE EFFECT OF CONQUEST ON PRIVATE PROPERTY AND CONTRACT RIGHTS

> Even in cases of conquest, it is very unusual for the conquerer [sic] to do more than to displace the sovereign and assume dominion over the country. The modern usage of nations, which has become law, would be violated; that sense of justice and of right which is acknowledged and felt by the whole civilized world, would be outraged; if private property should be generally confiscated, and private rights annulled.[1]
>
> [W]here the King of England conquers a country . . . by saving the lives of the people conquered . . . [he] gains a right and property in such people, in consequence of which he may impose upon them what law he pleases.[2]

I. INTRODUCTION

The confiscation of private property during wartime is prohibited under customary international law.[3] This chapter examines how well this rule has held up. To do so, I will discuss a 1905 House of Lords decision that explicitly found the rule against extinction was preempted by the prerogatives of the Crown. I will also discuss how Native American ownership of land in early American history was treated as mere possession upon conquest and in the various peace treaties between the United States and Spain, whereas similar possession of land by white colonial settlers was held to constitute unimpeachable private property interests.

This chapter in effect lays the historical backdrop for my argument in the next chapter. In Chapter 3, I will show that confiscation of private property in the war and occupation of Iraq was not exceptional but part of a long history of the uneven application of international law in

---

1. *United States v. Percheman*, 32 U.S. (7 Pet.) 51, 51 (1833).
2. *W. Rand Cent. Gold Mining Co. v. King*, 2 K.B. 391, 406 (1905).
3. There is a varied range of private property and contract rights that may be protected from confiscation upon conquest. The range includes rights, interests, or titles to bank accounts; all manner of securities (such as debentures, bonds, annuities, stock, shares, etc.), and beneficial interests therein; fixed and intellectual property rights; insurance on goods or other property; life insurance policies; shareholder rights and obligations; judicial awards; and so on.

situations of colonial and imperial conquest and the routine disregard and subordination of non-European peoples to the interests of European powers.

The primary reason accounting for its uneven and inconsistent application has been to facilitate the political expediencies and hegemony of conquering States over weaker and vulnerable States. Hence, domestic courts in conquering States have held treaties embodying this rule, that private property rights shall be inextinguishable upon conquest, are subject to the overriding constraint of their compatibility with national policy during times of war.[4] In the United States, such views have been fortified by judicial attitudes reluctant to use international law to restrain the Executive Branch,[5] especially with regard to wartime decisions.[6]

---

4. See *Clark v. Allen*, 331 U.S. 503, 513–14 (1947) ("Where the relevant historical sources and the instrument itself give no plain indication that it is to become inoperative in whole or in part on the outbreak of war, we are left to determine . . . [as *Techt v. Hughes* indicates] whether the provisions under which rights are asserted is [sic] incompatible with national policy in time of war."); *Techt v. Hughes*, 128 N.E. 185 (N.Y. 1920), *cert. denied*, 254 U.S. 643 (1920) (discussing the compatibility of a treaty granting rights to an alien of an enemy State to inherit land with national policy in times of war).

5. See *Guzman v. Tippy*, 130 F.3d 64, 66 (2d Cir. 1997) (holding that Executive decisions prevail over international law); *Gisbert v. U.S. Att'y Gen.*, 988 F.2d 1437, 1448 (5th Cir. 1993) (regarding immigration issues, legislative, executive, or judicial decisions may prevail even if contrary to international law); *Garcia-Mir v. Meese*, 788 F.2d 1446, 1453–54 (11th Cir. 1986) (deciding that the Attorney General has the power to detain aliens indefinitely despite general principles of international law forbidding prolonged arbitrary detention). But see *Rodriguez-Fernandez v. Wilkinson*, 505 F. Supp. 787, 789 (D. Kan. 1980) (holding that although Rodriquez-Fernandez did not have rights to avoid detention under the Fifth or Eighth Amendments to the U.S. Constitution, the indefinite nature of his detention violated principles of customary international law which create a right to be free from such detention). *See also Rasul v. Bush*, 124 S. Ct. 2686, 2696–97 (2004) and *Boumediene v. Bush*, 128 S. Ct. 2229 (2008) (both finding that aliens held as enemy combatants outside the United States under its control and jurisdiction were entitled to habeas relief).

6. See *Hamdi v. Rumsfeld*, 316 F.3d 450, 463–64 (4th Cir. 2003) (explaining that courts are bound to defer to Executive Branch decisions during wartime, since the Executive Branch, rather than the courts, is best equipped to make such decisions); *see also Al Odah v. United States*, 321 F.3d 1134, 1150 (D.C. Cir. 2003) (Randolph, J., concurring) (stating that "[military decisions]

It follows that the prohibition against extinguishing private property and contract rights on conquest is more likely honored by conquering States when it is most compatible with their interests.[7] For example, the prohibition is often enforced to secure the private property rights of nationals from a powerful belligerent State who are domiciled in a weaker State, vulnerable to conquest.[8]

---

have traditionally been left to the exclusive discretion of the Executive Branch, and there they should remain."); *See also Rasul*, 542 U.S. at 466, *superseded by* Detainee Treatment Act of 2005, 42 U.S.C.S. § 2000dd (2008); *Hamdan v. Rumsfeld*, 464 F. Supp. 2d 9 (D.D.C. 2006), *cert. denied, Hamdan v. Gates*, 128 S. Ct. 207 (2007), *inj. denied, Hamdan v. Gates*, 2008 U.S. Dist. LEXIS 54768 (D.D.C., July 18, 2008).

7. *See Foster v. Neilson*, 27 U.S. (2 Pet.) 253, 308 (1829) (interpreting the Treaty of Amity, Settlement and Limits, between the United States and Spain, under which the United States was required to confirm land grants made by the Spanish sovereign before 1818 in territory that later became U.S. territory). Here the court construed the treaty as a contract between the United States and Spain, upon which the United States was required to respect the Spanish title grants. However, in later cases, Foster was distinguished by the principle that a treaty might not create legal obligations except between State parties. *See, e.g., Percheman*, 32 U.S. (7 Pet.) 51 (holding that the United States agreed to recognize titles derived from Spanish grants without further legislative acts). Notably, it was in the interest of the United States to have regard for its treaties with the Spanish crown, not only because the United States was not as powerful a country then as now, but also because the treaties were crucial to the construction of the government of the United States. *See* Stewart Jay, *The Status of the Law of Nations in Early American Law*, 42 Vand. L. Rev. 819, 849 (1989) (discussing the shift in U.S. world power and its impact on U.S. responses to international law), *see also* Part 3.1. *infra* (discussing *Percheman*).

8. For example, the United States argued that Iraq's invasion of Kuwait in 1990 violated Article 23(g) of the Hague Regulations because Iraq had destroyed private property, including oil wells operated by multinational corporations, which they set on fire. *See* Convention (IV) respecting the Laws and Customs of War on Land and Its Annex: Regulation Concerning the Laws and Customs of War on Land, Oct. 18, 1907, art. 23, 36 Stat. 2277, T.S. 539 [hereinafter Hague Regulations] (prohibiting the destruction of enemy property unless the destruction is demanded by the necessities of war). Note that the Hague Regulations are an annex to the 1907 Hague Convention with Respect to the Laws and Customs of War on Land, first adopted at the International Peace Conference of 1899 and revised at the Second International Peace Conference of 1907. Additionally, in the 1970s, the U.S.

II. THE PROHIBITION OF CONFISCATION OF PRIVATE PROPERTY UNDER CLASSICAL CUSTOMARY INTERNATIONAL LAW

The prohibition against destruction of enemy property by belligerents is embodied in Article 23(g) of the 1907 Hague Convention respecting the Laws and Customs of War on Land, which *especially* forbids the destruction or seizure of an "enemy's property, unless such destruction or seizure be imperatively demanded by the necessities of war."[9] Some have argued that such military necessity has to be determined given the prevailing circumstances during wartime, rather than retrospectively.[10]

This rule against extinction of private property upon conquest and its underlying justifications is an ancient, indeed, classical rule of customary international law. It was recognized by Emer de Vattel, the eighteenth-century Swiss international lawyer, who wrote:

> In the conquests of ancient times, even individuals lost their lands. Nor is it a matter of surprise that in the first ages of Rome such a custom should have prevailed. The wars of that era were carried on between popular republics and communities. The State possessed very little, and the quarrel was in reality the common cause of all the citizens. But at present war is less dreadful in its consequences to the subject: [M]atters are conducted with more humanity: [O]ne sovereign makes war against another sovereign, and not against the unarmed citizens. The conqueror seizes on the possessions of the State, the public property, while private individuals are permitted to retain theirs.[11]

State Department took the position that Israel's occupation of the Gulf of Suez did not authorize it to violate the concessionary rights granted by Egypt to an American corporation, as these rights were protected under the law of belligerent occupation. U.S. State Department Memorandum of Law on Israel's Right to Develop New Oil Fields in Sinai and the Gulf of Suez, Oct. 1, 1976, 16 I.L.M. 733, 750–53 (1977) [hereinafter Department of State Memorandum].

9. Hague Regulations, *supra* note 8.

10. MYRES S. MCDOUGAL & FLORENTINO P. FELICIANO, LAW AND MINIMUM WORLD PUBLIC ORDER: THE LEGAL REGULATION OF INTERNATIONAL COERCION 678–79 (1961) (noting such circumstances include factors such as the decision makers' position in the hierarchy of military command, the nature of the property, intelligence reports, every pressure, and even the ambiguity of the rule allegedly violated).

11. EMER DE VATTEL, THE LAW OF NATIONS 388 (Joseph Chitty trans., T. & J. W. Johnson & Co. 1861) (1758). Vattel further opined: "[t]he whole right of

This rule also forbids the confiscation of debt due to the citizens of a belligerent who has been defeated at war from the citizens of the victorious belligerent.[12] However, as we shall see below, this rule has not been consistently or evenly applied, particularly in the context of colonial relations established through conquest.

A. Rationales Underlying the Exemption of Property and Contract Rights from Extinction upon Conquest

1. **The distinction between civil and military aspects of war** The laws of war are predicated on a distinction between civilian and military aspects. This distinction arose in the practice of States that have professional militaries.[13] Pursuant to this distinction, the laws of war seek to reduce the effects of war's adverse consequences to noncombatants, particularly to civilians, the sick, and the wounded of the belligerent and neutral States.

Thus, the laws of war apply considerations of equity and justice and are embodied in the obligation of belligerent States to treat civilians, neutrals, and prisoners of war humanely. By contrast, under

---

the conqueror is derived from justifiable self-defence" and "doing of harm to an enemy is no further authorized by the law of nature, than in the precise degree which is necessary for justifiable self-defence, and reasonable security for the time to come." *Id.* at 388–89.

12.
Nearly all modern writers (*e.g.*, Calvo, Heffter, Funck-Brentano and Sorel, Martens, Twiss, Wheaton, and others) declare debts due by the subjects of one belligerent State to the subjects of the other to be free from confiscation....

... It has thus become a rule of international law that neither the principal nor the interest of a State debt can be sequestrated or confiscated. Hall maintains that a State contracting a loan is "understood to contract that it will hold itself indebted to the lender, and will pay interest on the sum borrowed under all circumstances."

COLEMAN PHILLIPSON, THE EFFECT OF WAR ON CONTRACTS AND ON TRADING ASSOCIATIONS IN TERRITORIES OF BELLIGERENTS 38–40 (1909). *See also* Vienna Convention on Succession of States in Respect of States Property, Archives and Debt, Apr. 8, 1983, art. 32–36 (1983) 31:1 SELECT DOCUMENTS ON INT'L AFF. 10 (1983) [hereinafter Vienna Convention] (establishing the survival of State debts).

13. PHILLIPSON, *supra* note 12, at 29. However, as we shall see in Chapters 6 and 7, this distinction is hardly the case today, particularly in light of developments commercializing war and in wars over natural resources.

the doctrine of military necessity, the laws of war acquiesce to the application of forcible means as necessary and proportionate to defeat the enemy and to bring the war to an end.[14]

2. **War is between states not between individuals: the rousseau-portalis doctrine** Another justification for the rule that private property and contract rights are not affected by conquest is that the rules of international law governing the conduct of warfare are based on a presumed set of clear distinctions: between States and individuals; between a relatively stronger occupying State in relation to a weaker State; between the government and the people; between public and private property; and between civilians and combatants. Thus, under classical customary international law, war was conceived as something that occurs between States, rather than between individuals.[15] Where an individual of enemy nationality and his or her property are domiciled abroad, his or her property is not regarded as having an enemy character, and if seized, cannot be confiscated.[16] Where citizens of an enemy State are domiciled within the territory of the opposing belligerent State, they and their property may assume an enemy character.[17] In particular, where the resources of such citizens were applied toward aiding the enemy, they and their property automatically acquire an

---

14. *See* Burrus M. Carnahan, *Lincoln, Lieber and the Laws of War: The Origins and Limits of the Principle of Military Necessity*, 92 AM. J. INT'L L. 213, 213–15 (1998) (defining and giving examples of military necessity in the Civil War); *See also* DAVID KENNEDY, OF WAR AND LAW (2006); Nathaniel Berman, *Privileging Combat? Contemporary Conflict and the Legal Construction of War*, 43 COLUM. J. TRANSNAT'L L. (2004) (exploring the constitutive role law plays in constructing war including the civilian/combatant distinction).

15. According to Edmund H. Schwnck, the Hague Convention was developed at a time when war was "waged against sovereign and armies and not against subjects and civilians." *Legislative Power of the Military Occupant Under Article 43, Hague Regulations*, 54 YALE L.J. 393, 403 (1945). *But see El-Shifa Pharm. Indus. Co. v. United States*, 55 Fed. Cl. 751, 771 (2003) (observing in part that the "fact that Sudan, as a nation state, was not at war with the United States is not determinative. . . . Terrorism crosses national borders, even our own . . . [w]e do not regard a war against a non-state, non-insurgent group—stateless terrorists—to be any less a war.").

16. *See* PHILLIPSON, *supra* note 12, at 35.

17. *Id.* at 34.

enemy character and become subject to confiscation.[18] Thus, under customary international law, individuals were required to subordinate their property and contractual interests where they conflicted with the superior interest of the State.[19]

3. **It is unjust and impolitic for war to destroy or impair contracts between individuals for the convenience and continuity of commerce** Since at least the eighteenth century, it has been regarded as unjust and impolitic that debts and contracts between individuals, who had confidence in each other, and as a result entered into obligations, should have that trust and confidence between them destroyed as a result of national differences, or in the event of war.[20] Further, some authorities hold that it is prudent to suspend, rather than to abrogate, loan payments owed by subjects of an enemy to the subjects of the opposing belligerent until the conclusion of the war and the return to peacetime.[21]

---

18. *Id.* at 35.
19. For example, Justice Gray noted:
[T]he law of nations, as judicially declared, prohibits all intercourse between citizens of the two belligerents, which is inconsistent with the state of war between their countries. . . . At this age of the world, when all the tendencies of the law of nations are to exempt individuals and private contracts from injury or restraint in consequence of war between their governments, we are not disposed to declare such contracts unlawful as have not been heretofore adjudged to be inconsistent with a state of war.
Kershaw v. Kelsey, 100 Mass. 561, 572–73 (Mass. 1868).
20. *See* Treaty of Amity, Commerce, and Navigation, Nov. 19, 1794, U.S.-G.B., 8 Stat. 116, at art. 10, noting that,
Neither [d]ebts due from [i]ndividuals of the one [n]ation to individuals of the other, nor shares nor monies, which they may have in the public [f]unds or in the public or private [b]anks shall ever, in any [e]vent of war, or national differences, be sequestrated, or confiscated, it being unjust and impolitick that [d]ebts and [e]ngagements contracted and made by [i]ndividuals having confidence in each other, and in their respective Governments, should ever be destroyed or impaired by national authority, on account of national [d]ifferences and [d]iscontents.
Available at http://www.yale.edu/lawweb/avalon/diplomacy/brit/jay.htm (last visited Mar. 28, 2004).
21. PHILLIPSON, *supra* note 12, at 45. Further, it appears that rules of State succession do not allow for debts to disappear upon succession of one State

Although as a general matter the doctrine of nonintercourse prohibits commerce between belligerent States, the strictness[22] of this doctrine was held by the end of the nineteenth century to have been attenuated by the "rapid advances in civilization," "progressive public opinion," and the "influence of Christianity" such that it was possible to differentiate between military as opposed to civil affairs, and between the conduct of war and of commerce.[23] Thus, in the United States, as well as in the United Kingdom, trading with the enemy requires special licenses.[24]

4. Considerations of humanity Considerations of humanity are another justification given for the rule against extinction of property rights upon conquest. One of the most eloquent exponents of this view is John Basset Moore who argued that:

> The protection of property not militarily used or in immediate likelihood of being so used against destruction, not, as writers sometimes seem to fancy, because of humane regard for insensate things, but because of the belief that, in the interest of humanity, war-stricken peoples should not be reduced to a condition of barbarism or savagery, but should, on the contrary, be enabled to resume the normal processes of peaceful life as soon as possible.[25]

---

by another. Rather, debts are carried forward, see Vienna Convention, *supra* note 12, at art. 32–36.

22. The strict application of this rule is demonstrated in a Supreme Court decision from 1814, where Judge Johnson noted in part: "The universal sense of nations has acknowledged the demoralizing effects that would result from the admission of individual intercourse. The whole nation are [sic] embarked in one common bottom, and must be reconciled to submit to one common fate. Every individual of the one nation must acknowledge every individual of the other nation as his own enemy." *The Rapid*, 12 U.S. (8 Cranch) 155, 161 (1814).

23. PHILLIPSON, *supra* note 12, at 49. Notably, Montesquieu, the French eighteenth-century philosopher argued that "commerce . . . softens and polishes the manners of men." ALBERT O. HIRSCHMAN, RIVAL VIEWS OF MARKET SOCIETY AND OTHER RECENT ESSAYS 107 (1992).

24. For the United Kingdom, *see* F. A. Mann, *Enemy Property and the Paris Peace Treaties*, 64 LAW Q. R., 492, 499 (1948). For the United States, *see* Trading with the Enemy Act, Pub. L. No. 65–91, 65th Cong., Sess. I, Ch. 105, 106, Oct. 6, 1917, which forbids trade with enemies during times of war.

25. JOHN BASSETT MOORE, INTERNATIONAL LAW AND SOME CURRENT ILLUSIONS AND OTHER ESSAYS 5 (1924).

According to Moore, the basis of this rule lay in "a moral revolt, a new creed," a "loftier conception of the destiny of and rights of man and of a more humane spirit" according to which the confiscation of property was necessary to "assure the world's commerce a legitimate and definite freedom."[26] Moore's justification of the rule is a modernist emancipatory universalism, which is argued to have prevailed over the barbarity of war and similar dark forces.[27]

B. Unevenness and Inconsistency in the Application of the Traditional Canon Proscribing Extinction of Private Property Rights and Contracts

The classical customary international rule forbidding the extinction of contracts and private property rights upon conquest has been undermined by uneven and inconsistent application. One of the reasons advanced for this inconsistency is that the rule is ancient and therefore, does not reflect the practice of States. In addition to the justifications often advanced for these departures from the proscription of extinguishing private property rights and contracts, I will show that the political and hegemonic objectives of conquering States have been an important factor in the unevenness and inconsistency in the application of the rule.

1. The emergence of hegemonic militaries The Hague Regulations were negotiated at the end of the nineteenth century, at a time when it was in the interest of the United States to comply with rules of international law.[28] The growth of the United States' political and economic power over the twentieth century has been argued by some as a justification for a less significant role for international law in governing the role of the United States in international affairs.[29]

---

26. *Id.* at 13–14.
27. For a similar exposition of the expunging of religion from international law, see David Kennedy, *Images of Religion in International Legal Theory, in* THE INFLUENCE OF RELIGION ON THE DEVELOPMENT OF INTERNATIONAL LAW, 137, 142–43 (Mark Janis ed., 1991).
28. *See* Jay, *supra* note 7, at 845.
29. *See* Jules Lobel, *The Limits of Constitutional Power: Conflicts between Foreign Policy and International Law*, 71 VA. L. REV. 1071, 1104 (1985) (suggesting that "[a]s international relations changed and American military and economic power grew, the status of international law [in this country] also changed.").

One commentator concluded that international law serves as a tool for U.S. power as opposed to a restraint of U.S. power in the world today.[30] Thus, today, a little more than a hundred years after the Hague Regulations came into force, the United States has not infrequently asserted and sought to consolidate its global military and political dominance unilaterally,[31] and in a manner unthinkable a century ago when the United States was not a superpower. This global dominance, according to adherents of this view, has resulted in reducing the constraints of international law on the United States.[32]

---

30. See Nico Krisch, *Weak as Constraint, Strong as Tool: The Place of International Law in U.S. Foreign Policy*, in UNILATERALISM AND U.S. FOREIGN POLICY: INTERNATIONAL PERSPECTIVES 41 (David M. Malone & Yuen Foong Khong eds., 2003); Joel R. Paul, *The Geopolitical Constitution: Executive Expediency and Executive Agreements*, 86 CAL. L. REV. 671 (1998) (arguing that the United States presently uses international law as a tool to expand its power).

31. The best statement of American hegemony begins with the proclamation that "[t]he United States possesses unprecedented—and unequaled—strength and influence in the world." The National Security Strategy of the United States of America (The White House, Washington, D.C.) Sept. 2002, at 1 [hereinafter National Security Strategy]. The Strategy makes it the responsibility of the United States to make the world safe and better. It declares the doctrine of preemption:

> [D]efending the United States, the American people, and our interests at home and abroad by identifying and destroying the threat before it reaches our borders . . . [and] if necessary, to exercise our right of self-defense by acting preemptively against such terrorists, to prevent them from doing harm against our people and our country.

Id. at 6. *See also*, Henry J. Richardson III, *U.S. Hegemony, Race, and Oil in Deciding United Nations Security Resolution 1441 on Iraq*, 17 TEMPLE INT'L & COMP. L.J., (2003) 27; Jose E. Alvarez, *Hegemonic International Law Revisited*, 97 AM. J. INT'L L. 873 (2003) (commenting further on the U.S. National Security Strategy).

32. See Curtis A. Bradley, *The Charming Betsy Canon and Separation of Powers: Rethinking the Interpretive Role of International Law*, 86 GEO. L.J. 478, 519 (1998). (But it may suggest that, from the U.S. perspective, the perceived risks associated with lawbreaking have been reduced. Nor does the possible erosion of the connection between international law compliance and national security mean that it is morally right for the United States to ignore international law. Perhaps an argument can be made that the U.S. position regarding international law that developed in a time of relative weakness ought to be honored when the United States has reached its place in the sun).

EFFECT OF CONQUEST ON PRIVATE PROPERTY 53

In light of the foregoing, it is not surprising that in wars involving belligerent States with large military capacities, such as the United States, such States have defended the prohibition of the destruction of private property in war to be subject to the dispositions of their municipal law.[33] Thus, the view that it would be unjust and impolitic to adversely affect private property and contractual rights in contemporary times is often subject to the immediate political goals of conquering States. For example, Israel has argued that it is not legally bound by the Fourth Geneva Convention and thus, not by the Hague Regulations with regard to its occupation of the Gaza Strip and West Bank prior to its disengagement from the Strip and parts of the West Bank in 2005.[34] In the past, some commentators suggested that, in light of Israel's sui generis occupation over the West Bank and Gaza, the Fourth Geneva Convention can only be applied on a de facto basis with regard to Israeli occupation thereof.[35] In addition, the treaties

---

33. In *El-Shifa Pharm. Indus. Co. v. United States*, 55 Fed. Cl. 751 (2003) (where a U.S. Court of Claims rejected a property compensation suit arising from the destruction of a pharmaceutical company in Sudan by the U.S. military). See also PHILLIPSON, *supra* note 12, at 52. And *Miller v. United States*, 78 U.S. (11 Wall.) 268 (1871) (noting that the power to wage war includes the right to seize and confiscate all property of an enemy and to dispose of it at will and that this "has always been an undoubted belligerent right.").

34. Israel's argument was that neither the Gaza Strip nor West Bank were sovereign territories since in Israel's view the Fourth Geneva Convention only applies to sovereign territories. Since the 2005 disengagement plan, Israel has argued that it is no longer an occupying power and as such the Fourth Geneva Convention does not apply. This view is contested particularly because Israel still retains effective control and Security Council resolutions apply the Convention's obligations to Israel, see *Legal Consequences of the Construction of a Wall in the Occupied Palestinian Territory*, INERNATIONAL COURT OF JUSTICE (July 9, 2004), available at http://www.icj-cij.org/docket/index.php?pr=71&code=mwp&p1=3&p2=4&p3=6&case=131&k=5a; and Israel: *'Disengagement' Will Not End Gaza Occupation: Israeli Government Still Holds Responsibility for Welfare of Civilians*, HUMAN RIGHTS WATCH, October 28, 2004, available at http://www.hrw.org/en/news/2004/10/28/israel-disengagement-will-not-end-gaza-occupation.

35. Meir Shamga, *The Observance of International Law in the Administered Territories*, in ISRAEL YEARBOOK ON HUM. RTS. 262, 266 (1971) ("Accordingly, the Government of Israel distinguished between the legal problem of the applicability of the Fourth Convention to territories under consideration . . . and decided to act *de facto* in accordance in accordance with humanitarian

entered into after World War I and World War II gave the victorious powers the right to seize, retain, liquidate, or take such other action whose effect was to extinguish the private property rights of nationals of the defeated States.[36] The German property confiscation in the United Kingdom was justified as necessary to satisfy those British citizens indebted to German nationals. Thus, these confiscations, notwithstanding their clear departure from the traditional canon exempting private property rights and contracts from extinction or confiscation upon conquest,[37] were justified as "the only source of reparations open to" the United Kingdom.[38]

2. **The distinction between military and civilian aspects of war is hard to sustain as a result of the nature of twenty-first century warfare** Twenty-first century warfare, as meted out by powerful countries such as the United States, is vastly different from nineteenth-century warfare. Although it has been argued that warfare has become high-tech and therefore, more precise so that there has been a decrease in the death of civilians and destruction of their private property, this has not been the case. Rather, the trebled lethality of high-tech warfare has multiplied, rather than reduced, the impact of war on civilian populations and property.[39]

---

provision of Convention"). Nathaniel Berman has criticized liberals who supported the U.S. occupation of Iraq as nothing other than a projection of raw power rather and as such that the claims of the U.S. was an enlightened occupier were exaggerated. *See* Nathaniel Berman, *Enlightened Occupiers?*, N.Y. TIMES, Nov. 9, 2003, at A10.

36. Both the Treaty of Versailles, entered into after World War I, and the Treaty of Paris, entered into after World War II, provided that it was the responsibility of the enemy States to compensate those whose property was confiscated. *See* Mann, *supra* note 24, at 498–99 (discussing interpretations of the Treaty of Paris and the Treaty of Versailles).

37. Thus, some judges wrote opinions arguing that the confiscations authorized by the Treaty of Versailles were not consistent with the "common law," *See Daimler Co. v. Cont'l Tyre & Rubber Co., Ltd.*, 2 App. Cas. 307, 347 (Parker, dissenting); *Hugh Stevenson & Sons, Ltd. v. Aktiengesellschaft für Cartonnagen-Industrie*, App. Cas. 239, 244 (appeal taken from Eng.) (Lord Finlay's opinion); *Friedrich Krupp A.G. v. Orconera Iron Ore Co.* 88 L.J.R. 304, 309 (1919) (Lord Birkenhead's opinion).

38. Mann, *supra* note 24, at 498–99.

39. *See generally* Thomas W. Smith, *The New Law of War: Legitimizing Hi-Tech and Infrastructural Violence*, 46 INT'L STUD. Q. 355 (2002) (arguing

Several reasons account for the trebled lethality of presumably more precise weaponry. First, powerful States with such sophisticated weaponry have made sophisticated legal arguments to justify narrowing distinctions between soldiers and civilians that legitimize civilian casualties and destruction to civilian property as collateral damage.[40] In addition, at various times countries such as the United States have adopted doctrines justifying the use of overwhelming military force,[41] inter alia, the use of unchallenged heavy precision-guided aerial bombs and missiles to support few, but well-equipped battalions in enemy territory.[42] Second, the traditional humanitarian constraints on the use of military force have been mobilized to lend credibility to new visions of military necessity and military action.[43] For example, Anne Orford argued that the doctrine of militarized humanitarianism that began after the Cold War, which accelerated with the War Against Terrorism, has had adverse human rights and economic consequences for nondominant cultures and peoples.[44]

Thus, the premise of the classical rule prohibiting extinction of property rights and contracts upon conquest that was predicated on the distinction between military and civilian aspects of war is not any truer today than it was in the nineteenth century.[45] For example, in

---

that new legal interpretations of military necessity increase harm to long-term public health and human rights despite new technology's success in curbing immediate civilian casualties).

40. *See* Roger Normand & Chris af Jochnick, *The Legitimation of Violence: A Critical Analysis of the Gulf War*, 35 HARV. INT'L L.J. 387 (1994) (arguing that laws of war are drafted to subordinate humanitarian obligations to military necessities); *See also* KENNEDY, *supra* note 14; Berman, *supra* note 14.

41. For a description of the Powell doctrine, see *Doctrine of Digital War*, BUS. WEEK, Apr. 7, 2003, at 32.

42. *Id.* at 30–32.

43. *See* Smith, *supra* note 39, at 367–70 (discussing the erosion of fundamental rules and legal maneuvering to permit military necessity to supersede humanitarian law).

44. ANNE ORFORD, READING HUMANITARIAN INTERVENTION: HUMAN RIGHTS AND THE USE OF FORCE IN INTERNATIONAL LAW (2003).

45. For a similar point of view, see Michael W. Lewis, *The Law of Aerial Bombardment in the 1991 Gulf War*, 97 AM. J. INT'L L., 481, 508 (2003) (quoting Clausewitz to the effect that war is the realm of uncertainty and as such notwithstanding the technological advances of modern warfare, the uncertainties of war will continue to produce "unintended consequences").

the *Bankovic* case before the European Court of Human Rights, six Yugoslavian nationals sought orders against the seventeen North Atlantic Treaty Organization (NATO) member States concerning the bombing of the Serbian Radio and Television Headquarters in Belgrade during the course of the NATO air strike campaign in the Kosovo conflict.[46] This instance of bombardment of civilian facilities during war is not unusual. It shows that notwithstanding the improved accuracy of hi-tech warfare, mistaken bombardment of nonmilitary targets has not been eliminated. More importantly, the supposed accuracy of hi-tech weapons has not ended suspicion that consistent and repeated targeting of certain civilian targets,[47] as well as private property, was deliberate.[48]

3. **The war against terrorism** In the nineteenth century, the classical rule restricting the vitiation of contracts and private property upon conquest was founded on the view that war occurred between States. However, as I will show in Chapters 6 and 7, States are not the only actors involved in warfare. Indeed non-State actors such as pirates have been the staple of international law for centuries.[49]

---

46. *Id.* at 98–99. *See also* Michael Mandel, *Politics and Human Rights in International Criminal Law: Our Case Against NATO and the Lessons To Be Learned from It*, 25 FORDHAM INT'L L.J. 95 (2001) (discussing the failed attempt to commence an investigation of illegal aerial bombardments by U.S.-led NATO allies in the Kosovo intervention).

47. Examples include the bombing of the Red Cross camp in Afghanistan, the bombing of the Chinese Embassy in Serbia, etc.

48. For a discussion of a series of such incidents, see Lewis, *supra* note 45.

49. *See* EDWARD CHANNING, THE JEFFERSONIAN SYSTEM: 1801–1811, at 36–46 (1968) (discussing the Tripolitan War between the United States and pirates); RAY W. IRWIN, THE DIPLOMATIC RELATIONS OF THE UNITED STATES WITH THE BARBARY POWERS: 1776–1816, at 109–48 (1970) (discussing diplomatic relations between the United States and piratical States); DUMAS MALONE, JEFFERSON AND THE RIGHTS OF MAN 27–32 (1951) (discussing the difficulty Jefferson had in dealing with piratical States); DUMAS MALONE, JEFFERSON THE PRESIDENT FIRST TERM: 1801–1805, at 97–99 (1970) (covering the history of U.S. efforts, including war, to deal with disruption of U.S.-flag ships by the "stateless" Barbary (corsair) pirates stationed in a number of North Africa seaports. The pirates demanded ransom payments to allow ships to operate in the Mediterranean without capture. Although President John Adams sought to strike a diplomatic solution by seeking Congressional appropriations to satisfy the Barbary pirates, President Jefferson ordered the

The War Against Terrorism, declared after September 11, 2001, by the United States, and later endorsed by the United Nations, has contributed to the continued erosion of the view that war occurs between States.[50] The War Against Terrorism has come to be defined almost exclusively as against non-State actors. In its 2002 National Security Strategy, the United States argued that in its global War Against Terrorism: "The enemy is not a single political regime or person or religion or ideology. . . . The struggle against global terrorism is [therefore] different from any other war in our history. It will be fought on many fronts against a particularly elusive enemy over an extended period of time."[51] In addition to preemptive strikes against terrorists or those suspected of being terrorists or involved in terrorist activities, the United States adopted an aggressive effort to "disrupt and destroy" and disable terrorist organizations from planning and operating around the world through a variety of efforts, including disabling terrorist groups' material support and finances.[52] These efforts have been given imprimatur by the United Nations.[53] The Counter-Terrorism Committee, established by the United Nations to

---

U.S. navy to patrol and cruise the Mediterranean and blockade Tripoli to ensure safe passage of American ships. Notwithstanding the concerted military efforts of the United States to ensure safe passage of U.S. ships, war was not officially declared against the pirates).

50. *See* S.C. Res. 1483 U.N. SCOR, 4761st mtg., U.N. Doc. S/RES/1483, (May 22, 2003) 42 I.L.M. 1016 (2003) [hereinafter, S.C. Res. 1483] By this resolution, the Security Council appears to have effectively legitimated the Iraq War that it had previously declined to authorize.

51. National Security Strategy, *supra* note 32, at 5. The Obama administration has de-emphasized although not entirely abandoned the Bush administration's strong anti-terrorism policy. On the de-emphasis, see Vice President Joseph R. Biden, speech at the 45th Munich Security Conference, Feb. 7, 2009, *available at* http://www.securityconference.de/konferenzen/rede.php?menu_2009= &menu_konferenzen=&sprache=en&id=238& (Feb. 8, 2009). On continuity, see the Obama administration's arguments in favor of rendering terrorism suspects, *see* Greg Miller, *Obama Preserves Rendition as a Counter-Terrorism Tool*, L.A. TIMES, Feb. 1, 2009, *available at* http://www.latimes.com/news/nationworld/washingtondc/la-na-rendition1-2009feb01,0,4661244.story.

52. *Id.*

53. *See, e.g.*, S.C. Res. 1373, U.N. SCOR, 4385th mtg., U.N. Doc S/RES/1373 (2001) (establishing the United Nations Counter-Terrorism Committee).

monitor global antiterrorism activities, has legitimated broad powers to block and confiscate private property belonging to groups and individuals suspected of terrorism with little if any due process and inconsistently with United Nations human rights mandates as we saw in Chapter 1.[54]

III. HEGEMONIC EROSION OF A CUSTOMARY INTERNATIONAL LAW CANON OVER NON-EUROPEAN "PROPERTY"

As we have seen above, the necessities of national policy and political expediency as reflected in municipal law and the practices of belligerent States have modified and relaxed classical international law: that conquest does not extinguish preexisting private property and contract rights. As a result, conquest is often accompanied by the taking and confiscation of the private property of the nationals of the defeated belligerent State(s).

In this section, I will show that this rule against extinction of private property rights and contracts upon conquest has been most attenuated with reference to the conquest of non-Western peoples and States by Western States, as opposed to conquest among European States and peoples. This difference in the application of the rule against extinction of private property rights and contracts upon conquest is, I will argue, a systemic expression of the hegemonic power of conquering States that goes back decades in the history of international law. To show this hegemonic impulse to override the private

---

54. *See generally* Alvarez, *supra* note 31, at 878 (http://www.securityconference. de/konferenzen/rede.php?menu_2009=&menu_konferenzen= &sprache=en&id=238& (Feb. 8, 2009). On continuity, see the Obama administration's arguments in favor of rendering terrorism suspects. *Id. See, e.g., supra* note 51. See Chapter 1 for further detail. The Counter-Terrorism Committee's mandate of freezing financial assets departs from prior practice, under which peace treaties between belligerent States exempted property belonging to religious bodies and charitable organizations from confiscation and liquidation see Mann, *supra* note 24, at 503 (listing exemptions from liquidations and confiscations of property); *See also* G.A. Res. 60/288, U.N. Doc. A/RES/60/288 (Sept. 20, 2006) ("[E]ncourage[s] the [Counter-Terrorism Committee]" . . . to ensure, as a matter of priority, that fair and transparent procedures exist for placing individuals and entities").

property rights of non-Europeans upon conquest in the history of international law, a 1905 House of Lords decision that will be discussed explicitly found the prerogatives of the Crown preempted the rule against extinction. Furthermore, I will discuss the distinction between the Native American ownership of land in comparison to the white colonial settlers in the post-American Revolution period in American history to show that the colonial land was treated as private property interests whereas the Native American land was a possession upon conquest.

A. *West Rand Central Gold Mining Company v. The King*: Conquest Does Not Limit the Prerogative of the Crown to Extinguish Corporate Private Property

In *West Rand Central Gold Mining Co. v. The King*,[55] the question before the House of Lords was whether after annexation, a conquering State becomes liable to discharge the financial obligations of the conquered State due to individuals or corporations. The facts of the case were as follows.

In October 1899, the Republic of South Africa seized more than 2617 ounces of gold from the West Rand Central Gold Mining Company for "safe keeping." Following the Anglo-Boer War, Britain conquered the Republic of South Africa and by a proclamation dated September 1, 1900, all the territories of the Republic were annexed to and became part of the dominions of Queen Victoria. The Republic of South Africa thereby ceased to exist as it became part of the British Empire. West Rand Central Gold Mining Company brought suit seeking recovery of the gold seized by the Republic of South Africa that was now held by the British Crown. West Rand Central Gold Mining Company urged that conquest or change of sovereignty by cession ought not to affect preexisting contractual and property rights. Further, it was argued that, under international law, conquest does not destroy all private rights. According to West Rand Central Gold Mining Company, the seizure of the gold by the Republic of South Africa was a contractual obligation that the British government had assumed on conquering the Republic.

---

55. 2 K.B. 391, 391 (1905).

Relying on *United States v. Percheman*,[56] West Rand Central Gold Mining Company argued that the whole of the civilized world would be outraged if private property should be generally confiscated, and private rights annulled as a result of conquest of the Boers by the British. In addition, it argued that, although claims to enforce treaties or agreements between two sovereign powers were acts of State that courts had no power to inquire into, the repudiation of liability by the government for the seized gold belonging to an individual was not an act of State because the seizure had crystallized into a contractual obligation.

By contrast, the Crown refuted all arguments distinguishing private or contractual claims against the Crown, on the one hand, from public claims seeking to enforce obligations under treaties, on the other. The House of Lords, in agreeing with the Crown observed, "where the King of England conquers a country it is a different consideration, [from peaceable cession], for there the conqueror by saving the lives of the people conquered *gains a right and property in such people, in consequence of which he may impose upon them what law he pleases.*"[57]

In essence, the House of Lords declined to extend protection to the private property rights of a South African corporation by drawing a distinction between the circumstances under which such protection applies and those in which it does not.[58] Following this distinction, territory seized by conquest does not save personal rights arising

---

56. 32 U.S. (7 Pet.) 51, 86 (1833).
57. *W. Rand Cent. Gold Mining Co.* Ltd., 2 K.B. at 410–11 (emphasis added).
58. According to the court:
It must not be forgotten that the obligations of conquering States with regard to private property of private individuals, particularly land as to which the title had already been perfected before the conquest or annexation, are altogether different from the obligations which arise in respect of personal rights by contract. As is said in more cases than one, cession of territory does not mean the confiscation of the property of individuals in that territory. If a particular piece of property has been conveyed to a private owner or has been pledged, or a lien has been created upon it, considerations arise which are different from those which have to be considered when the question is whether the contractual obligation of the conquered State towards individuals is to undertaken by the conquering State.
Id. at 411.

under a contract, (as opposed to private property rights to land), from extinction upon conquest. By defining the interest in the confiscated gold as a personal right arising under a contract, the court declined to follow the classical rule under customary international law as adopted by American courts that private or contractual claims survive both conquest and cession of territory by peaceful means. The court reasoned that the American decisions were different because, unlike the seizure of the gold, they involved landed property in territories which had been ceded or annexed to the United States.[59]

In light of the court's observation that the Crown was freed of any constraints in deciding what law to apply to a conquered people, it is plausible to argue that the decision was made to match the demands of colonial expediency, rather than because the doctrine required such an outcome on any principled basis except those consistent with the designs of the expanding British Empire.

This case is compelling because it did not involve non-European claims to safeguard their private property upon conquest. It reveals the malleable, flexible, and contradictory applications of this customary international law rule's saving benediction of private property and contracts upon conquest. Sometimes it was held to apply, but in cases like this, the King's prerogatives over a conquered State overrode the applicability of the rule.

B. *Daniel F. Strother v. John B. C. Lucas*: Native American Land Claims Do Not Survive Conquest

The rule against extinction of private property rights was successfully applied in *Strother v. Lucas*[60] to facilitate the survival of land grants made by the Spanish crown to white settlers.[61] In addition, use and

---

59. *Id.* at 410.
60. 37 U.S. 410 (1838).
61. *Percheman*, 32 U.S. at 64 is another example. Similarly, in *Mitchel v. United States*, 34 U.S. 711, 733–34, 753–54 (1835), the Supreme Court held:
> [A] treaty of cession was a deed or grant by one sovereign to another, which transferred nothing to which he had no right of property, and only such right as he owned and could convey to the grantee. . . . [The U.S.] came in the place of the former sovereign by compact, on stipulated terms, which bound them to respect all the existing rights of the inhabitants. . . . They could assume no right of conquest which may at any time have been vested in Great Britain or Spain . . . new relations [had been] established

occupation of territory by Spanish and other white settlers that had not been recognized by the Spanish Crown or its administrators as constituting private property rights enjoyed the saving benediction of the rule against extinction of private property rights after Spain ceded her territories to the United States.[62] In this section, my claim is that conquest transformed the use and occupation of land into private property rights upon Spanish cession of territory to the United States. However, this transformation did not work in favor of a Native American who occupied and used the land in the same way as by the Spanish and other White settlers.

In essence, Native American use and occupation of land was held not to enjoy the same status as similarly used and occupied land of Spanish and other white settlers. This attitude of early American courts toward Native American land as falling below private property rights, is further evidenced by cases such as *Johnson v. M'Intosh*, where the Supreme Court held that conquest abrogated Native

---

between them by solemn treaties; nor did they take possession on any such assumption of right; . . . it was done under the guarantee of congress to the inhabitants. . . . They might, as the new sovereign, adopt any system of government or laws . . . consistent with the treaty and the constitution; but instead . . . all former laws and municipal regulations which were in existence at the cession, were continued in force.

62. *See Strother*, 37 U.S. at 438,

In following the course of the law of nations, this Court has declared, that even in cases of conquest, the conqueror does no more than displace the sovereign, and assume dominion over the country. . . . "A cession of territory is never understood to be a cession of the property of the inhabitants. The king cedes only that which belongs to him; lands he had previously granted, were not his to cede. Neither party could so understand the treaty. Neither party could consider itself as attempting a wrong to individuals, condemned by the whole civilized world. 'The cession of territory' would necessarily be understood to pass sovereignty only, and not to interfere with private property. . . ." No construction of a treaty, which would impair that security to private property, which the laws and usages of nations would without express stipulation have conferred, would seem to be admissible further than its positive words require.

This proposition is backed up by a series of treaties embodying the rule against extinction as the 1803 Treaty between Spain and France. *Id.* at 301 (referencing Convention of Neutrality and Subsidy between France and Spain, Oct. 19, 1803, 57 Consol. T.S. 201).

American rights to land.[63] The rationale for nonrecognition of Native American rights to land was espoused by Justice Marshall in *Johnson:*

[T]he tribes of Indians inhabiting this country were fierce savages, whose occupation was war, and whose subsistence was drawn chiefly from the forest. To leave them in possession of their country, was to leave the country a wilderness; to govern them as a distinct people, was impossible, because they were as brave and as high spirited as they were fierce, and were ready to repel by arms every attempt on their independence.[64]

In other words, conquest and cession applied differently as between Native Americans, on the one hand, and Spanish and white

---

63. *Johnson v. M'Intosh*, 21 U.S. 543, 574 (1823). According to Chief Justice Marshall, conquest "impaired" the rights of the indigenous people of North America because "their rights to complete sovereignty, as independent nations, were necessarily diminished, and their power to dispose of the soil at their own will . . . was denied by the original fundamental principle, that discovery gave exclusive title to those who made it." *Id.* at 574. The Court further held that conquest gives a title "which the [c]ourts of the conqueror cannot deny, whatever the private and speculative opinions of individuals may be, respecting the original justice of the claim." *Id.* at 588. Although *Johnson* was decided long after the doctrine of discovery was discredited among European nations, it may be said to represent a first generation case under which conquest and discovery were regarded as legitimate modes of acquiring sovereignty over territory. With the rise of the principle of self-determination after World War I, the doctrine of discovery as a legitimate mode of acquiring sovereignty over territory was eclipsed. For a discussion of this shift and its problems, see SHARON KORMAN, THE RIGHT OF CONQUEST: THE ACQUISITION OF TERRITORY BY FORCE IN INTERNATIONAL LAW AND PRACTICE (1996). For a critique holding that this shift toward self-determination was not immediately applied to non-Western peoples, such as Africans, see SIBA N'ZATIOULA GROVOGUI, SOVEREIGNS, QUASI-SOVEREIGNS AND AFRICANS (1996).

64. *Johnson*, 21 U.S. at 543, 590 (emphasis added). In *Mitchel*, the property rights of Native Americans in Florida were held to be rights of mere "occupancy and perpetual possession, either by cultivation, or as hunting-grounds, which was held sacred by the crown, the colonies, the states, and the United States." 34 U.S. at 752. Indeed the right of occupancy was considered "as sacred as the fee simple of the whites." *Id.* at 746. However, Indians did not enjoy full ownership because the "ultimate fee was in the crown and its grantees, which could be granted by the crown or colonial legislatures while the lands remained in possession of the Indians." *Id.* at 745.

settlers, on the other. Although Spanish and white settlers had their use and occupation of land as rising to the equivalent of land grants or titles that survived conquest or cession of territory, similar use and occupation of land by Native Americans did not get recognition as private property rights capable of surviving conquest or cession.

What is even more striking here is that in *Strother*, the U.S. Supreme Court, in determining whether prescriptive title[65] existed in favor of the plaintiff, recognized "local laws," "usages," and "customs"[66] as evidenced by "informal writings," "parol agreements," and "possession alone, for long time,"[67] and even common/collective as well as private ownership of property land all on behalf of the Spanish and white settlers but not for the Native Americans.[68] Thus the Court declares:

> [T]he law of this case is the law of all similar ones now existing, or which may arise, it is our plain duty to decide it on such principle. That while we do, as the law enjoins, respect ancient titles, possession and appropriation, give due effect to legal presumptions, lawful acts, and to the general and local laws, usages and customs of Spain and her colonies.[69]

The Court then engages in a lengthy exposition of the "laws, customs and usages of Spain in relation to grants to the grants, transfers and tenure of village property."[70] The description of how Spanish and

---

65. *Strother*, 37 U.S. at 300–01, 304–05, 306–14, 432 (referring to prescription as "uninterrupted cultivation" of the land).
66. *Id.* at 435.
67. *Id.*
68. *Id.* at 458. The Court observes that in Missouri, "derivative titles" to land include the "several right or rights in common" and "according to their several rights." *Id.* at 459.
69. *Id.* at 435.
70. *Id.* at 449. This exposition goes on in excruciating detail between pages 447–50. The Court justifies this exposition as follows:
> Thus connecting the law of nations, the stipulations of the treaty, the laws, usages and customs of Spain, the acts of [C]ongress, with the decisions of this court; we are furnished with sure rules of law, to guide us through this and all kindred cases, in ascertaining what was property in the inhabitants of the territory when it was ceded. As all the supreme laws of the land, the constitution, laws and treaties, forbid the United States to violate rights of property thus acquired, so they have never attempted it; but the state of the province required that some appropriate laws should

other white settlers acquired property rights over territory informally through usages, customs and local laws, parallels non-European settlement patterns, including those of the Native Americans as recorded by Europeans who came into contact with them.[71] For example, the informality of these processes in so far as they differed from formal grants conferred by written authority of the Crown or the Crown's representatives.[72] Thus, lack of formal Western education would not bar a settler from acquiring private property rights over land that had been settled and occupied in accordance with local laws, customs and usages.[73] Parole evidence to prove occupation and cultivation consistent with local laws, customs and usages was permissible[74] for the white settlers but not for the Native Americans who similarly occupied and cultivated their land in accordance with their customs, usages, and practices.

Notwithstanding Native American occupation of land that was analogous to settler practice, the Court found that lands not so occupied or cultivated by the settlers in Louisiana were parts of the King's dominions.[75] This effectively meant that land occupied by Native Americans did not enjoy the same status as that occupied or cultivated by the white settlers. Hence, those white settlers in this case, who had no formal grants were comparable to Native Americans in terms of the informality of occupation by dint of having no grants from the Crown, their lack of formal Western education, and the organization

---

be passed, in order to ascertain what was private, and what public property, to give repose to the possession, security to titles depending on the evidence of facts remote in time, difficult of proof, and in the absence of records and other writings.

Id. at 446–47.

71. *See* Carlos Scott Lopez, *Reformulating Native Title in Mabo's Wake: Aboriginal Sovereignty and Reconciliation in Post Centenary Australia*, 11 TULSA J. COMP & INT'L. L., 21 (2003) (noting that the communal nature of title to territory in Australia was also considered as unproductive). *But see* JOHN W. BRUCE & SHEM E. MIGOT-ADHOLLA, SEARCHING FOR LAND TENURE SECURITY IN AFRICA (1994) (challenging the view that communal title is unproductive).

72. *See* Strother, 37 U.S. at 439.

73. *See id.* at 440 (stating that private property rights do not change, only sovereignty).

74. *See id.*

75. *See id.* (stating that the royal ordinance of 1754 gave the king dominion).

of their tenure system in accordance with their local laws, customs, and usages. Yet these Native Americans did not enjoy the saving benediction of the customary international law norm precluding their land rights from being extinguished by cession. The Court reinforced this difference by noting that local authorities should treat Native Americans with "mildness, gentleness and moderation, with verbal, and not judicial, proceeding."[76]

It is remarkable that although the Court defines property as broadly as incorporating "any right, legal, equitable, inceptive or inchoate or perfect,"[77] Native American and occupation of land is not regarded as adding up to legal title. As such, Native Americans were regarded as merely entitled to be treated with the patronizing kindness of a "civilized State." In this manner the Court gives imprimatur to the colonial and racist notion that non-European use and occupation of land did not rise to private property rights and that treaties between colonial powers in the nineteenth and twentieth centuries effectively extinguished preexisting title to territory based on non-European use and occupation of land. In fact, as Justice Marshall held in *Johnson*, whereas conquest did not extinguish existing land rights, this rule did not operate in favor of "a people with whom it was impossible to mix, and who could not be governed as a distinct society."[78] For this reason, the same evidence of use, occupation, and cultivation by Europeans that was presented in *Strother*, was given the status of a private property right. Moreover, it was granted the saving benediction of the customary international law rule that preserves property rights upon conquest or cession that was not given to Native American property.[79]

---

76. *Id.* By contrast, with regard to the white settlers, the Court finds after examining their customs, usages and local laws: "Such are the laws, usages and customs of Spain, by which to ascertain what was property in the ceded territory, when it came into the hands of the United States, charged with titles originating thereby; creating rights of property of all grades and description." *Id.* at 446.

77. *Id.* at 406.

78. *Johnson*, 21 U.S. at 590–91.

79. I explore this theme at greater length in James Thuo Gathii, *Geographical Hegelianism in Territorial Disputes Involving Non-European Land Relations: An Analysis of the Case Concerning Kasikili/Sedudu Island (Botswana/Namibia)*, 15 LEIDEN J. INT'L L. 581 (2002).

There have been a few exceptional cases where courts of conquering powers have recognized the use and occupation of land by non-Europeans as a form of land tenure with a property rights system. In one such case, the House of Lords proceeded from the premise that among the indigenous Maori of New Zealand, there existed a system of land tenure which was known or was discoverable, and that this land tenure system was binding on the court with regard to the natives, rightful use and possession. The Crown could therefore not arbitrarily disregard this system of land tenure by appropriating land for sale inconsistent with the relevant statutory authority.[80] In effect, the House of Lords rejected the assertion by the Crown that no suit could be brought against it upon a native title.[81]

But, in the overwhelming number of cases where similar evidence of the existence of a land tenure system among non-Europeans was present, courts have found that there was no native title and if any such title existed, it was extinguished or abrogated by the conquering sovereign.[82] Hence, in *Ol le Njogo v. The Attorney General*, the East African Court of Appeal held that an agreement entered into between the Crown and a native tribe was a treaty, and therefore any cession of land inconsistent with the treaty was not cognizable in the courts of the Crown because it was an act of State.[83] In this case, the court said of the argument made by the Masai about their private property rights over their land: "[w]hether interference with the private rights of a subject by officers of the State to compel obedience to the terms

---

80. See *Nireaha Tamaki v. Baker*, 1 N.Z.L.R. 561, 577–80 (1901) (stating that the Crown could not extinguish native title).

81. *Id.* at 577 (allowing cases made by native titles).

82. For example, in *Ol Le Njogo v. The Att'y Gen.*, V E. Afr. L. Rep. 70 (1913), the Court held, without recognizing that the Masai had radical title to their territory, that they were nevertheless capable of entering into agreements with the Governor to cede their land, notwithstanding the fact that they were living in a protectorate. For an extensive analysis, see James Gathii, *Imperialism, Colonialism and International Law*, 54 BUFF. L. REV. 1013 (2007).

83. See *id.* at 78 (holding that the agreements in question are treaties). Similarly, in *Worcestor v. Georgia*, Justice Marshall held that the fact the Cherokee nation, a weaker State, had accepted the protection of the United States, a stronger State, did not mean that the Cherokee had surrendered their independence and right to self-government or to terminate their right to exist as a State. 31 US (6 Pet.) 515, 561 (1832).

of treaty could be authorised [sic] otherwise than by the Legislature is an open question."[84] More definitively, in *Sunmonu v. Disu Raphael*,[85] a case on appeal from the Supreme Court of Nigeria, the Privy Council held that there was a strong presumption that the title of a native to land was a usufructuary right, which is subject to the radical title of the Crown right and is held on behalf of the community or family.[86] Consequently, a native title was incapable of conferring exclusive possession of individual title against other members of the family. Although the effect of this decision was to protect family members from being dispossessed by the holder of land under a grant, it is nevertheless indicative of the second-class status African ownership to land and territory enjoyed in colonial jurisprudence.[87] Indeed, as the Privy Council held in the *Tijani* case:

> The title of the native community generally takes the form of a usufructuary right, a mere qualification of a burden on the radical or final title of whoever is sovereign.... Such a usufructuary right ... may be extinguished by the action of a paramount power which assumes possession or the entire control of the land.[88]

In essence, the Privy Council held that, because the Crown had radical title to territory, its acquisition of lands held under the rights, laws and customs of natives could not "legally interfere" or invalidate an exercise of the Crown's sovereign powers.[89] The upshot of these cases from Africa, unlike the *Nireaha Tamaki v. Baker* case from New Zealand, is that the Crown exercised unbridled and unaccountable

---

84. *Id.* at 113.

85. *See Sunmonu v. Disu Raphael*, A.C. 881 (H.L.) (1927) (holding that native titles cede to the crown).

86. *See Sunmonu*, A.C. at 883 (citing as authority the leading case of *Amodu Tijani v. Sec'y of S.Nig.* 2 A.C. 399 (1921)).

87. The treatment of Masubian occupation and use in the 1999 International Court of Justice case, *Namibia/Botswana* is also analogous to the treatment of non-European claims to land and territory in these African cases, see Gathii, *Geographical*, *supra* note 80.

88. *Sobhuza II v. Miller*, App. Cas. 518, 525 (1926) (citing as authority *Amodu Tijani*, 2 A.C. 399).

89. *Id.* at 528. *See also W. Rand Cent. Gold Mining Co. Ltd.*, 2 K.B. at 394. Here the House of Lords observed that "[w]here the Sovereign annexes a foreign country the terms on which he does so are settled by him, and no Court of law has any power to interpret or enforce those terms." *Id.*

power as the ultimate owner of the radical title to the territory upon conquest or peaceable cession. Native American land use and occupation, like African land use and occupation, did not rise to property rights under the Western system and its customs and usages. Thus, when the court referred to original title (property rights in land granted by the Crown) and derivative title (property rights in land arising from a transfer from original grantee or from such other mode as acquiescence, abandonment, adverse possession, prescription, or from local laws, usage, and custom) as the different modes of ownership of property in land, it did not contemplate that Native Americans had any such rights or even a land tenure system.[90]

In essence, American courts shared the view with British courts that international law and treaties between conquering colonial powers did not recognize non-European occupation and use of territory as establishing rights over territory; and, if such rights existed, they were extinguished by the superior title of the conquering sovereign. In both *West Central Grand Mining Company* and *Strother*, it is clear that both with regard to the private property interests of a corporation or the occupation, use and property of a non-European community over land, the Crown's authority upon conquest or cession more often than not overrides the customary international law rule's saving benediction of these property interests from extinction.

IV. CONCLUSIONS

In this chapter, I argued that the customary international law rule prohibiting extinction of private property rights is unevenly and inconsistently applied by conquering States. Indeed, as the House of Lords held in *West Grand Mining Company*, upon conquest, the King is free to impose whatever rules he wants upon his subjects, including disregarding rules of customary international law that constrain his power.

---

90. See *Strother*, 37 U.S. (12 Pet.) at 459 (differentiating between original and derivative titles).

In the next chapter, I argue that conquering States prioritize their hegemonic objectives, over conquest States in the name of maintaining or restoring international peace and security, achieving a variety of humanitarian objectives and even preempting attacks against them where there is no imminent threat. The broad agenda of militarized humanitarianism, preemptive, and unilateral strikes to ostensibly maintain or restore international peace and security has at least two different private property consequences.

First, hegemonic powers are far more interested in protecting the private property rights of Western multinationals and privatizing public wealth in conquered States in favor of these hegemonic States and Western multinationals.

Second, upon conquest or surrender of non-Western or non-European States, it is more likely that the private property and contract rights of non-Westerners and/or non-European nationals do not enjoy the saving benediction of the customary international law canon against extinction, or at least to the same extent as Western economic interests. Further, the hegemonic objectives of the conquering State to transform non-European States into liberal democratic political systems and market economies are used as a justification, pretext, or as military necessity to disregard, expropriate, or take without compensation the private property of defeated enemies. This trend is most earnest in European or Western conquest over non-Europeans or non-Westerners.

3. THE EFFECT OF OCCUPATION ON PRIVATE PROPERTY AND CONTRACT RIGHTS

"The right of conquest has no foundation other than the right of the strongest."[1]

This chapter examines the effect of occupation on private property and contract rights within the context of the U.S.-led invasion of Iraq in 2003. In doing so, I examine how the treatment of private property in the Iraqi occupation compares and contrasts with Japanese, Italian, and German occupations after World War II. Furthermore, I show how non-European occupations have been characterized by a disregard of occupation rules safeguarding private property as opposed to European occupations. This disregard of the private property under occupation is similar to the disregard with reference to territorial acquisitions of a much earlier period, which I addressed in Chapter 2.

In this chapter, I also demonstrate the importance placed on the private property of Europeans in non-European contexts and the lack of focus on the private property rights of non-Europeans. It is therefore not surprising that, following the U.S.-led conquest of Iraq in early 2003, most scholarly and press coverage focused on the status of foreign corporations' property in Iraq before the war.[2] By contrast,

---

1. JEAN-JACQUES ROUSSEAU, THE SOCIAL CONTRACT AND DISCOURSES 11 (G.D.H. Cole trans., E. P. Dutton & Co. 1950) (1920).
2. *See, e.g., Companies Who Had Contracts with Iraq's Previous Government Will Need Counseling as Will Companies Wanting to Do Business with Iraq's Future Government*, N.Y. L.J., Apr. 16, 2003; Stephen D. Davis & James L. Loftis, *Iraq's Opportunities for Energy Lawyers*, TEX. LAW., May 19, 2003 (noting that American and British government indications that active negotiations regarding twenty of the thirty to thirty-five known major oil fields prior to the war "would form the core of any plans to restore Iraqi oil production to levels in excess of 3 million bpd."); Chip Cummins, *U.S. Probes Its Iraq-Oil Rights: International Law Gives Occupying Power Freedom to Maneuver*, WALL ST. J., Jan. 29, 2003, at A16 (discussing ramifications of U.S. control over Iraqi oil policy); Robert S. Greenberger et al., *U.N. Lifts Iraq Trade Sanctions, Clearing*

there has been little attention given to the impact of the conquest on the private property and contracts that Iraqi citizens entered into before the war. In addition, even though the 2003 war was ostensibly waged to protect the human rights of the Iraqi people, in reality their rights took a backseat during the conquest and only emerged as significant during the planning stages to return sovereign control back to Iraqis.[3]

One of the reasons why the U.S.-led coalition took such a large a role in Iraq is because the United States made its own national security interests the primary aim. As such, if its role meant having no regard for international law, this did not seem to bother the United States. At the same time, lawyers for the Bush administration advised

---

Way for Oil Exports, WALL ST. J., May 23, 2003, at A3 (discussing foreign companies from various countries involved with purchasing Iraqi oil); Neil King Jr. & Jess Bravin, *U.S. May Spurn U.N. Iraq Sanctions: Sidestepping Rules Studied as a Way to Avoid Delay of Reconstruction Efforts*, WALL ST. J., May 5, 2003, at A3 (explaining how the United States found a loophole in sanctions by declaring contract work in Iraq as humanitarian); Michael M. Phillips, *New Iraqi Laws Target Economy, Foreign Access*, WALL ST. J., Sept. 22, 2003, at A16; Jeanne Whalen, *Nations Begin Tussle Over Control of Post War Iraq: Russia's Lukoil to Protect Claims to Iraqi Oil Field*, WALL ST. J., Apr. 9, 2003, at A10 (noting that Lukoil, a Russian oil company, will oppose any steps to develop the West Qurna oil fields that the Saddam Hussein government awarded to it under a contract in late 2002); and Pieter H. F. Bekker, *The Legal Status of Foreign Economic Interests in Occupied Iraq*, AM. SOC'Y INT'L L. NEWS. (2003) (analyzing the property interests and contracts of foreign parties before, during, and after U.S. occupation), *available at* http://www.asil.org/insights/insigh114.htm (last visited Mar. 28, 2004).

3. Notably Article 12 of the Law of Administration for the State of Iraq for the Transitional Period, adopted March 8, 2004 by the Iraqi Governing Council provided that:

> All Iraqis are equal in their rights without regard to gender, sect, opinion, belief, nationality, religion, or origin, and they are equal before the law. Discrimination against an Iraqi citizen on the basis of his gender, nationality, religion, or origin is prohibited. Everyone has the right to life, liberty, and the security of his person. No one may be deprived of his life or liberty, except in accordance with legal procedures. All are equal before the courts.

LAW OF ADMINISTRATION FOR THE STATE OF IRAQ FOR THE TRANSITIONAL PERIOD, art. 12, *available at* http://www.cpa-iraq.org/government/TAL.html (last visited Mar. 28, 2004). The 2005 Iraqi Constitution contains a similar provision.

the government that it was permissible to.[4] The administration was also advised that it could hold these prisoners indefinitely. This attitude of the United States has often found expression among scholars who have argued in favor of changing the laws relating to belligerent occupation, such as those prohibiting the confiscation of private property. Take the following proposition, for example:

> Violations of the law of belligerent occupation are frequent at least in part because the law is too restrictive today; this unrealistic restrictiveness tends to delegitimize international law, increasing the likelihood of continued and extensive violations. In order to bring this problem under control, a change in the purpose of the rules of belligerent occupation must be recognized along with a change in the rules themselves.[5]

These and similar justifications for changing the laws of belligerent occupation are more often written from the perspective of powerful belligerent nations with superior military capabilities. In one recent example of the claims for changing rules of belligerent occupation, it has been argued that occupations with a transformative presence in failed States or States with tyrannical regimes, rules of international human rights can provide legitimacy for transforming those societies.[6] These arguments are also founded on the view that considerations of policy and prudence, rather than legality justify a more permissive international legal regime governing belligerent occupation on the need to maintain legitimacy for international law. Such a permissive regime of belligerent occupation may in turn lend legitimacy to the political agenda of the powerful belligerent States extending their influence over weaker, less powerful States without having to worry about the constraints of international law.[7]

---

4. See KAREN J. GREENBERG ET AL. (EDS.), THE TORTURE PAPERS: THE ROAD TO ABU GHRAIB (2005).

5. See Davis P. Goodman, *The Need for Fundamental Change in the Law of Belligerent Occupation*, 37 STAN. L. REV. 1573, 1582 (1985); Adam Roberts, *Transformative Military Occupation: Applying the Laws of War and Human Rights* 100, AM. J. INT'L L. 580–622 (2006) (arguing occupation rules are ill suited for the challenges of occupation today). See also GREGORY FOX, HUMANITARIAN OCCUPATION (2008).

6. Roberts, *supra* note 5.

7. For example, the National Security Strategy of the United States of America (Sept. 2002), at 30 [hereinafter National Security Strategy], *available at*

Thus, the goals of introducing democracy,[8] the rule of law,[9] and free markets[10] in Iraq and Afghanistan particularly between 2003 to 2008 seemed to override any considerations about the legality of such actions under international law.[11] For example, in seeking to

---

http://www.whitehouse.gov/nsc/nss.pdf. President George W. Bush stated: The United States must and will maintain the capability to defeat any attempt by any enemy-whether a state or non-state actor-to impose its will on the United States, our allies, or our friends. *Our forces will be strong enough to dissuade potential adversaries from pursing a military build-up in hopes of surpassing, or equaling, the power of the United States* (emphasis added).

8. *Id.* at 6. The document further states as an objective to win the war against international terrorism: "supporting moderate and modern government, especially in the Muslim world, to ensure that the conditions and ideologies that promote terrorism do not find fertile ground in any nation." *Id.*

9. *Id.* at 17.

10. *Id.* at 1, 17–20.

11. *See, e.g., id.* at 29, states:

It is time to reaffirm the essential role of American military strength. We must build and maintain our defenses beyond challenge. Our military's highest priority is to defend the United States. To do so effectively, our military must: assure our allies and friends; dissuade future military competition; deter threats against U.S. interests, allies, and friends; and *decisively defeat any adversary if deterrence fails* (emphasis added).

This seems to set the stage for declaring the need to adapt the international legal prohibition against use of force in self-defense unless attacked:

For centuries, international law recognized that nations need not suffer an attack before they can lawfully take action to defend themselves against forces that present an imminent danger of attack. Legal scholars and international jurists often conditioned the legitimacy of preemption on the existence of an imminent threat—most often a visible mobilization of armies, navies, and air forces preparing to attack. We must adapt the concept of imminent threat to the capabilities and objectives of today's adversaries. Rogue states and terrorists do not seek to attack us using conventional means. Instead, they rely on acts of terror and . . . weapons that can be easily concealed, delivered covertly, and used without warning . . . the United States cannot remain idle when dangers gather.

Id. at 15. This doctrine of preemptive war where there is no imminent threat is inconsistent with customary international law, *see* Oscar Schachter et al., *Recourse to Force: State Action Against Threats and Armed Attacks*, 97 AM. J. INT'L L. 721, (2003) (arguing that the privileging of the Security Council would make the law available to serve the interests of powerful at the expense of weak States). *But see* Lori Damrosch & Bernard H. Oxman, *Agora: Future*

remake Iraq into the most idealistic type of free market economy, the United States placed the interests of its leading multinational corporations at the forefront in transforming public and private wealth into engines of new profit for the United States. Thus, the apparently enlightened occupier mission of ending a dictatorial regime by replacing it with idealistic visions of free markets and liberal democracy, may have turned into an excuse to legitimize new forms of oppression in Iraq. The Iraq and Afghanistan wars have given the United States a foothold to establish military bases in the Middle East and in Central Asia.[12] These bases will play an important role in protecting the interests of well-heeled oil companies with oil interests. The U.S.'s ambitions in Central Asia predated the 2001 war against Afghanistan.[13]

Implications of the Iraq Conflict, 97 AM. J. INT'L L., 553 (2003)(discussing the legality of the Iraqi conflict, especially contributions by William H. Taft and Todd F. Buchwald, John Yoo and Ruth Wedgewood arriving at a different conclusion).

12. For example, National Security Strategy, supra note 5, at 29 states:
The presence of American forces overseas is one of the most profound symbols of the U.S. commitments to allies and friends. Through our willingness to use force in our own defense and in defense of others, the United States demonstrates its resolve to maintain a balance of power that favors freedom. *To contend with uncertainty and to meet the many security challenges we face, the United States will require bases and stations within and beyond Western Europe and Northeast Asia, as well as temporary access arrangements for the long-distance deployment of U.S. forces* (emphasis added).

13. See Marjorie Cohn, Cheney's Black Gold: Oil Interests May Drive U.S. Foreign Policy, CHI. TRIB., Aug. 10, 2000, available at http://patriotaction. us/100Reasons/51.html (last visited Mar. 16, 2004) (reporting that Cheney, then CEO of oil company Halliburton had referred to Caspian oil as black gold and that he favored the repeal of section 907 of the 1992 Freedom Support Act, which severely restricts U.S. aid to Azerbaijan because of its ethnic cleansing of the Armenians in Nagorno-Karabakh, a mountainous enclave in Azerbaijan, to facilitate American oil corporations from getting access to Caspian oil). See also Michael T. Klare, Blood for Oil: The Bush Cheney Energy Strategy, in THE SOCIALIST REGISTER 2004: THE NEW IMPERIAL CHALLENGE 166 (Colin Leys & Leo Panitch eds., 2003) (arguing that U.S. foreign policy is predicated on a two-pronged strategy, one energy-driven and the other security-driven, that in the Bush-Cheney energy plan, these two strategies have become forged into a militarist agenda). For a critique of the

I. THE IRAQI OCCUPATION

In Chapter 2, I demonstrated that the classical international law rule that forbids the extinction of private property rights has been applied unevenly and inconsistently in the history of international law. In this section, I explore whether the occupation of Iraq from 2003 exhibited a parallel process of privileging and protecting foreign economic interests while under-protecting the property rights of Iraqis under the U.S.-led occupation. To do so, I first outline the law governing the treatment of private property under occupied territory before discussing the international legal regime that ought to have secured the private property rights of Iraqis in general and Iraqi women in particular following what was effectively a conquest of their country by the U.S. led coalition.

In this section, I also discuss the international law governing treatment of Iraqi public assets under occupation and how the de-Baathification of Iraq compared to and contrasted with similar occupation reconstruction programs in Nazi Germany, Fascist Italy, and Japan. In doing so, I show that there is a difference in treatment between Fascists and Nazis, whom the Allied powers authorized to continue receiving certain payments, such as pensions, after they lost their employment, as opposed to Japanese or Iraqi Baathists. Thus, although the Fascists and Nazis were defeated by conquest, their private property rights were relatively better protected than those of the defeated Japanese after the World War II and more recently, those of the Baathists in Iraq after the U.S.-led war against Iraq.

An additional issue addressed in this section is the process of transforming the Iraqi economy into an open market economy and how the doctrine of military necessity and the political and hegemonic objectives of transforming Iraq, as espoused by the United States in particular, have justified expansive occupying powers beyond those contemplated by Article 43 of the Hague Regulations. These powers include the authority to expropriate private property rights and the privatization of formerly publicly owned wealth, in

---

enlightened occupier view, see Nathaniel Berman, *Enlightened Occupiers?*, N.Y. TIMES, Nov. 9, 2003, at A10.

what is an unprecedented transformation of the Iraq economy into an almost utopian form of a market economy.

A. Private Property under Occupation: The Applicable Law and Available Remedies

Under customary international law, conquest does not vitiate preexisting private property and contract rights. However, under military occupation these rights enjoy a much lower threshold of protection under international law.[14] Although the occupying power is required to respect private property,[15] interferences with it are permissible where they accord with the following rules: Existing rules of "assessment and incidence" where the occupant collects taxes and tolls, in addition, the proceeds of such taxes and tolls must be used to defray the costs of administering the territory.[16] Further, no general punitive pecuniary penalties can be imposed on the population on account of acts involving specific individuals not imputing the general population jointly and severally.[17] All contributions must be made under a written order and can only be effective where it is "as far as possible in accordance with rules of assessment and incidence of the taxes in force."[18] Requisitions, where so demanded from individuals, for the needs of the army of occupation shall as far as is possible be paid

---

14. *See* Convention (IV) Respecting the Laws and Customs of War on Land and its Annex: Regulation Concerning the Laws and Customs of War on Land, Oct. 18, 1907, art. 42, 36 Stat. 2277, T.S. 539 [hereinafter Hague Regulations] (providing that "territory is considered occupied when it is actually placed under the authority of the hostile army").

15. *Id.* at art. 46 (requiring military authorities occupying the territory of a hostile State to respect "[f]amily honour [sic] and rights, the lives of persons, and private property, as well as religious convictions, and practice . . . [and] [p]rivate property cannot be confiscated").

16. *See id.* at arts. 48, 49 (explaining that Article 49 further provides that where the occupant "levies other money contributions in the occupied territory, this shall only be for the needs of the army or of the administration of the territory in question").

17. *See id.* at art. 50 (forbidding general penalties on individuals where they are not jointly and severally liable).

18. *See id.* at art. 51 (providing that a receipt shall be given to the contributors).

in cash.[19] Only assets belonging to the State may be taken into possession, and where the assets and resources of individuals are seized, they must be returned and "compensation fixed when peace is made."[20] Where there are submarine cables between the occupied and neutral territory, seizure is prohibited and restoration and compensation must be fixed when "peace is made."[21] The property of municipalities, religious institutions, charities, educational institutions, and the arts and sciences, are to be treated as private property whose seizure, destruction, or willful damage is forbidden.[22]

Some scholars have maintained that since World War II, the prohibition against interfering with private property rights by an occupying force is no longer governed by the foregoing framework of the Hague Regulations.[23] To support this position, reference is made to Article 46(2) of the second edition of the Fourth Geneva Convention,[24] which states: "restrictive measures affecting [protected persons] property shall be cancelled, in accordance with the law of the Detaining Power, as soon as possible after the close of hostilities."[25]

There are doubts whether Article 46(2) was intended to displace the Hague Regulations as the legal framework governing treatment of private property in occupied territory[26] and therefore, this position

---

19. *See id.* at art. 52 (stating that, in proportion to the resources of the country, requisitions cannot involve inhabitants taking part in military operations against one's own country).

20. *Id.* at art. 53.

21. *Id.* at art. 54.

22. *See Id.* at art. 56 (including damage to historic monuments and works of art and science).

23. Eyal Benvenisti & Eyal Zamir, *Private Claims to Property Rights in the Future Israeli-Palestinian Settlement*, 89 AM. J. INT'L L. 295, 303 (1995) (arguing, in part, that the original owners of private property destroyed, taken or damaged by an occupier "hold nothing more than the expectation of getting their property back").

24. Geneva Convention Relative to the Protection of Civilian Persons in Time of War, Aug. 12, 1949, art. 46, 6 U.S.T. 3516, 75 U.N.T.S. 287, *available at* http://www.un-documents.net/gc-4.htm (last visited Aug. 21, 2009).

25. *Id.*

26. *See* COMMENTARY ON THE GENEVA CONVENTIONS OF 12 AUGUST 1949: GENEVA CONVENTION RELATIVE TO THE PROTECTION OF CIVILIAN PERSONS IN TIME OF WAR 271 (Oscar Uhler & Henri Coursier eds., 1958).

is not very tenable. An authoritative and comprehensive examination of U.S. requisitions in occupied Japan after its unconditional surrender has argued that the United States generally complied with the Hague Regulations.[27] Indeed, it seems plausible to argue that departures from the customary international law norms embodied in the Hague Regulations do not establish an alternative norm acquiesced to by Article 46 of the Fourth Geneva Convention but are, in fact, violations of the Hague Regulations.[28] Departures from the rule requiring occupying powers to respect the private property rights in occupied territory, therefore, confirm this customary international law rule rather than create an alternative rule.

Further, there is no definitive State practice indicating that private property damaged, taken, or destroyed during war merely entitles its owners to an expectation of compensation following total defeat, belligerent such as Iraq was by the U.S. coalition.[29] Violations of customary international law rules laid down in the 1907 Hague Regulations, where such claims are proved, require compensation to be paid. However, in the United States, where courts often treat issues relating to foreign affairs, especially in the context of war, as raising separation of powers issues, it is unlikely that relief would be available.[30] Yet, this

---

27. See NISAKE ANDO, SURRENDER, OCCUPATION AND PRIVATE PROPERTY IN INTERNATIONAL LAW 104 (1991) (describing the history of U.S. requisition in Japan following World War II).

28. In Military and Paramilitary Activities In and Against Nicaragua (Nicar. v. U.S.) I.C.J. ¶ 186 (June 27) (describing the International Court of Justice in expounding on the inconsistency between actual practice and opinio juris noted:

> In order to deduce the existence of customary rules, the Court deems it is sufficient that the conduct of States should, in general, be consistent with such rules, and that *instances of State conduct inconsistent with a given rule should generally have been treated as breaches of that rule, not as indications of the recognition of a new rule.* If a State acts in a way prima facie incompatible with a recognized rule, but defends its conduct by appealing to exceptions or justifications within the rule itself, the significance of that attitude is to confirm rather than to weaken the rule (emphasis added).

29. See Benvenisti & Zamir, *supra* note 21, at 303 (arguing, in part, that the original owners of private property destroyed, taken or damaged by an occupier "hold nothing more than the expectation of getting their property back").

30. See Curtis A. Bradley, *The Charming Betsy Canon and Separation of Powers: Rethinking the Interpretive Role of International Law*, 86 GEO. L.J. 479

does not change the international law rule that a violation of international law is not excused because it is permissible under domestic law.[31] Were the U.S.-led occupiers found liable for such violations, they could not use their domestic law as a defense to a violation of norms of customary international law.[32] Violations of the Hague Regulations, would at minimum, result in liability to pay damages both under the Hague Regulations,[33] as well as under general international law.[34]

The occupying authorities in Iraq were also bound by the principle of humanity which supersedes the justifications founded on the military necessity of belligerent occupiers.[35] This principle, which goes to the heart of the laws of war,[36] was recognized even in the territorial conquests of the nineteenth century.[37]

(1998) (arguing that foreign affairs issues raise separation of powers constraints that prevent the judiciary from giving relief so as to maintain the integrity of the separate domains of governmental decision making); Hamdi v. Rumsfeld, 316 F.3d 450, 476–77 (4th Cir. 2003) (holding that "judicial review does not disappear during wartime, but the review of battlefield [decisions] is a highly deferential one").

31. RESTATEMENT (THIRD) OF THE FOREIGN RELATIONS LAW OF THE U.S. § 311(3). In addition, Article 46 (1) of the Vienna Convention of the Law of Treaties provides that States cannot invoke domestic laws to invalidate its consent to be bound by a treaty unless such violation of the treaty "was manifest and concerned a rule of its internal law of fundamental importance." Article 46(2) of the Convention further obliges State parties to carry out their treaty obligations in good faith.

32. Id.

33. Hague Regulations, supra note 12, at art. 3.

34. Factory at Chorzow (Ger. v. Pol.), 1927 P.C.I.J. (ser. A) No. 9, at 21 ("It is a principle of international law that the breach of an agreement involves an obligation to make reparation in an adequate form. Reparation therefore is the indispensable complement of a failure to apply a convention and there is no necessity for this to be stated in the convention itself.").

35. See ANDO, supra note 25, at 31, 76–78, 108 (stating that no ideological basis for war can prevent the principle of humanity from applying to a post-surrender occupation).

36. Id.

37. Thus, in the notorious Johnson v. M'Intosh, 21 U.S. 543, 589–90 (1823), the authority of the conquering power was regarded as being subject to "a general rule, [required by the constraints of humanity and public opinion],

B. Private Property Claims of Iraqis

During the war, thousands of Iraqis had their private property, including agricultural land, destroyed.[38] In addition, several thousand Iraqis deserted their property in the wake of war.[39] Some of the buildings were occupied by the advancing forces to secure supply lines and to restore law and order. In addition, the looting of the period immediately following the fall of the Saddam Hussein regime in early 2003[40] resulted in loss of private and public property and significant cultural artifacts.[41] The insecurity resulting from the looting, as well as from the insurgency against the opposition, developed into a low-intensity

---

that the conquered shall not be wantonly oppressed . . . without injury to his [the conqueror] fame, and hazard to his power."

38. Brian MacQuarrie, *For Iraqis, A Struggle to Recoup Loss*, BOSTON GLOBE, Aug. 6, 2003, at A1 (reporting that U.S. military officials have received about 2500 Iraqi claims of damage or loss of property related to the war); *U.S. Forces Demolish Iraq Homes*, Mar. 3, 2004 (reporting that the U.S. military was destroying Iraqi homes as punishment for the insurgency during the occupation period), available at http://www.news.com.au/common/story_page/0,4057,7942137%5E1702,00.html (last visited Mar. 4, 2004); Occupation Watch Center in Baghdad and the National Association for the Defense of Human Rights in Iraq, Joint Report on Civilian Casualty Casualties and Claims Related to U.S. Military Occupations (on file with author) [hereinafter Joint Report].

39. UNITED NATIONS, HUMANITARIAN APPEAL FOR IRAQ: REVISED INTER-AGENCY APPEAL 1 APRIL–31 DECEMBER, 2003, at 12–13, 15, 45, 49, and 54 (2003) (detailing displacement and damage resulting from the war) available at http:// www.reliefweb.int/appeals/2003/files/irq03flash2.pdf (last visited Mar. 29, 2004).

40. *See* John Daniszewski & Geoffrey Mohan, *Looters Bring Baghdad New Havoc*, L.A. TIMES, Apr. 11, 2003, at A1 (commenting on the disarray of Iraq after being conquered).

41. Article 56 of the Hague Regulations provides that the property of municipalities and institutions dedicated to education, the arts and sciences shall be treated as private property. In addition, the Article forbids the seizure, destruction, and willful damage of the foregoing properties and historic monuments and works of art and science. Article 47 prohibits pillage. The pilfering by looters, including U.S. soldiers, of Iraq's rich cultural artifacts in its Baghdad museums clearly violated the foregoing provisions of the Hague Regulations. Hague Regulations, *supra* note 12, arts. 56, 47. *See* S.C. Res. 1483, U.N. SCOR, 58th Sess., 4761st mtg., U.N. Doc. S/RES/1483, 42 I.L.M. 1016 (2003) [hereinafter S.C. Res. 1483], addressing this problem.

violence that disproportionately affected Iraqis, both in terms of human loss and suffering, as well as in further destruction of their private property during the occupation. Add to these casualties those resulting from U.S. cluster munitions, "accidental" bombings, and other military related activities that evidence the "inescapable brutality of modern warfare."[42]

However, there are many other claims relating to property damage arising from the movement of occupying power tanks and military vehicles including injury or death to Iraqi livestock, bicycles, and so on.[43] The U.S. Air Force runs a program under the Foreign Claims Act to compensate such losses that are unrelated to combat. The Judge Advocate General's Corps, who make determinations for compensation in such cases, applies local law and custom. This exercise is made difficult by problems of language difference and determining compensation schemes for claims such as camels injured or killed by the occupying forces or their civilian employees.[44]

C. Private Property Claims of Iraqi Women

Women are affected differently and arguably more adversely by conquest and war than men.[45] That was not different in Iraq. Although, at a formal level in the 1970s, equal protection was extended to women, and efforts were made to facilitate their access to the ballot box, the education system, the political system, and even to own private

---

42. Nehal Bhuta, *A Global State of Exception? The United States and World Order*, 10 CONSTELLATIONS 2003, at 3, *available at* http://www.constellationsjournal.org/Bhuta.pdf (last visited Feb. 4, 2004).

43. *See* Vanessa Blum, *After the War, A Time to Pay: How JAG Lawyers Settle Foreign Claims Over Non-Combat Damage*, LEGAL TIMES, Apr. 21, 2003 at 1 (describing cooperation to Iraqis for property damage by the occupying troops).

44. *See id.* (exploring the roles of Army lawyers in the compensation scheme).

45. JUDITH G. GARDAM & MICHELE J. JARVIS, WOMEN, ARMED CONFLICT AND INTERNATIONAL LAW, 19–51, 20 (2001) (noting in part that "one of the most significant factors leading to the disproportionate impact of armed conflict on women is the endemic discrimination that they experience in all societies,"); *see also* CYNTHIA ENLOE, MANEUVERS: THE INTERNATIONAL POLITICS OF MILITARIZING WOMEN'S LIVES (2000) (showing how women's lives and society in general has been militarized both deliberately and consciously in complex and ever-changing ways).

property, the 1991 Gulf War reversed these gains as the Saddam Hussein regime resorted to a conservative Islamic religious and traditional family law system as part of the nationalist response to Iraq's defeat in the 1991 Gulf War. The sanctions imposed by the United Nations (UN) following this war further eroded the gains women had made in the formal economy.[46]

According to the UN Educational, Scientific and Cultural Organization, about 75 percent of Iraqi women were literate in 1987. By 2000, less than 25 percent were literate.[47] In addition, the government purged women from government jobs to make way for men, thereby restricting chances of formal employment for women. This in turn facilitated their staying at home consistently with the advent of the new conservative nationalism after the 1991 Gulf War.[48] With Iraq's economy getting even worse at the end of 2003, as indicated by household income decreasing from $3600 per person in 1980 to $450 to $610, the position of women became all the more vulnerable.[49] The Interim Governing Council, appointed by the U.S.-led Occupation Iraqi Provisional Authority, was initially unclear on how to resolve the status of personal and religious laws in relation to guarantees of equality.[50] Eventually the Coalition Provisional Authority (CPA) approved an Interim Administrative Law granting equality rights to women without arriving at a formula on how to balance equality rights for women, on the one hand, and the cultural, social and religious

---

46. *See Background on Women's Status in Iraq Prior to the Fall of the Saddam Hussein Government*, Nov., 2003 (discussing the effects of U.N. sanctions on women in the Iraqi economy), *available at* http://www.hrw.org/backgrounder/wrd/iraq-women.htm (last visited Mar. 29, 2004).

47. *Id.*

48. *Id.*

49. Steve Schifferes, *Iraq's Economy Declines by Half*, BBC NEWS ONLINE, Oct. 10, 2003, *at* http://news.bbc.co.uk/2/hi/business/3181248.stm (last visited Mar. 29, 2004).

50. *See* Jim Lobe, *Women's Rights in Iraq Under the IGC: A Crisis is Brewing*, ZNET, Feb. 5, 2004 (discussing Iraqi Governing Council Resolution 137, which would, if approved by the Coalition Provisional Authority (CPA), create religious laws to be administered by clerics form the countries' different faiths) *at* http://www.zmag.org/content/showarticle.cfm?SectionID=43&ItemID=4936 (last visited Mar. 28, 2004).

practices of Iraqi society, including those of Islam, on the other.⁵¹ The U.S.-led occupation was typical of belligerent treatment of issues relating to women as peripheral to the larger war effort, and to the extent that women's involvement is called into question; it is in the position of wives, mothers, widows, or prostitutes who support the war effort on the home front and in the theater of war and are in need of the benevolent protection of the belligerents.⁵² The United States has also invented a postwar role for women in reviving the Iraqi economy, all of course consistent with the free market vision of the U.S.-led coalition.⁵³

The private property rights of Iraqi women were made even more precarious by the thousands of deaths of Iraqi men in and out of the military and the thousands being held in Iraq and outside the country. As women increasingly came to head families and become the breadwinners of their families, the liberalizing economic reforms further exacerbated their situation. The application of traditional and customary norms in the investigation of damage to property and human lives undertaken by the United States under the Foreign Claims Act in Somalia indicated the likelihood of the occupying authorities doing the same in Iraq: A Somali man's life was valued at

---

51. Law of Administration for the State of Iraq for the Transitional Period, art. 12 (Mar. 8, 2004), *available at* http://www.cpa-iraq.org/government/TAL.html. However, Article 13(f) provides that "Each Iraqi has the right to freedom of thought, conscience, and religious belief and practice. Coercion in such matters shall be prohibited." For insightful essays on the relationship between women's rights, culture, the market and international institutions, see Symposium, *Globalization and Comparative Family Law*, 67(2) ALB. L. REV. 54, (2004) (with a foreword by James Thuo Gathii & Patricia Youngblood Reyhan).

52. GARDAM & JARVIS, *supra* note 43, at 35–37.

53. Paula Dobriansky, Under-Secretary of State for Global Affairs, ensured that the United States engaged in the activities that advanced the interests of Iraqi women in areas of human rights, politics, economics, and education. The first priority of the United States, according to Dobriansky, is the security of Iraqi women and their families. Ensuring their security will bring about a revival of economic freedom in Iraq, and will facilitate greater participation of Iraqi women in the reconstruction efforts. *See* Paula Dobriansky, *Standing Up for Iraqi Women*, WASHINGTON POST, July 2, 2003, at A23.

100 camels, whereas that of a woman at 50 camels.[54] This mode of applying the Foreign Claims Act showed the danger of reinscribing the sexist differentiation between the lives, assets, and property of women, on the one hand, and the lives and assets of men, on the other. The vulnerability of women was further suggested by the fact that women were more likely than not to claim title to movable assets, as opposed to more valuable immovable property that may be registered in their husbands' names in the current economy in Iraq.[55]

II. TRANSFORMING OCCUPIED IRAQ

A. The Applicable Rules

Under the Hague Regulations, an occupying power is an administrator or usufructuary.[56] Article 55 reiterates the obligation of an occupying State to safeguard the capital of public properties and "to administer them in accordance with the rules of usufruct."[57] Pursuant to this

---

54. Blum, *supra* note 41, at 17. By contrast, the report notes that the highest award granted under the Foreign Claims Act was a $1 million settlement arising from a golf course accident involving a member of the U.S. Navy that struck an Australian woman with a golf ball and caused her serious injury. *Id.*

55. In Iraq, the process of filing claims under the Foreign Claims Act was also complicated by security, language and other barriers, *see* Joint Report, *supra* note 38; and Jon Tracy, *Sometimes in War, You Can Put a Price on Life*, NEW YORK TIMES, May 16, 2007, *available at* http://www.nytimes.com/2007/05/16/opinion/16tracy.html (noting the author's experience in handing out payments for wrongful deaths amounting to $ 1,500 for each lost life). This would suggest that Iraq did not experience the sexist differentiation in compensation that occurred in Somalia. With regard to the problems relating to recovery of claims filed by Iraqis, *see Adding Insult to Injury: US Military Claims System for Civilians*, CAMPAIGN FOR INNOCENT VICTIMS IN CONFLICT, *available at* http://www.civicworldwide.org/storage/civic/documents/civic%20military%20claims%20white%20paper.pdf.

56. *See* Hague Regulations, *supra* note 12, at art. 55 ("The occupying State shall be regarded only as administrator and usufructuary of public buildings, real estate, forests, and agricultural estates belonging to the hostile State, and situated in the occupied country."). *See also* JUSTINIAN'S INSTITUTES 61 (Peter Birks & Grant McLeod trans., 1987) (defining "usufruct" as the right to use the fruits of another person's property with the duty to preserve its substance).

57. Hague Regulations, *supra* note 12, at art. 55.

rule, an occupant does not own public property in occupied territory and cannot, therefore, "sell or otherwise transfer ownership of the property to third parties."[58] Consequently, the occupier is only authorized to "take possession"[59] of movable assets including cash, funds, realizable securities, depots of arms and so on, but only where necessary for use in military operations.[60] Seizure of private property for use in military operations "must be restored and compensation fixed when peace is made."[61] It follows that Article 53 of the Hague Regulations does not authorize taking possession of objects which cannot be used for military purposes.[62]

Article 43 of the Hague Regulations governs the scope of the authority of an occupying power. It provides:

> The authority of the legitimate power having in fact passed into the hands of the occupant, the latter shall take all the measures in his power to restore, and ensure, as far as possible, public order and safety, while respecting, unless absolutely prevented, the laws in force in the country.[63]

The right of an occupying power to administer occupied territory under Article 43 must be justified by its duty to restore and ensure public order, and it must respect the laws of the occupied territory unless "absolutely prevented." As such, large-scale social and economic transformations of an occupied territory, unless justified by considerations of public safety, are outside the purview of Article 43. In some contexts, such massive societal transformations by an occupant fall within the debellatio doctrine, which presumes the complete dissolution of the occupied State.[64] Proceeding from analogous reasoning, the allied powers of the post-World War II period justified their occupation of the Axis States on the basis of "New Order in Europe."[65] Such expansive powers on the part of occupier States suggest an agenda of

---

58. Benvenisti & Zamir, *supra* note 21, at 313.
59. Hague Regulations, *supra* note 12, at art. 53.
60. *Id.*
61. *Id.*
62. ERNEST H. FEILCHENFELD, THE INTERNATIONAL ECONOMIC LAW OF BELLIGERENT OCCUPATION, 52, (1942).
63. Hague Regulations, *supra* note 12, at art. 43.
64. *See* EYAL BENVENISTI, THE INTERNATIONAL LAW OF OCCUPATION 57–58, 92–96 (1993).
65. *Id.* at 64–65.

imposing their social, economic, and political systems and values on less powerful conquered and occupied States.[66] In fact, occupation invariably involves a "relationship of power, of domination [and] varying degrees of a complex hegemony"[67] between the occupying and occupied States. Thus, powerful occupying States seek to remake occupied States to adopt their ostensibly superior norms of economy, society, and politics. Occupying States justify the imposition of such goals by linking them to humanitarianism and showing how conquest is really intended to serve noble objectives such as preserving international peace and security, and enhancing the human rights protections of the "oppressed" populations of the conquered country.[68]

While occupying States justify their transformative agenda to protect and promote international human rights norms, international human rights have been held to apply to occupation by the International Court of Justice (ICJ) in the *Uganda v. DRC case*,[69] as well as in its *Wall* decision.[70] The application of human rights in occupation contexts was also upheld by the European Court of Human Rights in the 1974 occupation of Northern Cyprus by Turkey. While acknowledging the application of human rights protections in occupied territory, Israeli courts have shown more deference to security interests.[71]

---

66. Guttieri, Karen. "Making Might Right: The Legitimization of Occupation" *Paper presented at the annual meeting of the International Studies Association, Le Centre Sheraton Hotel, Montreal, Quebec, Canada*, Mar 17, 2004 <Not Available>. 2009-05-26 http://www.allacademic.com/meta/p73837_index.html (arguing that the UN recognition of the US led occupation of Iraq resulted in a legitimization of might).

67. EDWARD W. SAID, ORIENTALISM 5 (1979).

68. *But see,* Mustapha Kamal Pasha, *Predatory Globalization and Democracy in the Islamic World,* 581 ANNALS ACAD. POL. SCI. 121–32 (2002) (exploring how universal claims of economy and democracy fail to deal with the internal crisis of illegitimate Islamic States and their illiberal cultural politics).

69. Case Concerning Armed Activities on the Territory of the Congo (Dem. Rep. Congo v. Uganda) 2005 I.C.J. (Dec. 19), *available at* http://www.icj-cij.org.

70. Legal Consequences of the Construction of a Wall, Advisory Opinion, 2004 I.C.J. (July 9).

71. Aeyal Gross, *The Construction of a Wall between the Hague and Jerusalem: The Enforcement and Limits of Humanitarian Law and the Structure of Occupation,* 19 LEIDEN J INT'L L. 393–440 (2006).

B. The Iraqi Conquest and Occupation Reforms

The 2003 Anglo-American war against Iraq was primarily premised on finding weapons of mass destruction to preempt their use in future terrorist attacks. Prewar planning was especially poor[72] and ad hoc reasons for a decision to go to war with Iraq without Security Council authorization ranged from enforcement of Security Council Resolutions going back a decade to ending mass murder and torture.[73] Since the late 1990s it had been a policy of the United States to assist in regime change by replacing Saddam Hussein.[74] Lurking behind these justifications and the inability of the United States and the United Kingdom to build a coalition authorized by the Security Council, was the question of Iraqi oil—could all the other reasons have been a pretext for seeking control of one of the richest oil sources

---

72.
The United States risks being seen as an imperialist in the Middle East rather than a liberator if it doesn't allow the Iraqis to manage their own oil fields.... There is an ongoing debate... on whether a U.S. general should run a post-Saddam Iraq ... or whether there should be a quick transition to international agencies, then to Iraqis.... Even the kind of democracy to be introduced is unclear.... It's two minutes to midnight, and Americans are justifiably nervous. We appear to be unprepared for the cost of war, the price of occupation, and the demands of ensuring long-term peace.
The War: What Washington Won't Tell Us, BUSINESS WEEK, Mar. 3, 2003, at 140.

73. For a restatement of this view, see William H. Taft IV and Todd Buchwald, *Preemption, Iraq and International Law*, 97 AM. J. INT'L L., 557 (2003). For a discussion of whether the United States had the mandate to decide whether prior Security Council Resolutions authorized the use of force, see Thomas Franck, *What Happens Now? The United Nations After Iraq*, 97 AM. J. INT'L L., 607 (2003).

74. See the Iraqi Liberation Act of 1998 at Section 7, which provided that:
It is the sense of the Congress that once the Saddam Hussein regime is removed from power in Iraq, the United States should support Iraq's transition to democracy by providing immediate and substantial humanitarian assistance to the Iraqi people, by providing democracy transition assistance to Iraqi parties and movements with democratic goals, and by convening Iraq's foreign creditors to develop a multilateral response to Iraq's foreign debt incurred by Saddam Hussein's regime.
Available at http://www.iraqwatch.org/government/US/Legislation/ILA.htm (last visited Aug. 21, 2009).

EFFECT OF OCCUPATION ON PRIVATE PROPERTY AND CONTRACT RIGHTS 89

in the world today, or was it to demonstrate the unparalleled military might of the United States to other *rogue* States?

On arrival in Baghdad following the ouster of the Saddam Hussein regime, the question arose whether the U.S.-led coalition would follow the laws governing occupants of a territory upon conquest or if they would turn over the country to the United Nations to transition it toward a new government. The coalition initially opted to occupy Iraq without committing to be governed by the law of occupation. However, without a role for the United Nations, the application of this law lacked an institutional context outside the coalition that would hold the coalition accountable under the law of occupation. In addition, the coalition needed the legitimacy it had failed to get by going to war without Security Council authorization. By the vaguely worded Resolution 1483 of May 2003,[75] the Security Council gave the coalition authority the imprimatur of legitimacy to administer Iraq.[76] Although the preamble to the resolution called on the occupying powers to comply with the Fourth Geneva Convention and the Hague Regulations of 1907,[77] it did not expressly decide that the scope of the power of the occupying CPA would be determined by either of these sets of international obligations. In addition, the Security Council did not establish an accountability mechanism. Such vagueness and lack of an accountability mechanism, in turn, provided wiggle room for the occupying States to justify expansive powers under the ostensible cover of maintaining international peace and security.[78]

However, as I note below, the U.S.-led occupation of Iraq was bound not only by the Hague Regulations, but also by rules of

---

75. *See* S.C. Res. 1483, *supra* note 39 (calling on the "Authority, consistent with the Charter of the United Nations and *other relevant international law*, to promote the welfare of the Iraqi people through the effective administration of the territory" [emphasis added]).

76. *Id.*

77. *Id.* For circumstances under which the Preamble (or object and purpose clauses) may be regarded as part of the substantive provisions of an international legal instrument, see James Gathii, *The Legal Status of the Doha Declaration on TRIPS and Public Health under the Vienna Convention of the Law of Treaties*, 15 HARV. J.L. & TECH. 291, 305 (2002).

78. *See* Alvarez, *supra* note 55, at 882–83; King & Bravin, *supra* note 9 (noting that as the United States reconstruction of Iraq was subject to UN rules).

international humanitarian law that form part of customary international law. For now it will suffice to note that the U.S. State Department had previously referred to the Hague Regulations of 1907 regulating private property as codifying existing international law.[79] U.S. federal courts also recognized the application of the Hague Regulations. For example, in 2002, the Ninth Circuit found that the seizure of property by the Austrian government during World War II was a violation of the Hague Regulations.[80]

In addition, the U.S. Uniform Code of Military Justice recognizes these rules, and there is persuasive authority that multilateral conventions apply to belligerent occupation as well.[81] Yet, the U.S.-led occupiers of Iraq in 2003 decided to craft their own rules to guide their conduct of the occupation, justifying conduct such as torture and indefinite detention that were clearly impermissible under international law. Then U.S. Secretary of Defense Donald Rumsfeld even argued that U.S. soldiers were not obliged to stop the looting of Iraqi property when the invading forces arrived in Baghdad where invaluable cultural artifacts were being pilfered from Iraq in clear violation of rules of international law.[82]

---

79. Department of State Memorandum, *supra* note 8, at 734–35.

80. *Altmann v. Republic of Austria*, 317 F.3d 954, (9th Cir. 2002). Cultural property is protected from seizure in the context of war by the United Nations Educational, Scientific and Cultural Organization's Convention on the Means of Prohibiting and Preventing the Illicit Transport, Export and Transfer of Ownership of Cultural Property, Nov. 14, 1970, 823 U.N.T.S. 231; the 1954 Hague Convention for the Protection of Cultural Property in the Event of Armed Conflict, May 14, 1954, 249 U.N.T.S. 215; and the Hague Convention (IV) of 1907, Oct. 18, 1907, 36 Stat. 2777, 1 Bevans 631.

81. *See* Theodor Meron, *Applicability of Multilateral Conventions to Occupied Territories*, 72 AM. J. INT'L. L., 542 (1978); Theodor Meron, *The Humanization of Humanitarian Law*, 94 AM. J. INT'L. L., 239, 243 (2000) (noting the tension between "military necessity and restraint on the conduct of belligerents"); Theodore Meron, *The Martens Clause, Principles of Humanity, and Dictates of Public Conscience*, 94 AM. J. INT'L. L, 78, 79 (2000) (noting that until there is a more comprehensive code of laws of war, principles of international law apply to belligerents).

82. Mary Ellen O'Connell, *Beyond Wealth: Stories of Art, War and Greed*, 59 ALA. L. REV. 1075, 1099–1100 (2008) (also discussing disregard of rules of international law protecting cultural artifacts in armed conflict situations in the United States and elsewhere).

As we saw in Chapter 1, the US led coalition sought to reorganize Iraq along a free market model. The occupying U.S.-run administration saw privatization as a way of giving U.S.-based firms the ability to make Iraq assets and resources more productive. The private ownership of these assets following the defeat of the Saddam Hussein regime was understood to be preferable to public ownership of these assets. In addition, these reforms were predicated on the view that a future Iraqi government organized around a model of free market democracy would be unlikely to become as dictatorial and inclined to developing weapons of mass destruction as the Saddam Hussein regime was. These reforms were widely seen as being thinly veiled plans to give multinational corporations access to Iraqi assets.[83]

The exercise of these expansive powers to transform Iraq into a free market economy incorporating controversial elements such as a flat tax have been justified as falling within the scope of the CPA's mandate of promoting "the welfare of the Iraqi people through the effective administration of the territory"[84] and assisting in the "economic reconstruction and the conditions for sustainable development."[85] Although this Security Council Resolution was at best a controversial source of such expansive authority,[86] it is scarcely arguable that the powers exercised by the CPA in signing privatization contracts lacked legitimacy among a broad range of Iraqis.[87]

---

83. *E.g.,* Sara Flounders, *The Corporate Looting of Iraq*, WORKERS WORLD NEWS SERVICE, (July 24, 2003) *at* http://www.globalresearch.ca/articles/FL0307B.html (last visited Feb. 13, 2004); *The Rape of Iraq*, World Socialist Web Site, *available at* wsws.org/articles/2003/may2003/iraq-m09.pdf (last visited Feb. 13, 2004).

84. S.C. Res. 1483, *supra* note 39, at ¶ 4.

85. *Id.* at ¶ 8(e).

86. For example, in March 2003, the top legal advisor to UK Prime Minister Tony Blair wrote a subsequently leaked memo warning that "'the imposition of major structural economic reforms' might violate international law, unless the Security Council specifically authorized it." Daphne Eviatar, *Free-Market Iraq? Not So Fast*, N.Y. TIMES, Jan. 10, 2004, at B9.

87. *See* Cummins, *U.S. Probes, supra* note 2 (noting in part that the "Bush administration . . . would have to consider how the Iraqi public and the international community would react to a postwar oil policy" in developing the oil industry); *See also* Andrew Newton & Malaika Culverwell, *Legitimacy Risks and Peace-Building Opportunities: Scoping the Issues for Businesses in Post-War*

Further, such a broad occupation mandate was very reminiscent of the "sacred trust of civilization" under which European countries justified their mission of colonial rule and administration.[88]

These expansive powers of radically transforming the Iraqi economy and society are also questionable under Article 43 of the Hague Regulations. As Nisuke Ando argued, such major transformations without the consent of the occupied people are inconsistent with the temporary nature of occupation governance and the principle of self-determination under international law.[89] Indeed, an occupier engaged in regulating and transforming social and economic values and institutions, beyond restoring and ensuring order as envisaged under Article 43, is invariably an interested party and cannot claim to be in the position of a neutral trustee.[90]

In the midst of those free market reforms, then U.S. President Bush issued an Executive Order 13303, entitled "Protecting the Development Fund for Iraq and Certain Other Property in which Iraq Has an Interest."[91] This Order prohibited all judicial process, including, but not limited to, "attachment, judgment, decree, lien, execution, and garnishment" with respect to the Iraq Development Fund and all interests in Iraqi oil products. This broadly drafted order precluded suit to recover Iraqi assets with respect to which any country or individual of any country may have an interest. Simply put, it extinguished rights of Americans and others from pursuing judicial redress for any injuries that they may suffer with respect to any interests touching on Iraqi oil or the Iraq Development Fund. It covered almost all aspects of the CPA mandate. In effect, the Executive Order immunized the

---

Iraq (published under the auspices of the Royal Institute of International Affairs in the United Kingdom) *available at* http://www.cfr.org/pdf/highlight/Legitimacy_risks_Iraq.pdf (last visited Mar. 10, 2004).

88. *See* James Thuo Gathii, *Geographical Hegelianism in Territorial Disputes Involving Non-European Land Relations: An Analysis of the Case Concerning Kasikili/Sedudu Island (Botswana/Namibia)*, 15 LEIDEN J. INT'L L. 581, 614–15 (2002) (discussing the role of racism and arrogance played in the European colonization of African nations, and the contempt locals felt towards colonizers).

89. *See* ANDO, *supra* note 25, at 125.

90. *See* BENVENISTI, *supra* note 62, at 210.

91. Exec. Order No. 13,303, 68 Fed. Reg. 31,931 (May 22, 2003). The Supreme Court has upheld this sort of Executive Order, in *Dames & Moore v. Regan*, 453 U.S. 654 (1981), suggesting a wide scope for executive power during war.

CPA and its contractors from all legal process, an issue I shall revisit in Chapter 7.

In particular, the Executive Order preempted the use of the Alien Tort Act, which confers federal district courts in the United States "original jurisdiction of any civil action by an alien for a tort only committed in violation of the law of nations or a treaty of the United States."[92] The Executive Order in effect immunized private contractors, and other actors engaged in the occupation and reconstruction of Iraq from lawsuits for a broad range of torts including personal injury, death, damage to or loss of property committed in Iraq for which liability would be imposed by U.S. or international law.

III. THE EFFECT OF CONQUEST AND OCCUPATION ON IRAQI PRIVATE AND ECONOMIC RIGHTS IN A COMPARATIVE CONTEXT AND REMEDIAL OPTIONS

A. Comparing and Contrasting De-Fascistization, De-Baathification, De-Nazification, and the Liquidation of Japanese Zaibatsu

The de-Fascistization program of the Allied forces in Italy involved the impounding of the private property and assets of Fascist organizations and their affiliates that had been disbanded.[93] Individual members and sympathizers of these organizations had property that they had illicitly acquired, and confiscated, and they were ejected from government jobs. However, "they were allowed to maintain their pension rights."[94] In addition, since a majority of government jobs were held by members of the Fascist party, the Allied powers did not eject all of them to allow the continuity of Italian civil administration.[95] After the occupation, Italian courts invited to test the validity of occupation measures found them consistent with the Hague Regulations.[96]

In Germany, the Allied occupation was justified as necessary to ensure the elimination of Nazism and Militarism, and to engage in

---

92. 28 U.S.C. § 1350 (1879).
93. ANDO, *supra* note 25, at 53.
94. *Id.*
95. *Id.*
96. *Id.* at 69–71.

disarmament, recover reparations, control industry and all aspects of the economy, reform education, as well as to ensure the democratic reconstruction of Germany through political decentralization.[97] The United States' occupation of Japan was motivated by similar objectives of demilitarization and democratization through measures aimed at purging militarists and ultranationalists, as well as liquidating of big business combines (Zaibatsu) and the private property of individuals involved in these businesses.[98]

The similarity of the foregoing occupation measures in Italy and Japan, on the one hand, and Iraq, on the other, is that they all sought to fundamentally change the very foundations and values of the political, economic, and social institutions in these countries, as they existed before occupation. However, in Japan, unlike in Italy and Germany,[99] the U.S. occupation measures, such as the transfer to the Japanese government of the private property of individual members of the liquidated Zaibatsu combines, the restriction of economic transactions on the part of some of these individuals, denials of pensions, and expropriation of their farmland, were arguably inconsistent with the Hague Regulations.[100]

---

97. *Id.* at 59, 73.

98. *Id.* at 105 (arguing that the German instrument of surrender, the complete collapse of the German government, as well as the period of occupation, conferred on the occupiers more authority than the Hague Regulations).

99. Because in Japan many government officials depended almost entirely on pensions to sustain their own lives and those of their dependents after retirement, there can be no doubt that the flat prohibition of pension payment caused great difficulties to the lives of the persons involved. . . . It might be recalled that, in the implementation of de-Fascistization measures in occupied Italy, many members and collaborators of the Fascist party were removed from public service and part of their wealth illicitly acquired under the Fascist regime was confiscated. But they were allowed to maintain their pension rights. Even in the case of the de-Nazification of Germany, members and collaborators of the Nazi party were allowed to retain in their hands the minimum of livelihood. *Id.* at 112–14.

100. *Id.* at 106 (arguing that since the Japanese occupation was followed by an unconditional surrender and the Japanese government was still in place during the occupation, there is room to argue that the Hague Regulations of 1907 did not apply to the occupation).

EFFECT OF OCCUPATION ON PRIVATE PROPERTY AND CONTRACT RIGHTS 95

The de-Baathification of Iraq was one of the most important occupation objectives of the U.S.-led occupation objectives as we saw in Chapter 1.[101] It involved the dissolution of not just the Baath party but a whole continuum of entities affiliated with Saddam Hussein, including defense, security, information, and intelligence organs of government, and the entire structure of the Iraqi military including paramilitary units.[102] All the property and assets of the Baath party were ordered to be seized and transferred to the CPA "for the benefit of the people of Iraq."[103] Individuals in possession or control of Baath party property were required to turn it in to the Coalition.[104] An Iraqi Property Claims Commission was authorized to return seized private property.[105] The Iraqi De-Baathification Council, which like the Claims Commission was continued in the 2005 Iraqi Constitution,

---

101. The Preamble to the first order of the CPA on de-Baathification provided in part
that the Iraqi people have suffered large scale human rights abuses and depravations over many years at the hands of the Baath Party [and] the grave concern of Iraqi society regarding the threat posed by the continuation of Baath Party networks and personnel in the administration of Iraq, and the intimidation of the people of Iraq by Baath Party officials.
Coalitional Provisional Authority Memorandum No. 1: Implementation of De-Baathification Order No. 1 (May 16, 2003), *available at* http://www.cpa-iraq.org/regulations/ (last visited Mar. 29, 2004).

102. Coalitional Provisional Authority Order No. 2: Dissolution of Entities (May 23, 2003), *available at* http://www.cpa-iraq.org/regulations/ (last visited Mar. 29, 2004).

103. Coalitional Provisional Authority Order No. 4: Management of Property and Assets of the Iraqi Baath Party, § 3(1) (May 25, 2003) *available at* http://www.cpa-iraq.org/regulations/ (last visited Mar. 29, 2004).

104. *Id.* at § 3(3).

105. Coalitional Provisional Authority Regulation No. 8: Delegation of Authority Regarding Establishment of a Property Claims Commission (Jan. 16, 2004), *at* http://www.cpa-iraq.org/regulations/ (last visited Mar. 29, 2004). Although the Property Rights Commission, a quasi-judicial agency, has its regulations designed by the Governing Council, there is a Property Reconciliation Facility, which is charged with administration of conflicting claims to real property and is more of an executive agency under the direction of the Administrator. Coalition Provisional Authority No. 4: Establishment of the Iraqi Property Reconciliation Facility, (June 25, 2003), *available at* http://www.cpa-iraq.org/regulations/ (last visited Mar. 29, 2004).

was charged with the location of Baathists officials and the assets of the Party and its officials with a view to eliminating the party and its potential to intimidate the population.[106]

The de-Baathification of Iraqi institutions, such as the judiciary, proceeded apace with its Americanization.[107] As Tony Blair, then UK Prime Minister, stated in his address to the U.S. Congress:

> [O]urs are not Western values, they are the universal values of the human spirit. . . . Anywhere, anytime ordinary people are given the chance to choose, the choice is the same: freedom not tyranny; democracy, not dictatorship; the rule of law, not the rule of the secret police. The spread of freedom is the best security for the free. . . . And just as the terrorist seeks to divide humanity in hate, so we have to unify it around an idea. And that idea is liberty. We must find strength to fight for this idea and the compassion to make it universal.[108]

For Blair, American and British values are universal, and so it followed that the de-Baathification and reconstruction of Iraq was no less neutral than those universal values. Yet, although repressive regimes that violate people's rights must be held accountable, military action that legitimizes wholesale reorganization of a militarily weaker society also necessarily involves the imposition of the will of the conquering and occupying State(s).[109] Hence, unsurprisingly, otherwise well-intended processes such as de-Baathification resulted in the loss of employment and income for thousands of Iraqi professionals in the health and education sectors for simply being ordinary

---

106. Coalition Provisional Authority No. 5: Establishment of the Iraqi De-Baathification Council, (June 17, 2003), *available at* http://www.cpa-iraq.org/regulations/ (last visited Feb. 20, 2004).

107. *See* Jim Edwards, *Re-Building Iraq's Judicial System from the Ground Up*, N.J. L.J. Oct. 27, 2003, (reporting that a Judicial Assessment Team sent to Iraq by the Justice Department recommended detailed judicial reforms in Iraq along the lines of the U.S. legal system including: extension of Miranda style rights, attorney compensation, case management, and so on). For an alternative model of legal reform in Iraq that would involve exiled Iraqi jurists, the U.S. State Department and a multinational group of experts, see Ori Nir, *Long Path Ahead For Establishing Rule of Law in Iraq*, FORWARD, Apr. 18, 2003.

108. Prime Minister Tony Blair, Address to a Joint Meeting of Congress (July 17, 2003), 149 CONG. REC. H7059 2003).

109. Maxine Marcus, *Humanitarian Intervention without Borders: Belligerent Occupation or Colonization*, 25 HOUS. J. INT'L. L., 102, 133–34 (2003).

members of the Baath party.¹¹⁰ The related dissolution of the Iraqi army added to the unemployment and disillusionment of thousands of Iraqis. These and other outcomes of the de-Baathification process had a negative and cascading effect on the families and dependents of those who lost their incomes and are a reflection of the unilateral and undemocratic nature of the unaccountable authority of the CPA, which assumed all legislative, judicial, and executive powers combined.¹¹¹

Hence, as in Japan, but not in Italy and Germany, the process of recreating the occupied country resulted in adversely affecting the private property rights of these non-Western nationals to a far greater degree than similarly situated individuals in the Western States of Italy and Germany. This outcome could be coincidental or random, but in light of the unevenness and inconsistency of applying norms of international law as highlighted in Chapter 2 and in this chapter, this difference suggests that there is more to it.

It is important to note here, that under Article 3 of the Hague Convention respecting the Laws and Customs of War on Land, if a belligerent violates any of the provisions of the Regulations, it will be liable to pay compensation.¹¹² Thus, where an occupying power has taken the oil wealth of the occupied country to expand the occupying power's war readiness, it has been held to be a violation of this

---

110. Jonathan Steele, *U.S. Decree Strips Thousands of Their Jobs*, GUARDIAN, Aug. 30, 2003, at 16. The 2005 Iraqi Constitution does not criminalize ordinary members of the Baath party.

111. Coalition Provisional Authority Memorandum Number 1: Implementation of De-Baathification Order No. 1 (CPA/ORD/16 May 2003/01) § 1, *available at* http://www.cpa-iraq.org/regulations/ (last visited Feb. 20, 2004). *See* Brian Whitaker, *Iraq's Fresh Start May Be Another False Dawn*, GUARDIAN, Sept. 5, 2003. *See also* Amnesty International, Iraq: Memorandum on Concerns Relating to Legislation Introduced by the Coalition Provisional Authority, (MDE 14/14/176/2003, Dec. 4, 2003) (expressing concerns about the nature of powers reserved to the Coalitional Provisional Authority in light of international human rights concerns).

112. The provision further states that a belligerent party would also be liable for acts performed by its armed forces. In addition to art. 3 of the Hague Regulations, compensation would also be available under general principles of international law. *See Factory at Chorzow* (Ger. V. Pol.), *supra* note 34.

prohibition and of customs of war, particularly Article 53 of the Hague Regulations of 1907.[113]

Clearly, during the period of occupation, Iraq was under the effective control of the United States, the United Kingdom, and other members of the coalition. The United Kingdom is a contracting State of the European Convention on Human Rights and this, together with the United Kingdom's occupation of Iraq, renders its actions amenable to the jurisdiction of the European Convention on Human Rights. For example, reliance could be placed on the property protections of Article 1 of the First Protocol of the European Convention on Human Rights[114] for redress for confiscated and damaged property attributed to the United Kingdom and other members of the coalition that are parties to the Convention. Because Article 1 subjects deprivations of property to the general principles of international law, it follows that

---

113. *Singapore Oil Stocks*, 23 INT'L L. REP. 810 (1956). Similarly, the destruction of Kuwaiti oil fields by Iraq in the 1991 invasion was argued to constitute a violation of Article 23(g) of the Hague Regulations and Article 53 of Hague Convention IV, see Richard Carruthers, *International Controls on the Impact on the Environment of Wartime Operations*, 10 ENVT'L PLAN. L.J. 38, 48 (1993); L. Edgerton, *Eco-Terrorist Acts During the Persian Gulf War: Is International Law Sufficient to Hold Iraq Liable?*, 22 GA. J. INT'L & COMP. L. 151, 172 (1992). But see Rex J. Zedalis, *Burning of Kuwaiti Oilfields and the Laws of War*, 24 VAND. J. TRANSNAT'L L. 711, 729–33 (1990/2) (noting that Article 53 of Hague Convention IV is restricted to destruction of property where the occupation was uncontested and because the U.S.-led coalition of the Gulf War struck at Iraq, the occupation was contested and therefore Article 53 was inapplicable).

114. Article 1 of the Protocol to the European Convention on Human Rights provides:

Every natural or legal person is entitled to the peaceful enjoyment of his possessions. No one shall be deprived of his possessions except in the public interest and subject to the conditions provided for by law and by the general principles of international law. The preceding provisions shall not, however, in any way impair the right of a State to enforce such laws as it deems necessary to control the use of property in accordance with the general interest or to secure the payment of taxes or other contributions or penalties.

Convention for the Protection of Human Rights and Fundamental Freedoms, 1955 U.N.T.S. 220 (no. 2889), amended by The Protocol, Mar. 20, 1952, *available at* http://www.echr.coe.int/NR/rdonlyres/D5CC24A7-DC13-4318-B457-5C9014916D7A/0/EnglishAnglais.pdf.

the Hague Regulations[115] fall within the scope of the norms applicable within the jurisdiction of the European Court of Human Rights. There is already precedent for admissibility of petitions seeking relief for violation of international humanitarian law in the context of military occupation by non-State parties against State parties of the European Convention. In one such case, the European Court of Human Rights observed:

> [T]he responsibility of a Contracting Party may also arise when as a consequence of military action—whether lawful or unlawful—it exercises effective control of an area outside its national territory. The obligation to secure, in such an area, the rights and freedoms set out in the Convention derives from the fact of such control whether it be exercised directly, through its armed forces, or through subordinate local administration.[116]

Similarly, analogous jurisprudence exists within the Inter-American Court of Human Rights and the Inter-American Commission on Human Rights. In fact, the Inter-American Commission on Human Rights has, in a case involving U.S. military action in Panama, rejected the U.S. government's contention that the Fourth Geneva Convention and the general international laws governing use of force and armed conflict, which include the Hague Regulations, do not fall within its jurisdiction.[117]

---

115. As already alluded to before, the Hague Regulations are a statement of customary international law.

116. *Loizidou v. Turkey* (Preliminary Objections), 310 Eur. Ct. H.R. (ser. A) ¶ 62 (1995). *See also Hussein v. Albania* (Admissibility Decision), Eur. Ct. H.R. App. No. 23276/04 (2006) (holding that when the applicant was transferred to the interim Iraqi government for trial he was no longer under the jurisdiction of the coalition forces, and therefore his application to the court is inadmissible); and *Al-Saadoon & Mufdi v. The United Kingdom* (Admissibility Decision), Eur. Ct. H.R. App. No. 61498/08 (2009) (declaring partly admissible the application of two Iraqi citizens who are accused of murdering two British soldiers in 2003 because there are questions of fact as to whether there is substantial grounds for believing the two men were at real risk of being subjected to an unfair trial and executed).

117. Here, the Inter-American Commission argued that
> Where it is asserted that a use of military force has resulted in noncombatant deaths, personal injury, and property loss, the human rights of noncombatants are implicated. In the context of the present case, the guarantees set forth in the American Declaration are implicated. This case sets forth allegations

IV. CONCLUSIONS

In this chapter, I have shown that rules of international law, governing what happens upon conquest and occupation favor the interests of powerful Western States at the expense of conquered States, especially where the conquered States are non-Western. I have also shown that the rules of occupation with regard to private property rights protect peoples of non-Western States less than they protect the property of Western owners similarly situated and affected by conquest and occupation. This vulnerability is enhanced with regard to States such as Iraq and Afghanistan, in part because the image of a terrorist as a sunglasses-wearing, bearded Muslim in a turban, which existed long before September 11, 2001,[118] has become ensconced in occidental culture, particularly in the United States, and, although based on a simplistic stereotype, has been effectively mobilized to lend credence to loosening both the civil liberties protections and the private property rights for Arabs and Persians of the Muslim faith. Edward Said captured the difficulty of the dilemma in the following terms:

> One aspect of the electronic post-modern world is that there has been a reinforcement of the stereotypes by which the Orient is viewed. Television, the films, and all the media's resources have forced information into more and more standardized molds [not to mention September 11, 2001]. . . . This is nowhere more true than in the ways by which the Near East is grasped. Three things have contributed to making even the simplest perception of the Arabs and Islam into highly politicized, almost raucous matter: one is the history of popular anti-Arab and anti-Islamic prejudice in the West, which is immediately reflected in the history of Orientalism; two, the struggle between the Arabs and Israeli Zionism, and its effects upon American Jews as well as upon both the liberal culture and the population at large; three, the almost total absence of any cultural position making it possible either to identify with or dispassionately to discuss the

---

cognizable within the framework of the Declaration. Thus, the Commission is authorized to consider the subject matter of this case.
Salas v. United States, Inter-Am. C.H.R. 312 OEA/ser.L/V/II.85, Doc.9 rev., (1994), *reprinted in* 123 I.L.R. 116, 134–35 (Inter-Am. C.H.R. 1993).

118. *See* Ileana M. Porras, *On Terrorism: Reflections on Violence and the Outlaw*, *in* AFTER IDENTITY: A READER IN LAW AND CULTURE, 294, 306–307 (Dan Danielsen & Karen Engle eds., 1995) (discussing the view of terrorists as illegitimate combatants).

Arabs or Islam. Furthermore, it hardly needs saying that because the Middle East is now so identified with Great Power politics, oil economics, and the simple-minded dichotomy of freedom-loving democratic Israel and evil, totalitarian, and terroristic Arabs, the chances of anything like a clear view of what one talks about in talking about the Near East are depressingly small.[119]

Indeed, as I have demonstrated in this chapter, the peculiar nature of the international law applied toward non-European peoples is a reflection of a unique form of Western, American, or European power rather than a direct translation of these forms.[120] As Harold Hongju Koh,[121] Anne Marie Slaughter,[122] and Mariano-Florentino Cuellar,[123] among others, have demonstrated, the Iraqi invasion and the transgressions of international law that have occurred were the result of a small but growing group of "well-positioned individuals, who, by serving as key institutional chokepoints, have successfully promoted particular well-publicized acts of American exceptionalism."[124]

Needless to say, the importance of the rule of law in international relations, especially with regard to relations between powerful hegemonic States on the one hand, and weaker vulnerable States on the other, cannot be overstated. Indeed, the official discourse of American exceptionalism and unilateralism is not new in the context of relations between conquering and conquered States. Neither is the sanctification of the economic interests of American and Western investors in the so-called developing countries a new phenomenon as far more fully explored in the context of international investment in

---

119. SAID, *supra* note 64, at 26–27.

120. For more on this point, see Ann Laura Stoler, *Rethinking Colonial Categories: European Communities and the Boundaries of Rule*, 31 COMP. STUD. SOC'Y. AND HIST. 134, 136–37 (1989).

121. Harold H. Koh, *American Exceptionalism*, 55 STAN. L. REV. 1479 (2003).

122. Anne Marie Slaughter, *A Rallying Cry*, AMER. SOC'Y. INT'L L. NEWSL., Nov./Dec. 2003, at 6 (regretting the growing convergence between the right and left in the United States in supporting the weakening if not the disappearance of the commitment to a rule-based international order and calling supporters of international law to fight back).

123. Mariano-Florentino Cuellar, *The International Criminal Court and the Political Economy of Antitreaty Discourse*, 55 STAN. L. REV. 1597 (2003).

124. Harold H. Koh, *American Exceptionalism*, 55 STAN. L. REV. 1479, 1496 (2003).

Chapter 5.[125] These discourses must be exposed, as I hope I have done here, and resisted, challenged, and protested.[126] Otherwise, there shall be successive waves of their evocation and reenactment awaiting moments such as the unfortunate terrorist attacks of September 11, 2001, in the United States for reinforcement and reiteration. By resisting, challenging, and protesting hegemonic goals of powerful countries, institutions, and corporations, we also serve to delegitimize the American and European self-images of privilege and rule over non-European peoples.[127]

The findings of this chapter regarding the difference in the application of both the rule against extinction of private property and contract rights, and the status of private property rights under occupation as between Europeans and non-Europeans may be mistakenly traced to a theory of cultural politics that suggests that non-Europeans do not recognize private property rights, and that only Europeans or Westerners recognize them because they are an inherent feature of European and Western society. This view is mistaken to the extent to which it does not recognize that the disregard of non-Western private property rights is born out of the crucible of the encounter between a self-righteous Western cultural project and non-Western civilizations often designated as backward, barbaric, poor, and lazy, but which nevertheless, have and continue to have their own political and ethical virtue.[128]

---

125. *See, e.g.*, MOHAMMED BEDJAOUI, TOWARDS A NEW INTERNATIONAL ECONOMIC ORDER, (1979) (discussing the role of international law in shaping the international economic order); M. SONARAJAH, INTERNATIONAL COMMERCIAL ARBITRATION: THE PROBLEM OF STATE CONTRACTS, (1990).

126. Balakrishnan Rajagopal, *International Law and Social Movements: Challenges of Theorizing Resistance*, 41 CULUM. J. TRANSNAT'L L. 397, 400 (2003) ("[I]nternational law requires a theory of resistance to remain relevant.").

127. Gerry Simpson, *The Great Powers, Sovereign Equality and the Making of the United Nations Charter*, 21 AUST. Y.B. INT'L L. 133 (2002) (showing that international order is organized around two contrasting versions of liberalism, one based on the sovereign equality and another based on the view that it is the special responsibility of the great powers to "police" the world and maintain order, especially to ensure that "rogue" States "toe the line").

128. For an excellent analysis, see Anthony Anghie, *Francisco De Vitoria and the Colonial Origins of International Law*, 5 SOC. & LEGAL STUD. 321 (1996); Anthony Anghie, *Finding the Peripheries: Sovereignty and Colonialism in*

Further, the massive privatization of publicly owned Iraqi assets by the U.S.-led occupation raised questions about its legality under the Hague Regulations and the international norms recognizing the Iraqis' sovereignty over their resources. Placing the massive resources of the Iraqis in the hands of foreign firms without giving Iraqis an opportunity to participate in their ownership and management raised questions about the legitimacy of the process with the end of occupation.

Part of the challenge confronting the Iraqi people at the moment is a larger question of seeking the best arrangements at the national level that would simultaneously recognize the human rights of all individuals, irrespective of their background, while at the same time respecting their diverse cultures and religions particularly those of minorities and women. At the international level, the challenge is not different. It requires an acknowledgment of the human rights of all non-Western people vulnerable to conquest, and further recognizing that projects of imperial conquest that are facilitated by orientalist images of Arabs and Persians as terrorists do not serve the goals of global security but actually work against global security. By upholding these rights, the peoples of the vulnerable States of the world would not have to live in the fear that powerful countries will run over them and appropriate or confiscate their private property while privatizing their public assets.

> — Overly simplistic worldview on flimsy evidence.
> — Gathii has a view, and is stating "evidence" as if it proves it.

Nineteenth Century International Law, 40 HARV. INT'L L.J. 1 (1999); Anthony Anghie, "The Heart of My Home": Colonialism, Environmental Damage, and the Nauru Case, 34 HARV. INT'L L.J. 445 (1993); Anthony Anghie, Creating the Nation State: Colonialism and Making of International Law (1995) (unpublished S.J.D. thesis, Harvard Univ.) (on file with the Harvard Univ. Library); Mahmood Mamdani, Good Muslim, Bad Muslim: A Political Perspective on Culture and Terrorism, 104 AM. ANTHROPOLOGIST, 766 (2002).

4. THE CREATIVE TENSION BETWEEN COMMERCIAL FREEDOM AND BELLIGERENT RIGHTS

> *To have submitted our rightful commerce to prohibitions and tributary exactions from others would have been to surrender our independence. To resist them by arms was war, without consulting the state of things or the choice of the nation.*[1]

I. INTRODUCTION

In the early part of the twenty-first century, the United States has been invoked less as a country that conforms to its international legal obligations than as an "exemplar of might."[2] This has not always been the case.[3] The early U.S. republic of the late eighteenth century was a relatively weak military and economic country. The United Kingdom, France, the Netherlands and even Spain were more prosperous economically and militarily superior countries than the United States. In this chapter, I focus on the international legal jurisprudence of the

---

1. This is a quote of President Jefferson justifying the Embargo Act of 1807 and resisting pressure for its suspension. Under this Act, foreign ships were banned from sailing from any American port. Some limited exceptions were made but the Act served as a withdrawal of American commerce from the world in retaliation to British and French confiscations of American ships and resisting pressure to suspend it and to allow the continuance of commerce. *See* Benson J. Lossing, Pictorial Field-Book of the War of 1812 170 (1869).

2. Pratap Bhanu Mehta, "Empire and Moral Identity," 17 Ethics & Int'l Aff. 49 (2003). *See also* Nat'l Security Council, National Security Strategy of the United States of America 1 (2002), (acknowledging that the United States possesses "unprecedented—and unequaled—strength and influence in the world.").

3. The Obama administration that took over from the George W. Bush administration in early 2009 has promised to use U.S. power around the world wisely and softly rather than through the use of force as the preceding Bush administration had.

Marshall Court during this period of U.S. military and economic weakness.

An examination of this jurisprudence leads to three conclusions. First, that the Marshall Court, primarily motivated by the young country's relative economic and military weaknesses, adopted a policy of neutrality in international commerce. Second, that in seeking to ensure the United States' commercial relations conformed to international legal obligations of a neutral nation, the Marshall court played a constructive role in solidifying the early regime of international economic governance through law. Third, that this early regime of international economic governance through law was bifurcated between a regime of complete reciprocity between States, and a second regime of nonreciprocity or unequal exchange between States and entities regarded as not rising to the status of statehood in eighteenth- and nineteenth-century international law. Although the regime of complete reciprocity governed relations between and among European States and the emerging United States, the regime of nonreciprocity was espoused as governing relations between conquering European States, as well as the United States, on the one hand, and non-European entities, on the other.

In short, my thesis in this chapter is that the Marshall Court was the crucible within which international economic legal norms, such as those of reciprocal or equal exchange and neutrality, were sought to be solidified as a counterweight against the depredations of the more militarily superior naval forces of the United States' European trading partners. However, just at the moment when the Marshall Court was solidifying strong rules of reciprocity and equal exchange, it was simultaneously producing a jurisprudence of conquest and of nonreciprocal relations with the Native American populations of the United States.

Military force and economic power were factors in the solidification of reciprocal and nonreciprocal norms. Inferior military force and economic power were crucial in the creation of reciprocal norms, as these norms were being crafted and interpreted by the courts of a country facing States with superior military and economic might. These more powerful countries had, in the eyes of the weaker United States, engaged in creating the "rule of the jungle" in international commerce. The Marshall Court intervened by announcing norms that sought to ensure that commerce got safe passage, particularly during wartime or in times of international political and economic divisions.

These norms were, in effect, crafted to counter the rule of the jungle in international commercial relations preferred by the more economically and militarily stronger States. Superior military force was also a factor in the establishment of the nonreciprocal regime of U.S.-Native American relations, because the Court justified its jurisprudence on the basis of the military conquest of Indian territory. Thus, when the Marshall Court was announcing the most liberal rules of reciprocity in its international trading and economic relations with its European counterparts, it was concurrently establishing an illiberal regime of subjugating the non-European inhabitants of North America to a regime of nonreciprocity and inequality.

In Section II, I will discuss the United States' military weaknesses and its economic dependency on European countries in the late eighteenth to early nineteenth century. In Section III, the judicial creativity of the Marshall Court, particularly in establishing rules of equal exchange between neutrals and belligerents during war will be examined. In Section IV, I will show how the Marshall Court at the same time created rules of unequal exchange between the United States and Native American nations.

II. THE UNITED STATES' MILITARY WEAKNESSES AND ECONOMIC DEPENDENCE IN THE LATE-EIGHTEENTH CENTURY

The United States in the late eighteenth century was a militarily and economically weak country. Its military and naval capability could not rival that of the British or French. Its economy was also heavily dependent on these European countries for credit, as well as both a source of imports and as a market for its goods.

With regard to its economy, a large segment of U.S. federal revenue in the late eighteenth century was derived from import taxes primarily from Great Britain. Although France had hoped to replace Great Britain's position in this economic relationship with the United States, it failed in doing so. In addition, Alexander Hamilton and his followers felt it was the United States' trade relationship with Britain that kept the United States together.[4]

---

4. See FORREST MCDONALD, THE PRESIDENCY OF GEORGE WASHINGTON 119–120 (1974).

In fact, Hamilton, the Secretary of the Treasury in the George Washington administration, believed that supporting France while it was at war with Britain would be akin to commencing an indirect war between the United States and Britain. This would, in turn, undermine the important United States trade relationship with Great Britain.[5] The relative weakness of the United States vis-à-vis France and Great Britain was as such not an insignificant factor in the decision by the United States to remain neutral in its relationships with these European powers. Congress affirmed an impartial U.S. position by passing the Neutrality Act in 1794.[6] The Act endorsed President Washington's neutrality proclamation and made it illegal for United States citizens to "enlist in the service of a foreign power" and banned foreign-armed vessels from being fitted in U.S. ports.[7]

Thus, notwithstanding heavy prompting by France to take hostile action against the British, the United States demurred. The United States' dedication to neutrality was not taken well by the French, who felt the United States was being disloyal after the French had recently assisted the United States against the British in its fight for independence.

The upper hand of the British in its relations with the United States is epitomized by the Jay's Treaty of 1794.[8] Although intended by the Washington administration to have ended British captures of American cargo unrelated to war from the seas and the impressments of American men by the British navy, the Jay's Treaty failed to do so. Further, it effectively abandoned the neutrality principles to which the United States had committed itself. Hence, rather than affirm its freedom of the seas under which "free ships make free goods," the United States agreed to a different rule—that "neutrals have the right to trade freely in noncontraband goods with belligerents," and that "contraband lists must be limited to war materials,"[9] in Jay's Treaty. This agreement to a different rule showed the United States had

---

5. See id.
6. Neutrality Act, ch. 50, 1 Stat. 381 (1794). Today, the Neutrality Act is codified at 18 U.S.C. § 962, et. seq. (1982).
7. McDonald, supra note 4, at 145.
8. Jay's Treaty, U.S.-Gr. Brit., Nov. 19, 1794, available at http://memory.loc.gov. (last visited Oct. 1, 2006) [hereinafter Jay's Treaty].
9. McDonald. supra note 4, at 154.

acquiesced to British supremacy in the high seas. Further, under the terms of the treaty Britain revived the "Rule of 1756," under which neutrals were foreclosed from trading with British enemy ports during wartime.[10] By contrast, the United States gave exclusive rights to usage of American ports to the British under the treaty.[11] The Washington administration was heavily criticized in the United States for the unevenness of its concessions and for giving in too much to the British at a time when they were experiencing losses around the world.[12]

In response to this cozying up to the British, France began targeting and attacking American merchant ships. In less than a one-year period between 1796 and 1797 the French had captured more than 300 American Merchant ships.[13] The United States was practically defenseless against such French aggression because it lacked warships to defend its merchant ships. By 1800, the United States lost more than 2000 merchant ships.[14] While America suffered these losses at home, France went from victory to victory in Europe. France now had its aggression directed toward America, particularly with aspirations of creating a French colony in America and ending its westward expansion.[15] These plans were a real threat to the United States. France's army of 800,000 men had proven to be skilled in battle and would have surely made short work of America's then small 3000-man army.[16]

This military inferiority in turn molded the United States' response to France's aggressive actions. The actions taken in retaliation to the French actions were not military in nature, because such actions were likely to be futile and could lead to a disastrous result for the United States if France's military should retaliate.[17] Congress refused to allow

---

10. *See* Jay's Treaty, *supra* note 8, at art. XVIII.
11. *See* Gregory E. Fehlings, *America's First Limited War*, 53 NAVAL WAR C. REV. 103, 108 (2000).
12. *See* MCDONALD, *supra* note 4, at 152–53.
13. Fehlings, *supra* note 11, at 108.
14. *Id.*
15. *Id.*
16. *Id.*
17. *See id.*

vessels to carry arms for self-defense purposes and also used revenue cutters as an attempt to thwart French attacks.[18]

In an effort to avoid a war with France, President Adams sent a delegation of three prominent United States political figures to France in 1797.[19] These figures included future Supreme Court Chief Justice John Marshall, founding father Charles Cotesworth Pinckney, and Elbridge Gerry, who signed the declaration of independence. The French informed the delegation that they would not negotiate until the United States government assumed French debts to American suppliers, indemnified France against claims by American ship owners, extended a large loan to France, and apologized on behalf of President Adams for earlier comments made against France.[20] The delegation refused to accept these terms, not only because they were heavily prejudicial to the United States, but also because extending a loan to France would risk the appearance of the United States not being neutral in its relations with Britain. French representatives threatened that if all three members of the delegation left France, France would declare war on the United States. As a result of this threat one member remained in France.[21] President Adams announced that the French negotiations had failed and now sought to prepare the United States for a possible French attack.[22] President Adams pushed Congress to allow merchant ships to carry arms for self defense. Earlier, President Washington had imposed a restriction against arming merchant ships. President Adams lifted this restriction.[23] This action caused a furious reaction by the Democratic-Republican party led by Vice President Thomas Jefferson. Then Congressman James Madison called Adams' action "a usurpation by the Executive of a legislative power."[24] Once the American public heard of the insulting offer made by France to the United States, popular

---

18. *Id.* at 109.
19. *Id.*
20. *Id.*
21. *Id.* The remaining member was Elbridge Gerry, who stayed at the insistence of French foreign minister Charles Maurice de Talleyrand-Périgord.
22. *Id.* at 110.
23. *Id.*
24. *Id.*

opinion bayed for a war against the French. Adams chose to wage a defensive, undeclared, and limited naval war. Adams' objectives were to repel French aggression, and force France to respect American autonomy. Congress provided for national defense but never declared war against France.[25]

In 1798 Congress responded to Adams' requests for increased security by creating the Navy and Marine Corps. Fearing an invasion by France on United States soil, President Adams convinced a reluctant, retired President George Washington to come out of retirement and lead the United States Army. The United States was ill-prepared, both militarily and politically, to handle a French invasion. However, the Democratic-Republican party, also called Jeffersonians, were still loyal to the French and would not support a war against France.[26]

The War of 1812 was yet another occasion illustrating the military weakness of the United States in its relations with the British. In his Second Inaugural Address, James Madison described the war as necessary to maintain national sovereignty, particularly on the sea, as well as in maintaining the United States' equality as a nation to other nations around the world.[27] Madison asserted that the war was the result of the grave abuse and injustice inflicted on U.S. commerce by the British.[28] President Madison pointed out that the United States had reluctantly declared war as a last resort.[29] Madison said in his speech that war was not verbally declared against the United States, but physically war had already been waged against it.[30] Madison gave examples of U.S. mariners who were being forced from their vessels into foreign vessels.[31] In addition to the taking of American vessels, the British had often failed to give those captured the status of prisoners of war. Instead, the British treated them as traitors and deserters— quite unjustly in Madison's view.[32] Madison advocated for the United

---

25. Id.
26. Id.
27. See U.S. Gov't Printing Office, Inaugural Addresses of the Presidents of The United States 26 (1974).
28. Id.
29. Id.
30. Id.
31. Id. at 27.
32. Id.

States to fight for its rights in order to avoid having to do so again anytime in the immediate future.³³

Thus, it was argued that the United States chose to invade Canada during the War of 1812 as a means of rectifying the abuse inflicted on it by the British at sea.³⁴ A Canadian invasion would give the United States more weight when negotiating with Great Britain. Therefore, the rationale for this invasion was that, because the United States could not compete with the British at sea, prevailing on the Canadian front would force Britain to respect the United States' maritime rights.³⁵ In 1812, Canada served as Britain's access to American resources as well as a growing source of other raw materials essential to British industry, including timber for the Royal Navy.³⁶ For this reason, Madison felt that an attack on Canada would be an appropriate response to the maritime problems that existed between the two nations.³⁷

Merchants in the United States were also fed up with depredations they had been suffering at the hands of the British. Merchants from across the East Coast created memorials to express their views to Congress. Mr. Jefferson delivered the memorials' message to Congress, expressing the merchants' resentment of the British.³⁸ Monroe, who served as the U.S. minister to Britain, was instructed by the U.S. President to insist on the rights of the United States.³⁹ The merchants' pro-war views toward the British were significant because they had traditionally sought to avoid war, as it would be harmful to commerce. These same merchants were now pushing for the United States Army and Navy to protect their rights against the British. Boston merchants urged the United States to adopt a policy that would avoid the continued embarrassment of the nation and that would "support the dignity of the United States."⁴⁰

---

33. Id. at 28.
34. See J.C.A. Stagg, *James Madison and the Coercion of Great Britain: Canada, the West Indies, and the War of 1812*, 38 WM. & MARY Q. 3, 3 (1981).
35. See id. at 4.
36. See id. at 26–27.
37. See id. at 6.
38. See id. at 140.
39. See id. at 141.
40. Id.

American merchants also complained about the harm they suffered as a result of British Orders in Council. These British Orders were intended to be countervailing measures against the American Embargo Act that Congress had passed in 1807. American merchants viewed these Orders as constituting aggressive action against the United States.[41]

Napoleon further harmed American commerce in November of 1806 by declaring that the British Islands were to be in a state of blockade, forbidding all trade with England, and deeming possession of British products to be contraband. This decree was made from the Imperial Camp at Berlin. In addition, the British prohibited any neutral trade with France, unless it was made through Great Britain itself. The British claimed this move was in retaliation to the Berlin Decree.[42] This course of action by the British then set in motion even more aggressive commercial assaults on British commerce. Thus, by the Article of Milan Decree of 1807 Napoleon declared that any vessel that submitted to British search or tax or that was coming from a British port, was to be considered denationalized.[43] This took a devastating toll on U.S. sea commerce, resulting in the near removal of all American vessels from the sea.[44] In effect, the commercial war between the British and French had a very negative and devastating impact on American sea commerce.

Another furor arose when British deserters boarded an American vessel, the *Chesapeake*. Eager to maintain peaceful relations with Britain, the United States had negotiated a deal whereby they would return to the British any British deserters. Having knowledge that the British deserters were enlisted for service on board the *Chesapeake*, the *Leopard*, a British vessel, followed the *Chesapeake* out to sea. A British boat came alongside the *Chesapeake* and showed orders demanding all deserters. Within a short time, a shot was sent from the *Leopard* to the *Chesapeake*. The British vessel assaulted the *Chesapeake* with round after round, resulting in the death of three Americans and injuring eighteen more. After the brutal and unprovoked assault, two

---

41. See id. at 151.
42. See id. at 153–54.
43. REGINALD HORSEMAN, THE CAUSES OF THE WAR OF 1812, 121, 141–42 (1962).
44. Id. at 154.

British lieutenants boarded the *Chesapeake* to retrieve the deserters. America united in fury against the British and wanted them to pay for their assault on the *Chesapeake*. Some even desired an immediate declaration of war against the British.[45] The events at the *Chesapeake*, combined with the British decree, resulted in the President recommending to Congress the passage of Embargo legislation.[46] This legislation prohibited all vessels from sailing to foreign ports, except for foreign ships in ballast. This embargo was an attempt to force the rest of the world, specifically the French and British, to respect American commerce. Under international law, this withholding of commercial intercourse by an embargo was an attempt to pressure France and Britain into respecting the rights of a neutral nation.[47]

This prohibition was seen as a last attempt to avoid going to war with more powerful European nations.[48] Thus, between 1809 and 1811, the United States stopped all trade with France. The United States viewed this as a means to prevent France from world domination.[49]

Ultimately, by the 1814 Treaty of Ghent, the United States and the British agreed to stop further hostilities at sea and on land. Additionally, all property and territory taken during the war was to be returned.[50] The Third Article of the treaty provided that all prisoners of war shall be returned at the end of the hostilities.[51] Thus, through diplomacy and treaty-making, the United States sought to address its inability to militarily respond to interference with its commerce on the high seas. In the next section, I will explore how the Supreme Court responded to the depredations of U.S. commerce at the mercy of militarily powerful countries.

---

45. *See id.* at 158–59.
46. Embargo Act, 2 Stat. 451 (1807) and 2 Stat. 506 (1809).
47. HORESEMAN, *supra* note 43, at 163. *See also* Non-Intercourse, 3 Wharton DIGEST § 319, at 103.
48. Stagg, *supra* note 34, at 163.
49. *See id.* at 4.
50. *See* Treaty of Ghent, U.S.-Gr. Brit., Dec. 24, 1814, *available at* http://www.yale.edu/lawweb/avalon/diplomacy/britain/ghent.htm. (last visited Sept. 20, 2006).
51. *Id.* at art. III.

III. INTERNATIONAL LEGAL RESPONSES TO U.S. MILITARY AND ECONOMIC WEAKNESSES

Section II demonstrated the military and economic weaknesses of the United States in the late eighteenth century to early nineteenth century. In this section, I focus on the international legal jurisprudence of the Marshall Court during this period. The main innovations of the Court during this period are: the invocation and refinement of rules of neutrality and the rule that commerce should have safe passage in times of war (as evidenced by cases in which the court found that confiscation of private property during wartime was forbidden). In each of these areas, the Marshall court helped to solidify emerging rules of liberal trade as a counterweight to the abuses of free trade occasioned by depredations of American ships by countries with superior naval and military capabilities. These rules were eventually adopted in the Hague Regulations of 1907 following the Hague Peace conference of the early twentieth century.[52]

Although analyzing the birth of these innovations in international legal jurisprudence is important, equally important is observing the evolution and growth of Justice Marshall himself; for most of these new rules were products of his experience as attorney, Minister to France,[53] Secretary of State,[54] and Chief Justice of the Supreme Court.[55]

A. The Early Justice Marshall: Defending Virginian Debtors Against British Creditors

To appreciate the importance of the innovations of the Marshall Court under the law of nations, it is important to go back to Justice

---

52. *See, e.g., Berg v. British and African Steam Navigation* (The S.S. Appam), 243 U.S. 124 (1917).

53. According to Francis Howell Rudko, Marshall's experience as Minister to France prepared him for the "issues raised in the cases involving prize and neutrality." FRANCIS HOWELL RUDKO, JOHN MARSHALL AND INTERNATIONAL LAW: STATESMAN AND CHIEF JUSTICE 68 (1991). Marshall was appointed Minister to France by President Adams in early June 1797. *Id.* at 47. For his role as Minister to France, see *id.* at 47–82.

54. Marshall was appointed Secretary of State by President Adams in 1800. Regarding his role as Secretary of State, see *id.* at 96–120.

55. I address Marshall's role as a Justice and Chief Justice in Section III.

Marshall's career prior to becoming a Justice of the Supreme Court. As a Virginia lawyer, John Marshall defended Virginians who owed pre-Revolutionary War debts to British creditors.[56] He litigated in part to overcome the provisions of Article IV of the 1783 Treaty of Paris, which declared in part that these creditors should not "meet lawful impediments" in recovering the full value of these debts that had been contracted in a bona fide manner.[57] Marshall defended these debtors and Virginian debtor relief laws, in part, on the premise that the treaty supremacy clause of the federal Constitution did not entitle the federal government to enter into the 1783 Treaty of Paris. He argued that this treaty abrogated the rights of the State of Virginia by allowing British debtors to recover their debts, which Virginia had confiscated and sequestered by state law.[58]

It is important to note that, in this respect, John Marshall supported the Virginian debtors because like the anti-Federalists of the period, he supported the rights of states such as Virginia, as victors in the Revolutionary War that were now entitled to confiscate British debt. The anti-Federalists also saw confiscation as a way of easing the burden of poverty and famine for former colonists.[59] As I shall show below, as a Justice of the Supreme Court, John Marshall, by contrast,

---

56. See *Ware v. Hylton*, 3 U.S. 199 (1796).
57. Treaty of Paris, U.S.-Gr. Brit. Sept. 3, 1783, *available at* http://www.archives.gov/exhibits/american_originals/paris.html (last visited Oct. 1, 2006) [hereinafter Treaty of Paris].
58. *Ware*, 3 U.S. at 202.
59. Notably, Marshall had in the House of Delegates following the Philadelphia Convention supported the interests of creditors as opposed to those of debtors. For example, Marshall supported provisions in the draft Constitution that would have impeded the collection of British debts. The provision in question here is U.S. Constitution, Article 3, Section 2, which would grant to federal courts jurisdiction over "[c]ontroversies . . . [b]etween a State, or the Citizens thereof, and foreign states, Citizens, or Subjects" to intrude the national government into economic matters properly left to individuals and the states. *See* U.S. CONST. art. III, § 2. Marshall had also helped to draft the repeal law passed on December 12, with an amendment suspending it until Britain complied with all terms of the peace treaty of 1793; he voted against including the amendment. In addition, Marshall helped write a bill for establishing district courts, which creditors had long sought to speed up debt suits that tended to languish in the county courts. Marshall voted against the final bill, but for reasons unrelated to debtor-creditor matters. *See* JOURNALS OF THE

became one of the leading proponents of giving commerce safe passage during war—a position quite at odds with the arguments he advanced in defending Virginian debtors.

As an attorney, the most numerous classes of cases Marshall took on during his legal career—more than 100 during the 1790s—concerned suits initiated in the 1790s by British subjects to recover debts[60] that Virginians had contracted before the Revolution.[61] These actions stemmed from pervasive anti-British sentiment in Virginia during the 1780s. Although the fourth article of the 1783 Peace Treaty with Great Britain stated that "creditors on either side shall meet with no lawful impediment to the recovery of the full value in sterling money, of all bona fide debts heretofore contracted,"[62] as we saw above, the Virginia Assembly in 1783 directed that state courts remain closed to British creditors. Virginians feared an onslaught of suits that would undermine the State's already jeopardized finances. The federal courts, established under the Judiciary Act of 1789, offered a better opportunity for British creditors.[63] There, Federalist judges, who held an overwhelming majority of seats on the federal bench, were regarded as being more sympathetic to British interests than were the mostly anti-Federalist judges on the Virginia courts. During the next several years, the U.S. Circuit Court in Virginia heard hundreds of such cases—approximately three-fourths of its docket.[64]

In these cases, Virginia debtors entered, in addition to the regular common law pleas, a set of special pleas that raised questions of law that the courts would have to decide before juries could address any issues of fact. These pleas, eventually numbering four, declared that (1) the debtors' payments made to the state loan office under a 1777 sequestration law legally discharged the debt; (2) that two other wartime acts, which vested all British subjects' property in the state government

---

HOUSE OF DELEGATES OF THE COMMONWEALTH OF VIRGINIA, OCT. 1787 SESS., 79–95 *passim* (Richmond: Thomas W. White, 1828).

60. In 1791, the British government estimated that the value of the debt exceeded £2,300,000.

61. DAVID ROBARGE, A CHIEF JUSTICE'S PROGRESS: JOHN MARSHALL FROM REVOLUTIONARY VIRGINIA TO THE SUPREME COURT 132 (2000).

62. *See* Treaty of Paris, *supra* note 58, at art. IV.

63. Judiciary Act, ch. 20, 1 Stat. 73 (1789).

64. ROBARGE, *supra* note 62.

and prohibited recovery of British debts not assigned before May 1777, were still in effect; (3) that British violations of the seventh article of the peace treaty, pertaining to the confiscation of slaves and the continued occupation of forts in the Northwest, abrogated the peace treaty; and that (4) dissolution of the colonial relationship on July 2, 1776, annulled the British plaintiffs' rights of recovery.[65]

No courts heard any arguments on the British debt cases until November of 1791 when Marshall represented a Thomas Walker in *Jones v. Walker*.[66] For a variety of reasons, this case was not decided until the end of 1792.[67] A full circuit court, consisting of Chief Justice John Jay, Associate Justice James Iredell, and District Judge Cyrus Griffin, finally convened in May of 1793. By then, plaintiff Jones had died, and all of his many suits had to be revived by special writs in the name of his estate's administrator, John Tyndale Ware. To prevent another postponement, the court ordered that one of those suits, against prominent Richmond merchant Daniel Hylton, be revived in Ware's name. *Ware v. Hylton*[68] thus became the new test case for the special pleas. The court heard the case from May 24 to June 7; Marshall argued his points on the May 29 and 30. Although Marshall's notes have been lost, Justice Iredell kept several pages of words and phrases which, when joined with materials on the 1796 appeal of the case, make Marshall's main contentions evident.[69] Besides extrapolating from the special pleas, he also discussed some of the constitutional issues, such as the authority of states relative to the federal treaty-making power that judges had previously avoided. His essential point was that the peace treaty repealed conflicting state laws prospectively but could not undo actions taken while the Virginia sequestration act was in effect.[70]

---

65. See RUDKO, *supra* note 54, at 24–25.
66. 2 Paine 688 (1832).
67. See Charles F. Hobson, *The Recovery of British Debts in the Federal Circuit Court of Virginia, 1790 to 1797*, 92 VA. MAG. HIST. & BIOGRAPHY 176–87, 193 (Apr. 1984).
68. 3 U.S. 199 (1796).
69. Rudko, *supra* note 54, at 25 (citing 5 THE PAPERS OF JOHN MARSHALL: SELECTED LAW CASES, 1784–1800, at 300–13 (Charles F. Hobson, ed. 1987)).
70. See LEONARD BAKER, JOHN MARSHALL: A LIFE IN LAW 158–60 (1974).

It is interesting to note that *Ware v. Hylton* was Marshall's only appearance before the Supreme Court arguing a case. In the case, Marshall avoided directly disputing the plaintiff's constitutional point that treaties were supreme over state laws. Instead, he sought to persuade the Justices that "fair and rational construction" of the peace treaty would lead them to conclude that Virginia was correct in this instance—that loan office payments were not lawful impediments.[71] In a 4–1 decision issued on March 7, the Court rejected Marshall's "ingenious, metaphysical reasoning and refinement upon the words, debt, discharge, [and] extinguishment" as contradicting accepted principles for interpreting treaties, and held that Article 4 of the peace treaty annulled Virginia's 1777 debt law and allowed British creditors to pursue recovery.[72] In essence, the Court struck down the claim that Virginia could confiscate private debts because they were the property of enemy aliens.[73]

B. Marshall's Government Experience: Development of International Legal Jurisprudence Grounded in the Policy of Neutrality

To fully appreciate the foundation on which Justice Marshall grounded his reasoning in later Supreme Court cases, it is important and necessary to examine his experiences in the political milieu of the 1790s.

Although the Treaty of Paris in 1783 formally ended the revolutionary war between the United States and Great Britain, the political hostility between the two States did not cease.[74] At the same time, the political environment was also divided within the young nation, as it attempted to formulate its policies regarding domestic and foreign issues.[75] When, in 1793, France declared war against Great Britain,

---

71. THE PAPERS OF JOHN MARSHALL: VOLUME III 7–14 (William C. Stinchcombe et al. eds., Univ. of N.C. Press 1979) (1939); *see* THE PAPERS OF JOHN MARSHALL: VOLUME V 317–25 (Charles F. Hobson et al. eds., Univ. of N.C. Press 1987) (1939); *see also* ALBERT J. BEVERIDGE, THE LIFE OF JOHN MARSHALL: VOLUME III 192 (1916).

72. ROBARGE, *supra* note 62, at 136.

73. Burrus M. Carnahan, *Lincoln, Lieber and the Laws of War: The Origins and Limits of the Principle of Military Necessity*, 92 AM. J. INT'L L. 213, 217 n.23 (1998); *see also* RUDKO, *supra* note 54, at 26–30.

74. RUDKO, *supra* note 54, at 13.

75. *Id.*

these divisions grew deeper as nascent political parties adopted either a pro-British or pro-French stance.[76] President Washington, cognizant of the "importance of neutrality to American commerce and national survival,"[77] issued on April 22, 1793, the Proclamation of Neutrality.[78] Although there was much domestic opposition to the Proclamation, Marshall embraced it.[79] He viewed the opposing sentiments, especially those of the Republicans, who favored alliance with the French, as signs of "repudiation of national union and a tendency erroneously to equate national interest with French or foreign interest."[80] In essence, Marshall, who "perceived himself to be above party, dedicated only to preserving the nation's independence,"[81] was convinced that such pro-French feelings "[were] inimical to the survival of the United States as a nation."[82]

After the French declared war against the British and the subsequent adoption of the policy of neutrality by the Washington administration in 1793, relations between the United States and France, who felt that the Proclamation did not honor the United States' obligations under treaties executed in 1778, deteriorated.[83] Therefore, as mentioned above,[84] in an effort to mend U.S.-France relations, in 1797 President Adams sent John Marshall, Charles Cotesworth Pinckney, and Elbridge Gerry to France "to redefine French-American relations, to restore diplomatic harmony, and to assert the sovereignty of the United States."[85] Notably, Marshall's role, in congruence with his Federalist philosophy, was to assert and preserve both the "independence and neutrality" of the United States.[86]

Marshall's experience during his mission to France helped to shape and cultivate his understanding of the importance of the United

---

76. *Id.*
77. *Id.* at 53.
78. *See id.* at 13–14.
79. *Id.* at 14.
80. *Id.*
81. *Id.* at 49 (citation omitted).
82. *Id.* at 16.
83. *Id.* at 46.
84. *See* Fehlings, *supra* note 18 and accompanying text.
85. RUDKO, *supra* note 54, at 47.
86. *Id.* at 49 (citation omitted).

States' role as a neutral State.[87] The purpose of the policy of neutrality was strict self-interest: "The United States, attempting to become an *independent commercial nation*, adopted the relatively undeveloped concept in international law of neutrality."[88] Indeed, the prevalence of "intense maritime warfare," which characterized much of the end of the 1790s, increased the importance of the law of neutrality.[89] Without structuring the legal principles supporting the policy of neutrality, it would have been indeed difficult, if not impossible, for the United States to emerge as an independent commercial nation.

As will be seen later,[90] Marshall's experience in France not only prepared him to deal with issues raised by the prize cases, but was also essential to his ability to deal with those issues.[91] His experience as a Secretary of State in 1800, just prior to joining the Supreme Court, where Marshall represented the Adams administration, particularly in its protestations of the partiality of British admiralty courts for acquiescing to illegal captures and other practices inimical to U.S. commerce under the law of nations also influenced him.[92] He made similar protests to Spain and relied on the eighteenth-century international legal jurist, Vattel, in so doing.[93]

C. The Later Marshall: Using the Court to Solidify the Commercial Rights of Non-Belligerents and Neutrals During Wartime

Although John Marshall the attorney often argued in favor of Virginian debtors, as a Supreme Court Justice, he became the leading

---

87. *Id.* at 56 (quoting Marshall's response to French demands: "I told [Mr. Hottinguer] that . . . no nation estimated [France's] power more highly than America or wished more to be on amicable terms with her but that our object was still dearer to us than the friendship of France which was *our national independence. That America had taken a neutral station.*") (citing 3 THE PAPERS OF JOHN MARSHALL 173 (Stinchcombe & Cullen, eds. 1979)) (emphasis added).
88. *Id.* at 53 (emphasis added). The author further states that "[t]he United States' policy of neutrality toward all of Europe was prompted by the developing nation's desire to trade." *Id.* at 73.
89. *Id.* at 69.
90. *See infra* Part II.C.
91. *Id.* at 68.
92. RUDKO, *supra* note 54, at 106–09.
93. *Id.* at 110–11.

exponent of the rights of creditors and a defender of transnational commerce in the face of the depredations of American commerce on the high seas. There were already courts in the late eighteenth century that had begun recognizing the precarious predicament of U.S. commerce at the hands of more powerful military and maritime states. Thus, in 1793, the District Court of Pennsylvania observed that it was "difficult for a neutral nation, with the best dispositions, so to conduct itself as not to displease one or the other of belligerent parties, heated with the rage of war, and jealous of even common acts of justice or friendship on its part."[94]

During Marshall's time on the Supreme Court, it was generally asserted that a successful belligerent had a right to confiscate the private property of enemies and neutrals. The Supreme Court was, however, confronted not only by debtors from states such as Virginia, but also by foreigners asserting belligerent rights, such as confiscation or defending their cargo from confiscation. As a result, the Court came to assume the status of a quasi-international tribunal, particularly in prize cases arising from the various wars of the period.[95] In addition, as one scholar has asserted, the Court in this period, "suggested itself as a useful means to deal with sensitive U.S. treaty controversies in a way the States might perceive as mindful of their respective internal sovereignties, and foreign states might perceive as credibly neutral."[96] As indicated earlier, neutrality was indeed the policy of early U.S. administrations.[97]

As a militarily and economically weak country in the late eighteenth century, various early U.S. administrations sought to adhere

---

94. *Findlay v. The William*, 9 F. Cas. 57, 59 (D. Pa. 1793) (No. 4790) (emphasis added). *Findlay* also held, inter alia, that as a neutral nation, the United States does not have the right to affect the confiscation practices of another sovereign, but can forbid the sale of confiscated goods on American soil. *Id.*

95. James E. Pfander, *Rethinking the Supreme Court's Original Jurisdiction in State-Party Cases*, 82 Cal. L. Rev., 555, 633 (1994).

96. Thomas H. Lee, *The Supreme Court of the United States as Quasi-International Tribunal: Reclaiming the Court's Original and Exclusive Jurisdiction over Treaty-Based Suits by Foreign States Against States*, 104 Colum. L. Rev., 1765, 1849 (2004).

97. "From the beginnings of its history, this country has been careful to maintain a neutral position between warring governments." *Berg*, 243 U.S. at 149; *see infra* Part II.B.

strictly to the "acknowledged laws of civilized nations," to ensure that U.S. commerce was not swept from the ocean by the ruinous and lawless depredations of more powerful States.[98] The challenge for the Supreme Court, however, was that the rules of the law of nations relating to belligerent rights and obligations were not as clear-cut. Many controversies that landed in the court required judicial innovation, as they presented issues without clear answers under the law of nations or in the precedents of the court. As I will show, the Court more often than not decided such cases in favor of the most liberal rules that permitted the continuation of commerce in the face of war—notwithstanding the fact that those cases would equally have been decided in favor of belligerent rights with the consequence of frustrating free commerce by confiscating and sequestrating the cargo of neutrals and others in the high seas. My analysis below shows that the Marshall Court sought to conform the young country's views to its international legal obligations, primarily motivated by its relative economic and military weaknesses. Second, that in seeking to ensure that the United States conformed its international legal obligations, the Marshall Court played a constructive role in solidifying the early regime of international economic governance through law.

The sense one gets in reading the decisions that Marshall helped craft as a Justice of the Supreme Court was consistent with the policy of the Adams administration and, as agreed at the Continental Congress,[99] the United States was laying by the rules of the law of nations in its commercial relations with the warring States of Europe. However, these States seldom played by these rules, and as such, it was necessary to develop a jurisprudence that could encourage resort

---

98. Lossing, *supra* note 1, at 154.

99. Jay Stewart, *The Status of the Law of Nations in Early American Law*, 42 VAND. L. REV. 825 n.24 (1989) ("The Continental Congress resolved to insist on strict compliance with the law of nations when determining the legality of captures on the high seas"). *See* 14 JOURNALS OF THE CONTINENTAL CONGRESS 635 (W. Ford ed., 1909); *see also* J. S. Reeves, *The Influence of the Law of Nature Upon International Law in the United States*, 3 AM. J. INT'L L. 547, 556–57 (1909).

to complete reciprocity between these States and the United States as a neutral power.[100]

I want to begin this discussion with Chief Justice Marshall's 1801 decision in *Talbot v. Seeman*.[101] The following is the background of this case. In the 1790s, France commissioned its war vessels to seize certain U.S. ships. A French Executive Directory also permitted the seizure of any ship containing any item of English manufacture.[102] This led to the United States' first quasi-war. In retaliation to French privateering,[103] Congress authorized the capture of French military vessels,[104] and the seizure of French cargo.[105] Although the Congressional Acts gave American vessels the right to seize French

---

100. So for example, Benson J. Lossing, notes that a French decree of December 17, 1807, promulgated in response to British decrees in turn sparked similar decrees from Spain and Holland. As a result, the commerce of the United States was "swept from the ocean" within a few months, even though it had been conducted *"in strict accordance with the acknowledged laws of civilized nations."* LOSSING, *supra* note 1, at 154. As a result, Lossing notes that the United States was "utterly unable, by any power it then possessed, to resist the robbers upon the great highway of nations [and] the independence of the republic had no actual record. It had been theoretically declared on parchment a quarter of a century before, but the nation and its interests were now as much subservient to British orders in council and French imperial decrees as when George the Third sent governors to the colonies of which it was composed. . . ." *Id.* Most importantly, Lossing argues that "trade between the United States and the European possessions of Great Britain were placed on a footing of perfect reciprocity, but no concessions could be obtained as to the trade of the West Indies. . . ." by Jay's Treaty of 1794. *Id.* at 150.

101. *Talbot v. Seeman*, 5 U.S. 1, 6 (1801).

102. *See Law which Determines the Character of Vessels from Their Cargo, Especially Those Loaded with English Merchandise*, 29 Nivose *an* 6 (Jan. 18, 1798), *in* COLLECTION COMPLETE, DECRETS, OND ONNACES, REGLEMENTS ET AVIS DU COUNSEIL D'ETAT 214 (1825).

103. *See Talbot*, 5 U.S. at 6.

104. *See* Act of June 25, 1798, ch. 60, § 1–2, 1 Stat. 572 (1798) (providing authority for the defense of the merchant vessels of the United States against French depredations).

105. *See* Act of March 2, 1799, ch. 2, § 6, 1 Stat. 613, 615–16 (1799) (providing further suspension of the commercial intercourse between the United States and France, and the dependencies thereof).

property, the laws were not unfettered[106] and contained a number of restrictions regarding the nature of property to be confiscated.[107] One act provided that aliens of hostile nations could depart the United States with their property intact.[108] *Talbot v. Seeman* involved the capture, authorized by the foregoing congressional legislation, of an English vessel that had been privateered under the authority of the French directory. The captor of the French commandeered vessel sought payment of salvage charges. Hence, in *Talbot*, Marshall and his fellow justices confronted the novel and unsettled question under the law of nations: whether recaptured neutrals were liable for salvage.[109] The neutrality of the vessel was not in question, as it had sailed from Hamburg, and Hamburg and France were neutrals to each other—unlike the hostile relations of the French and the English and both of these countries and the United States throughout the late eighteenth to early nineteenth century.

Marshall and his fellow justices could well have answered this question of whether salvage was payable in one of several ways: They could have placed themselves in the position of a French admiralty court; they could have determined the case as if it was regulated by Congressional legislation authorizing defense or reprisals against French vessels destructive of U.S. commerce; or they could have decided that the case had to be determined under the laws of war, which were effectively the law of nations. All these alternatives placed the Court in the difficult position of having to decide on a question arising out of France's superior naval capabilities—either way the

---

106. *See* Fehlings, *supra* note 11, at 111. Congress specifically withheld the right to prey on unarmed French vessels in fear of an all-out war between the French and the United States. The United States' reluctance to authorize seizure of unarmed French vessels was less a product of enlightened thinking and more the product of America's fear of an all-out war and possible French invasion. *See id.*

107. *See* Act of Feb. 9, 1799, ch. 94, 50 Stat. 613 (1799) (providing further suspension of the commercial intercourse between the United States and France, and the dependencies thereof).

108. *See id.* at 615; JAMES KENT, 1 COMMENTARIES ON AMERICAN LAW 132 (1826).

109. Justice Marshall asserted years later in *The Nereide*, that "Even in the case of salvage . . . no fixed rule is prescribed by the law of nations." 13 U.S. 388, 423 (1815).

question implied was whether French privateering was permissible or a derogation of either French or U.S. law, or of the law of nations. The cautious manner in which Marshall asserted what Congress authorized is evident in the following quote:

> The substantial question here is, whether the case of the Amelia (the captured vessel under French command) is a *casus-belli*—whether she was an object of that limited war. The kind of war which existed was a war against all French force found upon the ocean, to seize it and bring it in, that it might not injure our commerce.[110]

Marshall frames the war as one not against France as such—but rather upon such French force as had injured U.S. commerce. In fact, Marshall goes on to distinguish between the intention of destroying French armed forces and French property. Marshall argues the object of the war was not to destroy French property. By arguing as such, Marshall was able to contend that it "made no difference in whom the absolute [title] property of the vessel was."[111] This is a crucial distinction because it lays down the boundary between war and commerce—war could be severed from commerce. In other words, the belligerent character of those privateering or commanding a vessel did not automatically infuse the character of the cargo. The character of the vessel's cargo was distinguishable from the hostile command of a vessel. The recapture of the vessel from France—the object of the limited war—did not interfere with the title to the property of the neutral owner of the cargo in the vessel.[112]

Further Marshall was careful in answering the question of whether the vessel's capture by France was justifiable by noting that, if France had violated the law of nations, this gave the United States no justification for violating this law by retaking the privateered vessel.[113] In any event, Marshall justified the retaking of the vessel by the United States on the basis that it was a neutral vessel captured by a belligerent[114] and further, that recaptures are "one of the incidents of war."[115] Marshall defended jurisdiction over the case on the view that federal

---

110. *Talbot*, 5 U.S. at 9.
111. *Id.*
112. *See id.*
113. *Id.* at 22.
114. *Id.* at 32, 36.
115. *Id.* at 42.

courts had jurisdiction to determine whether the capture, recapture and payment of salvage on recapture were due under the laws of war.[116] In responding to the view that the law of nations only allowed the United States to protest French privateering and no more, Marshall noted that it is only after having failed in its protests or its remonstrates against this conduct that the United States had authorized "limited hostilities" against France.[117] Thus, according to Marshall, the "respect due to France is totally unconnected with the danger in which her laws had placed the *Amelia.*"[118] Thus, the danger placed on the *Amelia*, according to Marshall, was the way in which it would be determined as to whether salvage was payable under the law of nations.[119] Marshall was of course not unaware of the ruinous nature of French depredations of U.S. commerce. As he noted:

> Much has been said about the general conduct of France and England on the seas, and it has been urged that the course of the latter has been still more injurious than that of the former. That is a consideration on to be taken up in this cause. Animadversions on either, in the present case, would be considered extremely unbecoming the judges of this court, who have only to enquire what was the real danger in which the laws of one of the countries placed the Amelia, and from which she has been freed by her re-capture.[120]

Thus by finding that the hostilities between the United States and France justified the recapture of the *Amelia*, Marshall placed the question of France's sovereignty and independence,[121] not on the altar of a victor justifying it as the spoils of war, but rather as justified by the state of hostilities between France and the United States. In essence, Marshall adroitly declined to frame the issue of the vessel's recapture as one involving the superiority of the United States over France. Ultimately, Marshall finds without the citation of any authorities

---

116. *Id.* at 36.
117. *Id.* at 41.
118. *Id.* at 40.
119. *Id.* at 41.
120. *Id.* at 41.
121. On the part of France, it had been urged that "France is an independent nation, entitled to the benefits of the law of the law of nations; and further that if she has violated them, we ought not to violate them also, but ought to remonstrate against such misconduct." *Id.* at 40.

that, because the *Amelia* had been placed in "real and imminent" danger, her captors were entitled to salvage.¹²²

The next case I want to discuss to illustrate how Chief Justice Marshall helped in the solidification of liberal rules of international commerce is *The Nereide*.¹²³ The issue in *The Nereide* was whether war gives a belligerent the right to condemn, capture and confiscate the goods of a neutral or friend if carried in the armed vessel of an enemy. Justice Marshall took the opportunity to make the case for the expansive rights of neutrals during wartime. According to Marshall, armed neutrality had effected "a great revolution in the law of nations."¹²⁴ His observation that it was a maxim of the law of nations that "free ships should make free goods" became the basis of his conclusion that the converse maxim was equally true—that "a neutral may lawfully put his goods on board a ship for conveyance on the ocean."¹²⁵ He even concluded that this rule was "universally recognized as the original rule of the law of nations"¹²⁶ that dated back into antiquity,¹²⁷ and he could find no writers contradicting it.¹²⁸

In refuting that the right of a belligerent to search a neutral vessel was superior to the right of a neutral to carry cargo in a belligerent's vessel, Marshall asked:

> Is it a substantive and independent right wantonly, and in the pride of power, to vex and harass neutral commerce, because there is a capacity to do so? Or to indulge the idle and mischievous curiosity of looking into neutral trade? Or the assumption of a right to control it? If it be such a substantive and independent right, it would be better that cargoes should be inspected in port before the sailing of the vessel, or that belligerent licenses should be procured.¹²⁹

This revealing passage suggests Justice Marshall's conclusion that the hostile character of a vessel does not attach to the goods of a neutral on board. According to Marshall, it mattered not that the

---

122. *Id.* at 41–42.
123. *The Nereide*, 13 U.S. 388 (1815).
124. *Id.* at 420.
125. *Id.* at 425.
126. *Id.*
127. *Id.* at 426.
128. *Id.* at 426.
129. *Id.* at 427.

vessel was a belligerent one or that it was armed. The goal of the neutral is the transportation of their goods, which is permissible as long as the neutral does not participate in arming the vessel.[130] He went even further to observe that, if the belligerent vessel resisted the right of the enemy to search the vessel, this did not affect the neutral character of the goods on board.[131] Thus, a neutral in this position only exposes themselves to "capture and detention, but not to condemnation."[132]

Although Justice Marshall disavowed using the power of the Court to "tread the devious and intricate path of politics,"[133] Justice Johnson, who agreed with him, nevertheless singled out Spain as the only "civilized nation" that had declined to "unequivocally acknowledge" this right of neutrals.[134] Justice Johnson went further to conclude that even if Spain had adopted a different doctrine, "the practice of one nation, and that one not the most enlightened or commercial, ought not to be permitted to control the law of the world."[135] Both Justice Marshall and Johnson's opinions in *The Nereide* disclose their bias in favor of open commerce and against doctrines that would constrain the rights of neutrals during war to engage in trade. Thus, even while disavowing a political role for the court in making rules, which he identified as a legislative function,[136] or in sorting out the political differences between warring belligerents, Justice Johnson too participated in solidifying the announced policy of various U.S. administrations in favor of neutral commerce at a time of U.S. military and economic weakness in relation to her trading partners.[137]

Although Justices Marshall and Johnson were unequivocal in announcing that belligerents had no right to condemn without compensation the goods of a neutral on board a belligerent vessel, Justice

---

130. *Id.* at 428.
131. *Id.* at 429–30.
132. *Id.* at 432.
133. *The Nereide*, 13 U.S. at 423.
134. *Id.* at 433.
135. *Id.* at 434.
136. *Id.* at 435.
137. Notably, Marshall praised the "talents and virtues which adorned the cabinet of that day, on the patient fortitude with which it resisted the intemperate violence with which it was assailed, on the firmness with which it maintained those principles which its sense of duty prescribe ... [and] on the wisdom of the rules it adopted." *Id.* at 422.

Story found little support for it in the law of nations or in "the elaborate treatises of Grotius, or Puffendorf, or Vattel."[138] For Justice Story, "modern commerce" had raised many intricate questions for prize tribunals for which there no clear rules.[139] After parsing through the cases and the law, Justice Story concluded

> [T]hat the act of sailing under belligerent or neutral convoy is of itself a violation of neutrality, and the ship and cargo if caught in *delicto* are justly confiscable; and further, that if resistance be necessary, as in my opinion it is not, to perfect the offence, still that the resistance of the convoy is to all purposes the resistance of the associated fleet.[140]

That Justices Marshall and Johnson, on the one hand, and Justice Story on the other, could arrive at such contradictory conclusions illustrates one of my central theses—that the law of nations on the questions in prize cases of the late eighteenth century were often novel and that the Marshall court played a crucial role in solidifying the emerging norms.

Perhaps no other statement in Justice Story's dissent is more telling than his observation that if the rule his brethren were espousing was adopted, "[i]t would strip from the conqueror all the fruits of victory, and lay them at the feet of those whose singular merit would consist in evading his rights, if not collusively in aiding his enemy."[141] For Justice Story, the rights of victorious belligerents to essentially condemn cargo of neutrals in belligerent vessels prevailed over the "false and hollow neutrality" of the rule that Justices Marshall and Johnson espoused in their opinion. Such false and hollow neutrality would in turn be "more injurious than the most active warfare"[142] much to the "dismay and ruin of inferior maritime powers."[143] The reason, according to Justice Story, that the Marshall/Johnson rule would be more ruinous to "inferior maritime powers" was that it would swallow the right of search and as such, allow belligerents "to

---

138. *Id.* at 437.
139. *Id.* at 438.
140. *Id.* at 445.
141. *Id.* at 449.
142. *Id.*
143. *Id.*

keep up armaments of incalculable size" under the disguise of carrying a neutrals goods.[144] Clearly then, the ability of neutrals, or inferior maritime powers as Justice Story referred to them, was a consideration in the outcome of *The Nereide*. This is unsurprising as late eighteenth- to early nineteenth-century U.S. administrations were committed to neutrality in the face of the depredations of U.S. commerce by the maritime powers of the period. My point is that Justice Marshall contributed to the then emerging rules of liberal commerce even when it seemed that the espousal of such rules were could not be easily reconciled with "the privileges of an inoffensive neutral."[145]

Justice Marshall continued his adherence to the policy of neutrality by upholding the rights of neutrals in a series of other cases arising from the quasi-war with France. For example, in *Maley v. Shattuck*,[146] William Maley, the commander of a public armed vessel belonging to the U.S. government, took as prize a vessel belonging to Jared Shattuck, a U.S.-born merchant who was now a subject of neutral Denmark.[147] Justice Marshall reiterated the general rule that "a vessel libeled as enemy's property is condemned as prize, if she act in such a manner as to forfeit the protection to which she is entitled by her neutral character."[148] Nonetheless, Marshall, in scrutinizing the evidence, determined that Maley did not have sufficient cause to justify seizure, and therefore assessed damages against Maley.[149]

In *Little v. Barreme*,[150] two U.S. vessels captured a Danish vessel near Hispaniola pursuant to a nonintercourse law passed by Congress in 1799, whose purpose was to proscribe maritime commerce between the United States and France.[151] The act, in short, provided that a ship owned, hired, or employed by a citizen of the United States was prohibited from proceeding to any French port; and, if such

---

144. *Id.* at 448–49.
145. *Id.* at 454 (Story, J., concurring).
146. 7 U.S. 458 (1806); *see also* RUDKO, *supra* note 54, at 71.
147. *Id.* at 459.
148. *Id.* at 487.
149. *Id.* at 490.
150. 6 U.S. 170 (1804); *see also* RUDKO, *supra* note 54, at 71.
151. *Id.* at 170.

vessel were discovered, it would be subject to seizure.[152] Further, the act empowered the president of the United States to instruct public armed vessels to stop and examine any such vessel on suspicion, and if warranted, seizure of the vessel.[153] The district court, which denied damages, held that the captors did not provide "sufficient proof to bring this vessel and cargo so far within the provisions of these statutes as to incur a forfeiture thereof."[154] Ultimately, Justice Marshall affirmed the decision of the district court and thereby reinforced the rights of neutrals.[155]

Also, in *Sands v. Knox*,[156] a U.S. resident owned a vessel, *The Juno*.[157] The vessel proceeded from Connecticut to St. Croix, which was under the power of Denmark—a neutral State.[158] At this point the vessel was sold to a Danish subject; the vessel then proceeded to the French-governed St. Domingo before returning to the United States.[159] Pursuant to the nonintercourse law, the customs collector in New York seized and detained the vessel.[160] Rejecting arguments, which interpreted the nonintercourse law strictly so as to condone the seizure, Justice Marshall, in upholding the rights of neutrals, held that the nonintercourse law "did not intend to affect the sale of vessels of the United States, or to impose any disability on the vessel, after *bona fide* sale and transfer to a foreigner."[161]

As Frances Howell Rudko summarizes:

> These cases arising from the Quasi-War illustrate that Marshall . . . construed the law to effect the rights of neutrals. He was aware . . . that search and seizure was a right to be exercised only on belligerent goods

---

152. *Id.*
153. *Id.* at 171.
154. *Id.* at 172.
155. *Id.* at 178. Justice Marshall, in affirming the district court's decision, stated: "Of consequence, however strong the circumstances might be, which induced captain *Little* to suspect [the Danish vessel] to be an *American* vessel, they could not excuse the detention of her, since he would not have been authorized to detain her had she been really *American*." *Id.*
156. 7 U.S. 499 (1806); *see also* RUDKO, *supra* note 54, at 71.
157. *Id.* at 499.
158. *Id.* at 500.
159. *Id.* at 499–500.
160. *Id.* at 499.
161. *Id.* at 503.

and vessels. By objectively allowing damages, he helped to police a practice subject to abuse. In this way, he continued to protest the violation of neutral rights.[162]

I would also like to credit or at least associate Justice Marshall with endorsing the innovation in the rules of war that where private property belonging to a national of an enemy State is within the other belligerent State's territory, it does not become automatically extinguished by the conquest. Instead, as Justice Marshall held in *Brown v. United States*,[163] such property is regarded as being held in suspension, pending its return to its owner on cessation of hostilities. Marshall's strong stance against a victorious belligerent's right to confiscate the private property of the nationals of an enemy State is evidenced by his assertion in *Brown v. United States* that the "practice of forbearing to seize and confiscate debts and credits" is universally received, and that if confiscated, such debts and credits revive to their owner "on the restoration of peace."[164] This principle was later followed in British courts. In one case, the Chancery Division held "it is a familiar principle of English law held that the outbreak of war effects no confiscation or forfeiture of enemy property."[165]

---

162. RUDKO, *supra* note 54, at 72.
163. *Brown v. United States*, 12 U.S. (8 Cranch) 110 (1814).
164. *Id.* at 127. In a more forthright statement of the principle, Marshall observed that the "proposition that a declaration of war does not in itself enact a confiscation of the property of the enemy within the territory of the belligerent, is believed to be entirely free from doubt." *Id.* at 127. However, Marshall conceded that war gives a sovereign the "full right to take the persons and confiscate the property of the enemy," but that this "rigid rule" had been moderated by "the humane and wise policy of modern times." *Id.* at 122–23. By contrast, Justice Story dissented, arguing that whereas mere declaration of war did not ipso facto operate as a confiscation of the property of enemy aliens, such property is liable to confiscation "at the discretion of the sovereign power having the conduct and execution of the war" and that the law of nations "is resorted to merely as a limitation of this discretion, not as conferring authority to exercise it." *Id.* at 154 (Story, J., dissenting). Justice Marshall appeared to have affirmed the modern rule prohibiting confiscation under the law of nations, and the sovereign power to confiscate enemy property. *See id.*; *see also United States v. Percheman*, 32 U.S. 51, 51 (1833) (affirming the rule against confiscation under the law of nations unambiguously).
165. *Fried Krupp Aktiengesellschaft v. Orconera Iron Ore Co.*, (1919) 88 Eng. Rep. 304, 309 (Ch.).

It is, however, only fair to observe that the Supreme Court's embrace of broader rights in favor of commerce and the consequential contraction of belligerent rights predated Marshall's entry into the court. As already noted above, Marshall the attorney lost his only case before the Court in *Ware v. Hylton*.[166] In this case, Marshall supported the rights of a Virginian businessman who owed pre-Revolutionary War debts to British creditors. One of Marshall's losing arguments was that Virginia, as having prevailed over the British in the Revolutionary War, was entitled to extinguish debts its citizens owed British creditors. In his concurring opinion, Justice Paterson noted:

> Considering . . . the usages of civilized nations, and the opinion of modern writers, relative to confiscation, and also the circumstances under which these debts were contracted. . . . [W]e ought to admit of no comment that will narrow and restrict their operation and import. The construction of a treaty made in favor of such creditors, and for the restoration and enforcement of pre-existing contracts, ought to be liberal and benign.[167]

Justice Chase had been more emphatic about the importance of creditor rights observing that:

> Congress had the power to sacrifice the rights and interests of private citizens to secure the safety and prosperity of the public . . . [and as such] ample compensation ought to be made to all the debtors who [were] injured by the treaty, for the benefit of the public.[168]

Thus, although there existed a doctrine of nonintercourse prohibiting commerce between belligerent States, the strictness of this doctrine had began to be attenuated by the late eighteenth century.[169] Some commentators have dated the attenuation of this rule to end

---

166. *Ware*, 3 U.S. (3 Dall.) 199.
167. *Id.* at 255–56.
168. *Id.* at 245.
169. The strict application of this rule is demonstrated in a Supreme Court decision from 1814, where Judge Johnson noted in part:
The universal sense of nations has acknowledged the demoralizing effects that would result from the admission of individual intercourse. The whole nation are embarked in one common bottom, and must be reconciled to submit to one common fate. Every individual of the one nation must acknowledge every individual of the other nation as his own enemy.
The Rapid, 12 U.S. (8 Cranch) 155, 161 (1814).

of the nineteenth century, when it is said that "rapid advances in civilization," "progressive public opinion," and the "influence of Christianity" made it possible to differentiate between military as opposed to civil affairs, and between the conduct of war and of commerce.[170] However, as the foregoing materials show, this rule was already under steady erosion under rather dissimilar geopolitical and military circumstances for the United States a century earlier. As the U.S. international legal jurist of that period, John Bassett Moore observed attitudes favorable toward commerce even during war were informed by "a moral revolt" and a "new creed," a "loftier conception [of] the destiny of and rights of man and of a more humane spirit" according to which the elimination of the confiscation of property was necessary to "assure to the world's commerce a legitimate and definite freedom."[171] Moore's justification of the rule is a modernist emancipatory universalism, which is argued to have prevailed over the barbarity of war and similar dark forces in the interest of avoiding the adverse consequences of war.[172]

To conclude this discussion, I will go back to Justice Marshall for a moment. Another of his significant decisions in support of commerce in the face of the assertion of rights of prevailing belligerents is *United States v. Percheman*.[173] Here Justice Marshall asserted that:

> The modern usage of nations, which has become law, would be violated; that sense of justice and of right, which is acknowledged and felt by the whole civilized world, would be outraged; if private property should generally be

---

170. COLEMAN PHILLIPSON, THE EFFECT OF WAR ON CONTRACTS AND ON TRADING ASSOCIATIONS IN TERRITORIES OF THE BELLIGERENT 49 (1909). Notably, Montesquieu, the French eighteenth-century philosopher argued that "commerce . . . softens and polishes the manners of men." ALBERT O. HIRSCHMAN, RIVAL VIEWS OF MARKET SOCIETY AND OTHER RECENT ESSAYS 107 (1992).

171. JOHN BASSETT MOORE, INTERNATIONAL LAW AND SOME CURRENT ILLUSIONS AND OTHER ESSAYS 13–14 (1924).

172. For a similar exposition of the expunging of religion from international law, see David Kennedy, *Images of Religion in International Legal Theory*, in THE INFLUENCE OF RELIGION ON THE DEVELOPMENT OF INTERNATIONAL LAW, 137, 142–43 (Mark Janis ed., 1991).

173. 32 U.S. (7 Pet.) 51 (1833).

confiscated and private rights annulled, on a change in the sovereignty of the country. The people change their allegiance . . . but their relations to each other, and their rights of property remain undisturbed.[174]

Justice Marshall's viewpoint is also evidenced in his criticisms of the decisions of the British Courts. He attributed the breakdown of negotiations over British debts "'to the wild, extensive, and unreasonable construction'" of Article VI of the Jay's Treaty.[175] For example, although the Jay's Treaty defined "contraband" as anything that might directly serve to equip a vessel, Marshall contended that the British construction of the definition essentially ignored "directly" by construing the term loosely.[176] Marshall also expressed disapproval of British courts' for lacking respect for the law by condoning illegal captures or denying damages.[177] Although Marshall respected Sir William Scott, Judge of the British High Court of Admiralty, the former noted that the decisions of the latter definitely favored the British and did not support international law; according to Justice Marshall, Sir Scott's jurisprudence seemed to have been influenced by an unconscious bias of Britain being a "great maritime country."[178] In particular, Marshall took issue with Sir Scott's decisions involving determination of the domicile of a person whose property had been confiscated by mere residence in a foreign country, without reference to what the person may have intended.[179] He also critiqued his brethren in *The Venus* for failing to inquire into the intentions of such a person, a failure which Marshall regarded as leading to the injustice

---

174. *Id.* at 51. The government's position in the case is captured by the following quote:
What, indeed, can be more clearly entitled to rank among things favourable [sic], than engagements between nations securing the private property of faithful subjects, honestly acquired under a government which is on the eve of relinquishing their allegiance, and confided to the pledged protection of that country [sic] which is about to receive them as citizens?
Id. at 68.
175. RUDKO, *supra* note 54, at 106 (citing Marshall to Rufus King, Sept. 20, 1800, 4 THE PAPERS OF JOHN MARSHALL 285 (Cullen, ed. 1984))
176. *Id.* at 106.
177. *Id.* at 107.
178. *The Venus*, 12 U.S. 253, 299 (1814).
179. *Id.* at 316.

of confiscating the property of such a person by virtue of their mere presence abroad. Thus, throughout his career in the Supreme Court, Justice Marshall consistently asserted the rights of those involved in commercial activity against claims of the superiority of rights of victorious belligerents. His jurisprudence had a definite mark in solidifying commercial rights when they came in tension with the privileges of belligerents. Unsurprisingly, the *Percheman* decision was cited in a South Africa court not long thereafter.[180] That this jurisprudence had already become that far known at the time is suggestive of the innovations of Justice Marshall in carving out spaces for legitimate commerce at a time when the assertion of the rights of belligerents was in the ascendant. In addition, as a further testament to the importance of Marshall's contribution to the law of prize, which at the time was the most critical and pertinent branch of international law, some commentators during Marshall's time counted him amongst the leading international jurists, including Sir William Scott, Robert Joseph Pothier, and Cornelius van Bynkershoek.[181] Further, as already noted, these liberal principles espoused by Justice Marshall were, about a century later, to be enshrined in the Hague Regulations of 1907.[182] Yet, notwithstanding these liberal rules of commercial relations that Justice Marshall espoused, in Section IV, I will show how he played a central role in justifying the power of conquest and discovery in the deprivation of Native Americans of their territory and their equal status as nations with whom the emerging United States could engage in commerce with complete reciprocity.

IV. A DIFFERENT RULE FOR UNITED STATES–NATIVE AMERICAN ECONOMIC RELATIONS[183]

Just at the moment he was announcing the most liberal rules for commerce between European nations and the early United States,

---

180. *W. Rand Century Gold Mining Co. v. King*, (1905) 2 K.B. 391.
181. RUDKO, *supra* note 54, at 72.
182. Regulations Concerning the Laws and Customs of War on Land. The Hague, 18 Oct. 1907.
183. This part borrows heavily from James Thuo Gathii, *Commerce, Conquest and Wartime Confiscation*, 31 BROOK. J. INT'L L. 709 (2006).

Justice Marshall was simultaneously contributing to the emergence of a jurisprudence that strongly favored the view that conquest[184] and discovery[185] give conquerors a legitimate title to the territory of Native Americans. In *Johnson v. M'Intosh*,[186] the question was whether two Indian chiefs had the power to pass on a valid title to private individuals that was recognizable in the Courts of the United States.[187] For Marshall, the question at the end of the day was whether, after the assumption of dominion over all the U.S. territory, first by the British Crown and subsequently by the United States, Native Americans had any title over their territory to pass on. In short, for Marshall the issue was whether "a title acquired from the Indians would be valid against a title acquired from the Crown."[188]

For Justice Marshall, the rule of decision in the case had been necessitated by the desire to reduce inter-European conflict over title to "this immense continent," which he noted that the "great nations of Europe' sought appropriate."[189] This rule, he held, was the principle of discovery that was consummated by the possession of territory by

---

184. In *Johnson v. M'Intosh*, Marshall held that "[c]onquest gives a title which Courts of the Conqueror cannot deny, whatever the private and speculative opinions of individuals may be respecting the ordinal justice of the claim which has been successfully asserted." 21 U.S. 543, 588 (1823).

185. According to Marshall,

However extravagant the pretension of converting the discovery of an inhabited country into conquest may appear; if the principle has been asserted in the first instance, and afterwards sustained; if a country has been acquired and held under it; if the property of the great mass of the community originates in it, it becomes the law of the land, and cannot be questioned.

Id. at 591. In affirming this, Marshall further notes,

This opinion conforms precisely to the principle which has been supposed to be recognised [sic] by all European governments, from the first settlement of America. The absolute ultimate title has been considered as acquired by discovery, subject only to the Indian title of occupancy, which title the discoverers possessed the exclusive right of acquiring. Such a right is no more incompatible with a seisin in fee, than a lease for years, and might as effectually bar an ejectment.

Id. at 592. *See also id.* at 595.

186. *Id.*
187. *Id.* at 572.
188. *Id.* at 604.
189. *Id.* at 573.

the subjects of respective European countries. Such discovery, in turn, operated to prevent other European States from claiming title to the discovered territory.[190] What of the Native Americans who occupied the territory? According to Justice Marshall, the "exclusive right of the United States to extinguish their title, and to grant the soil" had never been doubted.[191]

Having recognized the title of the United States over their land, Marshall concluded that this title was incompatible with an "absolute and complete title in the Indians."[192] It is at this point that Marshall then justified the title of the United States on the basis of conquest. According to Marshall, conquest gave valid title that the "courts of the conqueror cannot deny," notwithstanding questions about the "original justice" of the assertion of this title.[193] Such a title acquired by conquest was maintainable by force.[194]

The reason the title was maintainable by force, according to Justice Marshall, was because Indians were "fierce savages, whose occupation was war, and whose substance was drawn chiefly from the forest."[195] Marshall therefore argued that it was necessary to enforce European claims to the land they occupied "by the sword."[196]

Thus, although he had spoken eloquently against the rights of belligerents insofar as they undermined free commerce in U.S. international relations with its European counterparts, for Native Americans, war was the solution for their subjugation. Marshall further endorsed this subjugation by arguing that "European policy, numbers, and skill, prevailed" over Indian aggression.[197]

---

190. *Id.*; see also id. at 584.
191. *Id.* at 586.
192. *Id.* at 588.
193. *Id.*
194. *Id.* at 589.
195. *Id.* at 590.
196. *Id.* Marshall claimed that the Indians were incapable of legally owning the land and that they merely possessed it and, as such, could not pass on valid title to the white population. Marshall claimed that the Indians were merely the ancient inhabitants of the land and that the territory was held by the British Crown prior to its occupation by white settlers. *Id.* at 591.

197. *Id.* at 590. Note also his justification of the doctrine of discovery in the later case of *Worcester v. Georgia*:

After lying concealed for a series of ages, the enterprise of Europe, guided by nautical science, conducted some of her adventurous sons into this

[handwritten note: Reflected views of his time.]

As Marshall's holding in *Johnson v. M'Intosh* illustrates, the Supreme Court endorsed the power of belligerent confiscation, not simply out of a belligerent's absolute power, but rather out of the presumed backwardness of those whose territory or property had been seized by virtue of the proclaimed superiority of Europeans over these peoples. It was because Indians were so different that he held the law that applies as between conqueror and conquered was inapplicable to them and, instead, a "new and different rule, better adapted to the actual state of things was unavoidable."[198] This, according to Justice Marshall, was the rule of discovery under which Indians were recognized as mere occupants of their land.

In *Cherokee Nation v. Georgia*,[199] Justice Marshall announced that the relation of Native Americans to the United States was that of "a ward to his guardian."[200] Indians, according to Marshall, were essentially like children in relation to the United States, rather than sovereign nations. As such, they were obliged to look to the U.S. government for protection, kindness, and power, as well as well as to seek its help in fulfilling their needs.[201] Further, rather then proceeding to give the

---

western world. They found it in possession of a people who had made small progress in agriculture or manufactures, and whose general employment was war, hunting and fishing. . . . [D]iscovery gave title to the government by whose subjects or by whose authority it was made, against all other European governments, which title might be consummated by possession.
U.S. 543, 588 (1823).

198. *Id.* at 591. The basis of this doctrine of the supremacy of Europeans over non-Europeans in the common law finds expression in the landmark 1602 *Calvin's Case* where Lord Coke noted:

And upon this ground there is a diversity between a conquest of a kingdom of a Christian King, and the conquest of a kingdom of an infidel; for if a King come to a Christian kingdom by conquest, seeing that he hath *vitæ et necis potestatem*, he may at his pleasure alter and change the laws of that kingdom: but until be doth make an alteration of those laws the ancient laws of that kingdom remain. . . . But if a Christian King should conquer a kingdom of an infidel, and bring them under his subjection, there *ipso facto* the laws of the infidel are abrogated, for that they be not only against Christianity, but against the law of God and of nature, contained in the decalogue.

Calvin v. Smith, (1608) 77 Eng. Rep. 377, 397–98 (K.B.).

199. 30 U.S. (5 Pet.) 1, 17 (1831).

200. *See id.*

201. *See id.* For a further exploration of this theme, see James Gathii, *Colonialism, Imperialism and International Law*, 54 Buff. L. Rev. 1013 (2007)).

Cherokees protection from their forcible eviction from Georgia onto the deadly Trail of Tears that ensued, Justice Marshall declared that, even if the Cherokee Nation had rights they could assert, the Supreme Court was "not the tribunal which can redress the past or prevent the future."[202] On his part, Justice Johnson regarded the forcible exertion of authority over the Cherokees by the State of Georgia as not only legally permissible but as "a contest for empire."[203] By contrast, Justice Thompson's dissent would have recognized the sovereignty of the Cherokee Nation and allowed them jurisdiction to order the State of Georgia from forcibly evicting them from their lands.[204]

Finally, in *Worcester v. Georgia*,[205] Justice Marshall affirmed the doctrine of discovery and further justified the subjugation of Native Americans on the unsuccessful attempts the United States had made in negotiating and regulating trade with them.[206] According to Marshall, war was necessary to deal with the Indians because regular commercial contact could not be established with them.[207] In any

---

202. *Id.* at 20.
203. *Id.* at 29.
204. *See id.* at 50–80 (Thompson, J., dissenting).
205. 31 U.S. 515 (1832), *superseded by statute*, 43 U.S.C. § 666 (2000).
206. *Id.* at 558.
207. *Id.* In a groundbreaking analysis of the writings of Vitoria, the sixteenth-century international legal jurist credited with being one of the founders of international law, Antony Anghie shows that although Vitoria exhibited a progressive approach to dealing with the Native Americans by arguing in favor of incorporating them within the universal law of *jus gentium*, their incorporation into this universal law, in turn, served as the basis for justifying the imposition of Spanish "discipline" on them. Vitoria argued that because the Indians were resisting the right of the Spanish to sojourn on their territory, the Spanish were entitled to use forcible means to enforce this right. In addition, Vitoria argued that the ordinary prohibitions of waging war do not apply to Indians. *See* Antony Anghie, *Francisco de Vitoria and the Colonial Origins of International Law*, 5 Soc. & Legal Stud. 321, 331 (1996). In Vitoria's words:

> And so when a war is at that pass that the indiscriminate spoliation of all enemy-subjects alike and the seizure of all their goods are justifiable, then it is also justifiable to carry all enemy subjects off into captivity, whether they be guilty or guiltless. And inasmuch as war with pagans is of this type, seeing that it is perpetual and that they can never make amends for the wrongs and damages they have wrought, it is indubitably lawful to carry off both the children and women of the Saracens into captivity and slavery.

Id. at 330.

event, we know that Marshall had already concluded the Indians were incapable of being integrated into the United States, and that relations with them were that of a ward and its guardian.[208]

Marshall's jurisprudence sounds eerily similar to sixteenth-century jurist Francisco de Vitoria's justification of the Spanish conquest of the Indians. Vitoria justified as lawful the killing of Native Americans in the course of Spanish colonization, noting that this is "especially the case against the unbeliever, from whom it is useless ever to hope for a just peace on any terms."[209] War and the destruction of all the Indians who could bear arms against the invading Spanish conquerors—or in contravention of the right of the Spanish to sojourn on Indian territory—was the only remedy available to the Spaniards.[210]

As with Vitoria, the racial charge in Justice Marshall's jurisprudence with respect to non-Christian and non-European peoples is strikingly evident. This is radically different from the jurisprudence of neutrality that Justice Marshall helped crystallize in relations between the United States and its European counterparts. In effect, one could surmise from our discussion in Section III above that the Marshall court espoused and helped consolidate two very different legal regimes of international commercial governance. On the one hand, there was the regime of liberal commerce he promoted against the countervailing rights of belligerents, and on the other hand, there was the illiberal regime of conquest and subjugation that he helped establish in U.S.-Native American relations.

Marshall's federal Indian-law jurisprudence arose in the encounter between metropolitan policy and the resistance of non-Europeans

---

208. For further analysis, see similarly, Robert A. Williams, *The Algebra of Federal Indian Law: The Hard Trial of Decolonizing and Americanizing the White Man's Indian Jurisprudence*, 1986 WIS. L. REV. 219, 246 (1986), which argues that under this Eurocentric jurisprudence, conquest was thought necessary to bring "the Infidels and Savages [of America] to human Civility, and to a settled and quiet Government . . . " *Id.*

209. Anghie, *supra* note 208, at 27.

210. Similarly, Robert A. Williams argues that under this Eurocentric jurisprudence, conquest was thought necessary to "bring the infidels and savages of America to human civility, and to a settled and quiet Government." Williams, *supra* note 209, at 246.

against colonization.[211] As Laura Benton argued, the expansion of metropolitan authority over colonial peoples produced predictable "routines for incorporating groups with separate legal identities in production and trade and for accommodating (or changing) culturally diverse ways of viewing the regulation and exchange of property."[212] The Marshall solution for ordering these relations with the Native Americans was "Christian subjugation and remediation."[213] By contrast, Marshall announced the most liberal rules in relations between the weak maritime United States of the late eighteenth century. Ordering the economic relations of the late eighteenth century, United States was thus ultimately a question of power.[214]

V. CONCLUSIONS

The demand for rules of liberal commerce is often traced to market forces or population growth.[215] Market-oriented, "Smithian," and demographic accounts of the rise of liberal rules of international commerce, however, understate the importance of military and economic weakness as factors in the development and consolidation of liberal rules of commerce. The rules of neutrality that the Marshall court promoted in the face of depredations of U.S. commerce were eventually recognized in the 1907 Hague Regulations.[216] These regulations overwhelmingly give commerce and private property safe passage during wartime.[217]

---

211. Here I am heavily influenced by LAUREN BENTON, LAW AND COLONIAL CULTURES: LEGAL REGIMES IN WORLD HISTORY, 1400–1900, at 4–5 (2002).

212. *Id.* at 5.

213. Williams, *supra* note 209, at 247.

214. Judith Resnik, *Dependent Sovereigns: Indian Tribes, States, and the Federal Courts*, 56 U. CHI. L. REV., 671, 675 (1989) (Resnik similarly argues that the issues of power and jurisdiction dominate federal courts jurisprudence).

215. *See* DOUGLASS C. NORTH, INSTITUTIONS, INSTITUTIONAL CHANGE AND ECONOMIC PERFORMANCE (1990); *see also* DOUGLASS C. NORTH, THE RISE OF THE WESTERN WORLD: A NEW ECONOMIC HISTORY (1973). *But see* Robert Brenner, *The Origins of Capitalist Development: A Critique of Neo-Smithian Marxism*, 104 NEW LEFT REV., 25, 58 (July/Aug. 1977).

216. *See* Regulations *supra* note 183.

217. *See* Berg, 243 U.S. at 150–51.

Today, this legacy of unequal regimes in international economic governance largely remains intact. Reciprocity between Western industrialized countries has largely been achieved. However, a nonreciprocal regime remains embedded with the international economic order in relations between Western industrialized economies and contemporary, developing economies that largely remain agrarian. For example, for approximately the last five or so decades there has been more or less full reciprocity of the industrialized products of Western economies within the international trade regime established under the aegis of General Agreement on Tariffs and Trade (GATT) in 1948,[218] while within the same time period there has been no full reciprocity for the agricultural products of developing countries in Western markets within this regime.

This account of the relevance of military and economic power or lack thereof leads to the following crucial insight: Economically and militarily weak countries are very likely to seek the promotion and protection of international legal norms to safeguard their commercial rights from violation and abuse from more economically and militarily powerful countries. In essence, weaker countries have big incentives to persuade more powerful countries to build and to play by some common rules that are beneficial to all countries, whether rich or poor or militarily powerful or not. Although there is an already established literature demonstrating the incentives of economically prosperous countries promoting, shaping, and imposing their preferred norms of international economic behavior on less prosperous nations,[219] it is in the interests of less prosperous nations to promote the promulgation of rules of international economic governance beneficial to all States.

---

218. For a further exploration of this theme, see James Gathii, *Process and Substance in WTO Reform*, 56 RUTGERS L. REV. 885 (2004); *See also* The General Agreement on Tariffs and Trade, (1948) T.I.A.S. 1700, 55 U.N.T.S. 194.

219. This is of course not to suggest that militarily and economically powerful countries have no incentive to develop or comply with international legal norms. *See* JOSEPH S. NYE, JR., THE PARADOX OF AMERICAN POWER: WHY THE WORLD'S ONLY SUPERPOWER CAN'T GO IT ALONE 17 (2002).

5. WAR, INVESTMENT, AND INTERNATIONAL LAW

I. INTRODUCTION

Recent scholarship has celebrated the peaceful consequences of regimes of the international economic order.[1] The advent of the Bretton Woods institutions and the United Nations were in fact, institutional responses to the World War II that embodied a set of goals and principles as alternatives to resolving conflict by war. It is not therefore surprising that the pragmatism and functionalism of the post-World War II period also regarded these institutions as a victory over the dark forces and passions that led to the outbreak of World War II.

Rules and institutions of international trade and investment also provide alternatives to the role of territorial conquests as ways of facilitating access to resources in formerly colonized countries needed by multinational firms. In addition, as shown in this chapter, rules of international investment law and arbitral forums were seen as alternatives to the forcible collection of debts. In short, although territorial conquest in the nineteenth century facilitated the extraction of mineral and other resources from poor countries, in the twenty-first century international legal regimes ensure their continued nonviolent access.

---

1. Symposium, *Trade as Guarantor of Peace, Liberty and Security: The Role of Peace in the Bretton Woods Institutions*, 20 AM. UNIV. L. REV. 1113 (2005); Donald Markwell, JOHN MAYNARD KEYNES AND INTERNATIONAL RELATIONS: ECONOMIC PATHS TO WAR AND PEACE (2006); For other views, see Symposium, *War and Commerce*, 31 BROOK. J. INT'L L. (2006); Nathaniel Berman, *Economic Consequences, Nationalist Passions: Keynes, Crisis, Culture and Policy*, 10 AM. UNIV. J. INT'L L. & POL'Y, 619 (1995); AM. SOC. INT'L L., TRADE AS THE GUARANTOR OF PEACE, LIBERTY AND SECURITY? CRITICAL, HISTORICAL AND EMPIRICAL PERSPECTIVES 97 (Padideh Alai, Tomer Broude, & Colin B. Picker eds., 2006).

This chapter explores the role war has played in the formation and consolidation of rules and institutions of international investment law. In so doing, this chapter shows how notwithstanding the guarantees of self-determination, equality of States and permanent sovereignty over natural resources, private international law to date continues to guarantee regimes of economic governance that protect rights of alien investors often at the expense of the former colonies. This continuity has an uncanny resemblance to the era when conquest and war were permissible means of international economic interaction.

This chapter begins by discussing the origins of the Drago doctrine in the Venezuelan blockade of 1902 by Great Britain, Germany, and Italy. It then traces the origins of binding international arbitration to this incident. Various efforts to address problems arising in commercial disputes between capital importing and capital exporting countries such as the Calvo clause and the New International Economic Order are then addressed. There is an examination of how arbitral forums have resolved cases involving State responsibility for war destruction. The last major section of the chapter reflects on how the resolution of war destruction cases tells us about the move from forcible to unequal economic relations between capital importing and exporting States.

II. THE RELEVANCE OF WAR IN SHAPING RULES OF INTERNATIONAL ECONOMIC GOVERNANCE

This section examines continuities and discontinuities of rules of international economic governance particularly as they relate to issues surrounding war from the colonial to the postcolonial era. Although protecting commerce from the scourge of war was a primary inspiration for the post-World War II international economic order, war was also an animating factor for former colonies in designing new rules of international economic governance. The relevance of war for postcolonial economic governance, particularly in the nineteenth century for newly independent Latin American countries, is often understated or simply regarded as an instance of economic nationalism.

Two of the best examples of the influence of war in shaping rules of international economic governance is the nineteenth-century Latin American innovation required in contracts between foreign investors and nationals and Latin American governments, known as the Calvo clause and the Drago doctrine. The origins of the Calvo clause arose as a response to the nineteenth-century practice of European States that engaged in aggression and conquest against militarily and economically weaker Latin American States as a means of collecting debts owed to their citizens. The Drago doctrine arose from a 1902 warlike blockade of Venezuela by Great Britain and Germany with the diplomatic support of Italy. Following unrest and turmoil in Venezuela, the Venezuelan government refused to settle claims it owed to bondholders from Great Britain, Germany, and Italy. Venezuela proposed that it would only settle those claims in a Commission comprised of Venezuelans.[2] This blockade quickly coerced Venezuela into compliance.[3]

In a letter dated December 29, 1902, the Venezuelan Secretary of Foreign Affairs, Luis M. Drago, protested the "collection of loan by military means" for its inconsistency with Venezuela's sovereignty. He argued that forcible collection of loans not only amounted to a form "territorial occupation" of Venezuelan territory, but also signified the "suppression or subordination" of Venezuela to these creditor nations.[4] The letter then stated what became known as the Drago doctrine: "That the public debt cannot occasion armed intervention nor even the actual occupation of the territory of American nations by a European power."[5]

The Drago doctrine was therefore both a nonintervention principle as well as a statement of the special nature of public bonds and loans taken by States. It was a noninterventionist principle because it was aimed against armed interventions and occupation of debtor States by creditor States. It was a statement of the special nature of bonds and loans borrowed by governments because the doctrine was

---

2. Luis M. Drago & H. Edward Nettles, *The Drago Doctrine in International Law and Politics*, 8 HISP. AM. HIST. REV. 204 (1928). There is some controversy regarding the purpose of this blockade. Some suggested it was not so much to protect bond-holder rights as to protect the lives, liberty, and property of British subjects, *id.* at 205–06. However, the forcible collection of debts was undoubtedly the primary reason for the Drago doctrine.
3. *Id.*
4. *Id.* at 209.
5. *Id.* For a full exploration of this, Luis M. Drago, *State Loans in their Relation to International Policy*, AM. J. INT'L L. 692–726 (1907).

based on distinguishing the kinds of remedies that were available to creditors when the borrower was a private individual rather than the government. According to Drago, a lender who lends to a sovereign knows that "no proceedings for the execution of a judgment may be instituted or carried out against it."[6] The Drago doctrine is therefore closely associated with the now obsolete theory of absolute sovereign immunity in commercial transactions involving sovereigns.[7] I will return to this point below to show how the now obsolete rule of absolute immunity enunciated in the Drago doctrine represented an effort to move from the justifiable use of force in the collection of sovereign debt toward a juridical framework in which the use of force was impermissible.

The Drago doctrine was an effort aimed at finding juridical proscription of the use of force in the economic relations between militarily weak debtor Latin American countries, on the one hand, and militarily powerful European States, on the other. Law for Latin American countries represented the best hope for restraining the use of force against them by countries with more military power than they had. In fact, Drago specifically argued against the use of violence as inapplicable to Venezuela because it involved conquest.[8] In so doing, he was advocating against the views of scholars of international law of his day such as W. E. Hall who held the view that States had the right to engage in forcible interventions to collect public debt.[9] In fact, U.S. Secretary of State Elihu Root, while asserting that

---

6. Drago, *supra* note 5, as quoted in Drago & Nettles, *supra* note 2, at 211.

7. Today, it is generally recognized that foreign states are not immune from jurisdiction in a judicial forum when they have engaged in commercial conduct equivalent to that which private actors engage in. There is therefore no absolute immunity for *acta jure imperii*, (acts of state of a commercial nature) because they will be regarded as *acta jure gestionis* thereby subjecting the State to suit. *See* SIENHO YEE, TOWARDS AN INTERNATIONAL LAW OF CO-PROGRESSIVENESS 280–85 (2004). *See also* Robert Wai, *The Commercial Activity Exception to Sovereign Immunity and the Boundaries of Contemporary Legalism*, in TORTURE AS TORT: COMPARATIVE PERSPECTIVES ON THE DEVELOPMENT OF TRANSNATIONAL HUMAN RIGHTS 213 (Craig Scott ed., 2001).

8. Drago, *supra* note 5, at 725.

9. W. E. HALL, INTERNATIONAL LAW (1880); Thomas H. Lee, *The Safe-Conduct Theory of the Alien Tort Statute*, 106 COLUM. L. REV. 830, 821 (2006) also argued that "[u]nder traditional state-based principles of international

the use of armed forces by a State for the collection of ordinary contracts debts on behalf of its citizens was regrettable, left open the possibility that it was justifiable to use force over nonpayment of public debts "when accompanied by such circumstances of fraud, wrong-doing or violation of treaties."[10]

When the Second Hague Conference met in 1906 and negotiated the Convention Respecting the Limitation of the Employment of Force for the Recovery of Contract Debts, the contracting parties agreed not "to have recourse to armed force for the recovery of contract debt claimed from the Government of one country by the Government of another country as being due to its nationals."[11] However, consistent with Root's reservation that the use of armed force was unjustifiable in all cases, a proviso to this prohibition in the Hague Convention provided that use of force would be permissible where a "debtor state refuses or neglects to accept an offer of arbitration, or after accepting the offer, prevents any compromise from being agreed upon, or, after the arbitration, fails to submit to the award."[12]

In 1957, the International Court of Justice endorsed this interpretation in the *Case of Certain Norwegian Loans* when it noted that the Convention Respecting the Limitation of the Employment of Force for the Recovery of Contract Debts, although not requiring compulsory arbitration over contractual debts, imposed an obligation "that an intervening power should not have recourse to force before it had tried arbitration."[13] As Judge Sir Hersch Lauterpacht noted in his separate opinion in this case,[14] Article 52(2) of the Hague Convention

---

law—i.e., those from the eighteenth to the early twentieth centuries—the safe conduct promise was enforceable through the offended sovereign's right to make war in the event of a breach," *id.* However, see Amos S. Hershey, *Hague Convention Restricting the Use of Force to Recover on Contract Claims*, 1 AM. J. INT'L L. 78 (1908)

10. Root's instructions to the 1906 Hague Conference, as cited in Drago & Nettles, *supra* note 5, at 218.

11. Convention Respecting the Limitation of the Employment of Force for the Recovery of Contract Debts, Oct. 18, 1907, art. 1, 36 Stat. 2241, T.S. 537 [hereinafter Hague Regulations on Debt Recovery].

12. *Id.*

13. Case of Certain Norwegian Loans (*Fr. v. Nor.*) 1987 I.C.J. (July 6).

14. *Id.* (Lauterpacht, separate opinion).

for the Pacific Settlement of International Disputes gave the Permanent Court of Arbitration competence to settle by agreement disputes "arising from contract debts claimed from one Power by another Power."[15] Sir Lauterpacht interpreted the recognition of the contract debts among sovereigns for arbitration as an indirect recognition that controversies relating to debts between States were "suitable for settlement by reference to international law."[16] In other words, international law came to be regarded as a substitute for war as means of collecting contract debt. Indeed, as President Roosevelt stated in support of the provision seeking to limit the use of force in the collection of debts in the Hague Convention Respecting the Limitation of the Employment of Force for the Recovery of Contract Debts "such a provision would have prevented much injustice and extortion in the past."[17] International law was clearly being seen as an antidote to forcible measures.

Clearly then, during the negotiations and subsequent recognition of the principle of pacific settlement of disputes in the 1906 Hague Conference, the right claimed by States, particularly in the late nineteenth and early twentieth centuries, to collect debt by forcible means was sought to be limited under rules of international law. Although the early twentieth-century prohibition of the use of force to collect debts in the Hague Conventions was only partial, it represented an important step toward the eventual prohibition of the use of force between States in the United Nations Charter.[18] For my purpose here,

---

15. Hague Convention for the Pacific Settlement of International Disputes, Oct. 18, 1907, 36 Stat. 2199, T.S. 233.

16. *Case of Certain Norwegian Loans* (Lauterpacht, separate opinion), at 38 ¶ 33.

17. *Cited in* James Brown Scott, *The Work of the Second Hague Peace Conference*, 1 AM. J. INT'L L. 15 (1908).

18. Article 2(4) of the United Nations Charter, which is regarded as a jus cogens norm under international law provides that "[a]ll members, shall refrain in their international relations from the threat or use of force against the territorial integrity or political independence of any state, or in any other manner inconsistent with the Purposes of the United Nations." In addition, UN General Assembly Resolution 3314 (XXIX) of 1974, on the Definition of Aggression defined aggression as "the use of armed force by a State against the sovereignty, territorial integrity or political independence of another State, or in any other manner inconsistent with the Charter of the United Nations," (art. 1) and further defined the "blockade of ports or coasts of a State

the move toward arbitration and away from the use of force to enforce contract debts shifted the concerns of weak, mostly non-Western countries from the fear of forcible interventions to the bias against them in the rules, processes, and outcomes of arbitral forums.[19] These countries saw these biases as a reflection of their unequal bargaining power vis-à-vis the wealthy countries and their giant multinational firms on which they depended on for finance, technology, and trade.

Thus, whereas the principle of the pacific settlement of disputes and the partial rejection of the use of force to enforce debt contracts were important advances in the relations between capital-exporting and capital-importing States, peaceful settlement of disputes through forums such as arbitration did not necessarily eviscerate the coercion that was characteristic in contractual relations between economically stronger and weaker parties. In addition, without an explicit prohibition on the use of force, there was still the possibility that armed force could still be used in the collection of public debts after the Hague Conventions came into force. Without such an explicit prohibition on the use of force, defaulting States therefore lived under the threat that capital-exporting States might wage war against them to enforce their rights, rather than to submit to compulsory or obligatory arbitration as proposed in the course of the First and Second Hague conferences.[20]

---

by armed forces of another state" (art. 3(c)) as constituting aggression. Notably, the Drago doctrine arose precisely out of this kind of a blockade. Article 5 of the Aggression Resolution provides that "No consideration of whatever nature, whether political, economic, military or otherwise, may serve as a justification for aggression," *id*. In addition, it is notable that although the use of force "must be avoided as far as possible" when it is inevitable "it must not go beyond what is reasonable and necessary under the circumstances," M.V. Saiga No. 2, (*Saint Vincent & the Grenadines v. Guinea*),Vol. 10 INT'L TRIBUNAL L. Sea Rep. ¶ 155 (1999).

19. One of the best articulations of this bias is Amr Shalakany, *Arbitration and the Third World: A Plea for Reassessing Bias under the Specter of Neo-Liberalism*, 41 HARV. INT'L L.J. 419 (2000); see also, M. SORNARAJAH, INTERNATIONAL COMMERCIAL ARBITRATION: THE PROBLEM OF STATE CONTRACTS (1990).

20. Amos S. Hershey, *Hague Convention Restricting the Use of Force to Recover on Contract Claims*, 1 AM. J. INT'L L. 78 (1908), "arguing that every State which considers itself aggrieved enjoys the sole right to decide the redress which it shall exact and, also, whether in a given case it has exhausted

Thirteen of what were termed the "small powers" at the Second Hague Conference who were likely to be subject to forcible collection of debt, supported "obligatory arbitration." By contrast, the big powers, such as the United States and Great Britain, sought to reserve their right to protect what they termed their "vital interests, independence and honor" through the use of force.[21]

Today, high transaction costs, as well as prohibitions on the use of force, have reduced, if not entirely eliminated, the resort to war for the collection of contract debt.[22] In addition, wars for debt collection came to be discredited as between "civilized nations," but also against "small and weak nations." The use of force to collect private debts against small and weak nations came to be regarded as a "violation of

---

all peaceful remedies it should pursue in order to secure redress. *The use of force is a recognized legal remedy by which states may settle their differences." Id.* at 85 (emphasis added). *But see* MICHAEL TOMZ, REPUTATION AND INTERNATIONAL COOPERATION: SOVEREIGN DEBT ACROSS THREE CENTURIES (2007) (arguing that the use of force to collect Venezuelan debt was exceptional and not motivated solely by default).

21. William I. Hull, *Obligatory Arbitration and the Hague Conferences*, 4 AM. J. INT'L L. 737 (1908).

22. CHARLES LIPSON, STANDING GUARD: PROTECTING FOREIGN CAPITAL IN THE NINETEENTH AND TWENTIETH CENTURIES (1985). Addressing the use of forcible interventions to address bond defaults notes,

Britain's naval capacity and its diplomatic network were formidable. Direct and frequent interventions promised immediate and tangible gains. *Yet such a course was both risky and costly. It was costly, even in the short run, if the desired results could be won diplomatically. It was risky in the long run because direct interventions undermined the basis of local political authority and social control.* British policy in Latin America demonstrated a clear understanding of these alternatives. *It was based on the idea that it was cheaper to bear the immediate costs of bond defaults than to risk sabotaging local governments by frequent interventions.*

Id. at 44–45 (emphasis added).

Peter Liberman, *The Spoils of Conquest*, 18 INT'L SECURITY, 125, 150 (1993) (also argues that the costs of imperial adventures, among other factors such as nationalism, now outweigh the benefits of such adventures). *See also* Stephen Brooks, *The Globalization of Production and the Changing Benefits of Conquest*, 43 J. CONFLICT RESOL. 646–70 (1999) (arguing that the central role of foreign direct investment in contemporary globalization may allow governments to substitute that instrument of external economic influence for older instrument of conquest).

the doctrine of international law that independent nations should stand upon a footing of equality."[23]

As the use of force to collect debt fell into disuse, and the liberalization of financial markets grew in pace from the nineteenth century and accelerated even more in the twentieth century with the removal of obstacles to the flow of finance across national boundaries, the enforcement costs of contract debt became "as high if not higher than in the nineteenth century."[24] The enormous debt owed to capital-exporting States by capital-importing States has therefore unsurprisingly been a major theme in international economic relations at the end of the twentieth century and the beginning of the twenty-first century.[25]

Suffice it to say, the declining significance of the use of force to collect contract debt merely relocated from the battlefield to arbitral and judicial forums the same concerns that inspired the Drago doctrine. The belief of early international lawyers, including Luis Drago, was that rules and institutions of international law were neutral and apolitical alternatives to the use of force would soon be under scrutiny. Influenced by the classical legal thinking of their time, these lawyers believed that there were only two ways of achieving harmony or reconciliation through either force or law.[26] Arbitration for them was an example of a larger set of voluntary and consensual processes that States could use to resolve conflicts rather than resorting to war.[27] These lawyers celebrated international law as a noncoercive solution through which problems, domestic and international, could

---

23. *Wars for Debt Collection*, N.Y. TIMES, May 12, 1903, at 8.

24. Gerald Epstein, *International Capital Mobility and the Scope for National Economic Management*, in STATES AGAINST MARKETS: THE LIMITS OF GLOBALIZATION 211–24, 217 (Robert Boyer & Daniel Drache, eds., 1996).

25. WORLD BANK, CAN AFRICA CLAIM THE 21ST CENTURY? (2000) (noting the significance of debt and aid dependence as one of the major constraints on Africa's development prospects in the twenty-first century).

26. Joseph Beale, an early classicist for example argued that there "are only two methods of reconciliation: force, and law. Either the will of the physically strongest, or of the mentally alertest, must prevail—the way of the beast; or conflicting wills must be restrained by law—the way of organized human society," cited in Jonathan Zasloff, *Abolishing Coercion: The Jurisprudence of American Foreign Policy in the 1920's*, 102 YALE L.J. 1689, 1698 (1993).

27. *See* Richard H. Steinberg & Jonathan M. Zasloff, *Power and International Law* (Centennial Essay), 100 AM. J. INT'L L. 66 (2006).

be cooperatively and beneficially resolved.[28] Not only did this early thinking of international law therefore assume a harmony of interests that could be worked out impartially if not scientifically, but it also denied that "coercion was the basis of [international] legal efficacy."[29]

This early faith in the neutrality and impartiality of the law denied the role of power and coercion in international relations and institutions[30] and in rules of law.[31] Rules of law, after all, are more often than not politics by other means. For example, gross inequalities and disparities of bargaining power in contracts between indebted sovereign nations and financially sophisticated multinational firms could very well lead to the conclusion that such contracts are no more than a "power order"[32] than consensually bargained deals. Thus, while poor countries now enjoy the autonomy to freely enter into commercial contracts, they continue to be concerned about the reciprocity or underlying fairness of these deals.[33] For them,

---

28. Id. at 69. See also Robert Wai, Transnational Liftoff and Juridical Touchdown: The Regulatory Function of Private International Law in an Era of Globalization, 40 COLUM. J. TRANSNAT'L L. 209 (2002) (examining the benefits and challenges of international cooperation).

29. Steinberg &. Zasloff, supra note 26, at 68; Zasloff, supra note 25.

30. Steinberg & Zasloff, supra note 26, at 72 (discussing realism in international law and international relations).

31. Duncan Kennedy, The Stakes of Law, or Hale and Foucault!, XV LEG. STUDIES FORUM 327 (1991) (arguing in part that early conservative economic rhetoric justified the existing capitalist system as being based on freedom in contrast to socialism, which replaced freedom with state coercion and how realists showed that freedom or agreement was a product of coercion "by which they meant that neither party got what the wanted (the whole joint product) and that each had the experience of being 'forced to settle for less,'" id. at 328.

32. ROBERTO MANGABEIRA UNGER, THE CRITICAL STUDIES MOVEMENT 70 (1983).

33. MICHAEL J. SANDEL, LIBERALISM AND THE LIMITS OF JUSTICE (1982) notes that "Unlike obligations voluntarily incurred, obligations arising under the ideal of reciprocity must presuppose some criterion of fairness independent of contract, some way in which the objective fairness of an exchange may be assessed," id. at 107–08. See also NAGLA NASSAR, SANCTITY OF CONTRACTS REVISITED: A STUDY IN THE THEORY AND PRACTICE OF LONG-TERM INTERNATIONAL COMMERCIAL TRANSACTIONS (1995), arguing that

> If as claimed by classical theorists, legal rules are merely concerned with resource allocation, then the unfairness of the classical rule in denying

simply having an agreement, institution or process is insufficient to establish its fairness. That is why, in arbitral forums, rules of private international law much like the right to use force to collect debt were challenged by poor countries as "furthering colonial inequalities"[34] very much like the wars for debt collection. The Calvo clause, which I will turn to shortly, was an early effort to reform private international law to address such inequalities and the concerns of Latin American States.

The upshot of my argument so far is that the legalization and institutionalization of international commercial disputes did not end the concerns about the exercise of coercion and power by capital-exporting over capital-importing States. Perhaps nothing illustrates better the legalization and institutionalization of international commercial disputes than the arbitral proceedings that arose from the Allied blockade (British, German, and Italian), of Venezuela that inspired the Drago doctrine in the first place. Having set aside 30 percent of all

---

adjustment is somewhat but not completely, justifiable. From a societal perspective, the adjustment rule, according to the classical model, is considered inefficient, for it wastes society's revenue on an unnecessary reallocation of resources. . . . The validity of the above argument is very doubtful. First, it is misleading to assume that society has no interest in the equitable reallocation of resources. . . . Secondly, arguing that the main concern of the rule of law is to maximize wealth is a misleading proposition. Laws have been created . . . to establish social peace and promote exchange. . . . This is particularly true of international society where actors come from different societies at different levels of economic development and with different legal rules. . . . In the absence of a strong institutional organization, actors need to be assured that their interests will not be sacrificed because of an event they could not have known about or controlled."

Id. at 233–34.

34. ANTONY ANGHIE, IMPERIALISM, SOVEREIGNTY AND THE MAKING OF INTERNATIONAL LAW 239 (2005). For a different view, see Duncan Kennedy, *Distributive and Paternalist Motives in Contract and Tort Law, with Special Reference to Compulsory Terms and Unequal Bargaining Power*, 41 MD. L. REV. 563, 580 (1982) (arguing that the "real problem with freedom of contract is that neither its principles, nor is principles supplemented by common moral understanding, nor its principles supplemented by historical practice, are definite enough to tell the decision maker what to do when asked to change or even just to elaborate the existing law of agreements").

customs receipts of two Venezuelan ports to settle the claims of all her creditors, the Allied powers demanded preferential payment over all other creditor nations.[35] Venezuela and the Allied powers decided, as a condition for lifting their blockade, that they would accept arbitration over the question of preferential treatment before the Permanent Court of Arbitration in the Hague.[36] For Venezuela, the arbitration proceedings in this case were superior to enforcement of the contract claims by forcible means. Yet, in many ways Venezuela's agreement to arbitral proceedings was in no small way influenced by the vastly superior military/naval power of the allied forces while Venezuela was still subject to the allied powers blockade.[37] So powerful were these blockading powers that they used the arbitral process, against Venezuela's protestations, to win a right to preferential treatment above all other creditors.[38] In fact, not only did the Permanent Court of Arbitration grant the blockading powers the right to preferential treatment, but it also rejected Venezuela's argument on jurisdictional grounds to decide whether the allied powers had exhausted all other remedies prior to engaging in the use of force.[39]

In the next section, I will examine how the legalization and institutionalization of international commercial disputes set the stage for more skirmishes between these countries. The debates about the Calvo clause represent one early episode in these disagreements between capital importing and capital exporting States.

---

35. *The Venezuelan Preferential Case* (Ger., Gr. Br., Italy, Venez., et. al.), *in* IX REPORTS OF INTERNATIONAL ARBITRAL AWARDS, 103 (United Nations ed., 1904).

36. *Protocol between Germany and Venezuela for the Reference of Certain Questions to the Permanent Court of Arbitration at the Hague* (signed at Washington, May 7, 1903) *in* INTERNATIONAL ARBITRAL AWARDS, *supra* note 34, at 105–06; *Protocol between Great Britain and Venezuela Relating to the Settlement of the British Claims and Other Matters* (signed Washington, Feb. 13, 1904) *in* INTERNATIONAL ARBITRAL AWARDS, *supra* note 34.

37. *See In Fear of the Hague: Every Effort Making to Settle Venezuela Case in Washington,* N.Y. TIMES Feb. 5, 1903, at 1 (noting in part that negotiations were proceeding and that referring the matter to the Hague would prolong the blockade and would be of no good).

38. *The Venezuela Preferential Case: Award of the Tribunal of Arbitration, in* IX REPORTS OF INTERNATIONAL ARBITRAL AWARDS *supra* note 34, at 107–10.

39. *Id.* at 108.

III. THE CALVO CLAUSE AND ITS PROGENY

As we noted above, the Calvo clause proclaimed the sovereign equality of Latin American countries with more powerful States, and their independence from diplomatic interference with regard to matters arising out of contractual relations.[40] In effect, both the Calvo clause and the Drago doctrines represented efforts by the newly independent Latin American countries to overcome the unequal economic relations they had with capital-exporting States.

The Calvo clause required foreign investors to submit to the remedies available within the judiciaries of Latin American countries, rather than to be governed by rules of their home countries or rules of international law. It was designed to circumvent capitulation treaties, which were imposed by capital-exporting States requiring capital-importing States to protect the rights of alien investors through the use of the law of the capital-exporting State. The Calvo clause, in essence, required foreign investors to forfeit the option of pursuing alternative remedies, such as diplomacy or war to collect on their debts. Under the Calvo clause, foreign investors had the same degree of protection as domestic investors. It was a rule of equal treatment in the protection of foreign and national investors of Latin American countries.

As such, the Calvo clause was predicated on the view that there did not exist a universal or "international standard of justice" that alien investors were entitled to under customary international law. Instead, under the Calvo clause foreign investors were entitled to exactly the same remedies as domestic investors. Domestic, rather than international law, was the source of rights for foreign investors. Only where a denial of justice occurred, under some Latin American Calvo clauses, could foreign investors resort to rules of international law for remedies. A violation of the Calvo clause resulted in the termination of the rights that a foreign investor had under the contract in question. As a Mexican jurist argued in 1944, the purpose of the Calvo clause was to prevent foreigners from using the diplomatic protection of

---

40. M. R. Garcia-Mora, *The Calvo Clause in Latin American Constitutions and International Law*, 33 MARQ. L. REV. 4, 205–06 (1950).

their countries as "an instrument of oppression . . . by strong States against weak ones."[41]

IV. AFRICAN AND ASIAN CHALLENGES TO INTERNATIONAL ECONOMIC LAW AND GOVERNANCE

If the nineteenth-century system of capitulations and forcible enforcement of contractual rights was rejected by Latin American countries, neither was the post-World War II regime of international economic law and governance embraced without severe reservations by newly independent countries of Asia and Africa. The best example of the objections these countries had to the old regime of international economic governance was the clean slate theory. States that adhered to this theory argued that they should be freed from having to assume obligations that legitimized colonial conquests and acquisitions upon independence. The Nyerere doctrine, for example, advocated that countries should be able to select only those treaty commitments that best comported with their newly acquired sovereignty.[42]

However, as Antony Anghie has shown, efforts by these newly independent countries to undo treaty commitments and customary international law rules in the international investment area were strongly challenged by capital-exporting States.[43] Several arguments were deployed against the clean slate theory and the Nyerere doctrine. One of the primary means by which the continuity of prior treaty and customary rights was assured was through the assertion of the doctrine of State succession. Rules of State succession require new States to undertake treaty and other rights assumed by the old State.[44]

---

41. Id.
42. E. E. SEATON & S. E. MALITI, TANZANIA TREATY PRACTICE (1973). See also M. BEDJAOUI, TOWARDS A NEW INTERNATIONAL ECONOMIC ORDER 110 (1979) (arguing that international law could not easily assume the task of transforming international relations because it had been "confined to protecting a type of international relations not yet purged of inequality and imperialism").
43. ANTONY ANGHIE, IMPERIALISM, SOVEREIGNTY AND THE MAKING OF INTERNATIONAL LAW 196, 226–44 (2005).
44. Vienna Convention on Succession of States in Respect of States Property, Archives and Debt, Apr. 8, 1983, art. 32–36 (1983) 31:1 SELECT

Under this doctrine, it is irrelevant how those treaties were procured or indeed, how illegitimate and unequal the commitments in these treaties and agreements were. Developed countries and their supporters also invoked the doctrine of acquired rights, under which rights that preexisted the independence of the new States were required to be upheld. Whereas newly independent countries argued in favor of revising treaty commitments and mineral concessions that they had played no part in making while they were under colonial rule, developed countries argued that they were seeking to unilaterally modify these commitments, inconsistent with the principle of *pacta sund servanda*. Indeed, several international law jurists from developed countries[45] argued that changing these acquired rights or the customary international law rules that guaranteed the rights of alien investors would result in unraveling the very international legal order that had brought these countries into existence. One such jurist argued that, in so far as the rules newly independent countries wanted to repudiate were customary international law, they could only have done so when the rules were in formation.[46] Because these rules were already in force, they had been in formation long before the independence of African and Asian countries.[47]

DOCUMENTS ON INT'L AFF. 10 (1983) [hereinafter Vienna Convention] (establishing the survival of State debts).

45. Sir Humphrey Waldock, *General Course on Public International Law*, 106 REC. DE COURS 1, 49–53 (1962-II). This rule is also reflected in Restatement (Third) of Foreign Relations Law of the United States § 102 (c) Comment d. *See also* Norbett Horn, *Normative Problems of a New International Economic Order*, 16 J WORLD TRADE L. 343 (1982); ROBERT H. JACKSON, QUASI-STATES: SOVEREIGNTY, INTERNATIONAL RELATIONS AND THE THIRD WORLD 202 (1991) (arguing that the NIEO was "unduly ambitious in that it attempted to replace free trade and cumulative justice with economic democracy and distributive justice").

46. *Id.*

47. Notably, in the interwar years, Soviet and Eastern European jurists of international law challenged international legal rules on foreign investor protection. These jurists argued that rules of international law could not regulate property relations within States. Within the socialist approach to economic governance, domestic law governed the rights of foreign investors and international adjudication of foreign investor rights was not permitted. Rules of international economic governance were also critiqued for being

In the 1970s, developing countries sought to change various rules of international economic governance that they perceived as prejudicial to them through the legislative agenda of the United Nations General Assembly. They argued that rules of State responsibility gave them jurisdiction to regulate foreign investors within their territory, to enable them to regulate the conditions of under which these investors could enter into their economies, and in particular the jurisdiction to: exclude foreign investors from certain sectors of their economies, as well as to regulate the permissibility and scope of repatriating capital and profits and the conditions under which technology could or could not be transferred to their economies. As in the Calvo clause era, these countries argued that international law was only valid in so far as it required these newly independent countries to treat foreign and domestic investors similarly.[48]

These efforts included the 1970s initiative to inaugurate a New International Economic Order (NIEO). Using their majorities in the United Nations General Assembly and acting together as the Group of 77, developing countries also drafted and campaigned for the adoption of the Charter of Economic Rights and Duties of States (CERDS). The Charter reintroduced the Calvo doctrine's requirement of a uniform standard of treatment for domestic and foreign investors.[49] It also recognized the right of a State to nationalize foreign-owned property and the right of such a State to use its own law, as opposed to international law, to measure compensation after nationalization. The NIEO agenda sought to restructure international economic relations to establish a balance between the predominantly raw material producing economies of the capital-importing States and Western industrial economies. The NIEO challenged unfair international

---

incompatible with a State-led model of economic governance. Thus, like Latin American jurists of the nineteenth century, these jurists contested the laissez faire underpinnings of the rules' international economic governance such as the inviolability of private property and the sanctity of contracts.

48. Guha-Roy, *Is the Law of Responsibility of State for Injuries to Aliens a Part of Universal International Law*, 55 AM. J. INT'L L. 863 (1961). *See also* S. K. B. Asante, *Stability of Contractual Relations in the Transnational Investment Process*, 28 INT'L & COMP. L.Q. 401 (1979); S. SELL, POWER AND IDEAS: NORTH SOUTH POLITICS OF INTELLECTUAL PROPERTY AND ANTITRUST (1998).

49. *See* B. H. Weston, *The Charter of Economic Rights and Duties of States and the Deprivation of Foreign-Owned Wealth*, 75 AM. J. INT'L L. 441 (1981).

trading, investment and finance rules and advocated in favor of a right to development.[50] The NIEO approach was informed by the theoretical work of dependency theorists who argued that countries that were formerly under colonial rule had failed to develop economically because of their peripheral position in the international economy. Under some of these dependency theories, capital-importing economies were thought vulnerable as a result of the poor terms of trade for their unprocessed raw materials and because of the downward trend in prices of their agricultural exports. Dependency theories attributed the shape of poorer economies on Western sources of aid, investment, and loans that favored industrial development at the expense of agriculture. Such policies, in turn, exploited the peasantry while enriching a comprador class. Rather than trace uneven development to internal problems within poor economies, dependency theorists emphasized the structural limitations of the global economy posed by huge multinational corporations, unequal exchanges between the north and the south, and the reliance on a few primary products for export among poor economies.[51] Some scholars even proposed that poorer economies should unlink from the richer industrial economies to resolve the relational foundations of maldistribution of global wealth.[52] The debate on the content, authority, and fairness of international investment rules particularly those relating to compensation for nationalization of alien property were captured in the following terms by the United States Supreme Court:

> Certain representatives of the newly independent and underdeveloped countries have questioned whether the rules of state responsibility toward aliens can bind nations that have not consented to them and it is argued

---

50. Garcia-Mora, *supra* note 39, at 205–06.
51. F. H. CARDOSO & E. FALETTO, DEPENDENCY AND DEVELOPMENT IN LATIN AMERICA, (1978).
52. S. AMIN, ACCUMULATION ON A WORLD SCALE: A CRITIQUE OF THE THEORY OF UNDERDEVELOPMENT (Brian Pearce trans., 1974). *See also* CARDOSO & FALETTO *supra* note 47. For a critique that the agenda of the NIEO replicated the old rules, strategies and institutions of liberal modernity it sought to overcome and therefore could not promise fundamental change, see Dianne Otto, *Subalternity and International Law: The Problems of Global Community and the Incommensurability of Difference*, 5 Soc. & LEG. STUD. 348 (1996).

that the traditionally articulated standards governing expropriation of property reflect "imperialist" interests and are inappropriate to the circumstances of emergent states. The disagreement as to relevant international law standards reflects an even more basic divergence between the national interests of capital importing and capital exporting nations, between the social ideologies of those countries in favor of state control of a considerable portion of the means of production and those that adhere to a free enterprise system. It is difficult to imagine the courts of this country embarking on adjudication in an area which touches more sensitively the practical and ideological goals of the various members of the community of nations.[53]

While developing countries were challenging the fairness of rules of international economic governance in the 1960s to the 1970s as the foregoing observation suggests, some of them were also cautiously embracing these rules as well as market-based models of national economic policy. For these countries, rules of international investment law including bilateral investment agreements provided a context within which they could enter into credible commitments with foreign investors.[54] The adoption of market-based models of economic development resulted in the spectacular economic success of the East Asian economies such as South Korea.[55] Whereas most of the East Asian economies were experimenting with market reforms from the 1960s, many other developing economies were far too skeptical.[56]

This rejection of market-led development on the part of some States was evident in the debates on the drafting of the Convention on the Settlement of Investment Disputes between States and

---

53. *Banco Sabbatino de Cuba v. Sabbatino*, 376 U.S. 398 (1964).

54. *See* Andrew T. Guzman, *Why LDCs Sign Treaties That Hurt Them: Explaining the Popularity of Bilateral Investment Treaties*, 38 VA. J. INT'L L. 639 (1998).

55. M. Sornarajah, *ICSID Involvement in Asian Foreign Investment Disputes: The Amco and AAPL Cases*, 4 Asian Y.B. INT'L L. 69 (1994). For a view of the particular variation of free markets in the rise of the East Asian economies, relative to the neoliberal model known as the Washington Consensus, see Alice Amsden, *Why Isn't the Whole World Experimenting with the East Asian Model to Develop?: Review of World Bank's East Asian Miracle Report*, 22 WORLD DEV. 4 (1994).

56. On this, see DEEPAK LAL, THE POVERTY OF "DEVELOPMENT ECONOMICS" 24–36 (2000).

Nationals of Other States in the late 1960s.[57] Representatives of Asian States, such as Sri Lanka, feared that this new international investment tribunal would simply continue unequal economic relations between capital-importing and capital-exporting States.[58] Scholars from third-world States have often noted how the rulings of the Tribunals of the International Center for the Settlement of Investment Disputes work against the interests of their States.[59] This attitude is also reflected in the Libyan defense in arbitration proceedings that its decision to nationalize oil concessions in 1973 and 1974 was a nonarbitral sovereign act. In perhaps one of the most well-known arbitration investment decisions that followed, Arbitrator Rene-Jean Dupuy rejected Libya's decision.[60] He held that Libya's nationalization of the concessions it had granted alien investors could not be determined exclusively under Libyan law and in Libyan courts. In his view, the provision in the Charter of Economic Rights and Duties of States, which would have allowed for such an outcome, was adopted with 86 votes but more importantly 11 votes against and 28 abstentions.[61] Among the objectors were capital-exporting States including the

---

57. Sornarajah, *ICSID Involvement, supra* note 49, at 69–70. Clearly, developing countries had a love-hate relationship to international law; they loved its promise of autonomy but criticized its continuation of colonial inequalities. One of the best examples of this attitude is BEDJAOUI, *supra* note 42. For a further discussion, see James Gathii, *A Critical Appraisal of the International Legal Tradition of Taslim Olawale Elias,* 21 LEIDEN J. INT'L L. 317 (2008) (arguing that a defining question for the first generation of scholars from the former colonies after World War II was "how to establish a doctrinal basis or a set of principles to address not only their frustration with international law, but also how its rules and institutions could contribute to the challenges of the newly independent states," *id.* at 318–19).

58. *Id.* at 70 n.4.

59. For example, M. SORNARAJAH, INTERNATIONAL LAW ON FOREIGN INVESTMENT (1994); Ibironke Odumosu, *Locating Third World Resistance in the International Law on Foreign Investment,* 9 INT'L COMMUNITY L. REV. 427 (2007). For a view skeptical of these reservations, see AMAZU A. ASOUZU, INTERNATIONAL COMMERCIAL ARBITRATION AND AFRICAN STATES: PRACTICE, PARTICIPATION AND INSTITUTIONAL DEVELOPMENT (2001).

60. *Texas Overseas Petroleum Co. v. Libyan Arab Republic,* 17 I.L.M. 1 (1978). The outcome in this case contrasts sharply with that in the Sabbatino case discussed above, *supra* note 54 and accompanying text.

61. *Id.* at ¶ 85.

United States, Germany, Belgium, Spain, France, Japan, and the United Kingdom. Having found that the "most important [W]estern countries"[62] had not consented to disregarding international law in determining compensation for nationalization, Arbitrator Dupuy then turned to the United Nations General Assembly Resolution on the Permanent Sovereignty over Natural Resources of 1962[63] (PSNR). Dupuy noted that the PSNR, which was passed with the approval of "many States of the Third World, but also [by] several Western developed countries with market economies, including the most important one, the United States."[64] Dupuy concluded the appropriate compensation standard adopted in that resolution reflected the *opinio juris communis* because it reflected a "consensus by a majority of states belonging to the various representative groups."[65] Arbitrator Dupuy's efforts to precisely define the rules applicable to compensation for nationalization were also in issue in the *Sabbatino* decision of the U.S. Supreme Court about a decade earlier. Thus, in *Sabbatino*, the Court noted that its decision on a question related to the content of rules of compensation for takings would hardly be regarded as "disinterested expressions of sound legal principles by those adhering to widely different ideologies."[66] This self-consciousness about the controversies surrounding the efficacy and authority of rules of international law in this period was also a reflection of the heated debates surrounding the large-scale nationalizations of natural

---

62. *Id.* He also noted that a number of developing countries abstained on this question and attributed their abstention to their disagreement with disregarding international law on compensation for nationalizations.

63. G.A. Res. 1803 (XVII) U.N. Doc. A/RES/1803 (Dec.14 1962) (declaring in Article 4 that "[n]ationalization, expropriation or requisitioning shall be based on grounds of public utility, security or the national interest . . . [and] in such cases the owner shall be paid appropriate compensation").

64. *Id.* at ¶ 84.

65. *Id.* at 87.

66. *Sabbatino*, 376 U.S. at 429. For another decision indicating a limited rather than expansive view of the duty of compensation in international investment law, see *Case Concerning Barcelona Traction, Light & Power Co. (Belg. v. Swed.)* 1970 I.C.J. 4 (Feb. 5) (holding that shareholder interests are indirect interests that do not qualify for international legal protection, and a claimant State cannot espouse the claim of its nationals who have invested in foreign corporations absent treaties or agreements providing for such protections).

resource concessions and entire industries that characterized the period following decolonization.[67] The debate continues to date on the appropriate standard for compensation for expropriation.[68] Although international law is now widely accepted as governing international investment and commercial disputes, the uncertainty about the precise content of many of its governing rules and the

---

67. For perhaps this reason in *Sabbatino, supra* note 54, Justice Harlan in similar circumstances as those in the Libyan case declined to invoke international law as Arbitrator Dupuy. Justice Harlan instead held that, "[w]e decide only that the Judicial branch will not examine the validity of a taking of property . . . in the absence of a treaty or other unambiguous agreement regarding controlling legal principles, even if the complaint alleges that the taking violates customary international law." *Sabbatino,* 376 U.S. at 428; *see also* RICHARD FALK, THE STATUS OF LAW IN INTERNATIONAL SOCIETY 409–13 (1970); RICHARD LILLICH, THE PROTECTION OF FOREIGN INVESTMENTS 77–78 (1978); Jordan Paust, *Correspondence,* 18 VA. J. INT'L L, 601–03 (1978).

68. The "prompt, adequate and effective compensation" formulation of the Hull diplomatic note has been rejected by many capital-importing States. For example, Mexico rejected it in 1938. *See 1938 Correspondence between United States and Mexico, excerpted in* 5 G. HACKWORTH, DIG. INT'L L. 655–65 (1942); *see also* Oscar Schachter, *Compensation for Expropriation,* 23 COLUM. J. TRANSNAT'L L. 615, 616 (1985) (arguing that there is a dispute as to whether the Hull formula represents customary international law). In addition, three UN resolutions have embraced the view that national treatment rather than prompt adequate and effective compensation is the rule governing expropriations. *See* G.A. Res. 3171, U.N. GAOR, 28th Sess., Resolution on the Permanent Sovereignty over Natural Resources, G.A. Doc. 3171/XXVII (1973); G.A. Res. 3201, Declaration on the Establishment of a New International Economic Order, 29th Sess., G.A. Doc. 3201/VI-6 (1974); G.A. Res. Charter of Economic Rights and Duties of States, 30th Sess., G.A. Doc. 3281/XXIX (1975). On the uncertainty of customary international law relating to foreign investment particularly in relation to bilateral investment treaties (BITs), see Bernard Kishoiyan, *The Utility of Bilateral Investment Treaties in the Formulation of Customary International Law,* 14 NW. J. INT'L L. & BUS. 327 (1994) (exploring the various compensation standards in a variety of BITs and concluding there is no universally agreed standard because the practice evidences "so much uncertainty and contradiction" as well as "so much fluctuation and discrepancy," *id.* at 372). For an overview of various standards applied in a variety of contexts, see R. DOAK BISHOP, JAMES CRAWFORD & W. MICHAEL REISMAN, FOREIGN INVESTMENT DISPUTES: CASES, MATERIALS AND COMMENTARY 1298–325 (2005).

growing propensity particularly in bilateral investment treaties[69] (BITs) to overprotect the rights of investors has led a leading first-world scholar to refer to BITs, which often provide the applicable rules for International Centre for Settlement of Investment Disputes (ICSID) tribunals, as "bills of rights for foreign investors."[70] In the recent past, Bolivia denounced the ICSID Convention and withdrew from it, arguing multinational corporations used ICSID Tribunals to resist the exercise of sovereign responsibilities such as environmental laws. There are also several other Latin American countries including Bolivia, Venezuela, and Nicaragua that announced their opposition to and intention to denounce the ICSID Convention.[71] For precisely this reason, the United States Congress in 2002 enacted the No Greater Rights Than principle, under which foreign investors

---

69. Other notable examples here include the North American Free Trade Agreement (NAFTA), which includes an investment chapter that effectively guarantees investors compensation for losses arising from a regulatory measure that a NAFTA member may take to protect the environment. On this, see Frederick M. Abbot, *The Political Economy of NAFTA Chapter Eleven: Equality Before the Law and the Boundaries of North American Legal Integration*, 23 HASTINGS INT'L & COMP. L. REV. 303 (2000).

70. Jose Alvarez, *North American Free Trade Agreement's Chapter Eleven*, 28 U. MIAMI INTER-AM. L. REV. 303, 308 (1996–97) (also arguing that NAFTA is a "bilateral investment treaty on steroids," *id*. at 304). This theme is further echoed in PHILIPPE SANDS, LAWLESS WORLD: AMERICA AND THE MAKING AND BREAKING OF GLOBAL RULES FROM FDR'S ATLANTIC CHARTER TO GEORGE W. BUSH'S ILLEGAL WAR 117–42 (2005) (noting the tendency to interpret international investment rules in isolation of other international law rules and to give priority to investor rights over rules that protect human rights and the environment). *See also* UPENDRA BAXI, THE FUTURE OF INTERNATIONAL HUMAN RIGHTS 235 (1999) (noting the ascendance of a trade-related, market-friendly approach to human rights under the aegis of globalization).

71. For an analysis, see Igacio Vincentelli, *The Uncertain Future of ICSID in Latin America*, available at http://ssrn.com/abstract=1340816. On Bolivia's denunciation, see International Centre for Settlement of Investment Disputes (ICSID), *List of Contracting States and Other Signatories to the Convention (as of Nov. 4, 2007)*, available at http://icsid.worldbank.org/ICSID/FrontServlet?requestType=ICSIDDocRH&actionVal=ContractingStates&ReqFrom=Main (last visited Jan. 25, 2009). In addition, note that Venezuela in 2008 denounced its BIT with the Netherlands. In addition, the Venezuelan Supreme Court has decided that any decision of an ICSID Tribunal inconsistent with Venezuelan law would be unenforceable in Venezeula, see Vincentelli, *supra* note 71.

have no greater rights than a U.S. citizen under the U.S. Constitution and local laws. In effect, whereas a U.S. corporation abroad has the full protections of an investor to challenge foreign laws and regulatory regimes standing in the way of their investment opportunities, foreign investors in the United States enjoy no such rights.[72]

Ultimately, arbitration proceedings before bodies such as the ICSID are an indication of how international investment law has empowered private actors, such as multinational corporations, to bring suit against States hosting their investments. By giving private actors the power to sue and have a choice with regard not only as to forum but as of the applicable law as well, vests these actors with enormous legal authority over host States over which they may already exercise significant market leverage. In short, although the significance of the diplomatic protection of foreign investment through forcible means has largely declined, the role of privatized investment dispute forums that have no oversight has grown.[73] This, together with the retaliatory threats exercised by capital-exporting States to protect their investors and interests in capital-importing States, in

---

72. The immediate reason relating to U.S. concern about Chapter 11 of NAFTA arose from a suit filed against the United States by Methanex, a Canadian company claiming $970 million compensation for business it would lose because of California's plan to phase out the use of methyl tertiary butyl ether (MTBE), an oxygenate that cleans gasoline, because of concerns the additive was contaminating drinking water supplies. Methanex argued that the ban was not based on scientific evidence, and the water pollution could be solved by fixing leaking underground storage tanks at gas stations. California was the largest market for Methanex and was important because it sets environmental standards that are adopted by other states. Methanex alleged in the suit that the ban was necessitated by political considerations including the financial contributions to the campaign of Governor Gray Davis of California by Archer Daniel Midlands Corporation, which produces a competing oxygenate from corn. In August 2002, a binational panel decided not to proceed with the case since there was inadequate evidence to make a determination. *See* Allen Dowd, *NAFTA Panel Says Cannot Rule on Methanex MTBE Case*, REUTERS (Aug. 7, 2002) *available at* http://www.mindfully.org/WTO/Methanex-MTBE7aug02.htm.

73. For an excellent view, see Ibironke T. Odumosu, *Locating Third World Resistance in the International Law on Foreign Investment*, 9 INT'L COMMUNITY L. REV. 427 (2007). *See also* Ibironke T. Odumosu, *The Antinomies of the (Continued) Relevance of the ICSID to the Third World*, 8 SAN DIEGO J. INT'L L. 345 (2007).

many ways tilts international economic governance in favor of investors from capital exporting States.[74] To continue this exploration of the power of international investment law over capital-importing States, Section V examines a decision of the ICSID in the context of State responsibility for war destruction.

V. STATE RESPONSIBILITY FOR WAR DESTRUCTION IN INVESTMENT DISPUTES

Asian Agricultural Products Limited (AAPL) v. Democratic Socialist Republic of Sri Lanka was an ICSID case that raised the question of State responsibility for war destruction.[75] AAPL, a foreign-owned firm

---

74. One of the best-known retaliatory threats is Super 301 contained in the Trade Act of 1974, 19 U.S.C. § 2242 (2000), *amended by* Omnibus Trade and Competitiveness Act of 1988, Pub. L. No. 100-416, 102 Stat. 1105. Under this section, the United States Trade Representative (USTR) is required within thirty days after the submission of the annual National Trade Estimates (foreign trade barriers) to report to Congress those foreign countries that (1) "deny adequate and effective protection of U.S. intellectual property rights" and (2) those countries under (1) "that are determined by the USTR to be priority foreign countries." *Id.* The USTR identifies as priorities only those countries "that have the most onerous or egregious acts, policies, or practices that . . . have the greatest adverse impact on the relevant United States products and that are not entering into good faith negotiations or making significant progress in bilateral or multilateral negotiations to provide adequate and effective intellectual property rights" protection. *Id.* The United States blacklisted India and Brazil leading up to the conclusion of the Uruguay Round of negotiations thereby effectively ending their opposition to the Uruguay Round bargain. *See* James Gathii, *Construing Intellectual Property Rights and Competition Policy Consistently with Facilitating Access to Affordable Aids Drugs to Low-End Consumers*, 53 FLA. L. REV. 756 (2001). In a challenge at the World Trade Organization (WTO), this provision of U.S. law was sustained. *See* World Trade Organization Report of the Panel, *United States–Sections 301–310 of the Trade Act of 1974*, WT/DS152/R ¶ 7.22 (Dec. 22, 1999).

75. *Asian Agric. Prod. Ltd. v. Democratic Socialist Republic of Sri Lanka*, ICSID Case No. ARB/87/3, *available at* http:// www.worldbank.org/icsid (follow "cases" hyperlink; then follow "List of Cases" hyperlink; then follow "Concluded Cases" hyperlink; then scroll to "Asian Agricultural Products Limited v. Democratic Socialist Republic of Sri Lanka (ICSID Case No. ARB/87/3)") [hereinafter *AAPL v. Sri Lanka*].

operated a prawn farm under the name, Serendib Seafoods Limited, a Sri Lankan public company in which the Sri Lankan government participated in as an equity partner. AAPL claimed damages for losses it suffered on the Prawn farm as a result of a military operation conducted by the Sri Lankan military against Tamil tiger fighters.

Besides claiming liability on a war destruction clause, AAPL primarily based its claim on the view that Sri Lanka bore "strict or absolute liability" under a BIT Sri Lanka had signed with Great Britain and Northern Ireland.[76] AAPL argued that the customary international law due diligence standard of State responsibility had been replaced by this new rule of "strict or absolute liability." AAPL claimed that the "most favored nation" and "full protection and security"[77] clauses in the treaty imposed "strict or absolute liability" even if it could be shown that AAPL's investments were destroyed by persons whose conduct could not be attributable to Sri Lanka and under circumstances beyond its control. In fact, as the Tribunal noted, AAPL exhibited "hostility to the general applicability of customary international law rules" and showed "reluctance to admit Sri Lankan domestic law as the basic governing law."[78] Suffice it to say here, AAPL's claims are consistent with the traditional attitude investors have of overstating the responsibility of host States beyond that recognized under customary international law. As Sri Lanka argued in response, with the concurrence of the Tribunal, the "full protection

---

76. *Id.* at ¶ 9. The Tribunal's majority opinion found that in light of the failure of the parties to agree on a choice of law, during the arbitration proceedings, they had presented their case in a manner that showed that they mutually agreed that the provisions Sri Lanka–UK BIT was "the primary source of the applicable legal rules," *id.* at ¶ 20. However, the dissenting opinion of one member of the Tribunal, S. K. B. Asante took issue with the tribunal's finding that the treaty was the primary source of rules for determining the dispute, see dissenting opinion of S. K. B. Asante *in* ICSID REV.-FOREIGN INV. L.J. 576–78 (1990).

77. *AAPL v. Sri Lanka, supra* note 75, at ¶ 26 (A), where AAPL argues argued that "the ordinary meaning of the words 'full protection and security' points to an acceptance of the host state of strict or absolute liability." Further AAPL argued that under the treaty, the "full protection and security clause" had to be read as "autonomous in character and independent of any link to customary international law." *Id.* at ¶ 26(B).

78. *Id.* at ¶ 23.

and security" clause of the treaty could not be construed to impose strict or absolute liability.[79] In fact, the Tribunal noted it could find no case in which such a clause had been construed to impose a strict or absolute liability on a host State.[80] This conclusion was also endorsed in the dissenting opinion of one of the arbitrators.[81]

Having rejected AAPL's novel but not unusual basis for seeking to hold Sri Lanka liable, the Tribunal then moved to consider Sri Lanka's liability under the war destruction clause of the treaty. Under this clause, the Contracting Parties were liable for losses suffered "owing to war or other armed conflict, revolution, a state of national emergency, revolt, insurrection or riot in the territory."[82] Sri Lanka argued that, for it to be held liable under this clause for failing to act reasonably under the circumstances, it had to be shown that it had been "negligent in the use of or in the failure to use, the forces at its disposal for the prevention or suppression of the insurrection."[83]

According to the Tribunal, the duty of vigilance required to establish the "degree of security reasonably expected" depended on the circumstances.[84] The Tribunal noted this degree of security could be established by Sri Lanka's failure to take by "all means reasonably necessary" steps to prevent acts of revolutionaries that caused injury or damage to AAPL's investment.[85]

AAPL argued that the destruction of its "office structure, repair shed, store and dormitory," as well as "the opening of its sluice gates to the grow-out ponds," and the resulting destruction of its prawn crop and the death of 21 of its staff members, was not necessary because "less destructive" measures short of the destruction and murders could have been taken by the Sri Lankan military.[86] Sri Lanka countered by arguing that its operation on AAPL's farm was

---

79. *Id.* at ¶ 32.
80. *Id.* ¶¶ 48–55.
81. *Id.* at ¶ 4 (Asante, S. K. B., dissenting).
82. *AAPL v. Sri Lanka, supra* note 75, at ¶ 65. Under the treaty, liability would be remediable by "restitution, indemnification, compensation or other settlement," *id.* at ¶ 66.
83. *Id.* at ¶ 69.
84. *Id.* at ¶ 73.
85. *Id.* at ¶ 73.
86. *Id.* at ¶ 79.

necessary to "prevent the spread of terrorism and the erosion of government control in the towns surrounding the shrimp farm."[87] The government also contended the farm had been used by the Tamil rebels as an operations base; that the farm's management had cooperated with the rebels' and that the Tamil fighters had engaged in fierce combat with the Sri Lankan Special Task Force on the day of the raid. Sri Lanka argued that it was the Tamil fighters who had actually occasioned the damage complained of by AAPL.[88] It was agreed by both Sri Lanka and AAPL that the area in which the farm on which the damage occurred was infiltrated by Tamil fighters and was out of the control of the Sri Lankan government for several months before the raid.[89]

The Tribunal found the Sri Lanka government had not acted reasonably because it had failed to use peaceful alternatives in dealing with Tamil fighters, an option in the Tribunal's opinion the government had because it had established a "high level channel of communication in order to get any suspect elements excluded from the farm."[90] According to the Tribunal, Sri Lanka's:

> [F]ailure to resort to such precautionary measures acquires more significance when taking into consideration that such measures fall within the normal exercise of governmental inherent powers—as a public authority—entitled to order undesirable persons out from security sensitive areas. The failure became particularly serious when the highest executive officer of the Company [AAPL] reconfirmed just ten days before his willingness to comply with any governmental requests in this respect.[91]

Having no evidence of either Sri Lankan forces being directly responsible for the damage or even having had control of AAPL's premises or that the Tamil fighters caused the damage, the Tribunal nevertheless found Sri Lanka liable. In the Tribunal's view, the appropriate course of conduct was either to "institute judicial investigations against them to prove their culpability or innocence, or to get them off the Company's farm."[92]

---

87. *Id.* at ¶ 82(a).
88. *Id.* at ¶ 82(b)-(e).
89. *Id.* at ¶ 85(a).
90. *Id.* at ¶ 85(b).
91. *Id.*
92. *Id.*

According to the Tribunal, Sri Lanka had failed to give full protection and security to AAPL's farm and it was therefore liable.[93] As such, Sri Lanka's decision to deal with, what was essentially a national security issue forcibly, particularly because it involved claims relating to terrorism was reviewable in international investment proceedings if it conflicted with its treaty obligations to protect AAPL's commercial rights.

The dissenting opinion in the case regretted that the Tribunal's decision failed "to appreciate the full implications of the formidable security situation and the grave national emergency that confronted the Sri Lankan authorities."[94] It went on to note that it was not in dispute that the entire province within which the investment losses had occurred had been embroiled in civil war pitting the government against "a powerful and well-armed group" that were engaged in "sophisticated guerilla warfare against the Sri Lanka government forces,"[95] which had established its headquarters within 1.5 miles of the farm where the losses occurred.[96] As a result, even the managing director of AAPL had not been able to visit the farm for six months prior to the government's counter-insurgency operation during which the investment losses occurred.[97]

Article 4 of the Sri Lankan–Great Britain BIT provided for circumstances under which liability for compensation arises when investment losses result from war or other armed conflict, revolution, state of emergency, revolt or insurgency, and where the losses resulting are attributable to the host State or its agents.[98] Under this Article,

---

93. *Id.* ¶¶ 86–87.
94. *Id.* at ¶ 4 (Asante, S. K. B., dissenting).
95. *Id.* at ¶ 5.
96. *Id.* at ¶ 3.
97. *Id.* at ¶ 4.
98. Article 4 (Compensation for losses) (1) Nationals or companies of one Contracting Party whose investments in the territory of other Contracting Party suffer losses owing to war or other armed conflict, revolution, a state of national emergency, revolt, insurrection or riot in the territory of the latter Contracting Party shall be accorded by the latter Contracting Party treatment, as regards to restitution, indemnification, compensation or other settlement, no less favorable than that which the latter Contracting Party accords to its own nationals or companies of any third

State responsibility is precluded where investment losses are not attributable to a State or where the destruction is "not caused in combat action or by the necessity of the situation."[99] Quoting extensively from the literature on responsibility for war destruction, the dissenting opinion arrived at two conclusions. First, that the provisions of Article 4 of the treaty were a statement of the customary international law position on responsibility for war destruction. Second, that responsibility for war destruction did not prescribe a substantive obligation on the part of the host State to pay compensation where foreign investments sustain losses by reason of war or other armed conflict, revolution, a state of national emergency, revolt or other civil disturbance."[100] In other words, the treaty provision only contained the customary international law provision of property and/or investment protection, contrary to the Tribunal's interpretation as a specific undertaking on the part of Sri Lanka "to pay compensation to all aliens from all countries."[101]

State; (2) Without prejudice to paragraph (1) of this Article, nationals and companies of one Contracting Party who in any of the situations referred to in that paragraph suffer losses in the territory of the other Contracting Party resulting from (a) requisitioning of their property by its forces or authorities, or (b) destruction of their property by its forces or authorities which was not caused in combat action or was not required by the necessity of the situation, shall be accorded restitution or adequate compensation. Resulting payments shall be freely transferable.

Asante's dissenting opinion proceeded on the view that because Article 4 was more specific to issue in dispute than the full protection and most-favored nation clauses, it applied to the situation. Noted Asante, "Article 4(2) is crucial, first, because as the *lex specialis* between Sri Lanka and the U.K. spelling out specific grounds of liability in the particular situations defined in Article 4(1), it must prevail as the definitive source of liability in respect of the conduct of the armed forces of the host State." *Supra* note 57, at 585 (Asante, S. K. B., dissenting).

99. AAPL v. Sri Lanka, supra note 75, at art. 4(2).

100. Dissenting opinion of Asante, *supra* note 57, at 585–86.

101. *Id.* at 588. Asante notes that such an interpretation of Article 4(1) of the Treaty was more consistent with the understanding of the most favored nation (MFN) provision and as such, the majority opinion had in effect obliterated "the juridical distinction between the concept of most favored nation treatment, a creature of treaty, and the general requirements of customary international law," *id.* at 589.

The dissenting opinion noted that, even if the treaty clause could be interpreted as the Tribunal had done, Sri Lanka had effectively waived this obligation in its Constitution in so far as the obligation conflicted with its national security.[102] Thus, although the Tribunal's opinion focused primarily on the exceptional circumstances under which a State is responsible for war destruction relating to wanton destruction or unnecessary force, the dissenting opinion focused on the general rule of customary international law under which a State is not responsible for investment losses arising from war, armed conflict, insurrection, revolt, riot, a national emergency, or other civil disturbances where the destruction was caused in combat or by the necessity of the situation.

Applying this rule of customary international law, the dissenting opinion proceeded as follows. First, it was not in contention there was a general insurrection in the area where AAPL had its shrimp factory and that the government had been engaged in seeking to regain control of the area. Further, that this was "a legitimate and praiseworthy act of a sovereign government."[103] Second, both Sri Lanka and AAPL, as the Tribunal found, had insufficient evidence to definitively establish who destroyed AAPL's farm. As such, the dissenting opinion found that AAPL had "failed to establish the fundamental basis of the claim, namely that the Government's security forces had used excessive force in its military operation resulting in the wanton destruction of the farm."[104]

The dissenting opinion then proceeded to argue why it found the Tribunal's argument that Sri Lanka was liable for failing to use precautionary measures unconvincing. The dissent noted that the Tribunal raised the "fundamental question" regarding the propriety of the decision to engage in a military operation at that particular time, a question which "touches on the sovereign prerogatives of a Government fighting for its very life."[105] The dissent noted it would not have been feasible for the Sri Lankan government to be expected

---

102. *Id.* at 589. It is not unusual for commercial or trade treaties to have security exceptions. Article 21 of the General Agreement on Tariffs and Trade, 1948 as amended in 1994 embodies such an exception.
103. *Id.* at 592.
104. *Id.*
105. *Id.* at 593.

to have taken the sort of precautionary measures that the Tribunal held it should have, as it was engaged in sophisticated guerilla war fare against powerful insurgents.[106] Ultimately, the dissent noted that "the applicable rules and principles of customary international law, the regime of property protection under the Sri Lanka/Great Britain Treaty and Article 157 of the Sri Lankan Constitution all recognized that the requirements of national security warrant a departure from the normal principles of responsibility in respect of the protection of foreign property."[107]

Although the vigorous debate between the dissent and the opinion of the ICSID Tribunal in *APL v. Sri-Lanka* may be exceptional,[108] holding capital importing States responsible for war destruction is not unusual. In a later arbitration, *American Manufacturing & Trading, Inc. v. Republic of Zaire*,[109] the arbitrators found that the then Zaire had failed to fulfill its obligation of vigilance to prevent the occurrence of acts of violence on its territory that had resulted in the looting and destruction of investments made by American Manufacturing and Trading Inc. In this case, unlike in *AAPL v. Sri Lanka*, Zaire did not contest its responsibility for destroying and looting the investor's property, finished goods, raw materials, and other objects of value. However, consistent with the dissent in *AAPL v. Sri Lanka*, Zaire argued that, because it had not compensated domestic businesses and other foreign investors, Article IV of its BIT with the United States was unavailable. The arbitration panel, however, found that the

---

106. *Id.* at 594.
107. *Id.* at 594–95.
108. For critical commentary on the *AAPL v. Sri Lankan* case, see Stephen C. Vascianne, *Bilateral Investment Treaties and Civil Strife: The AAPL/Sri Lanka Arbitration*, 39 NETH. INT'L L. REV. 332 (1992) (noting respects in which the decision of the Tribunal would reduce its utility as a precedent in future cases) and A. Rohan Perera & Noel Dias, *Asian Agricultural Products Ltd v. The Republic of Sri Lanka*, 2 AM. REV. INT'L ARB. 217 (1991) (discussing the Tribunal's misinterpretation of Article 4(1)).
109. ICSID Case No. ARB/93/1. Award of Feb. 21, 1997, 36 I.L.M. 1531 (1992), *available at* http:// www.worldbank.org/icsid (follow "cases" hyperlink; then follow "List of Cases" hyperlink; then follow "Concluded Cases" hyperlink; then scroll to "American Manufacturing & Trading, Inc. v. Democratic Republic of the Congo (ICSID Case No. ARB/93/1)") [hereinafter *Am. Mfg. & Trading, Inc. v. Republic of Zaire*].

clause did not require such national treatment. The finding against Zaire was arguably much broader than in *AAPL v. Sri Lanka*. This is particularly so given that the primary basis for holding Zaire responsible was the full protection and security clause that the *AAPL v. Sri Lanka* Tribunal had avoided as a basis of holding Sri Lanka responsible. In addition, unlike in *AAPL v. Sri Lanka*, damage to the investors' property was not caused by its armed forces or army, but rather by rioters and looters.[110] Ultimately, unlike in *AAPL v. Sri Lanka*, the Tribunal found against Zaire primarily under the full protection and security clause of its BIT with the United States[111] and only secondarily under Article IV, the war destruction clause on which the *AAPL v. Sri Lankan* Tribunal had relied on to hold Sri Lanka responsible.

Finally, in *Wena Hotels Limited v. Arab Republic of Egypt*, the ICSID Tribunal, without much discussion, found that Egypt had violated the full protection and security clause of UK–Egypt Agreement for the Promotion and Protection of Investments in the forcible seizure of a hotel.[112] The Tribunal cited the *American Manufactures v. Zaire* case for the proposition that States have an obligation of vigilance "to ensure the full enjoyment of protection and security" of their investments and that a country could not "invoke its own legislation to detract from any such obligation."[113] Thus, the controversial origins of responsibility for war destruction in *AAPL v. Sri Lanka* have evolved in an ever-tightening obligation on States to take preventive measures to avoid loss or damage to the property of alien investors in the context of war and domestic unrest.[114] Therefore, although ICSID

---

110. *Id.* at ¶ 7.01, 7.09.

111. The Tribunal found that Zaire had "manifestly failed" to comply with its duty of vigilance and care by its failure to take precautionary measures to protect the investors property, *id.* at ¶¶ 6.04–6.11. The Tribunal found that the protection and security obligation in Article II of the BIT was reinforced by "a special Article IV on compensation for damages due to war, or similar events, including riots and acts of violence." *Id.* at ¶¶ 6.12–6.14.

112. *Wena Hotels Ltd. v. Arab Republic of Egypt*, ICSID Case No. ARB/98/4; 41 I.L.M. 896 (2002).

113. *Id.* at ¶ 84.

114. *See also* CME Czech Republic B.V. (The Netherlands) v. The Czech Republic, Partial Award, Sept. 13, 2001 and Azurix Corp. v. Argentina, ICSID Case No. ARB/01/12, Award, July 14, 2006, which show how ICSID Tribunals have heightened the responsibility of States under the full protection and

Tribunals cite *AAPL v. Sri Lanka* for the proposition that full security and protection do not embody absolute obligations,[115] the effect of these decisions has been to effectively heighten the obligations of States for war destruction toward such absoluteness and strictness.

This heightened standard of State responsibility for war destruction is clearly demonstrated when one compares the standard of vigilance States have in the investor context, with that in the context of ensuring their territory is not used for purposes inimical to other States. In *Democratic Republic of Congo v. Uganda*, the International Court of Justice (ICJ) strongly suggested that the duty of due diligence or vigilance expected of a government with respect to rebel activity that may result in violating the rights of a neighboring State may be lower if the geographical terrain was remote and difficult.[116] In fact, this is the customary international legal standard of due diligence that imposes a reasonable, rather than an absolute, standard of conduct. Under such a standard, a State is assumed to have the means to provide protection. As such if its ability to provide protection was remote, liability would not automatically attach.[117] In addition, this standard is based on the assumption that a State had the opportunity to "prevent the act but failed to do so."[118] Taken together, these tests

---

security clauses of BITs to go beyond the kind of security that may be provided by security forces and in particular to include a secure investment environment— arguably much superior to that enjoyed by domestic investors. For another example, *see* Occidental Exploration and Prod. Co. v. The Republic of Ecuador, Award, July 1, 2004 at ¶ 187, where Ecuador's amendment of its tax laws was found to constitute a violation of its obligation to provide full protection and security to investors.

115. E.g., *supra* note 112, at ¶ 84.

116. Case Concerning Armed Activities on the Territory of the Congo (Dem. Rep. Congo v. Uganda), 2005 I.C.J. 116 at ¶ 304 (Dec. 19).

117. Richard Lillich & Paxman, *State Responsibility for Injuries to Aliens Occasioned By Terrorist Activities*, 26 AM. UNIV. L. REV. 217 (1977).

118. *Id.* This view is also confirmed by the International Law Commission's Draft Articles on Prevention of Transboundary Harm from Hazardous Activities, which discusses the duty of due diligence and specifically explains that the degree of due diligence expected of a State differs from a State that has a "well-developed economy and human and material resources and with highly evolved systems and structures of governance is different from States which are not so well placed. Even in the latter case, *vigilance*, employment of infrastructure *and monitoring of hazardous activities in the territory of the State*,

require before imposition of liability that the conduct of the [S]tate be "judged by [its] reasonableness under the circumstances."[119] This, in my view, is the approach taken by the ICJ in *Congo v. Uganda*. Clearly, the heightening of the responsibility of States for war destruction is consistent with the heightening of the responsibility of States in the terrorism context that I discuss in Chapter 7. Yet, the obligations of investors have remained the same.

To be sure, there are arbitration decisions that have found essential security interests escape clauses in BITs between capital-importing and capital-exporting States that operate to preclude capital-importing States from being held responsible. Thus in *LG&E Energy Corp. v. Argentine Republic*,[120] the Tribunal found that Argentina's decision to convert tariff denomination from U.S. dollars to Argentinian pesos as a part of its economic recovery plan did not constitute a violation of its treaty obligations to the foreign investor. The Tribunal rejected the claimants contention that essential security interests had to be necessarily of a military nature or involving war to preclude State responsibility in the context of a severe economic crisis.[121]

---

which is a natural attribute of any Government, are expected," International Law Commission, *Draft Articles on Prevention of Transboundary Harm from Hazardous Activities*, at 395, *available at* http://untreaty.un.org/ilc/texts/instruments/english/commentaries/9_7_2001.pdf (last visited Aug. 16, 2006)

119. Lillich & Paxman, *supra* note 117.

120. *LG&E Energy Corp. v. Argentine Republic*, ICSID Case. No. ARB/02/1 (Decision on Liability), Oct. 3, 2006. Other victories outside the context of the war destruction clause in BITs include *Patrick Mitchell v. Democratic Republic of Congo*, ICSID Case No. ARB/99/7 (Decision on the Application for Annulment of the Award, Nov. 1, 2006) where an award was annulled on the grounds that the investment that had been the subject matter of the claim did not fall within the definition of an investment in a United States–Zaire BIT.

121. *Supra* note 120, at ¶ 238. In this case Argentina prevailed in showing that it faced a severe economic crisis that threatened its economic and political survival that precluded it on the basis of a state of necessity from being responsible for measure taken (these included freeing gas distribution tariffs and abandoning calculation of tariffs in dollars) to address the crisis that also occasioned losses to LG&E Energy Corporation investments in Argentina, *id.* at ¶¶ 236 and 266. *See also In re CMS Transmission Co. and the Argentine Republic*, Case No. ARB/01/08 (Award of May 12, 2005) (where the tribunal concluded that a State is free to adopt emergency measures "it consider appropriate without requesting the views of any court" pursuant to a provision

Such cases show that it is possible to imagine a different liability regime for war destruction in BITs. There are a few BITs between developed and developing countries that have an escape clause to safeguard security interests of the signatory countries in the same way that Article 21 of the General Agreement on Tariff and Trade (GATT) does.[122] This clause, already contained in some U.S. BITs provides "[t]his Treaty shall not preclude the application by either Party of measures necessary for the maintenance of public order, the fulfillment of its obligations with respect to the maintenance and restoration of international peace or security, or the protection of its essential security interests."[123]

Such an escape clause would work perhaps the same way the national security exception in GATT does. The GATT security escape clause allows member States to invoke national security as an excuse

---

of a BIT authorizing a State to adopt measures in response to threats to its security interests, *id.* at ¶ 373). For further analysis, see William W. Burke-White, *The Argentine Financial Crisis: State Liability Under BITs and the Legitimacy of the ICSID System*, 3 ASIAN J. WTO & INT'L L. & POL'Y 199 (2008) (this article analyzes four ICSID Tribunal rulings arising from Argentina's response to its financial crisis in 2001–2002. The author argues this jurisprudence is deeply problematic because the four tribunals gave different interpretations of Argentina's response, whereas in fact Argentina made the same arguments in all four cases). Inconsistent arbitration rulings in similar cases is not all that unusual, see Susan D. Franck, *The Legitimacy Crisis in Investment Treaty Arbitration: Privatizing Public International Law through Inconsistent Decisions*, 73 FORDHAM L. REV. 1521 (2005). *See also* Andrea K. Bjorklund, *Reconciling State Sovereignty and Investor Protection in Denial of Justice Claims*, 45 VA. J. INT'L L., 809 (2005) (arguing that denial of justice standard is malleable and may therefore not result in a well-reasoned body of jurisprudence).

122. Anne van Asken, *Perils of Success? The Case of International Investment Protection*, 9 EUR. BUS. ORG. L. REV. 1–27, (March 2008), available at http://papers.ssrn.com/sol3/papers.cfm?abstract_id=1020959 Even better would be having international investment decisions made in a manner that takes into account the circumstances in a country in the same way social and economic rights under international law are conditioned on availability of resources or on the principle of progressive realization. For further analysis, see Emily A. Alexander, *Taking Account of Reality: Adopting Contextual Standards for Developing Countries in International Investment Law*, 48 VA. J. INT'L L., 817 (2008)

123. *See* Anne van Asken, *supra* note 122, at 13.

to depart from the rules of nondiscriminatory trade without risking the imposition of compensating trade concessions for departing from these otherwise binding obligations.[124]

For example, in 1985, the United States prohibited the importation of all goods and services of Nicaraguan origin as well as exports from the United States into Nicaragua.[125] Nicaragua lodged a complaint before a GATT panel arguing in part that this prohibition had nullified and impaired trade benefits it had accrued inconsistently with U.S. GATT obligations.[126] Nicaragua further argued that the United States and Nicaragua were not at war, and that they had maintained diplomatic relations. Instead, Nicaragua argued that as "a small developing country," it had not attacked the United States and could not pose a security threat to the United States. Nicaragua argued that it was the United States that was using force against Nicaragua inconsistently with the prohibition against the use of force.[127] Nicaragua referred the GATT panel to a decision of the International Court of Justice, finding that the United States had violated the nonuse of force prohibition of the UN Charter. For Nicaragua, the GATT had to be interpreted in accordance with rather than inconsistently with international law.[128]

---

124. Art. XXI(b)(iii) of GATT provides that: "Nothing in this Agreement shall be construed ... to prevent any contracting party from taking ... in time of war or other national emergency in international relations ... any action which it considers necessary for the protection of its national security interests." Remarkably, this security exception in the GATT regime is very similar in substance to the doctrine of suspension that allowed belligerents to confiscate private property in war but to return it on cessation of hostilities.

125. Exec. Order No. 12,513, 3 C.F.R. 342 (1985). The only exception to this ban was goods intended for the democratic resistance. The order also banned air and naval transportation to and from Nicaragua to the United States. This ban was issued under the expansive authority the U.S. President enjoys under the International Emergency Economic Powers Act (IEEPA), *see Dames & Moore*, 453 U.S. at 699 noting that the language of the IEEPA is "sweeping and unqualified," *id.*

126. Report of the Panel, *United States—Trade Measures Affecting Nicaragua* (L/6053) (Oct. 13, 1986).

127. *Id.* at ¶ 4.5.

128. *Id.* Further, Nicaragua's argument in this case that "GATT did not exist in a vacuum but was an integral structure of international law" foreshadowed the Treaty Establishing the WTO of 1994, which affirmed this position.

The United States, by contrast, argued that the panel could examine neither the validity nor motivation for the invocation of national security as an excuse for departing from its GATT obligations. In short, the U.S. case was simply that a GATT member country could, in its sole discretion, determine when its national security was threatened and as such, it could to depart from its GATT obligations. In cases involving national security, the United States argued that the nullification or impairment of benefits under the GATT agreement could not be presumed.[129] In the U.S. view, the dispute was political and the judgment of the International Court of Justice was not only irrelevant to the dispute,[130] "but clearly outside the Panel's terms of reference."[131]

Agreeing with the United States, the GATT panel determined that it was precluded from examining the justification and as such the validity and motivation for the U.S. invocation of GATT's national security exception.[132] This issue of whether a security escape clause in a bilateral investment treaty can be invoked has arisen in arbitration *Proceeding between CMS Transmission Company and the Argentine Republic*.[133] In this case, the ICSID Tribunal held that such a clause authorizes a State to take whatever measures it deems necessary to protect its security interests without requesting the views of any court. However, the Tribunal added that the clause is not a self-judging clause because the legitimacy of a measure taken pursuant to such a clause may be challenged in an international tribunal, which would have jurisdiction.[134]

---

129. *Id.* at ¶ 4.9.
130. *Id.* at ¶ 4.15.
131. *Id.* at ¶ 4.16. This argument is completely analogical to the one made by Zaire in *Am. Mfg. & Trading, Inc. v. Republic of Zaire*, supra note 109.
132. *Id.* at ¶¶ 5.2, 5.3.
133. *CMS Gas Transmission Co. v. Argentine Republic*, ICSID Case No. ARB/01/8 (May 12, 2005), *available at* http://www.worldbank.org/icsid (follow "cases" hyperlink; then follow "List of Cases" hyperlink; then follow "Concluded Cases" hyperlink; then scroll to "CMS Gas Transmission Company v. Argentine Republic (ICSID Case No. ARB/01/8)").
134. *Id.* at ¶ 373. For further analysis see William W. Burke-White and Andreas von Staden, *Investment Protection in Extraordinary Times: The Interpretation and Application of Non-Precluded Measures Provisions in Bilateral Investment Treaties*, 48 VA. J. INT'L L., 307 (2008).

Thus although the security exception in the GATT regime creates a liability-free space within which trade rules would be suspended to enable a State to pursue a national security agenda without attracting responsibility for violating the rules of the trading regime, in the *Proceeding between CMS Transmission Company and the Argentine Republic*, the arbitrators decided a measure taken pursuant to this clause would be subject to international jurisdiction. Here the arbitration panel declined to agree with Argentina that Argentina should be allowed, consistent with U.S. practice, to construe its national security interests in the investment regime without having its decision reviewed by international tribunals. Thus in the trade regime, States arguably have more space to invoke the exception to advance their war agenda without attracting legal responsibility for departing from their trade obligations if they decide to do so.[135] That is why such a broad reading of Article 21 has generated much debate and opposition in the World Trade Organization (WTO) regime. This is particularly so because the entire post-World War II UN Charter system was predicated on prohibiting the use of force, and yet the system nevertheless created exceptional circumstances under which the use of forcible measures was nevertheless permissible.[136]

In short, although rules of international trade in the post-World War II era were designed to preserve the national security of their members, even if this resulted in departures from GATT obligations, the international investment regime has gone in the opposite direction. It has imposed ever heightened responsibilities on States for war destruction. Although there are differences in the substantive rules in GATT and with the typical war destruction clause that has been examined, my point is that national security in the GATT context

---

135. *See* CARL SCHMIT, THE NOMOS OF THE INTERNATIONAL LAW OF JUS PUBLICUM EUROPAEUM 99 (G.L. Ulmen trans., 2003) (noting a "historical and structural relation between such spatial concepts of free trade, and free world economy, and the idea of a free space within which to pursue free competition and free exploitation").

136. This would, of course, include the right to self-defense. However, my point here is less the self-defense exception than that the GATT regime, although intended to promote peaceful commerce following the experience of the World War II, nevertheless permitted a zone of discretion on States to unilaterally decide when to depart from this regime of trade rules to protect their national security as they perceived it.

can provide a safe harbor from attracting international legal liability. The opposite is true in the international investment context particularly as the *Proceeding between CMS Transmission Company and the Argentine Republic* shows. What is more, it is developing economies or capital-importing States that are more likely to be subject to the heightened obligations of State responsibility for war destruction in the investment context. In addition, as the Nicaragua case shows, escape clauses in the GATT context are more likely to benefit countries with enormous market power such as the United States.

My view is fortified by the ICJ's decision in the *Case Concerning Oil Platforms (Iran v. United States)*.[137] In that case, the United States was alleged to have violated the freedom of commerce and navigation clause contained in Article X(1) of the Treaty of Amity, Economic Relations, and Consular Rights it had signed with Iran. It was alleged to have done so by bombing and destroying Iranian Platforms. The Court held that the United States had not violated Article X(1). According to the Court, the United States could not have violated the freedom of commerce clause unless it could be shown that the platforms had directly and actually contributed to oil exports between Iran and the United States. In addition, the Court held that ships were only protected to the extent they were actually engaged in commercial transport at the time of their destruction.[138] In the Court's view, injury to potential commerce did not constitute injury to freedom of commerce.[139] According to the Court, "the possibility must be entertained that [freedom of commerce] could actually be impeded as a result of acts entailed by the destruction of goods destined to be exported" but only in so far as the goods to be exported were already in existence.[140] Thus, unlike in investment disputes where claimants often successfully claim both present and expected earnings from

---

137. 2003 I.C.J. 90 (Nov. 6), *available at* http://www.icj-cij.org (follow "Cases" hyperlink; then follow "List of All Cases" hyperlink; then follow "More . . . " hyperlink under "1992: Oil Platforms (Islamic Republic of Iran v. United States of America)") [hereinafter *Iran v. United States*].

138. The Court also observed that at the time of the attacks there was a U.S. oil embargo against Iran.

139. *Iran v. United States, supra* note 137, at ¶ 92.

140. *Id.*

their investments,[141] here the ICJ confined its findings to merely that which would have been physically lost by the bombings. It was irrelevant that the platforms were to be operational only within a "few days."[142] In this case, unlike in the Nicaragua GATT case discussed earlier, the Court rejected the U.S. argument that the bombing was necessary to protect international peace and security under Article XX(1)(d) of the Treaty. The court also rejected the U.S. counterclaim that certain attacks from Iran violated the freedom of commerce clause. Thus, although in this case the Court held against the U.S. claim that the attacks on the platforms were justifiable self-defense under the Charter, it nevertheless construed the freedom of commerce clause so narrowly[143] as if the clause could not be read to protect commerce generally—"whether or not there was actually any commerce going on at the time" of the bombing.[144] This decision was also inconsistent with an earlier decision in the preliminary stage of the case where the court had noted that treaty protected commerce generally and included "not merely the immediate act of purchase and sale, but also the ancillary activities integrally related to commerce."[145]

The upshot of my claim here is that by using a security lens, freedom of commerce will often take a back seat. The ICJ opinions in the *Nicaragua* decision as well as in the *Oil Platforms* case are arguably made from the vantage point of security. By contrast, in the investment context, I have shown that cases involving questions of responsibility for war destruction are decided mostly from the view of protecting alien investors. The outcome of this contrasting approach to the intersection of war and commerce is often to protect the security

---

141. For a discussion of restitution and compensation for unlawful, tortuous, and delictual conduct, see BISHOP, CRAWFORD & REISMAN, *supra* note 68, at 1278 ff (for methods of valuing losses see 1331 ff).

142. *Iran v. United States*, *supra* note 137, at ¶ 93.

143. *See Iran v. United States* (Al-Khasawheh, dissenting; Elarany, dissenting; Simma, separate opinion) *supra* note 137.

144. Separate Opinion of Judge Simma *id.* at ¶ 3.6. Notably the court's interpretation also excluded commerce with third parties other than the two contracting parties. Yet, Article VIII of the treaty seemed to contemplate such a broader view of commerce. That clause provided that in part that the treaty was intended to cover "products of the other High Contracting Party, from whatever place and by whatever type of carrier . . . by whatever route."

145. *Iran v. United States*, Preliminary Objections, 1996 I.C.J. Rep. at ¶ 819.

and investment interests of developed economies and their investors at the expense of those of developing economies and their investors.

VI. FROM FORCIBLE INTERVENTIONS TO COERCIVE AND UNEQUAL ECONOMIC RELATIONS

Briefly then, what we see here is a continuity of a structure of rules supportive of the rights of alien investors carried from the colonial past into the postcolonial present. As the public side of international law was guaranteeing the newly won right of political autonomy from colonial rule, thanks to the extension of the principle of self-determination to Africa and Asia, the continuity of rules of international economic governance oversaw continuity from the past to the present of colonial economic relations. For example, postcolonial countries in which there was European settlement were required as a condition of the grant of its independence by its former colonial power to guarantee white European settlers property and citizenship rights as well.[146] Paradoxically, the acquisition of the autonomy by the new States became the new basis on which unequal and inegalitarian relationships of international economic governance would be played out. After all, these new States were required to play by exactly the same rules that applied to the older States.

This in turn made possible the continuities of rules and obligations from the colonial past to the postcolonial present and exemplifies international law's role as "a systematic regime of accumulation"[147] in favor of rich multinational corporations with their third world allies. In Chapter 2, I examined how the conquest legitimized acquisition of territory and how colonial courts used conquest to legitimize these acquisitions of territory and those that had not been acquired by treaty or conquest. If law was central to legitimizing public and

---

146. In the Kenyan case, see Gary Wasserman, *The Independence Bargain: Kenya Europeans and the Land Issue, 1960–62*, 11 J. COMMONWEALTH POL. STUD. 99–120 (1973).

147. EDWARD SAID, ORIENTALISM 123 (1979). This is also the thesis in UGO MATTEI & LAURA NADER, PLUNDER: WHEN THE RULE OF LAW IS ILLEGAL (2008) (arguing that colonial relationships are now embodied in contemporary legal doctrines and approaches to economic reform including neoliberalism).

private acquisitions of territory and their subsequent exploitation, then postcolonial rules of international economic governance are not any different particularly as my discussion in this chapter and of resource wars in Chapter 6 shows. In this sense, rules of international economic governance seem less given than the result of the political economy of extraction and exploitation of wealth in Africa.

In this sense, rules of international economic law were as much a reflection of the exploitative nature of colonial interests as they once were of the intellectual strength of Europe. This strength dominated the doctrines and rules that governed relations between the West and non-West politically, legally, and economically.[148] From this perspective, these rules and doctrines could not immediately be expected to inaugurate a new era of equality that reversed what had become hardened and deepened rules of international economic governance. Capital-exporting States, of course, were using their intellectual strength to strenuously defend these rules by rejecting efforts to revise them.

From this vantage point, rules of international economic law then may be regarded as a set of assumptions and limitations that set the terms on which powerful and less powerful countries relate. These set of assumptions and limitations were, and continue to be based on assumptions of the superiority of Europe and the United States. The reverse is also true—the presumed inferiority of non-Europeans who lacked the technology, sophistication, and material progress that was argued to be possible only by virtue of commerce. International economic law is also a realm of specialized and privileged knowledge, such as in the arbitration proceedings involving host States and multinational investors. My contention is that this body of specialized knowledge primarily defined the prerogatives of the colonial powers and their business interests. Repeated efforts to counter and challenge this knowledge in each round of postcolonial skirmish from the nineteenth century to the present has not made much progress in loosening the hardened rules.

This hardening has been justified as necessary because of the dangerous investment area the developing world continues to be. In other words, alien investors need all the protection necessary against

---

148. *See* James Gathii, *International Law and Eurocentricity,* 9(1) Eur. J. Int'l L. 184–211 (1998).

the fragile investment climate resulting from chaos, disorder, war, and nationalization that characterizes these countries. Resistance to changing these rules therefore frequently invokes the very images of disorder and war that in the first place justified colonial conquest and the very inauguration of rules of international economic law in both the nineteenth-century Calvo clause era, as well as in the post-World War II era. To date, rules of international economic governance continue to be presented as effortlessly managing disorder in each period.

Just as rules of international law of the nineteenth century created consent for non-sovereign non-European entities to enable them to enter into treaties disposing of their territory with no other rights attached, international law today has created a sphere of rules allowing capital-importing States to be sued as private actors when they participate in market transactions without regard to whether the commercial transactions they engaged in were an exercise of a regulatory authority, rather than merely of commercial nature.[149] Thus, like colonial international law, contemporary international law rules such as the restrictive theory of immunity have stripped developing countries of their sovereign immunity and given private actors the right to sue and recover against third-world States in the courts of the developed world and in arbitral forums.[150] In addition, rules of international law such as the act of state and comity doctrines that were used by colonial governments to preclude judicial inquiry into their overseas conduct are now unavailable to defend capital-importing States when the exercise of the regulatory authority intersects with investor rights.[151] In short, rules of international law have hollowed out the sovereignty of capital-importing States when they engage in transnational commercial activity. This means that, even if a capital-importing State seeks to defend its inability to meet a commercial obligation

---

149. For an extensive analysis, see James Gathii, *The Sanctity of Sovereign Loan Contracts and Its Origins in Enforcement Litigation*, 38 GEO. WASH. INT'L L. REV. 251 (2006). *See also* Robert Wai, *The Commercial Activity Exception to Sovereign Immunity and the Boundaries of Contemporary International Legalism*, in 213 TORTURE AS TORT: COMPARATIVE PERSPECTIVES ON THE DEVELOPMENT OF TRANSNATIONAL HUMAN RIGHTS LITIGATION (C. Scott ed., 2001).
150. James Gathii, *The Sanctity of Sovereign Loan Contracts and Its Origins in Enforcement Litigation*, 38 GEO. WASH. INT'L L. REV. 251 (2006).
151. *Id.*

because of its role as a State superseded its contractual obligations, courts in first world countries would more likely still hold it liable.[152] In the international investment context with regard to State responsibility for war destruction, no case illustrates this point better than the *AAPL v. Sri Lanka.*

VII. CONCLUSIONS

At the end of the nineteenth century and the beginning of the twentieth century, the move toward institutions, such as arbitration forums, and rules as an alternative to the use of force gave new impetus to the growth of international commercial law and related institutions. These rules and institutions represented the hope that the use of force would be eclipsed as the world moved forward toward more cooperative, consensual, and noncoercive mechanisms of dispute settlement. In the nineteenth century, the capital-importing States in Latin America became acutely aware that these institutions and rules did not completely erase the coercive and uneven relations they had with capital-exporting States. In era after era of reformism from the Calvo era, to the NIEO and to the era in opposition to neoliberal economic governance, capital-importing States have had to contend with the coercive realities of the rules of international economic governance.

As such, although the rules and institutions of international economic governance have created possibilities and alternatives to the use of force in the economic relations between capital-importing and capital-exporting States, these rules have nevertheless not completely eliminated the power of capital-exporting States to influence the content and meaning of these rules.[153] Contrary to what international

---

152. *See Commercial Bank of Kuwait v. Rifidian Bank & Central Bank of Iraq*, where the Second Circuit held that a default occasioned by war, economic sanctions and the freezing of its assets making it impossible to obtain foreign currency to repay its debts did not preclude it from finding that Iraq had willfully defaulted, 15 F.3d 238, 242–43 (2d Cir. 1994).

153. Susan Strange refers to this ability to set "the rules of the game" as structural power. *See Conversation with Susan Strange, available at* http://www.geocities.com/jtrevino41/STRANGE.DOC (last visited June 4, 2003). Note,

lawyers of the early twentieth-century thought, these rules did not entirely represent a clean break from the coercive past. Instead, these rules and institutions in many ways repackaged the inequalities between capital-exporting and capital-importing States. In a variety of ways, these rules continue to perpetuate the subordinate position of these formerly colonial countries in a manner that uncannily reflects the imbalances that characterized colonial rule.

Although the denouement of forcible measures to resolve contract debt was overstated by early twentieth-century international lawyers, international law nevertheless provided avenues for dispute settlement outside the use of force in international commercial relations. The challenge for lawyers from non-Western capital-importing States therefore became whether their advocacy for revising these rules to accommodate the interests of their countries would be accepted as legitimate demands for the revision of international law. By contrast, for the most part, international lawyers of the capital-exporting States and their governments denounced the agenda of the NIEO as an illegitimate effort to exercise sovereignty over economic affairs whereas sovereignty was merely a political doctrine.[154]

I want to note in concluding that, although undemocratic capital-importing States fear loss of whatever economic sovereignty they have, rules of international investment law enable them to have access to foreign capital and investment without domestic democratic oversight. As such, the contractual nature of engaging in foreign investment decisions is often rife with corruption within capital-importing States.[155] This combination of especially friendly pro-investor rules

---

she gives the following example of the exercise of structural power: "An individual like the Pope has structural power because he manages the Catholic Church, and the Catholic Church, for example, prevents some Catholics from contraception or abortion in their range of options; so he is exercising structural power." *Id.* Further, she argues that it is "only by looking at the structural power exercised—often unconsciously—over other states, markets, private individuals, and firms by the agencies of the United States can the extent of the asymmetries of state power be appreciated." Susan Strange, *The Defective State*, 124 DAEDULUS 55, 64 (1995).

154. *See, e.g.*, Norbett Horn, *Normative Problems of a New International Economic Order*, 16 J WORLD TRADE L. 343 (1982)

155. In *World Duty Free Co. Ltd. v. The Republic of Kenya* (ICSID Case No. ARB/00/7) Award, Oct. 4, 2006, the arbitration tribunal was presented with

and corruption undermines the promise of foreign investment to contribute to increased productivity.[156] Such outcomes are even worse off in mineral-rich, war-torn, least-developed African countries that continue to attract increased amounts of foreign direct investment[157] and the accompanying human tragedy these wars result in.

---

convincing evidence of payment of a cash bribe to the then sitting head of state to procure a contract. The tribunal held that the contract was legally unenforceable because it was an affront to the public conscience.

156. See Kenneth J. Vandevelde, *The Economics of Bilateral Investment Treaties*, 41 HARV. J. INT'L L. 469 (2000) (arguing that BITs are inefficient in promoting foreign investment because they focus on "controlling and protecting the desired investment flow rather than on maximizing productivity through market allocations of capital," *id.* at 491.). Vandevelde argues that BITs merely "shift control of an asset from a local investor to a foreign investor without increasing the productive capacity of the asset" and this is occurs because these investors are more interested in controlling the movement of the capital rather than it's the promotion of its movement, *id.* at 492.

157. United Nations Conference on Trade and Development (UNCTAD), WORLD INVESTMENT REPORT 2001: PROMOTING LINKAGES (2001). This trend has continued because of the boom in natural resources in recent times, see UNCTAD, WORLD INVESTMENT REPORT: FDI FROM DEVELOPING AND TRANSITION ECONOMIES–IMPLICATIONS FOR DEVELOPMENT (2006). However as a share of global FDI flows, least-developed countries still receive a miniscule percentage.

6. SLIPPAGES OF THE PUBLIC AND PRIVATE IN RESOURCE WARS

I. INTRODUCTION

International law and international relations theory assume that States monopolize the means and the right to wage war.[1] Thus international law evaluates whether war is legally permissible given the role a State plays in initiating or conducting the war.[2] On this view, violence

---

1. John W. Meyer, *The World Polity and the Authority of the Modern State*, in STUDIES OF THE MODERN WORLD SYSTEM, 118–20 (Albert Bergesen ed., 1980); H. H. GERTH & C. W. MILLS, FROM MAX WEBER: ESSAYS IN SOCIOLOGY 78 (1946) citing Max Weber arguing that "a state is a human community that (successfully) claims the monopoly of the legitimate use of physical force within a given territory."; Nobert Elias, Power and Civility: The Civilizing Process (1982) Volume II, 104 (arguing that the "modern age is characterized by a certain level of monopolization. Free use of military weapons is denied the individual and reserved to a central authority of whatever kind . . . and likewise the taxation of the property or income of individuals is concentrated in the hands of a central social authority. The financial means thus flowing in this central authority maintain its monopoly of military force, while this in turn maintains the monopoly of taxation."); Charles Tilly, *War Making and State Making As Organized Crime*, in BRINGING THE STATE BACK IN, 169, (Peter Evans, Dietrich Rueschmeyer & Theda Skocpol eds., 1985) (arguing that the consolidation of state power in Europe was accompanied by the monopolization of violence by the State. Notably, Tilly argues that third-world states of today do not resemble sixteenth- or seventeenth-century states in their monopolization of violence, *id*. Even early international law scholars such as Grotius distinguished between public and private war and noted that public war could only be waged by those with the authority or sovereign power to conduct it, whereas private war was "an impermissible exercise of autonomy," see discussion in David Kennedy, *Primitive Legal Scholarship*, 27 HARV. INT'L L.J. 1, at 33 and 89 (1986). *See also* DAVID KENNEDY, OF LAW AND WAR (2006) (addressing how international law is mobilized to create sharp distinctions and formal boundaries including of course the public or private distinction).

2. In *Nicaragua v. United States*, the ICJ held that the right of self-defense under Article 51 of the United Nations Charter requires as a precondition that

affecting international security not attributable to a State raises difficult issues of responsibility as Judge Koijmans noted in his separate opinion in the 2005 decision of the International Court of Justice (ICJ), *Democratic Republic of Congo v. Uganda*.³ For example, there is no agreement among States, ICJ judges, or scholars of international law on whether a State has an international law right to use force in self-defense where an armed attack emanates from a non-State actor as opposed to that from a State.⁴

The assumption that States monopolize the use of force is misleading if not entirely inaccurate, particularly with regard to sham or collapsed States outside the West. Unlike their Western counterparts,⁵ many non-Western States do not have a monopoly on the use of

---

an armed attack be attributable directly or indirectly to a State. Military and Paramilitary Activities (Nicar. v. U.S.), 1986 I.C.J. (June 27). In *Congo v. Uganda*, the ICJ grappled with the complex conflict in the eastern part of the DRC where groups, whose conduct could not be attributed to the conduct of either the DRC or Uganda, were involved in wars that clearly violated both jus ad bellum and in bellum rules. Armed Activities on the Territory of the Congo (Dem. Rep. Congo v. Uganda), 2005 I.C.J. (Dec. 19).

3. Armed Activities on the Territory of the Congo (Dem. Rep. Congo v. Uganda), 2005 I.C.J. (Dec. 19). See discussion of Judge Koijmans's observations later in this chapter.

4. In *Congo v. Uganda*, the ICJ dodged this question much to the chagrin of Justice Kooijmans who reiterated his view in the *Wall* case that recent Security Council resolutions suggest that a right to self-defense against an armed attack by a non-State actor arises "without any reference to an armed attack by a State." Dem. Rep. Congo, 2005 I.C.J. at 28 (Kooijmans, separate opinion). For further analysis see James Gathii, *Case Concerning Armed Activities on the Territory of the Congo (Democratic Republic of the Congo v. Uganda) (International Decision)*, 101 AM. J. INT'L L. 142 (2007) (comment). Some scholars argue in favor of a right of self-defense even where an attack emanates from a non-State actor, e.g., Yoram Dinstein, WAR, AGGRESSION, AND SELF–DEFENCE, 204, (Cambridge Univ. Press, 4th ed. (2005) (1988) and Sean D. Murphy, *Terrorism and the Concept of "Armed Attack,"* 43 HARV. INT'L L.J. 41, 50 (Winter 2002). However, this chapter's focus is the intersection of war and commerce particularly in countries without effective governments where irregular forces control mineral resources.

5. On the monopolization of violence in Western states, see JANICE THOMPSON, MERCENARIES, PIRATES AND SOVEREIGNS: STATE-BUILDING AND EXTRATERRITORIAL VIOLENCE IN EARLY MODERN EUROPE (1994).

violence within their territory.[6] Yet, rules of international law continue to be predicated on the assumption that States monopolize the use of violence. Some of the clearest examples of the prevalence of war and violence outside the control of States, other than the obvious example of terrorist groups, include the use of force by bands of guerillas and mercenaries who control mineral resources such as diamonds often with no goal of capturing State power or without advancing a political cause where they operate. In such areas of lawlessness and minimum governance, the line between profit, which is often unrestrained, and murderous plunder over mineral resources is blurred. The disorder and violence caused by non-State groups therefore challenges international law's assumption that war is the business of States, rather than of private actors. It also demonstrates the extent to which violence has been democratized and marketed as a commodity beyond the presumed monopoly of the State.[7]

For example, in the context of resource wars in weak or collapsed States, non-State actors involved in the violent extraction of valuable minerals are linked to petty traders and ultimately to global chains of commerce.[8] These links are possible because of the demand for these minerals or resources as well as the fact that weak or collapsed States are not only administratively incapable, but also "badly financed, organizationally inept, corrupt, politically divided, and poorly informed about goings-on at the local level."[9] In such contexts, the Westphalian state with exclusive territorial jurisdiction, control,

---

6. JEFFREY HERBST, STATES AND POWER IN AFRICA: COMPARATIVE LESSONS IN AUTHORITY AND CONTROL (Princeton Univ. Press, 2000); Makau Wa Mutua, *Why Redraw the Map of Africa: A Moral and Legal Inquiry*, 16 MICH. J. INT'L L., 1113 (1995).

7. For an insightful analysis, see LAW AND DISORDER IN THE POSTCOLONY (Jean Comaroff & John Comaroff et al. eds., 2006) (they show that although most postcolonies thrive on disorder, they still fetishize the law).

8. As Jean and John Camaroff argue, there are "dangerous liaisons between north and south, about the ways in which 'respectable' metropolitan trade gains by deflecting the risks and moral outlaw of commerce 'beyond the border,'" Jean Comaroff & John Comaroff, *Introduction* to LAW AND DISORDER IN THE POSTCOLONY 17 (Jean Comaroff & John Comaroff eds., 2006).

9. James Fearon & David Laitin, *Ethnicity, Insurgency, and Civil War*, 97 AM. POL. SCI. REV. 80 (2003).

and jurisdiction has been the exception than the norm.[10] Yet, although conflicts over valuable tradable resources are often noninternational, access to global trade networks ensures these resources reach the world market.[11] Thus "domains of prosperity and order" in the markets where these minerals are sold "feed off, and perpetuate, zones of scarcity and violence" in collapsed, weak, and sham States.[12]

As such, an attribution analysis of where responsibility for the violent conduct of non-State actors lies, rather than revealing or merely revealing State actors, a whole array of non-State actors involved in commerce would surface.[13] Unfortunately, *ad bellum* rules of international law relating to the illegal use of force are not designed to track responsibility to non-State actors where their conduct cannot be tracked back to a State. Although international law's *jus in bello* rules certainly apply even to noninternational armed conflict, the very efficacy of these rules is called into question by State weakness, because States are primarily charged with the enforcement of these norms.[14]

---

10. Miles Kahler, *Territoriality and Conflict in an Era of Globalization*, in TERRITORIALITY AND CONFLICT IN AN ERA OF GLOBALIZATION (Miles Kahler & Barbara F. Walter eds., 2006), argues that "Scrutiny of the concept of territoriality leads to a more contingent and mutable formulation of unit variation rather than the conventional static view of territoriality within international relations—a 'Westphalian' system populated by precisely delimited territorial states." at 1.

11. *Id.* at 14.

12. COMAROFF & COMAROFF, *supra* note 8, at 18.

13. For example, one author notes that "smuggling within respected channels of the diamond trade is, like all else related to it, a very well-organized and long standing system. The largest cutting and polishing centers in the world, in Bombay and Surat, India, were founded on smuggled goods that made their way from DTC customers in Belgium via German courier, with the finished stones then being smuggled back," GREG CAMPBELL, BLOOD DIAMONDS: TRACING THE DEADLY PATH OF THE WORLD'S MOST PRECIOUS STONES 38 (2004).

14. *See* Article 17(a) and (b) of the Rome Statute, which respectively provide that a case will be inadmissible before the International Criminal Court if: (a) "The case is being investigated or prosecuted by a State which has jurisdiction over it, unless the State is unwilling or unable genuinely to carry out the investigation or prosecution; (b) The case has been investigated by a State which has jurisdiction over it and the State has decided not to prosecute the person concerned, unless the decision resulted from the unwillingness or

This chapter seeks to demonstrate that the public or private distinction that undergirds the view that States have a monopoly of violence of the means to wage war, although inaccurate, continues to inform contemporary debates in international law in the context of conflicts over resources such as diamonds. What is more, the doctrine of statehood guarantees States that have no effective control of their territory the benefit of Statehood in relations with other States and with international institutions although indeed they are sham States. Donors and international institutions such as the Bretton Woods institutions that continue their relations with sham States therefore contribute to the façade under which stateless groups operate under the shadow of sham States. States such as Somalia, which have had no functioning central government with any amount of control over its territory for more than a decade continue to be represented in international bodies like the United Nations, thereby legitimizing their sham existence.[15] William Reno, who refers to these sham States as *shadow States*, argues that they are "the product of personal rule, usually constructed behind the façade of de jure state sovereignty."[16] In these sham States non-State actors tend to exercise abundant authority often threatening the very existence of these weak States. In turn, political

---

inability of the State genuinely to prosecute." This chapter is not about the *jus in bello* law that applies in resource conflicts.

15. PAUL COLLIER, THE BOTTOM BILLION: WHY THE POOREST COUNTRIES ARE FAILING AND WHAT CAN BE DONE ABOUT IT 4–5 (2007); William Reno notes,

> Nearly all governments recognize shadow states as interlocutors in global society and conform to the practice of extending sovereignty by right to former colonies. This principles applies in cases where formal state capacity is practically nil. For example, Somalia holds a seat in the United Nations, exists as an entry in World Bank tables, and presumably has access to foreign aid, provided an organization there can convince outsiders that is the rightful heir to Somalia's existing sovereignty. . . . Jackson observed that this leads to external support for de jure sovereignty of states with very weak internal administrations, relieving rulers of the need to strengthen institutions to protect productive groups in society, from which regimes could extract income.

William Reno, *Shadow States and the Political Economy of Civil Wars*, in GREED AND GRIEVANCE: ECONOMIC AGENDAS IN CIVIL WARS 45 (Mats Berdal & David M. Malone, 2000).

16. *Id.*

actors in these States prefer to exercise authority through the market for resources such as minerals within their States.[17] Resource wars in weak States therefore exhibit competing factions of State and non-State actors all connected to networks of transnational commerce that buy their booty. Although the rules of international law prohibiting the use of force are directed against States, clearly non-State actors are no less capable of using force and violence in the same way States do in the scramble for control and extraction of resources to make the money that sustains their existence. Indeed, the history of international law is replete with the involvement of non-State actors using war and violence to advance commercial and other goals as this chapter shows.

A major purpose of this inquiry is to show how the sharp distinctions and boundaries between public and private realms in relation to the monopolization of violence contributes to the ambivalent commitments of the global legal order—and of international law in particular—in dealing with non-State actors engaged in initiating or starting wars in the context of resource wars. In short, my claim is that international law is split at the root. It is split at a number of levels: first, it is split in proceeding from the premise that the use of force (violence) can only be evaluated for its lawfulness if it fulfills certain criteria that relate to the conduct of a State, but where it involves the conduct of non-State actors such violence or use of force largely, although not exclusively—arguably falls outside the scope of the rules of *jus ad bellum*.[18]

---

17. *Id.* at 44.
18. The Nuremberg prosecutions of German industrialists are a rare exception to the prosecution of non-State entities (not individuals) for their role in supporting war. On this see, Hjalmar Schacht, *The Party and Big Business, in* THE TRIAL OF THE GERMANS: AN ACCOUNT OF THE TWENTY-TWO DEFENDANTS BEFORE THE INTERNATIONAL MILITARY TRIBUNAL AT NUREMBERG 23 (Eugene Davidson ed., 1966); For a recent view, see ANDREW CLAPHAM, HUMAN RIGHTS OBLIGATIONS OF NON-STATE ACTORS (2006) (discussing the obligations of rebel groups, mercenaries and other non-State actors for human rights obligations in the context of war). *See also* UN Econ. & Soc. Council [ESOSOC], Sub-Comm. on the Promotion and Prot. of Human Rights, *Human Rights Principles and Responsibilities for Transnational Corporations and Other Business Enterprises*, U.N. Doc. E/CN.4/Sub.2/2002/WG.2/WP.1 (Feb. 2002). It is important to note that individuals are liable for war-related

Contemporary international law is also split at its root because it has traditionally underplayed the role of private actors in creating and conducting the use of force and violence. Yet, eighteenth- and nineteenth-century chartered trading corporations in the colonies were explicitly mandated to wage war to expand the commercial interests of European States consistently with prevailing understanding of international law at the time. The resource conflicts of the twentieth and twenty-first centuries, which also primarily involve non-State actors, have strikingly similar parallels with mercantile and chartered trading corporations in the colonies—although today, international law arguably proceeds from the premise that only States have the monopoly of the means and the right to lawfully engage in violence and war.[19] In short, the resource conflicts of today are analogous in many respects with the use of violence by chartered companies. Like the chartered companies of earlier periods, the roving bandits, mercenaries, and guerillas controlling resource zones seek, protect, and expand their commerce in a manner in that demonstrates that violence has not been "dedemocratized, demarketized and deterritorialized,"[20] contrary to international law's premise that States have a monopoly of violence.

Ultimately, rules of international law relating to the use of force artificially separate the legality of the use of force as used by States, from the use of forcible measures by non-State actors even when the

---

offenses for the crimes defined in the Statute of the International Criminal Court. See also Report On the Meaning of Armed Conflict in International Law, INTERNATIONAL LAW ASSOCIATION COMMITTEE ON THE USE OF FORCE (2008), available at http://www.ila-hq.org/en/committees/index.cfm/cid/1022 (follow "Conference Report Rio 2008" hyperlink) (noting that acts of terrorism even when committed on a regular basis have not been treated as constituting armed conflict but rather as crimes). The Report is discussed in Mary O'Connell, Defining Armed Conflict, 13 J. OF CONFLICT & SEC. L. 393 (2008).

19. My argument is not that these private actors are not involved in war, in fact they are as I show in this chapter. Further, my argument is not to simply suggest that these private actors are involved in war especially in supporting their commercial interests and therefore that international law needs to catch up. Rather, my argument is an exposition of the discipline's pretense and therefore acquiescence as it were of the private uses of otherwise prohibited violence if it were meted out by States.

20. THOMPSON, supra note 5, at 4.

history of the role of international law is deeply implicated in acquiescing to and legitimating the spread of commerce and the acquisition of territory through the use of force.[21] What is more, to the extent that there are standards being developed to govern the extraction of mineral resources, this has involved developing "soft" rather than hard norms.[22] That is to say that those standards being formulated to govern the role of private actors in resource conflicts as evidenced by the Kimberley Transparency Initiative with regard to "blood diamonds," are not legally binding as rules relating to the resort to use of force by States.

This failure so far to establish explicitly categorical and enforceable rules prohibiting the use of force in the activities of local and transnational actors engaged in resource extraction in the third world is striking given the hardness of the rules prohibiting the use of force and regulating the use of force when the actors involved are States. What makes these differences all the more striking is that the prohibitions on resort to force where States are involved are predicated on safeguarding the territorial integrity and political independence of States, precisely the twin concerns that arise when non-State actors resort to the use of force. In short, non-State actors threaten the territorial integrity and political independence of States much the same way that resort to the use of force does with reference to State actors,[23] and yet rules of international law have been slow to begin addressing the use of force by non-State actors in the same way.

In effect, the emerging regimes of soft or voluntary rules and standards may be argued to have the effect of ineluctably facilitating the activities of local and transnational actors to extract mineral resources in so far as they do not categorically impose binding international legal sanctions on these non-State actors not to use force in the same way that they apply to States. This arguably results in the facilitation of the commercial interests of transnational and local actors. Even if one was not persuaded that the absence of a strict norm prohibiting non-State actors from engaging in forcible measures, it is clear that the thriving global trade in resources such as diamonds and hardwood

---

21. Of course today the acquisition of territory through the use of force is prohibited under international law.
22. Except perhaps in areas such as the War Against Terrorism.
23. See discussion of resource wars below.

timber benefit directly from the forcible extraction of these resources at lower costs than if these resources were peaceably extracted. This is because wars make it difficult for weak States to build institutions that can enforce the collection of taxes and royalties. Without the income that taxes and royalties generate from resources, these States have no income to build the kind of institutions necessary to provide alternative and legitimate avenues of resource extraction.

Wars over resources in these countries coincide with the promotion of free markets in mineral-extraction activities. For example, the World Bank has proposed mineral-rich countries should have minimal regulatory restrictions in the mining sector. On this view African governments have been advised to shed their "public sector orientation" in mineral-extraction activities by privatizing government-owned mines so that the private sector with experienced multinational firms can take the lead in the operation and management of these mines. The World Bank further recommends that these firms should not be encumbered with a taxing regime based on output but rather one based on earnings.[24] The Bank further calls for better regulation of informal mining activities.

This laissez-faire regulatory regime being recommended together with the soft norms that are being formulated to oversee mineral extraction involving the use of force by private actors in turn illustrates the split within international law between public and private uses of violence. As this chapter will demonstrate, the distinction between State and non-State violence[25] is hardly sustainable.[26]

Although I emphasize the nature of sham States and the manner in which they are overwhelmed by non-State actors that have a higher capability to mete out violence, than State militaries, to achieve their objectives, I do not subscribe to the view that the solution to these challenges is to expand the right of self-defense to give States a right to defend themselves if attacked by non-State actors. Neither do

---

24. World Bank, *Strategy for African Mining*, Africa Technical Department Series, Technical Paper No. 181 (1992).

25. See *infra* notes 61 ff and accompanying text below.

26. American legal realism has long challenged distinctions such as those between public and private state and market and so on, *see, e.g.*, Duncan Kennedy, *The Stages in the Decline of Public/Private Distinction*, 130 U. PA. L. REV. 1349 (1982).

I subscribe to the view that third States should have the right to forcibly intervene on behalf of these sham States. I also do not want to be read as advocating for a recolonization of these sham States. Rather, I am calling attention to the particular valence of the State form and its connections to transnational commerce in sham States.

To achieve the foregoing objectives, I track two genealogical antecedents to today's resource wars. First, I trace the role of mercantile companies with a special focus on King Leopold II's International African Association. Thereafter, I examine the acquisition of territory in Swaziland by the British through an examination of the legal skirmishes over a violation of a concession to reserve certain territory to the Swazi's as European settlement advanced. Finally, I briefly examine today's resource wars with special reference to the blood diamond trade.

II. GENEALOGICAL ANTECEDENTS TO TODAY'S RESOURCE WARS

A. Antecedent One: Mercantile Companies with Special Reference to King Leopold's International African Association

One of the major ways in which European countries established colonial rule was through chartering mercantile companies.[27] These companies used their private capital to establish trading and commercial monopolies over territories in the New World as well as in Asia and Africa. In sub-Saharan Africa at the end of the nineteenth century, various mercantile companies were engaged in a scramble for the vast unexplored hinterlands. Examples of such companies abound—from the East India Company to the Imperial British East Africa Company and so on.

---

27. RAMKRISHNA MUKHERJEE, THE RISE AND FALL OF THE EAST INDIA COMPANY: A SOCIOLOGICAL APPRAISAL, (1974); P. E. Roberts, *The East India Company and the State*, in 5 THE CAMBRIDGE HISTORY OF INDIA: BRITISH INDIA, 1497–1858 (H. H. Dodwell ed., 1929); William Seymour, *The Company That Founded an Empire: The First Hundred Years of the Rise to Power of the East India Company*, 19 HISTORY TODAY, Sept. 1969, at 641–50; Arnold A. Sherman, *Pressure from Leadenhall: The East India Company Lobby 1660–1678*, 50 BUS. HIST. REV., 329–53 (Autumn 1976).

European States chartered these mercantile corporations empowering them with "military, judicial and diplomatic power."[28] For example, the Dutch's East India Company was authorized "to make war, conclude treaties, acquire territories and build fortresses."[29] Although they were for the most part privately financed, these mercantilist corporations were therefore hardly private organization as they exercised quasi-sovereign authority.[30] The importance of these mercantile corporations for European States lay in the fact that the States did not have the economic wherewithal or political support at home to pursue territorial acquisitions or trade monopolies. As such, by chartering mercantile corporations these States could then evaluate whether to assume sovereignty over the territories and trade monopolies acquired by mercantile companies.[31] As Janice Thompson has persuasively argued, the conduct of mercantile companies broke down distinctions between "the economic and political, non-state and state, property rights and sovereignty, [and] the public and private."[32]

Take the example of King Leopold II of Belgium. Because Belgian law prohibited him from spending State funds to pursue territorial conquests and trade monopolies abroad, he established a private company, the International African Association. King Leopold then

---

28. THOMPSON, supra note 5, at 10.
29. Quoting Id. at 10–11.
30. SIBA GROVOGUI, SOVEREIGNS, QUASI-SOVEREIGNS AND AFRICANS: RACE AND SELF DETERMINATION IN INTERNATIONAL LAW, (Univ. of Minn. Press, 1996). See also Philip Jessup & Francis Deak, The Origins, in 1 NEUTRALITY: ITS HISTORY, ECONOMICS AND LAW (Colum. Univ. Council for Res. in Soc. Sci., 1935).
31. THOMPSON, supra note 5, at 10–11.
32. Id.; see also LUCY SUTHERLAND, THE EAST INDIA COMPANY IN EIGHTEENTH CENTURY POLITICS 51 (1957) (where in analyzing the workings of the East India Company notes: "The crucial weakness of the eighteenth century standard of political morality, seen through the eyes of its successors, was that private and public interests of those taking part in the political life were insufficiently distinguished either by the sanctions of political organization or by the influence of informed public opinion. To make a comfortable life fortune in the public service and to establish those dependent on him in situations of profit was the major . . . and the legitimate ambition of the ordinary politician.").

funded Henry M. Stanley, a naturalized American[33] explorer to *discover* the mineral-rich Congo region and the source of the Congo River while entering into hundreds of treaties with African chiefs. Stanley delivered these treaties to King Leopold's private company, the International African Association.[34]

King Leopold II then began seeking international legal recognition of his International African Association by European States as well as by the United States. He used the Berlin conference of 1884 at which European countries were defining their spheres of influence in the African continent to promote his vision of a Congo Free State. To achieve his objectives, he worked hard to convince the U.S. delegation to the conference of his vision of the Congo as a free State open to the commerce of all European States as well as the United States.

The United States was represented at the Berlin conference by three people: Henry S. Sanford, a credentialed associate delegate and a close confidant of King Leopold II of Belgium;[35] John A. Kasson, the American Ambassador to the conference;[36] and Henry M. Stanley, the explorer who had been procuring treaties for King Leopold II in the Congo. Like Sanford, Stanley shared King Leopold's stated goal of establishing free trade in the Congo river and free navigation of the Congo and Niger rivers and attended the conference as a technical advisor.[37]

---

33. Stanley was born in Britain. SYBIL E. CROWE, THE BERLIN WEST AFRICA CONFERENCE 1884–1885, at 14 (1942).

34. Stanley procured these treaties from more than 2000 treaties, which in part specified that the rights these chiefs had ceded "would be conceded by all to have been indisputable, since ages of succession, by real divine right." ARTHUR B. KEITH, THE BELGIAN CONGO AND THE BERLIN ACT 49 (1919).

35. Keith described Sanford as appearing to "have had a truly American enthusiasm for noble sentiments of philanthropy, as well as a keen appreciation of the business possibilities of opening to trade the Congo, and who won for the enterprise the respectful sympathy of the U.S." *Id.* at 35–36.

36. CROWE, *supra* note 33, at 97 (describing Kasson as having been distinguished "more by verbosity than by brains [and] an ardent sympathizer with Leopold's designs, as understood in American through the propaganda of Colonel Sanford").

37. CROWE, *supra* note 33, at 81 (according to Crowe, "Stanley remained throughout Leopold's faithful henchman, and only served the interests of the

Although this delegation did not officially represent the United States, the State Department and Congress endorsed the conference's primary goal of ensuring liberty of trade in the Congo basin particularly by U.S. citizens.[38] This endorsement followed intense lobbying on behalf of King Leopold by Henry Sanford who had hosted President Chester A. Arthur in his Florida ranch[39] and who had for a long time supported the Republican party.[40] President Arthur endorsed the benevolent mission of the International African Association in the Congo in a report to Congress that closely tracked a draft that Sanford had prepared for him.[41]

After the first preliminary report on the conference reached the United States Senate on April 10, 1884, the Senate decided to recognize the flag of the International Association of the Congo, (the new name of King Leopold's International African Association), and appointed a commercial agent for the Congo basin.[42] Sanford procured this recognition from the Senate through an intensive campaign that has been described as "probably the most sophisticated piece of Washington lobbying on behalf of a foreign ruler in the nineteenth century."[43]

United States in so far as these were themselves subservient to those of the King of the Belgians.").

38. Message from President of the United States to the House of Representatives on the Congo Conference at Berlin, 48th Cong. (2d. Sess. 1884–1885) 29 H.R. Exec. Docs. No. 247 at 179.

39. Adam Hochschild, King Leopold's Ghost: A Story of Greed, Terror, and Heroism in Colonial Africa 76 (1998).

40. Id. at 77.

41. Id. at 78.

42. The Senate resolution read in part that the "prospective rich trade in the Congo valley should be opened to all nations on equal terms." Id. at 3. Kasson was instructed that the United States' most important objective was "free participation in the trade and intercourse of that newly opened country by vessels and citizens of the U.S." Id. at 5. This resolution was largely based on Henry Sanford, the U.S. Trade Representative in Belgium whose business interests coincided with King Leopold's design of a free trade zone in the Congo. Id. at 80. On October 22, 1884, the U.S. Secretary of State issued a letter recognizing the International Association of the Congo. The letter inadvertently referred to the Association by its old name, the International African Association, see Thomas Packenham, The Scramble for Africa: White Man's Conquest of the Dark Continent, 1876–1912, at 246 (1991).

43. Hochschild, supra note 39, at 80.

Sanford had wined and dined members of the Senate in Washington to achieve this support. He in particular procured the support of Senator John Tyler Morgan of Alabama a former confederate brigadier general. Senator Tyler supported Sanford's claim that the International Association of the Congo's goal of establishing freedom of commerce within a free African State would provide a home for freed black slaves in the United States so that white America would not be threatened by their dreams of equality.[44]

The recognition of the Association by the United States was a huge diplomatic victory for King Leopold who sought to legitimize Belgian claims in the Congo. This recognition goes to fortify a major theme of this chapter, that without the close collaboration between the private entities such as the International Association of the Congo and State recognition by the United States and European States, the expansion of territorial, trade, and commercial presence that was often accompanied with the use of violence in the Congo and elsewhere may not have occurred as it did.

In fact, it was the recognition of the private International Association of the Congo by these States that legitimized King Leopold's ever-growing claims in an interior part of the Continent that rival European powers had little prior knowledge of.[45] King Leopold had appealed to the Senate and the President in a variety of ways and in particular by proclaiming his support for unrestricted free trade and by representing the Association as having similar goals of establishing a State in the Congo like Liberia, then only recently established by former U.S. slaves.[46] In addition, he promised to suppress the slave trade[47] and to secure the welfare of the barbarous people of the Congo under European tutelage.[48] It is noteworthy that

---

44. *Id.* at 79.
45. *Id.* at 86.
46. *See* HOCHSCHILD, *supra* note 39, at 77–78 (noting that the choice of Liberia could not have been better "since it had not been the United States government that had resettled ex-slaves in Liberia, but a private society, like Leopold's International Association of the Congo"). On the establishment of the U.S.-backed Liberian state and its subsequent related decay into anarchy, see IKECHI MGBEOJI, COLLECTIVE INSECURITY: THE LIBERIAN CRISIS, UNILATERISM AND GLOBAL ORDER (2003).
47. CROWE, *supra* note 33, at 80; HOCHSCHILD *supra* note 39, at 78.
48. HOCHSCHILD, *supra* note 39, at 80.

King Leopold was making these promises only about two decades after the banning of the Atlantic Slave Trade by treaty and two decades after the emancipation proclamation in the United States. As S. E. Crowe[49] and Adam Hochschild[50] have shown, Stanley and Sanford were crucial to Leopold's procurement of the support of the American government for the proclaimed beneficent goals of his private company and Belgium's ultimate acquisition of the Congo as a colony.

The recognition of King Leopold's company by the United States gave Belgium the visibility before Portugal, Britain, France, and Germany, which were all interested in extending their colonial conquests into the Congo but did not have as much information about the Congo as King Leopold had from Stanley's travels. The conflicting ambitions of these powers over the Congo laid the basis of Leopold's adroit suggestion at the Berlin conference for the formation of an independent State, the International Congo Commission, in Central Africa that would guarantee all European countries and the United States freedom of commerce in the Congo.[51] The Berlin conference was taking place against a backdrop of growing mistrust and mutual suspicion particularly of the designs of King Leopold's scheme of acquiring the Congo about which Stanley's travels had started revealing in the European and American press. There was suspicion about whether King Leopold would ultimately convert his private International African Association into the internationally recognized International Association of the Congo and ultimately into a State—the international Congo Commission—which he had advocated as a neutral territory free of any national interest to be governed on the basis of the idealism of philanthropists and explorers like Stanley.[52]

---

49. See generally CROWE, supra note 33.

50. See HOCHSCHILD, supra note 39, at 61–87.

51. See CROWE, supra note 33, at 84–85. According to Crowe, "The combination of Bismarck's wholehearted support of the International Association, born out of his fear of French tariffs on the Congo, with Great Britain's halfhearted support of it, born out of the same fear, qualified by an instinctive mistrust of Leopold . . . was destined to have important results at the conference." Id. at 90.

52. Leopold managed to payoff journalists in Europe and the United States about the Association's mission of "rendering lasting and disinterested services to the cause of progress." HOCHSCHILD, supra note 39, at 66.

In this episode then, we see how the establishment of a private company[53] by King Leopold and his private funding of Stanley to conduct an expeditionary force[54] disguised his plans to get an African colony.[55] Thus through a private association, King Leopold was doing what other European States had been doing in the rest of Africa—acquiring African territory or trading interests through private groups or chartered companies, which then sought the imprimatur of their governments.

Leopold's hiring of Stanley as his personal employee goes to show how private groups and chartered companies were jostling not simply for territorial administrative control, but rather jurisdiction over the fiscal resources with a view to sustaining a free trading system, that they had been establishing for decades before, unencumbered by the cost of territorial administration.[56] Further, this example also shows that these private entities were not too far off removed from the power of the European States of the time. Indeed, the nature of European rivalries in the last part of the nineteenth century was to open up new areas to European commercial activity or to consolidate existing commercial routes, stations, and trading posts, which were previously controlled and managed extraterritorially[57] by strong rules safeguarding the property rights of these European nationals rather than simply capturing territory for administration. Once private groups or chartered companies managed to procure trade and commercial monopolies, they approached their home States to buy them off. For example, the Imperial British East Africa sold its commercial and trade monopoly over East Africa for £250,000 in 1895 to the

---

53. *Id.* at 65.
54. *Id.* at 63.
55. *Id.* at 61 and 63. According to Hochschild, King Leopold II entered into five-year contract with Stanley under which Stanley would be paid 25,000 francs a year for time spent in Europe and 50,000 francs for time spent in Africa leading an expeditionary force there and setting up posts as he made his way into the interior of the Congo. As already noted, King Leopold changed the name of the essentially nonexistent International African Association into the International Association of the Congo just ahead of the Berlin Conference of 1884, CROWE, *supra* note 33, at 13.
56. J. D. Hargreaves, *The Making of the Boundaries: Focus on West Africa*, in PARTITIONED AFRICANS 21–22 (A. I. Asiwaju ed., 1985).
57. *Id.*

British government after British government refused to finance the operations of the Company.[58] This sale ended the Imperial British East Africa Company's seven-year trade and commercial monopoly.[59] The directors of the Imperial British East Africa Company decided to sell the Protectorate to the British government to make the company's commercial and trading ventures profitable, as the British government would assume thereafter the task and cost of administering the territory.[60]

What then is the lesson of the International Association of the Congo's experience and this brief rendition of the Imperial British East Africa Company? Through private entities both Britain and Belgian acquired colonies and all the mineral territory and mineral resources that came with these territories. In Belgium's case, once Belgium had acquired Congo, the stage was then set for one of the most brutal episodes of colonial governance and economic plunder. Clearly, the connections not only between the public and private as well as the commercial and the violent came very well together in the colonial context. These instances show that far from being distinct, public and private collaboration and violence often worked together to achieve the goals of commercial expansion and territorial acquisition.

B. Antecedent Two: The Acquisition of Swazi Territory by the British and the *Sobhuza II* Case

The main issue in the *Sobhuza* case arose in relation to a claim of trespass by a British corporation owned by two settlers[61] over territory that had been reserved for the sole and exclusive use of Swazi natives under a concession to the company made by the King of Swaziland on December 17, 1890.[62] As a protectorate, Swaziland was outside the

---

58. *See* Mwangi Wa Githumo, Land and Nationalism in East Africa: The Impact of Land Expropriation and Land Grievances upon the Rise and Development of Nationalist Movements in Kenya 1884–1939, at 204–05 (Feb. 1974) (unpublished PhD dissertation, New York Univ.) (on file with Bobst Library, New York Univ.).

59. *See id.* at 205.

60. *See id.* at 204–05.

61. The Court mentions the names of those granted the concession as Thorburn and Watkins. *Id.* at 529, 526.

62. *Id.* at 521.

jurisdiction of the Crown and was therefore considered a foreign country. However, the Privy Council held that de facto, Swaziland "approximated in constitutional status to a Crown Colony and was therefore de jure within the jurisdiction of the Crown. This status in turn gave the Crown the power to make laws for the peace, order and good government of Swaziland, and of all persons therein."[63] As such, the Court held, "[a]ny original native title had . . . been effectually extinguished."[64]

What is really peculiar about the *Sobhuza* case is that as individuals defending their occupation of Swazi territory in violation of the Concession of December 17, 1890, the respondents relied on little or nothing in their *private* capacity—as individuals or as the corporation that had entered into the Concession with the King of Swaziland.[65] Rather than invoking private law claims or defenses in the law of contracts or property, (e.g., a claim of adverse possession), the respondents relied on public law norms regarding the authority of the Crown. Intuitively, one would have expected that private individuals defending their right to use territory that did not belong to them would have relied less on a claim of authority of the Crown than on a claim of title connected to them in their individual or corporate capacities. Instead, the respondents relied exclusively on the authority of the Crown and its claim of ownership over Swazi territory even though Swaziland was not formally a protectorate of the Crown.

Here then we see a continuity between a claim to territory made by individuals or corporations, on the one hand, and those made by the Crown on the other. In effect, valid title to territory by the Crown over Swazi territory was good enough to legitimize title to territory held by British settlers rather than by the British Crown. In effect, the *Sobhuza* court concurred with the arguments of the respondents that what the Crown owned could be claimed by British settlers to be their own as well. It of course helped that the settlers could show they had a grant of the disputed land made to them by the Crown notwithstanding express limitations making the disputed land outside settler occupation, a stipulation to which the Crown itself had agreed to. What is

---

63. *Id.*
64. *Id.* at 522.
65. *Id.* at 521 (The Court refers to respondents Thorburn and Watkins as "the respondent company.").

more, defects in the title to land held by private individuals—because of the limitation in the December 17, 1890, concession making the disputed land for the sole and exclusive use of natives—could be cured by the overriding title to native territory held by the Crown. Thus since the December 17, 1890, concession did not authorize the respondents to use or occupy the land in question in the case, legislation conferring Swazi territory on the Crown that came into effect well after 1890 could be relied on to authorize private individuals— not the Crown—to defend their occupation and use of the land. Consequently, the fact that the 1890 concession had set aside the land for the exclusive and sole use of Swazi natives is rendered irrelevant and illusory.

Remarkably for our purposes in this chapter, the authority of the Crown to hold title to the territory is justified not only on legislative grounds, but also on the basis of the Crown's authority to acquire title to territory by conquest. Notably, the British victory over the Boers in the Anglo-Boer War of 1899 is argued to have conferred upon the Crown the territory the Boers held, including the Swazi territory in question in the *Sobhuza* case. Yet, this British victory over the Boers cannot be a stand-in for victory over the Swazis[66] given that it was Swazi territory, rather than Boer territory, that was the subject of the *Sobhuza* case and was held to have been acquired by conquest. According to this reasoning, Swazi agency or consent in ceding their territory to the British was rendered irrelevant. It seemed sufficient that because the British had conquered the Boers, they had effectively acquired Swazi territory. This justification for acquisition of native land had already been applied before in a similar context in an earlier case involving the authority of the Crown over South Africa. In that case, the House of Lords held, "[w]here the King of England conquers a country . . . by saving the lives of the people conquered . . . [he] gains a right and property in such people, in consequence of which he may

---

66. The reasoning in *Sobhuza* is that even though the 1890 concession did not grant the respondents the territory in question, the Crown did so by a proclamation made by the "High Commissioner . . . on March 16, 1917," which proclaimed lands including those in issue in the case to have been granted to the respondents. The Court argued that the Crown had acquired title to the territory in 1908. *Id.* at 527–28.

impose upon them what law he pleases."[67] Similarly, the *Sobhuza* court concluded that the authority of the Crown to acquire the disputed land and to give it to the respondents was validly exercised "either under the Foreign Jurisdiction Act, or as an act of State which cannot be questioned in a Court of law," and further that the Crown "could not excepting by statute, deprive itself of freedom to make Orders in Council, even when these were inconsistent with previous orders."[68]

This doctrinal strategy of legitimizing private claims to non-European territory using the power of the Crown is not peculiar to the *Sobhuza* case. The *Ole Njogo* case determined by the East Africa Court of Appeal in 1913 raised exactly the same issues in question in the *Sobhuza* case.[69] In *Ole Njogo*, the Masai alleged that the British government had acted inconsistently with a treaty entered into with them in 1904 by opening up land set aside for the sole and exclusive use by the Masai for European occupation. The East African Court of Appeal used reasoning very similar to that of the *Sobhuza* court and found against the Masai.

What is particularly striking though is that the same doctrinal strategy used in the *Ole Njogo* and *Sobhuza* cases in the context of British colonial occupation of native territory had been used across the Atlantic in the United States Supreme Court about a century before. *Johnson v. McIntosh*[70] involved two corporations defending their ownership of land claimed by Native Americans. Hence, we have again a native (American Indian) community claiming ownership of its territory against claims by private individuals. Like in the *Sobhuza* and *Ole Njogo* cases, the individuals do not defend their right to the disputed territory using private law defenses such as on contract or property law grounds, rather they rely on the authority of the U.S. government and its claim to ownership over all the land owned by the Indians.

However, in *Johnson v. McIntosh* unlike in *Sobhuza* and *Ole Njogo*, Justice Marshall holds the basis for the ownership of the territory by

---

67. W. *Rand Central Gold Mining Co. Ltd. v. The King*, 2 K.B. 391, 406 (1905).
68. *Id.* at 527–28.
69. For an extended analysis of the Masai case, see James Gathii, *Imperialism, Colonialism and International Law*, 54 BUFF. L. REV. 1013 (2006).
70. *Johnson v. McIntosh*, 21 U.S. 543 (1823).

the United States as a *civilized* inhabitant was valid because "discovery gave an exclusive right to extinguish the Indian title of occupancy, either by purchase or by conquest; and gave also a right to such a degree of sovereignty, as the circumstances of the people would allow them to exercise."[71] In fact, the court in *Johnson v. McIntosh* went further holding that "conquest gives a title which the Courts of the Conqueror cannot deny, *whatever the private and speculative opinions of individuals may be, respecting the original justice of the claim which has been successfully asserted.*"[72]

III. RESOURCE CONFLICTS AND SLIPPAGES OF THE PUBLIC AND PRIVATE DISTINCTION IN INTERNATIONAL LAW

The foregoing examples so far illustrate the continuities between private and public violence, on the one hand, the expansion of commerce particularly over claims over territory and trade monopolies, on the other. They undermine a telling of the relationship between war and commerce that presupposes the monopolization of violence by States. These examples also question assumptions about the safety of commerce from the vagaries of war and commerce.

Resource conflicts over valuable minerals such as diamonds in war-torn countries such as Sierra Leone further blur the lines between public and private violence and the assumption that a liberal kind of peace would best guarantee freedom of commerce. Rather, today's resource conflicts are characterized by "bandits, slave traders, religious-military orders, and nomadic raiders"[73] who have long engaged in violent activities beyond the reach of the State. Most of these conflicts are concentrated in resource-rich, economically poor African countries.[74]

Stateless bandits, mercenaries, and other non-State and State actors use labor often under slavish and cruel conditions to prospect for high-value minerals such as diamonds. These very easily portable minerals that can be hidden in any part of the human body are then sold to intermediary businesses in or around the prospecting areas

---

71. *Id.* at 587.
72. *Id.* at 588.
73. THOMPSON, *supra* note 5, at 156 n.19.
74. COLLIER, *supra* note 15, at x.

before they find their way to brand name stores and other outlets in Europe, Asia, the United States, and elsewhere.[75] In resource conflicts therefore, there is a symbiosis between ruthlessly violent non-State bandits such as the Revolutionary United Front (RUF)[76] of Sierra Leone, which chop off the limbs of innocent civilians in their terror campaigns, on the one hand, and privately owned multinational corporations, which control global diamond trade, on the other.

Non-State actors unleash violence to maintain control over extraction of resources such as diamonds, timber, and gold because of the lucrative illegal trade in these resources. Their aim differs from the traditional war objective of defeating an enemy. Instead, non-State actors or bandits involved in resource extraction seem to have economic motivations to keep fighting as way of maintaining the profitability of resource extraction activities. From this perspective valuable resources are perhaps thought of much better as sustaining and aggravating factors rather than as causes of conflict. The intensification of the scramble for these resources in the international economy in large and growing economies such as India and China is unsurprisingly strongly correlated with the wars in some resource-rich areas further pointing to the transnational connections these wars have

---

75. CAMPBELL, *supra* note 13 (Greg Campbell is one of the best at describing trade in valuable minerals under these conditions.).

76. The RUF has been described as defying
all available typologies on guerilla movements. It is neither a separatist uprising rooted in a specific demand, as in the case of Eritrea, nor a reformist movement with a radical agenda superior to the regime it sought to overthrow. Nor does it possess the kind of leadership that would be necessary to designate it as [a] warlord insurgency. The RUF has made history; it is a peculiar guerilla movement without any significant national following or ethnic support. Perhaps because of its lumpen social base and its lack of an emancipatory programme to garner support from other social groups, it has remained a bandit organization solely driven by the survivalist needs of its predominantly uneducated and alienated battle front and battle group commanders. Neither the peasantry, the natural ally of most revolutionary movements, nor the students, amongst whose ranks the RUF-to-be originated, lent any support to the organization during the [first] six years of fighting.

Ibrahim Abdallah & Patrick Muana, *The Revolutionary United Front of Sierra Leone: A Revolt of the Lumpenproletariat*, in AFRICAN GUERILLAS (Christopher Clapham ed., 1998), *cited in* CAMPBELL, *supra* note 13, at 72–3.

with global commerce.⁷⁷ In many cases resource wars span across entire regions sometimes crossing national boundaries. As Richard Reno, a leading researcher on this type of warfare argues:

> [These wars do] not mark a turn toward more rigid distinctions between spheres of state authority and private enterprise . . . Intensified transnational market transactions in the context of the shadow state relationships of internal authority and markets can lay the groundwork for further integration of markets and political control.⁷⁸

In this section, I will continue demonstrating the continuities between public and private violence illustrating that the monopolization of violence by States is not only a "distinctively modern"⁷⁹ phenomenon but one that has little relevance with respect to mineral-rich, non-Western States where there seems to have been little movement of violence from non-State actors to being monopolized by the State.⁸⁰

Scholars studying resource wars fall into two main groups. In the first group are those that show the strong correlation between resource abundance and large pools of unemployed youth, on the one hand, with the high likelihood of resource wars or conflicts on the other.⁸¹ In the second group, are scholars who argue that the

---

77. MICHAEL T. KLARE, RESOURCE WARS: THE NEW LANDSCAPE OF GLOBAL CONFLICT (2001) (arguing that conflict over valuable resources has become an increasingly prominent feature of the global landscape). *See also* Celine Moyroud & John Katunga, *Coltan Exploration in Eastern Democratic Republic of the Congo (DRC)*, *in* SCARCITY AND SURFEIT: THE ECOLOGY OF AFRICA'S CONFLICT 174 (Jeremy Lind & Kathryn Sturman, 2002) arguing that "In the absence of strong state apparatus and legitimate government, coupled with the strong need for high-technology development materials on international markets, multinational corporations and local entrepreneurs have allied themselves with specific African countries to access these minerals in the DRC."

78. Reno, *supra* note 15, at 44.

79. THOMPSON, *supra* note 5, at 11.

80. Reno, *supra* note 15, at 44–45: Weak States can however exercise power indirectly by sponsoring irregular groups to control resources that in turn generate revenues clandestinely for the State.

81. Paul Collier & Anke Hoeffler, *Resource Rents, Governance and Conflict*, 49 J. CONFLICT RESOL. (2005).

coincidence of large pools of unemployed youth and resource abundance is insufficient to precipitate a conflict without a grievance.[82]

Both approaches to resource conflicts acknowledge the centrality of resources such as diamonds and other precious minerals in sparking or fueling the continuation of conflict. In addition to the lootability of minerals, the high demand of minerals such as Coltan, which is used in the defense industry and is a major import of the United States from the war-torn Democratic Republic of Congo (DRC) is a factor in conflicts. The weaknesses of States in such countries as the DRC has meant that mercenaries and all sorts of bandits and non-State actors have taken the lead in exploiting these resources and finding markets for them particularly in industrialized countries.

Two of the most significant international responses to conflicts over resources are the Kimberley Process Certification Scheme and a variety of United Nations Security Resolutions that have had little or no impact on reducing trade in diamonds mined from conflict areas.[83] The Kimberley Process was forged on the initiative of nongovernmental organizations, and the diamond industry which did not want its brand name linked to conflict diamonds as well as three of the largest diamond producers, South Africa, Botswana, and Namibia and the largest consumers, the United States, Belgium, and the United Kingdom.[84] Nongovernmental organizations such as Global Witness and Partnership Africa Canada played a central role in negotiating and configuring the set-up of the Certification Scheme.[85] The Kimberley Process resulted in the creation of the World Diamond Council in 2003 to oversee a newly created diamond-tracking system. An annual meeting between the participating

---

82. Indra de Soysa, *The Resource Curse: Are Civil Wars Driven by Rapacity or Paucity?*, in GREED AND GRIEVANCE: ECONOMIC AGENDAS IN CIVIL WARS 113–36 (Mats Berdal & David M. Malone eds., 2000).

83. For example, UN Security Council Resolutions 1127(1997); 1306(2000) and 1343(2001) with respect to diamonds from Angola, Sierra Leone, and Liberia.

84. Clive Wright, *Tackling Conflict Diamonds: The Kimberley Process Certification Scheme*, 11 INT'L PEACEKEEPING, 698–699 (Winter 2004).

85. Both the United Nations Security Council and the United Nations General Assembly endorsed the Process.

countries and nongovernmental organizations who sit as observers is held to monitor the implementation of the certification process. The purpose of this certification system was to eliminate the use of diamonds for illicit purposes such as in fueling conflict.[86] Participating countries are required to establish laws establishing control systems that monitor the importation and exportation of rough diamonds, guaranteeing that each diamond would not be allowed in or out of their country without a Kimberley Process certificate. Thus only participating countries are allowed to trade in rough diamonds with each other. The exporting country, under this scheme, is expected to certify only diamonds mined from lawful sources.[87] The aim of the Process was to create conflict-free trade zones within which only non-conflict diamonds would be traded. By September 2007, there were 48 countries who were members of the Kimberley Process.[88]

The effectiveness of the Kimberley Process has been undermined by reports that significant volumes of diamonds from rebel areas such as Cote d'Ivoire have found their way into the international diamond market through Ghana where they had been certified. Similarly the continuing maze of conflicts in the DRC and weaknesses in the implementation of the Kimberley Process certification process have not prevented conflict diamonds from finding their way into international markets.

Some of problems facing the Kimberley Process include failure to maintain adequate export and import controls that document the origin of the diamonds from the mines they originate, to their

---

86. Julie L. Fishman, *Is Diamond Smuggling Forever? The Kimberley Process Certification Scheme: The First Step Down the Long Road to Solving the Blood Diamond Trade Problem*, 13 U. MIAMI BUS. L. REV. 217 (2005). Fishman argues that "A system that requires no international watchdog or universal guidelines, and instead merely suggests ways for nations to conduct their investigations and punish violators, invites abuse and inefficiency," *id.* at 218.

87. In 2003, the WTO issued a waiver allowing countries participating in the Kimberley Process to restrict trade in conflict diamonds without violating WTO Rules, see Agreement Reached on WTO Waiver for *Conflict Diamonds* (Feb. 26, 2003) *available at* http://www.wto.org/english/news_e/news03_e/goods_council_26fev03_e.htm (last visited Sept. 26, 2008).

88. Because the EU counts as an single participant, there are indeed 78 member states in the Process.

point of sale. As such the benefits intended to be accrued by the certification process and the licensing of mines where the diamonds originate are lost. Further, weak States do not provide sufficient oversight of the diamond industry through on-site monitoring and verification as well as border controls. The Process is financed and monitored by volunteers, which in turn limits its potential to be an effective monitoring mechanism. In addition, the Kimberley Process was not designed to deal with alluvial diamonds, which is a major economic activity often accompanied by conflict.[89] In these areas, governments have little or no data on mining making it hard to track the origin of diamonds.[90]

In addition to the weakness of the States charged with implementing the Kimberley Process, one of the most significant reasons accounting for the existence of nonbinding standards in resource extraction is the conspicuous absence of a binding legal regime over the violent extraction of mineral resources to which many actors in the trade are committed.[91] By contrast, public international law establishes an elaborate legal framework for inter-State wars providing for rules on the permissibility of the use of force as well as on the rules governing the use of force. Resource wars, unlike inter-State wars sometimes involve non-State actors especially irregular forces

---

89. There is a Working Group on Artisanal and Alluvial Producers in the Kimberley Process.

90. Greg Campbell provides an excellent exploration of this. *See* CAMPBELL, *supra* note 13, at 133. Campbell suggests the Kimberley Process is an evasive solution to the wars caused by the diamond trade. Campbell further argues, "for smugglers and criminals, UN resolutions mean little," *id.* at 185.

91. This is not to suggest that international law, for example, does not address mercenarism. The specific claim is in relation to resource conflicts and generally to the inconspicuousness and mostly nonbinding nature of the few available rules outlawing mercenarism. Additional Protocol 1 to the Geneva Convention of August 12, 1949 defines a mercenary. A lot of focus on mercenarism has been in the context of anticolonial wars, and the rules reflect the issues raised by the role in the era of self-determination. *See, e.g.*, The OAU Convention for the Elimination of Mercenarism in Africa, O.A.U. Doc. CM/433/Rev. L. Annex 1 (1972); The UN International Convention Against the Recruitment, Use, Financing and Training of Mercenaries, G.A. Res., A/RES/44/34 (Dec. 4, 1989). For further discussion, see Chapter 7.

SLIPPAGES OF THE PUBLIC AND PRIVATE IN RESOURCE WARS 217

operating independently or with direct or indirect support of States, politicians and other non-State actors including local and multinational companies.[92]

Thus a widely known phenomenon—the involvement of private capital, bandits and mercenaries directly or indirectly in resource wars—has been left with an inadequate legal framework. The Kimberley Process is a voluntary rather than a binding regime of legal rules.[93] Yet, as we have seen, the transnational commercial connections of trade in resources such as diamonds has been central to the conflicts and wars in weak States. The only legally binding rules available are on the public law side involving complicity in war crimes, genocide, and crimes against humanity.[94] The role irregular forces play in fanning war directly or indirectly is therefore irremediable under international law unless these non-State actors have links with State action or unless the individual participants are prosecuted for violations of international humanitarian law.

In light of the foregoing, I can say then that even outside the context of monopolizing violence, the theoretical construct of a State as a unitary category has been demonstrated to underestimate the reality of the enmeshment with non-State actors' networks outside and

---

92. For these reasons, the Security Council and the UN General Assembly have continued to give support to the strengthening of the Kimberley Transparency Initiative, see UNGA, The Role of Diamonds in Fuelling Conflict: Breaking the Link Between the Illicit Transaction of Rough Diamonds and Armed Conflict as a Contribution to the Prevention and Settlement of Conflicts, Agenda Item 13, Nov. 21, 2007, A/62/L.16.

93. Amnesty Int'l: *Beyond Voluntary Standards: Canadians Want New Rules to Make Sure Corporations Respect Human Rights Everywhere*, AI Index AMR 20/C09/2006 (Nov. 14, 2006), *available at* http://www.amnesty.ca/resource_centre/news/view.php?load=arcview&article=3789&c=Resource+Centre+News. Article 8 of the Statute of the International Criminal Court specifies crimes related to looting and plunder whereas Article 25 may be used to prosecute those complicit in such crimes. On the potential use of the International Criminal Court in this context, see William A. Schabas, *War Economies, Economic Actors and International Criminal Law*, in PROFITING FROM PEACE: MANAGING THE RESOURCE DIMENSIONS OF CIVIL WAR 425 (Karen Ballentine & Heiko Nitchske eds., 2005).

94. Exceptions under national laws could include Canada's Crimes against Humanity and War Crimes Act.

beyond the State.⁹⁵ Most importantly, resource conflicts demonstrate how assumptions such as those relating to States as monopolies of violence overstate the extent to which State power and sovereignty are "fixed principles of international order" rather than social and political principles that have and continue to be "constituted and reconstituted"⁹⁶ in actual praxis rather than defined exclusively as abstract and theoretical principles.⁹⁷

Such abstractions are evidenced by permitting the use of force in self-defense. For a State to liable for the use of force by a non-State group, the State has to have *"effective control* of the military or paramilitary operations in the course of which the alleged violations were committed."⁹⁸ At minimum, international law requires that the conduct of the non-State actor be attributable to a State.⁹⁹ Yet resource wars are precisely possible because of weakness or complete collapse of the African State, and in particular its inability to monopolize violence.¹⁰⁰ The inability of States to wield a monopoly of violence in places such as the Democratic Republic of Congo has given rebel groups autonomy because the money they make in extracting

---

95. ANNE MARIE SLAUGHTER, A NEW WORLD ORDER (2004).

96. R. B. J. Walker, State Sovereignty, *Global Civilization, and the Rearticulation of Political Space*, World Studies Program Occasional Paper No. 18, Princeton Univ. Center of Int'l Studies 3 (1998), cited in THOMPSON, *supra* note 5, at 13.

97. *See also* the excellent discussion in Robert Wai, *The Commercial Activity Exception to Sovereign Immunity and the Boundaries of Contemporary International Legalism, in* TORTURE AS TORT: COMPARATIVE PERSPECTIVES ON THE DEVELOPMENT OF TRANSNATIONAL HUMAN RIGHTS LITIGATION 213–45 (C. Scott, ed., 2001).

98. Nicar., 1986 I.C.J., at ¶ 195 (noting that the conduct of irregular forces attributable to a State could amount to an armed attack under Article 51).

99. *See* TARCISIO GAZZINI, THE CHANGING RULES ON USE OF FORCE UNDER INTERNATIONAL LAW, 139 ff (2005).

100. *But see Prosecutor v. Dusko Tadic*, Case No. IT-94-1-A, I.CT.Y. App. Ch., 15 July 1999, ¶ 70 (where the Tribunal recognized conflicts between non-State actors for the applicability of International Humanitarian Law and made no reference to the necessity of attribution of the armed conflict to a State unlike under Article 51. In addition, unlike in *Nicaragua* the Chamber applied a lower threshold of control, i.e., *overall control*, by a State "not only by equipping and financing the group, but also by coordinating or helping in the general planning of its military activity.").

and selling natural resources can buy them military equipment and other supplies.[101] For a long time now, there has been a consensus that several African States do not have effective control over their territories, yet they continued to enjoy their internationally guaranteed juridical statehood.[102] In these sham States, the bureaucratic separation of the private and public spheres presumed in the Weberian State is absent.[103] Resource wars represent private uses of state resources outside the control of the State. Yet, rebel and irregular groups, although often autonomous in their operations are known to pay off underpaid and poorly trained military officers and governmental officials to ensure the extraction of natural resources enjoys little interference. For these irregular groups, this extraction of natural resources plays a "conflict sustaining role."[104]

Not surprisingly therefore, in his separate opinion in the 2005 International Court of Justice Case, *Democratic Republic of Congo v. Uganda*, Judge Kooijmans expressed caution in evaluating the legality of *complex conflicts* in which "regimes under constant threat from armed movements often operating from the territory of neighboring States, whose governments sometimes support such movements but often merely tolerate them since they do not have the means to control or repel them."[105] Judge Kooijmans observed this was possible because weak or collapsed States lack the power and authority to effectively exercise their territorial sovereignty.[106] In such situations, irregular forces fill the void and thrive by controlling the exploitation of natural resources. Feuding over natural resources among such irregular groups results in complex conflicts that are in turn funded by the monies made from exploiting natural resources. For these irregular groups, continuing these conflicts becomes a logical extension of

---

101. Moyroud & Katunga, *supra* note 77, at 182.
102. Robert H. Jackson, *Juridical Statehood in Sub-Saharan Africa*, 45 J. INT'L AFFAIRS 1 (1992); Robert H. Jackson & Carl G. Rosberg, *Why Africa's Weak States Persist: The Empirical and the Juridical in Statehood*, 35 WORLD POL. 1 (1982).
103. MAX WEBER, ECONOMY AND SOCIETY, 1028–29 (1978).
104. Mayround & Katunga, *supra* note 77.
105. *Case Concerning Armed Activities on the Territory of the Congo* (Dem. Rep. Congo v. Uganda) (Dec. 23, 2005) (Kooijmans, separate opinion, ¶ 5) *available at* http://www.icj-cij.org.
106. *Id.*

their desire to continue profiting from natural-resource exploitation. As a result, Judge Kooijmans observed that commitments such as those prohibiting the use of force "entered into by governments unable to implement them are unworthy of reliance from the very start and hardly contribute to the creation of more stability."[107]

IV. CONCLUSIONS

This chapter has sought to show the artificiality of the distinction between public and private violence in the context of the international legal regulation of commerce. Rather than taking for granted the assumption that States monopolize violence, this chapter investigated how the boundary between public and private violence was blurred and contested in the specific contexts of territorial acquisitions, mercantile corporations, and resource wars. What this chapter shows therefore is that at least for more than a century, the boundary between public and private violence in the context of commerce did not simply reflect or produce the theoretical distinction between legitimate public and illegitimate private violence. Rather, a more complex, fluid, even arbitrary relationship between not only public and private violence, but also between national and transnational and international commerce, as well as between the political and economic emerges.[108] This means that perhaps only in a very traditionalist sense is it tenable to maintain a doctrinal position that authoritatively defends the monopolization of violence exclusively by States. Such a pursuit of conceptual clarity and coherence is belied by incoherencies and inconsistencies on the relationship between violence and public and private actors addressed in this chapter.

If this is the case, then international law's assumptions about the measuring the legality of violence on the baseline of state monopolization of it is demonstrated to be greatly undermined. In effect, international law is therefore split at its root in continuing to be based on a theoretical construct that has no bearing on the ground

---

107. *Id.*
108. For a scholar reaching a similar conclusion in the context of State-building see Obiora Okafor, *After Martyrdom: International Law, Sub-State Groups, and the Construction of Legitimate Statehood in Africa*, 41 HARV. INT'L L.J. 503, 506 (2000) (discussing what he refers to as the "violentization" of statehood).

particularly in places such as the Democratic Republic of Congo and other resource-rich non-Western countries. It may be argued that the African State is no more than a legitimization or Africanization of inherited regimes of colonial governance without removing the predatory actors who typified colonial rule.[109]

The demonstration in this chapter that non-State violence over commerce is a persistent historical fact has affirmed an important theme pursued in this book, namely that international law inaccurately portrays commerce as enjoying safe passage during war. Thus it may be an overstatement to argue that States (especially developing States) once monopolized control over war, and now there is a transformation dispersing or marketing war and therefore making it available to non-State actors.[110] Instead, this chapter through a series of examples including resource conflicts over precious minerals such as diamonds shows that non-State involvement in war and commerce recur quite frequently in the history of international law. Indeed, resource wars demonstrate that rather than undermining commerce entirely, wars indeed support and enable commerce especially over the mineral resources over which conflict arises. In resource wars, the relationship between "private power, commerce and state institutions in weak states" is seen most acutely.[111]

Yet, contemporary efforts to address the illegality and illegitimacy of the use of war and violence to support resource conflicts with regard to non-State actors have fallen short of being categorical in their prohibition of the use of violence in the same way international law prohibits use of force between States under Article 2(4) of the United Nations Charter. Thus although on the public side international law has a standard of especially higher normativity prohibiting the use of force between States, on the private side there is no equivalent norm prohibiting to the same extent the use of violence at the intersection of war and commerce.[112] It is for these reasons that international law is

---

109. Reno, *supra* note 15, at 63.
110. *See, e.g.*, MARTIN VAN CREVELD, THE TRANSFORMATION OF WAR (1991).
111. Reno, *supra* note 15, at 44.
112. My claim is limited to cases at the intersection of war and commerce where there is generalized state collapse or ineffective control by a State such as in the Democratic Republic of Congo. There are instances in which the conduct of irregular forces or non-State actors can be much more readily attributable to an effective State. For the approaches that may be taken to

split at its root between public and private consequences of the use of violence.

It must also be noted in concluding this chapter that unfortunately, the telling of the story of war has been dominated by what the leading military historian Jeremy Black has called "Eurocentrism."[113] The telling of the story of war has largely neglected war outside the West and has as such failed to provide categorizations that would make sense of the kind of wars not typified by the monopolization of violence by the State. In States without effective control over their territory, rather than being organized vertically, sovereignty is a "horizontally woven tapestry of partial sovereignties" that are and have become the "endemic condition of the postcolony."[114] By expanding the scope of what is defined as war to incorporate the experiences that constitute war in non-Western societies, international law could begin addressing its Eurocentric distinctions between the public and the private; the political and the economic as well as between the State and non-State.[115] Rules such as those relating to the permissible use of force in the context of irregular forces have come into sharp focus in the recent past precisely because they were not designed to take into account the discontinuous, overlapping sovereignties and pluralities that now characterize violent resource-rich postcolonies.

---

create state responsibility for the conduct of irregulars, see Vincent-Joel Proulx, *Babysitting Terrorists: Should States be Strictly Liable for Failing to Prevent Transborder Attacks?*, 23 BERKELEY J. INT'L L. 615 (2005); Derek Jinks, *State Responsibility for the Acts of Private Armed Groups*, 4 CHI. J. INT'L L. 83 (Spring 2003); Tom Ruys et al., *Attacks by Private Actors and the Right to Self Defense*, 10 J. CONFLICT & SECURITY L. 289 (2005).

113. Some of his leading works on this subject include, JEREMY BLACK, WAR AND THE WORLD, 1450–2000 (1998), WAR: PAST, PRESENT AND FUTURE (2000), WESTERN WARFARE 1775–1882 (2001), and WAR IN THE TWENTY-FIRST CENTURY (2001).

114. COMAROFF & COMAROFF, *supra* note 8, at 35.

115. Remarkably, violence in the postcolony as described here has much in common with violence in medieval Europe prior to the emergence of strong States where "conflict was funded to a large extent through plundering civilians, which compensated for inadequate provisioning and for pay that was generally low, late, or non-existent," David Keen, *Incentives and Disincentives for Violence*, *in* GREED AND GRIEVANCE: ECONOMIC AGENDAS IN CIVIL WARS, 28 (Mats Berdal & David M. Malone eds., 2000).

7. COMMERCIALIZING WAR
Private Military and Security Companies, Mercenaries and International Law

I. INTRODUCTION

With the end of the twentieth century and the beginning of the twenty-first century, the commercialization of war has greatly expanded and accelerated.[1] In fact, as shown in the discussion of resource wars in Chapter 6, war is as much a business as is the secretive trade in high-end resources, such as diamonds. In addition, although the work of mercenaries and mercenary-like groups is not new, the commercialization of war is increasingly becoming privatized within corporations with global operations managed by former military professionals offering a whole range of services.[2] The following chapter discusses this commercialization of war, and the limits and potential for holding its wielders accountable for violations international law.

Although transnational commerce has been increasingly militarized, States have lost their monopoly over the use of legitimate force, particularly in poor countries where violence and war have increasingly become commercialized. Thus, investors and States buy the services of paramilitary and other groups like they would buy other inputs to enable them to do what they do. Entrepreneurial paramilitaries, irregular groups, transnational security firms, bandits and irregulars, among others, supply this market of violence for profit. For example, the now defunct Executive Outcomes is alleged to have received mineral concessions for bringing a rebellion to an end and

---

1. *See, e.g.,* Craig Forcese, *Deterring "Militarized" Commerce*, 31 OTTAWA L. REV. 172 (1999–2000); Craig Forcese, *ACTA's Achilles Heel: Corporate Complicity, International Law and the Alien Tort Claims Act*, 26 YALE J. INT'L L. 487 (2001).

2. P.W. SINGER, CORPORATE WARRIORS: THE RISE OF THE PRIVATIZED MILITARY INDUSTRY 44–48 (2003).

restoring order for the Sierra Leonean government in the 1990s.[3] The Sierra Leonean Truth Commission noted that these concessions led to the "mortgaging of the nation's assets."[4] In addition to governments with no effective control of their territory and no armies to speak of, huge multinational corporations interested in guarding their investment, as well as nongovernmental and intergovernmental organizations, are among the consumers of this private market for security provisioning and warriors.[5]

Although commercialization of war has thrived, the opprobrium against mercenary violence has also grown. Yet, this high level of opprobrium has not been accompanied by a correlative heightening of the attendant international legal rules to hold violators accountable.[6] That, however, has not been because of a lack of effort to heighten the obligations of States to root out violence in the hands of private actors in all instances. For example, the United Nations has increased the obligations of States to deal with terrorists and terrorist groups that pose a threat to international peace and security. However, no analogous heightening of the responsibility of States to curb the violence of other non-State actors, such as mercenaries, as well as private military and security companies has occurred. Thus, threats posed by non-State actors that are more likely to threaten powerful countries are subject to enhanced international legal scrutiny through the very real possibility of mandatory United Nations Security sanctions. This, by contrast, is not the case for private military companies and mercenaries who largely operate in, and threaten weak and poor countries. This is caused by the fact that

---

3. *But see*, Michael Grunberg, *A Sierra Leone Contract: Letters to the Editor*, NEW YORK TIMES, Aug. 28, 7, 2001 (noting that the Contract between Executive Outcomes and Sierra Leone, which ran from May 1995 to January 1997 "did not include a sharing of mining profits" and that Sierra Leone was required to only make "purely monetary" payments).

4. The Sierra Leone Truth and Reconciliation Commission, *Witness to Truth: Report of the Sierra Leone Truth and Reconciliation Commission* ¶ 371 (2004) [hereinafter Sierra Leone TRC].

5. SINGER, *supra* note 2, at 9.

6. Joana Abrisketa, Comment, *Blackwater: Mercenaries and International Law*, PRIDE, Oct. 2007 (noting that international law needs to adapt and evolve in the same way that the nature of armed conflict is changing).

they are often conducting their activities without nearly any similar scrutiny, such as the mandatory decisions of the Security Council.[7] In addition to exploring the foregoing theme, this chapter examines the proliferation of efforts at self-regulation in the private military and security industry, and the international legal regime that applies to this group of non-State actors. I also argue that individuals who stand behind private security and companies that violate international humanitarian and human rights law can be prosecuted as accessories for complicity to such violations.[8] In effect, I argue in favor of closing the apparent gap between the high likelihood for prosecution of crimes causing violations of bodily integrity, such as killings and mutilations, versus the low likelihood for prosecution of economic actors in war who finance or provide arms to those who engage in crimes causing violations of bodily integrity.

II. COMMERCIALIZING WAR AND DEFERRING ACCOUNTABILITY

Perhaps the most dramatic example of the commercialization of war is the hiring of the now defunct Executive Outcomes, a private military firm, by the government of Sierra Leone in 1995.[9] Overwhelmed by

---

7. U.N. Charter art. 25 (which provides that "The members of the United Nations agree to accept and carry out the decisions of the Security Council in accordance with the present Charter." Article 24 of the Charter gives the Security Council, the primary responsibility for the maintenance of international peace and security).

8. *But see*, Allison Danner & Jenny S. Martinez, *Guilty Associations: Joint Criminal Enterprise, Command Responsibility and the Development of International Criminal Law*, 93 CAL. L. REV. 75 (2005) (arguing unlimited uses of joint criminal enterprise liability theories are likely to lead to guilt by association which would in turn undermine the legitimacy and effectiveness of international criminal law).

9. SINGER, *supra* note 5, at 45 (arguing that "[t]he newest eave of private military agents are commercial enterprises first and foremost. They are hierarchically organized into registered businesses that trade and compete openly (for the most part) and are vertically integrated into the wider global market place. They target market niches by offering a wide variety of military skill sets. The very fact that a coherent industry made up of these companies is identifiable provides evidence of their distinction.").

a rebellion led by the Revolutionary United Front (RUF), the Sierra Leonean government turned to Executive Outcomes. Executive Outcomes was the second private military firm that the government hired to deal with the violent RUF rebellion, in which hundreds of thousands had been displaced, maimed, or killed in one of the most brutal episodes of senseless mayhem.[10] For its efforts, Executive Outcomes is reported to have been paid in mineral concessions, as the Sierra Leonean government was reportedly bankrupt. Within a short time of being hired, Executive Outcomes restored some order in the country. It also reportedly deployed its "battalion-strength force" and its huge collection of armored vehicles, combat fighter aircraft, and gun ships to eventually remove the RUF from the diamond-rich fields of Sierra Leone. Executive Outcomes was familiar with operating in African war zones, having done so before in Angola in 1997 with one of its companies, Teleservices. Notwithstanding, the quick success of Executive Outcomes in putting down the RUF insurgency, the international community rallied against the hiring of a private military firm by a government. Although the International Monetary Fund, an ardent supporter of privatization, provided Sierra Leone financing to pay off Executive Outcomes, it nevertheless made its financing conditional on the Sierra Leonean government of President Kabbah reducing defense spending.[11] This, together with the Abdjian Peace Agreement of 1996, resulted in Sierra Leone ending its contract with Executive Outcomes and its withdrawal from the country in January 1997.[12] With a decrease of military spending, and because of the effect of the war on the economy, Sierra Leone had

---

10. The Sierra Leonean government initially hired Gurkha Security Guards, a South African security firm. Its leader, Robert Mackenzie, was killed in an RUF ambush following which the Gurkha Security Guards declined to engage the RUF further. Their contract, was cancelled and Executive Outcomes was hired. *See* GREG CAMPBELL, BLOOD DIAMONDS: TRACING THE DEADLY PATH OF THE WORLD'S MOST PRECIOUS STONES 74–75 (2004).
11. Michael Chege, *Sierra Leone: The State that Came Back from the Dead*, 25:3 WASH. Q. 147, 155 (2002).
12. Sierra Leone TRC, *supra* note 4, at ¶ 405. *See also Peace Agreement Between the Government of Sierra Leone and the Revolutionary United Front* of 30th art. 12 (Nov. 30, 1996) (requiring the withdrawal of Executive Outcomes From Sierra Leone within five months of the signing of the Agreement) *available at* http://www.sierra-leone.org/abidjanaccord.html.

no access to additional funds to pay Executive Outcomes.[13] As soon as Executive Outcomes left Sierra Leone, the country burst into a fullscale civil war again. A UN-supported Economic Community of West African States' Military Observer Group (ECOMOG) peacekeeping force replaced Executive Outcomes.

Another example of the commercialization of war is the outsourcing of several military-related functions in the conduct of recent inter-State wars by the U.S. military. This commercialization or privatization of military functions in the United States began in the mid-1980s. Commercialization coincided with the rise of neoliberal economic reforms, which are strongly committed to market solutions for social problems, including the supply of government services. Thus, although the international financial institutions and western governments condemned the hiring of private military firms in Sierra Leone in the mid-1990s, the biggest military spender in the world since the 1980s has been increasingly privatizing a range of military services. In addition, war veterans from any number of countries have been hired to fight in foreign wars. For example, Gurkha Security Guards, the firm that was initially hired by the Sierra Leonean government, was under the command of a U.S. veteran of the Vietnam War.[14]

So even in the United States where the government largely maintains the monopoly of violence, several military functions have been commercialized. These include basic support functions, such as laundering soldiers attire, providing dining services, and refueling military vehicles and aircrafts; but this commercialization has also spread into roles such as interrogating prisoners and conducting combat. Defense industry companies argue their services in training and providing logistical support and advice are legitimate and noncombative, and they do in fact provide services that were traditionally

---

13. Sierra Leone TRC, *supra* note 4, at ¶ 405 (noting that the cancellation of the Executive Outcomes contract saddled the country with substantial financial obligations and noting that the Sierra Leonean government conceded to pressure in the Abidjan Peace Agreement of 1996 to terminate its contract with Executive Outcomes). *See* Grunberg, *supra* note 3 (noting that under the contract Sierra Leone owed Executive Outcomes US$31 million and that he helped negotiate the payment of the balance after the contract was terminated).

14. CAMPBELL, *supra* note 9, at 77.

performed by national militaries, which operate under civilian control. When one of these defense-industry firms employed by the U.S. government was sued for wrongful deaths by their contract employees, it unsuccessfully argued that it could not be sued, because its supply of military services formed part of the military operations under the command of the President of the United States. In its view, courts had no jurisdiction to review its operations.[15] This argument in turn raises a question I will return to later—whether these companies for hire are legally unaccountable under international law as well.[16]

In this context, it is noteworthy that private military contractors have argued in favor of commercializing the provision of humanitarian assistance because international responses to humanitarian crisis are often too slow, expensive, and ineffective.[17] These contractors have therefore argued in favor of addressing humanitarian crisis, such as the genocide in Darfur, Sudan[18] and the piracy menace off the coast of Somalia,[19] for a fraction of the price that organizations such as the United Nations might expend on such responses.

Recently, the United States Department of Justice charged the multinational Chiquita Brands International, Inc. with the offense of engaging in transactions with a specially designated global terrorist group—the United Self Defense Forces of Colombia (AUC)—that has engaged in assassinations and guerilla activities.[20] Chiquita paid

---

15. Brief for Appellants, *Blackwater Security Consulting v. Nordan* (No. 06-857), 2005 WL 3730928 (C.A.4). Blackwater in effect argued that "The judiciary may not impose standards on the manner in which the President oversees and commands the private component of the total force in foreign military operations," *id.* at 17. Blackwater also invoked the political question doctrine arguing that because it was performing a classic military function, its role was not subject to civilian control," *id.* at 18.

16. Domestic courts are the primary enforcers of international law, see MARY O'CONNELL, THE POWER AND PURPOSES OF INTERNATIONAL LAW: INSIGHTS FROM THE THEORY AND PRACTICE OF INTERNATIONAL LAW 392 (2008).

17. JEREMY SCAHILL, BLACKWATER: THE RISE OF THE WORLD'S MOST POWERFUL MERCENARY ARMY 346–60 (2007).

18. *Id.* at 348–49.

19. NOAH SHACHTMAN, BLACKWATER: WE'LL FIGHT SOMALIA'S PIRATES, Oct. 16, 2008, *available at* http://blog.wired.com/defense/2008/10/blackwater-well.html.

20. This is the English translation for "Autodefensas Unidas de Colombia."

AUC and other violent groups with the knowledge and approval of senior Chiquita Executives, even with awareness that those payments were prohibited under U.S. law. These payments were made as protection money so that Chiquita's banana farms could not fall under the control of this and similar groups. Chiquita pleaded guilty to paying this group more than US$1.7 between 1997 and early 2004.[21] The Chiquita case illustrates the use of violent private-security forces by business owners, including plantation owners, ranchers, and miners, because the Colombian State and its military have no control over many parts of the country—particularly in rural areas. This is really the story in many weak States, as seen in the discussion on resource wars in Chapter 6. Thus, the regulation of private military companies and paramilitary groups, such as those in Colombia, would ideally include the conduct of both these suppliers of violence, as well as the consumers who pay for it.[22] This would include petroleum corporations involved in oil exploration and mining operations from Burma[23] and Sudan,[24] to Nigeria,[25] who have also been alleged to

---

21. Press Release, Department of Justice, Chiquita Brands International Pleads Guilty to Making Payments to a Designated Terrorist Organization And Agrees to Pay $25 Million Fine (Mar. 19, 2007).

22. *See* Katie Kerr, *Making Peace With Criminals: An Economic Approach to Assessing Punishment Options in the Colombian Peace Process*, 37 UNIV. MIAMI INTER-AM. L. REV. 53 (2005) (arguing in favor of a role for the international community to force the hand of Colombian government to take tougher sanctions against paramilitary groups including withholding financial aid and public disapproval by the United States and the European Union; the possibility of extradition for trial to the United States coupled together with the government's discretion not to extradite paramilitaries and others who are willing to demobilize among other options).

23. *Doe v. Unocol Corp.*, 248 F.3d 915 (9th Cir. 2002) (where Unocal is alleged of being complicit in the forced labor, rape and murder of Burmese workers by security workers the company hired to help build a pipeline).

24. *See* JOHN HARKER, THE HUMAN SECURITY IN SUDAN: THE REPORT OF A CANADIAN ASSESSMENT MISSION (PREPARED FOR THE MINISTER OF FOREIGN AFFAIRS) (2000) (investigating Talisman Energy, a Canadian Corporation's involvement together with the Sudanese state-owned joint venture firm in financing military operations and providing aircraft to attack and displace residents living in the locality of the Talisman-operated oil fields).

25. *See Wiwa v. Royal Dutch Petroleum Co.*, 226 F.3d. 88 (2000) (plaintiffs alleging Royal Dutch and Shell Nigeria coercively appropriated land for oil

funnel resources to government or paramilitary groups in the past to deal harshly with dissidents protesting or sabotaging their investment operations.

The foregoing examples are not intended to be an exhaustive list. They are simply illustrative. The British Parliament's Green Paper on Private Military Companies of 2002 compiled a long list of Africa's experience with mercenary, military, and private security and defense companies from the 1950s to the 1960s.[26] This comprehensive list indicates the extent of the involvement of foreign and private military defense and security firms, and mercenaries, particularly in the countries with the least effective control of their often remote and dangerous resource-rich territory.[27] In addition, this Green Paper noted, the ratio of private security guards to police is ten to one in less-developed countries as compared to a ratio of three to one in developed countries.[28]

III. INTERNATIONAL LAW AND MERCENARIES

Article 47 of the First Additional Protocol to the Geneva Conventions defines a mercenary extremely narrowly. To be regarded a mercenary

---

development without adequate compensation and with the support of Nigerian military and police resulting in torture, a violation of the law of nations).

26. HOUSE OF COMMONS, PRIVATE MILITARY COMPANIES: OPTIONS FOR REGULATION 28–38 (Annex A) (Feb. 12, 2002). *See also* Commission on Human Rights, *The Right of Peoples to Self-Determination and Its Application to Peoples Under Colonial or Alien Domination or Foreign Occupation: Report of the Working Group on the Use of Mercenaries as a Means of Violating Human Rights and Impeding the Exercise of the right of People to Self Determination on the Resumed First Session*, U.N. Doc. E/CN.4/2006/11Add.1 (Oct. 10–14, 2005 and Sept. 1–13, 2006) E/CN.4/2006/11Add.1 (3 Mar. 2006) (reporting cases of mercenaries active in Honduras (Sept. 2005); Papua New Guinea (1998); Panama (2005); Iraq (2004), Equatorial Guinea (2004), among other countries.

27. Notably, in its decision in *Congo v. Dem. Rep. Congo*, I.C.J., ¶ 304 (2005), the ICJ strongly suggested that the duty of due diligence or vigilance expected of a government with respect to rebel activity that may result in violating the rights of a neighboring state may be lower if the geographical terrain was remote and difficult.

28. *Id.* at 9.

under the protocol, one has to be: specifically recruited to fight in an armed conflict in which he or she takes part in and is motivated to do so by the desire for private gain. Such a person should also be neither a national of a party to the conflict, nor resident in the territory of a party to the conflict. In addition, such a person should not be a member of the armed forces of a party to the conflict and such a person should not have been sent by a State that is not a party to the conflict on official duty as a member of the armed forces. This definition is cumulative in the sense that a mercenary must fulfill all elements of the foregoing criteria. This definition also poses difficulties in determining motivations for involvement in mercenary or mercenary-like activities. A person could be motivated by mixed motives—a pecuniary and a nonpecuniary purpose, in which case concluding the motivation was only for private gain becomes problematic. In addition, mercenaries may, and indeed have been known, to be motivated by other motivations including religious and ideological, in which case the question of whether one is a mercenary becomes open to interpretation.

The Organization of African Unity's Convention for the Elimination of Mercenarism in Africa[29] defines a mercenary as someone who is not a national of the State, against which his or her actions are directed and is employed, enrolled, or willingly linked to a person, group, or organization whose aim is to forcibly overthrow a member government. The definition further includes mercenaries as those who aim to undermine the independence, territorial integrity, or normal working institutions of such a State, or blocks in any way the activities of a liberation movement recognized by the Organization of African Unity (OAU) (now renamed the African Union). This definition may be argued to exclude the activities of entities such as Executive Outcomes, whose primary goal was not interfering with the independence of the Sierra Leonean State, but rather to help it restore order.

---

29. O.A.U. Doc. CM/433/Rev. L. Annex 1 (1972). For a discussion of related United Nations anti mercenarism resolutions, see Ellen L. Frye, *Private military Firms in the New World Order: How Redefining "Mercenary"Can Tame the "Dogs of War,"* 73 FORDHAM L. REV. 2607, 2626–28 (2005). However, perhaps the best discussion is Sarah V. Percy, *The United Nations Security Council and the Use of Private Force, in* THE UNITED NATIONS SECURITY COUNCIL AND WAR (Vaughan Lowe et al. eds., 2007).

Further, Executive Outcomes' role in the mid-1990s in seizing oil facilities from rebels and providing security to the Angolan government has been argued to fall outside the scope of the Convention.[30]

The UN General Assembly's International Convention Against the Recruitment, Use, Financing and Training of Mercenaries,[31] which came into force in 2001 largely follows the OAU and the First Additional Protocol's definition of a mercenary. In addition, by 2001, only 21 countries had ratified or acceded to the Convention further eroding its usefulness in addressing the mercenary menace. As such, none of these Conventions adequately applies to mercenarism that is not inspired by profit or pay, but for ideological, religious, or such other nonmonetary reasons. The problem is that the Convention's definition of mercenarism leaves out instances in which non-State actors may engage in to further combat.

Hague Convention No. V Respecting the Rights and Duties of Neutral Powers and Persons in the Case of War on Land of 1907 makes it illegal for neutral powers to form and recruit mercenary armies on their territory.[32] However, it does not prohibit the passage of mercenaries through the territory of a neutral.

The argument that international law does not prohibit all instances of mercenarism or the provision of private military services is based on a literal or textualist interpretation of current rules of international law. According to this argument, those forms of mercenarism not explicitly prohibited, such as those not inspired by a profit motive, are permissible. To make such a claim would be to invoke the kind of high positivism exemplified in the Permanent Court of International Justice (PCIJ) decision in the *Lotus* case. In *Lotus*, the PCIJ held that, where there was no rule of international law prohibiting a particular conduct, then it was permissible as it would be inappropriate to make

---

30. This, of course, raises the question whether a government may invite a private military company to play such roles when it has been unable to do so itself. It is much clearer under international law that a state may invite another state to assist it in self-defense against another state, *see* Military and Paramilitary Activities in and against Nicaragua (Nicar. V. U.S.), 1986 I.C.J. 14 (June 27).

31. G.A. Res. A/RES/44/34 (Dec. 4, 1989).

32. Hague Convention (V), Respecting the Rights and Duties of Neutral Powers and Persons in the Case of War on Land, Oct. 18, 1907, 36 Stat. 2310, T.S. 540.

any presumptions against the sovereignty of a State.³³ This effectively acquiesces to the permissibility of mercenarism inconsistently with the prohibition of the use of force especially given that this prohibition is recognized both as jus cogens,³⁴ as well as a cornerstone principle of the United Nations charter.³⁵ In some recent cases, mercenaries, still pose the threat of deposing governments in weak States inconsistently with current antimercenarism international law rules or providing arms to rebel groups that pose a threat to governments and that reign terror on citizens.³⁶

In addition, the payment of mercenaries or private security and military companies by governments with natural or mineral resources is inconsistent with both the letter and spirit of the international legal norms on permanent sovereignty over natural resources, and the principles relating to the right to development.³⁷ International law is now understood to establish a right to use natural resources for

---

33. Bruno Simma, *Termination and Suspension of Treaties: Two Recent Austrian Cases*, GER. Y.B. INT'L L. 74 n.24 (1978) (noting that a Lotus argument is akin to the availability of an international gray zone in which States operate with "international legal freestyle"). *See* Justice Weeramantry's opinion *in* The Legality of the Threat or Use of Nuclear Weapons, Advisory Opinion, 1996 I.C.J. 226 (July 8) (expressing skepticism to the applicability of the Lotus approach where no clear rule of international law is available).

34. *Nicar. v. U.S.*, 1986 I.C.J. 14.

35. Case Concerning Armed Activities on the Territory of the Congo (Dem. Rep. Congo v. Uganda) 2005 I.C.J. 115 (Dec. 19) ¶ 148, *available at* http://www.icj-cij.org.

36. *E.g.*, Sir. Mark Thatcher was fined and given a suspended sentence for bankrolling the purchase of a helicopter that was to be used in a coup attempt in Equatorial Guinea in 2005. South Africa and the United Kingdom knew of the impending coup and did nothing *See* Steve Bloomfield, *Mercenaries Acquitted in 'Wonga Coup Case'*, THE INDEP. (Feb. 24, 2007) (reporting the outcome another related case). *See also* Peta Thornycroft, *Mercenaries Accused of Plotting to Overthrow Equatorial Guinea Government Sentenced in Zimbabwe*, *available at* http://www.voanews.com/english/archive/2004-09/a-2004-09-10-29-1.cfm?renderforprint.

37. *The Declaration on the Right to Development*, G.A. Res. 128 G.A.O.R., 41st Sess., Supp. No. 53, at 186, U.N. Doc. A/41/53(1986), at arts. 1(2), 2(1). *See also* Thomas Pogge, *Priorities of Global Justice*, 31 METAPHILOSOPHY (2001) (on international resource privilege).

national development.[38] Further, private military companies, mercenaries, and others privately engaged in combat in the shadows of war in weak States, often operate without being accountable for the violations of international law, including disregard of human rights,[39] plundering of resources, and emerging rules against official corruption.[40] This contrasts sharply with the kind of liability that governments may incur for war destruction as seen in the discussion of *AAPL v. Sri Lanka* in Chapter 5. Thus, another reason to bring these private actors under a legal regime of accountability is to remove the double standards between holding governments accountable for war destruction, while having little or nothing for private actors engaging in similar conduct.[41]

Clearly, although the treaty regimes banning mercenary conduct are narrowly tailored, and private military companies and mercenaries often operate without accountability, these non-State actors are, nevertheless, subject to international law, including both international human rights and humanitarian law, a topic I return to below. In my view, the current ban on mercenarism in the U.N. and OAU Conventions ought to be given a purposive and contextual construction to include instances of mercenary activity that, although not

---

38. Nico Schrijver, Sovereignty Over Natural Resources: Balancing Rights and Duties 269 (1997).

39. On human rights violations of mercenaries, see United Nations, *Use of Mercenaries as a means of Violating Human Rights and Impeding the Exercise of the Right Peoples to Self-Determination*, submitted by Mr. Enrique Bernales Ballesteros, Special Rapporteur, G.A. Res. 198/6.E/CN.4/1999/11 (Jan. 13, 1999). See also, ANDREW CLAPHAM, HUMAN RIGHTS OBLIGATIONS OF NON-STATE ACTORS (2006).

40. See, e.g., *United Nations Convention Against Corruption*, G.A. Res. 58/4, U.N. Doc. A/RES/58/4 (Oct. 31, 2003) and *African Union Convention on Preventing and Combating Corruption* (2003), available at http://www.africa-union.org. On the prevalence of corruption in the provision of private military and security companies, see COLONEL GERALD SCHUMACHER, A BLOODY BUSINESS: AMERICA'S WAR ZONE CONTRACTORS AND THE OCCUPATION OF IRAQ (2006); M. M. Harris, *Patriots and Profiteers: Combating False Claims By Contractors in the Iraq War and Reconstruction*, 59 ALA. L. REV. 1227 (2008).

41. On this see, Andrew Clapham, *Human Rights Obligations of Non-State Actors in Conflict Situations*, 88 INT'L L. REV. RED CROSS COMM. No. 863, at 491 (2006).

explicitly prohibited, are nevertheless inconsistent with the prohibition of mercenarism. Indeed, as shown earlier, there are other norms of international law, including the prohibition of the use of force and the related values of territorial integrity and political independence of States that are as relevant to understanding the ban of mercenarism.

For the moment, what is clear is that the United Nations Security Council has enhanced the obligations of States to take measures to prevent terrorism. These obligations have effectively changed the low threshold due-diligence obligation[42] States had until the U.N. Security Council Resolution 1373 of 2001 to prevent their territory from being used to launch terrorism conduct in other States to requiring States to compulsorily take all measures to prevent terrorism.[43] This resolution was framed in very categorical terms such as should and shall repeatedly. This categorical language emphasizes the obligations of States to prevent and suppress terrorist financing[44] and refrain in the provision of active or passive support of terrorism.[45] In Resolution 1735, the Security Council authorized States to freeze the financial or economic assets or funds of non-State actors including individuals, groups, and entities suspected of terrorism.[46] Indeed, these two resolutions are two of several resolutions declaring the Council's view that terrorism constitutes "one of the most serious threats to international peace and security."[47] The Security Council has not similarly

---

42. R. B. Lillich & J. B. Paxman, *State Responsibility for Injuries to Aliens Occasioned by Terrorist Activities*, 26 AM. U. L. REV. 217, 210ff (1976–77) (arguing the duty of due diligence is not absolute but rather requires only that the State exercises best possible efforts and therefore this has something to do with the capacity of a State, and as such, responsibility only attaches when a State fails to take reasonable steps under the circumstances). *Congo v. Dem. Rep. Congo*, I.C.J. (2005).
43. S.C. Res. 1372, U.N. Doc. S/RES/1372 (Sept. 28, 2001).
44. *Id.* at ¶ 1(a).
45. *Id.* at ¶ 2(a). *But see* Jimmy Gurule, Unfunding Terror: The Legal Response to the Financing of Global Terrorism, (2009) (arguing in favor of more effective international efforts to unfund terrorists).
46. *See* Andrew Hudson, *Not a Great Asset: The UN Security Council's Counter-Terrorism Regime: Violating Human Rights*, 25 BERKELEY J. INT'L L. 203 (2004).
47. *E.g.*, S.C. Res. 1540, U.N. Doc. S/RES/1540 (Apr. 28 2004) (requiring States not to provide any form of support to non-State actors to develop chemical

heightened the duty of States to counter mercenarism as it has with reference to terrorism.

A counter-argument may be made that Resolution 1373, and the Counter-Terrorism Committee it established, may have been an expression of a hegemonic international law to the extent that in so doing, the Security Council failed to balance the twin mandates of the United Nations in maintaining international peace and security, on the one hand, and ensuring the protection of fundamental rights and freedoms, on the other.[48] This notwithstanding, Resolution 1373 demonstrates a commitment to holding States liable under particularly high thresholds of responsibility for the conduct of non-State actors that might even be remotely attributable to them. In addition, the Security Council has not shied away from exercising its authority, particularly in the economic sanctions area, over non-State actors.[49] Thus, non-State actors, such as terrorists who threaten powerful countries and their interests, are subject to enhanced international legal scrutiny through the very real possibility of mandatory United Nations Security sanctions; whereas those such as private military companies and mercenaries, who threaten weak and poor countries, are conducting their activities without nearly any similar scrutiny or enhanced responsibility from the Security Council. In addition, both the United States and the United Kingdom, two of the primary source countries of private military and security companies, do not favor a ban or stringent international regulation of these companies.[50] This attitude is perhaps a reflection of their ambivalence toward the efficacy of rules of international law shaping the behavior of these firms, but it is also consistent with the view that these militarily powerful countries may view some of these private firms as contributing to, rather than undermining global security. If this is the case, then the security of rich and powerful countries arguably

---

or biological weapons or their delivery in particular for terrorist purposes); S.C. Res. 1333, U.N. Doc. S/RES/1333 (Dec. 19, 2000).

48. Jose E. Alvarez, *Hegemonic International Law Revisited*, 97 AM. J. INT'L. L. 873 (2003).

49. Kristen Boon, "*Coining A New Jurisdiction: The Security Council As Economic Peacekeeper*," 41 VAND. J. TRANSNAT' L. L. 991, 1033 (2008).

50. P. W. Singer, *War, Profits and the Vacuum of Law: Privatized Military Firms and International Law*, 42 COLUM. J. INT'L. L. 521, 544 (2004).

comes before those of poor and weaker countries. As such, threats posed by mercenarism and rogue military companies, particularly for poor countries, do not receive the same international attention and regulatory oversight as do threats to rich and powerful countries such as transcontinental terrorism does.

IV. THE ACCOUNTABILITY OF ECONOMIC ACTORS IN WAR

The operations of the violent paramilitaries and the involvement of military and private security and military firms in extrajudicial killings, as well as the breakdown of order in weak States exemplifies an unfortunate normalization of violence and the unaccountable exercise of power by non-State actors over unregulated zones of commerce and disorder. Thus, although mercenary activity is inconsistent with and operates outside prevailing rules, both national and international law, there is a danger that statutory incorporation of a business that behaves like a mercenary may give it a kind of respectability that distinguishes it from unincorporated entities such as paramilitary groups that are no less violent and that operate outside the realm of official law.[51] Yet, both paramilitary groups and incorporated military and security companies often operate within this zone of unregulated commerce and disorder that often defies the boundary between the legal and nonlegal.

Incorporation ought not to be used as a disguise for the conduct of individuals. The Nuremberg Tribunal took this into account when it noted that "crimes against international law are committed by men, not by abstract entities, and only by punishing individuals

---

51. BENEDICT SHEEHY, JACKSON MAOGOTO & VIRGINIA NEWELL, LEGAL CONTROL OF THE PRIVATE MILITARY CORPORATION 36 (2009) pose the following question before answering it: "What does the presence of the corporate form do to alter what in other contexts would be termed mercenarism? A global answer is simple: power." These authors relying on Peter Singer argue that "the distinctive features of mercenaries . . . [are] the following: foreigners, independent of the organized structured force, motivated by money and not political goals, recruited to avoid legal prohibitions, and focused on combat," *id*. The corporate form, the authors point out, gives private military companies, military, financial and political power which would not be as easily available for mercenary groups, *id*.

who commit such crimes, can the provisions of international be enforced."[52] In other words, the corporate shield is a veil that hides conduct that is directly traceable to individuals. Incorporation does not and cannot displace the individual criminal responsibility under international law.

Thus, although some private military companies distinguish themselves as respectable rather than rogue investors, both formal and informal groups operating in zones of unregulated commerce and disorder operate in a marketplace where violence is for sale, but where individual responsibility under international law still exists.[53] Thus, whereas incorporation may, for some entities, be simply a way of disguising their mercenary character,[54] individual criminal responsibility is not displaced by such incorporation. The limitations we have seen above with reference to defining mercenaries that makes this market of violence appear largely unregulated, therefore has less to do with the innate inadequacies of existing rules. Rather, war zones and other areas of lawlessness have increasingly become subject to the new norms and institutions, such as those related to the Rome Statute of the International Criminal Court. In addition, there have been ad hoc tribunals charged with seeking individual criminal responsibility from Rwanda, to the former Yugoslavia, as well as mixed courts from Sierra Leone to Cambodia. These courts and tribunals continue to generate a growing jurisprudence on individual responsibility for crimes against humanity, genocide and war crimes.[55]

The prosecutions in these tribunals have primarily focused on crimes related to "bodily integrity such as killings, mutilations, summary executions," sexual assault,[56] and genocide, which only indirectly

---

52. Trial of the Major War Criminal Before the International Military Tribunal, Nuremberg, Nov. 14, 1945–Oct. 1, (1946, at 223 (Nuremberg, Germany, 1947).

53. For the definitional issues and categorizations of companies involved in the supply of private force, see Sarah V. Percy, *This Gun's For Hire: A New Look at an Old Issue*, 58 INT'L J. 721 (2003).

54. JANICE THOMSON, MERCENARIES, PIRATES AND SOVEREIGNS: STATE BUILDING AND EXTRATERRITORIAL VIOLENCE IN EARLY MODERN EUROPE 90 (1994).

55. *See* ANTONIO CASSESE, INTERNATIONAL CRIMINAL LAW (2nd ed., 2008).

56. William Schabas, *War Economies, Economic actors and International Criminal Law, in* PROFITING FROM PEACE: MANAGING THE RESOURCE

focuses on the responsibility economic actors[57] including mercenaries and private military and security companies that often supply the arms in these conflicts. While noting the inadequacy of current rules of international law to deal with the responsibility of economic actors, William Schabas proposed charging such actors with complicity in crimes against humanity, war crimes, and genocide under theories such as joint criminal enterprise.[58] However, there have been few, if any, instances in which the often clandestine activities of the corporations involved arms dealing and the purchase of conflict resources, as well as their financiers and bankers have been charged with international criminal responsibility for their conduct.

This compartmentalization of crimes involving bodily integrity, however, from those of an economic nature, such as the illicit plundering and looting of mineral and other resources is artificial, and it does not reflect the reality in war-torn countries.[59] Take the example of the wars in the Democratic Republic of Congo, where the State has failed or been disabled from having effective control. Here, the International Court of Justice found Uganda liable for preventing the looting, plundering, and exploitation of the natural resources of the Democratic Republic of the Congo.[60] Looted resources, such as diamonds, would then find their way into markets outside the Democratic Republic of Congo through globally linked marketing, transportation and banking networks. In return, money and weapons flow back into such war economies from non-State actors, thereby contributing to the continued sustenance of the further violent extraction of resources.

In July 2003, the Prosecutor of the International Criminal Court acknowledged reports of the involvement of companies from African, Middle Eastern, and European countries, as well as organized crimes groups, which had financed their exploitation of the natural resources of the Democratic Republic of Congo through the

---

DIMENSIONS OF CIVIL WAR 431 (Karen Ballentine et al. eds., 2005).
57. *Id.* (giving the example of trade in diamonds in Sierra Leone, which fueled the war, "there was little existing law" could contribute to holding those responsible).
58. *Id.* at 426–29.
59. Ruben Carranza, *Plunder and Pain: Should Transitional Justice Engage with Corruption and Economic Crimes?*, 2 INT'L J. TRANSITIONAL JUST. 310 (2008).
60. *Congo v. Dem. Rep. Congo*, I.C.J. ¶¶ 242, 245–46, 249–50 (2005).

international banking system.[61] He promised not only to investigate, but to prosecute and punish those involved in these crimes. Although the Statute of the International Criminal Court does not confer jurisdiction to prosecute corporations, individual criminal responsibility could be pursued for corporate actors.

There are precedents for charging individuals with complicity for war crimes such as pillage against corporate actors. For example, in criminal proceedings against a Dutch national, Frank Cornelis Adrianus van Anraat before the Netherlands Court of Appeal, the defendant was found guilty for complicity as an accessory to a violation of the laws and customs of war that resulted in the death and grievous bodily harm, which was also part of a systematic policy of terror and wrongful acts against a population or specific group thereof. Van Anraat had formed a company to engage in trade in chemicals, a lucrative business he learnt about while living in Iraq. He sold the chemical raw material for mustard and nerve gas to the Iraqi government of Saddam Hussein between 1980 and 1988. This raw material was used to produce mustard gas, an asphyxiating and poisonous gas that the then Iraqi President Saddam Hussein and others proceeded to use against the Kurdish population, thereby causing not only death but terror as well. Van Anraat was sentenced to a 17-year term of imprisonment in 2007.[62]

The Nuremberg prosecutions of German industrialists are another precedent illustrating the potential for individual responsibility of corporate actors. For example, in The *Flick* Case, Flick and Steinbrinck

---

61. Press Release, Prosecutor of the Int'l Criminal Court, Communications Received By the Office of the Prosecutor of the ICC (July 16, 2003) (press release no.: pids.0092003-EN).

62. Criminal Proceedings Against Van Anraat, Hague Ct. Rep. (May 9, 2007) (Cause-list No 22-000509-06). *But see* The Vietnam Association for Victims of Agent Orange/Dioxin et al. Dow Chemical et al. 2005 U.S. Dist. Lexis 3644 (E.D.N.Y. 2005) (dismissing civil case against Dow Chemicals for supplying U.S. government a herbicide used in the Vietnam war. The Court held in part that the herbicide was not illegal in wars prior to 1975 under the War Crimes Act of 1996 and held against applying the Hague Convention IV Respecting the Laws and Customs of War on Land against the military use of the herbicide during war). For a discussion of holding military contractors accountable, *see* Laura A. Dickinson, *Filartiga's Legacy in an Era of Military Privatization*, 37 RUTGERS L.J. 703 (2006)

were charged with contributing money, as well as their influence and support to the SS, a criminal organization with knowledge of its criminal activities. Although the Nuremberg Tribunal noted that they did not approve or condone the SS activities, the Tribunal nevertheless found them guilty for lending their reputation and large contributions to it while knowing its atrocities and for their failure, like others, to withdraw their contribution and membership.[63] Weiss was charged and convicted for initiating orders for increased production of freight cars for military purposes, with the approval of Flick, and for using large numbers of prisoners of war from Russia, who they had procured for this purpose.[64] Flick was also convicted for the crime of economic plunder.[65]

This Nuremberg Tribunal rejected the defendants claim that "international law is a matter wholly outside the work, interest and knowledge of private individuals," and held that international law binds private individuals as much as it binds governmental officials.[66] The Nuremberg judgment in *The Flick Case* therefore, shows the availability of international criminal and humanitarian law to pursue corporate and other economic actors for violations of international humanitarian and human rights law, rules that today unquestionably apply to both international and noninternational armed conflicts.

As late as the 1990s international agreements between the United States on the one hand, and the government of Germany and German insurance companies, on the other, established a fund for the payment of Holocaust victims whose insurance policies had been confiscated or cancelled by these companies and the Nazi government. The U.S. federal government leveraged diplomacy and prevailed over California's preference of using litigation to get compensation for the victims.[67]

---

63. Trials of War Criminals Before the Nuremberg Military Tribunals Under Control Council No. 10, Oct. 1946–Apr. 1949, Vol. VI. For the rules relating to the protection of property in war and under occupation, see Chapters 2 and 3.
64. The violations here included the Hague Regulations of 1907 and the Prisoners of War Convention (Geneva, 1929).
65. For a full account, see Mathew Lippman, *War Crimes Trials of German Industrialists: The Other "Schindlers,"* 9 TEMP INT'L & COMP. L.J. 195 (1995).
66. *Id.* at 200.
67. *See Garamendi v. U.S. Dist. Ct.*, No. 05–73652 (9th Cir. 2005) (denying mandamus).

These precedents show that the plundering, pillaging, and looting of mineral resources and private property can subject corporate actors to individual and corporate criminal responsibility under international law and international humanitarian law. Such prosecutions would bring individuals behind mercenary firms and other non-State actors, who operate outside any democratic or legal controls, potentially within the prospect of being held liable. Such a possibility would be a helpful deterrent for weak States without effective control of foreign paramilitaries, as well as rogue security and military services firms.[68]

V. THE LIMITS OF SELF-REGULATION FOR PRIVATE MILITARY AND SECURITY COMPANIES

Private military and security companies have sought to distinguish themselves from what they regard as rogue or mercenary suppliers of military services. These private military and security companies have even formed industry associations. In this section, I will discuss the efforts of these industry associations to self-regulate.

One of these industry associations is the International Peace Operations Association (IPOA). IPOA distinguishes itself from rogue military service or mercenary providers by its commitment to providing professional military services transparently and subject to a Code of Conduct that *encourages* members to "follow all rules of international humanitarian law and human rights law," as well as all "applicable international protocols and conventions" applicable to their work.[69] IPOA also established an enforcement mechanism

---

68. *But see* Mark A. Drumbl, *The Expressive Value of Prosecuting and Punishing Terrorists: Hamdan, The Geneva Conventions, and International Criminal Law*, 75 Geo. Wash. L. Rev. 1165 (2007) (arguing that in the context of terrorism trials, prosecutions serve no more a symbolic purpose).

69. International Peace Operations, Code of Conduct, Version 11, *available at* http://ipoaworld.org/eng/codeofconductv11eng.html (last visited Jan. 2009). The Code of Conduct mentions the following international legal instruments: The Universal Declaration of Human Rights (1948); Geneva Conventions (1949); Protocols Additional to the Geneva Conventions (1977); Chemical Weapons Conventions (1993); and the Voluntary Principles on Security and Human Rights (2000).

under a Standards Committee that can issue nonlegally binding decisions.[70] Anyone or any organization can lodge a complaint against an IPOA member. However, the only corrective measure issued against a member of the IPOA who has been found to violate provisions of the IPOA's code of conduct is suspension from the IPOA.[71] Two other industry groups are the British Association of Private Security Companies (BAPSC) and the Private Security Company Association of Iraq. The BAPSC's Charter obliges its members to "comply with international statutes, with due regard for ethical practice and standards of governance, balancing the provisions of security services with the legitimate concerns of those that are or may be affected by the delivery of those services."[72] Yet, although the Charter states that members are obliged to comply with international statutes, it is not at all clear if this refers to international law and even if it does, it is not clear at all what the BAPSC's commitment to upholding international law is.

Although self-regulation within the private military services industry is laudable, its effectiveness as a matter of international law is demonstrated by the fact that IPOA's Code of Conduct simply encourages, rather than requires its members to conduct their activities in accordance with their international legal obligations,[73] whereas that

---

70. Preamble of the International Peace Operations Association Mechanism, Version 1, *available at* http://ipoaworld.org/eng/enforcementvo1.html (last visited January 2009) [hereinafter IPOA's Enforcement Mechanism].

71. Section 1.4 of the IPOA's Enforcement Mechanism, *supra* note 65. Similarly, if the subject matter of the complaint is subject to ongoing litigation, the Standards Committee is empowered to suspend the enforcement mechanisms until the litigation results are made public, *id.* at § 1.7.

72. Charter of the British Association of Private Security Companies.

73. The Foreign Affairs Committee of the UK Parliament also concluded that self-regulation of private military companies is insufficient, see SELECT COMMITTEE ON FOREIGN AFFAIRS, PRIVATE MILITARY COMPANIES: NINTH REPORT (Oct. 2002). *See also* MADELAINE DROHAN, MAKING A KILLING: HOW CORPORATIONS USE ARMED FORCE TO DO BUSINESS, 324 (2004) (concluding that voluntary codes of an industry or individual corporation will not work based on a review of several codes and their scanty reference to human rights and lack of effective sanctions regime). *See also* SHEEHY ET AL., *supra* note 51, at 140–41 (2009) concluding that self-regulation "is of limited efficacy in terms of

of the BAPSC merely makes reference to what it terms "international statutes" without more.

Private military companies and the IPOA have argued strenuously that insecurity, particularly in weak States, justifies the necessity for their kind of professional and efficient military services, but self-regulation does not nearly begin to address the concerns that arise where the provision of such security services may lead to or result in violations of existing rules of international human rights and humanitarian law.

It is not simply a conjecture that the provision of these services has often been accompanied by violations of international humanitarian law and international human rights law, not to mention of general international law in situations of armed conflict.[74] The inefficacy of self-regulation alone to ensure military service providers comply with international law and that rogue providers are outlawed is evidenced by the fact that Blackwater USA, which joined the IPOA in 2004, decided to withdraw from the Association in October 2007 after it came under scrutiny for its lethal use of force against civilians in Iraq. As a result, Blackwater USA continues to face numerous lawsuits alleging it to be a mercenary army and to have violated international law in its work.[75] Blackwater USA's withdrawal from IPOA came after the IPOA initiated an independent review of whether Blackwater USA had "processes and procedures that were fully sufficient to ensure compliance with the IPOA Code of Conduct."[76]

---

improving accountability and ethical operating procedures particularly if it is lacking in meaningful reporting, enforcement, or monitoring provisions."

74. See *Use of Mercenaries as Means of Violating Human Rights and Impeding the Exercise of the Right of Peoples to Self-Determination*, G.A. Res. 62/145, U.N. Doc. A/RES/62/145 (Mar. 4, 2008).

75. In one incident in Nisoor Square in Baghdad, Iraq on September 16, 2007, Blackwater employees allegedly shot and killed 17 Iraqi civilians. Two days later, Blackwater was barred from operating in Iraq. Suit was filed against Blackwater alleging Blackwater violated the human rights of the deceased by engaging in extrajudicial killings and war crimes and that the corporation operated in an atmosphere where its financial interests prevailed over human life, see *Atban v. Blackwater USA*, No. 1:07-CV-01831 (D.D.C. filed Oct. 11, 2007).

76. Press Release, IPOA Statement Regarding Membership Status of Blackwater USA (Oct. 12, 2007), *available at* http://ipoaonline.org/php/index.php?option=com_content&task=view&id=156&Itemid=80 (last visited

COMMERCIALIZING WAR 245

Another reason to be skeptical of self-regulation of private military or security companies is that they often operate in countries experiencing conflict or that are under occupation. As a result, State weakness in such cases makes it unlikely that self-regulation will result in compliance with rules of international law, inadequate as these may be for regulating these firms. For example, in 2004 the Coalition Provisional Authority, which oversaw Iraq's occupation, issued a memorandum on the Registration Requirements of Private Security Companies that made no reference whatsoever to international law.[77] Instead, the memorandum simply provided for a registration, vetting and licensing framework with an accompanying Code of Conduct that included a hortatory list of terms such as honesty, sincerity, fidelity, and morality.[78] The Code further provided that the companies would "conduct all operations within the bounds of legality, morality and professional ethics."[79] Given the antiseptic attitude of the Coalition Provisional Authority and the Allied Forces in Iraq at the time to conducting the operations there in accordance with international law, these generic honorific references to legality could hardly have been construed as committing private security companies to international law. In any event, by Executive Order, the United States had effectively exempted all the activities of private military companies from being sued in the United States, where a suit may have been brought for a violation of the law of nations.[80] Blackwater USA was

---

Jan. 2009). In mid-February 2009, Blackwater changed its name to Xe in what was widely regarded as a rebranding initiative as a result of the adverse publicity surrounding the allegations of misconduct by its employees.

77. Coalition Provision Authority Memorandum No. 17, Registration Requirements for Private Security Companies, (PSC) (Iraq) CAP/MEM/26 June 2004/17.

78. *Id.* at Code of Conduct for Private Security Companies Operating In Iraq, Annex B. *See also* Section 9(3) of Memorandum 17, which provided that private security companies "must comply with applicable criminal, administrative, commercial and civil laws and regulations, except those provided by law."

79. *Id.*

80. Exec. Order No. 13,303, 68 Fed. Reg. 31,931 (May 22, 2003), also discussed in Chapter 3. For an examination of the options for holding private military contractors accountable, see Laura A. Dickinson, *Government for Hire: Privatizing Foreign Affairs And the Problem of Accountability Under International Law*, 47 WM. & MARY L. REV. 135 (2005).

further immunized from suit in Iraq under the Coalition Provisional Authority's Order No. 17.[81] In addition, private security forces in Iraq were permitted to carry weapons with authorization and to use deadly force not only in self-defense, but also to defend persons who they had been contracted to defend and to prevent "life-threatening offences against civilians."[82] Such a broad writ for the use of deadly force by non-State actors for profit has been a major moral objection to the privatization of military and police functions.[83] Private military and security companies were eventually brought under Iraqi law in a Status of Forces Agreement signed between the government of Iraq and the United States at the end of 2008.[84]

The foregoing goes to show that private military and security companies enjoy very broad freedoms as commercial actors to enter into contractual relationships with States, without their services being explicitly subjected to international law. Given the contracts between States that need the services of private military and security companies invariably include a right to sue for breach of contract, such contracts in effect give these private actors the right to sue these States for failure to pay them for delivery of these services, even if the provision of these services and subsequent conduct violates international law. In effect, militarily weak States contracting for the services of these corporations are doubly disadvantaged. First, given their own utter governance failures, as well as the failure of multilateral or regional initiatives to help them out when they need help, they are vulnerable to domestic or regional paramilitary groups who control parts of the territory. Alternatively, these States may decide to procure the services of external military and security companies to maintain order or to perform specific functions that they are unable to perform.

---

81. *See* Coalition Provisional Authority Order No. 17 (Revised) (Status of the Provisional Coalition Authority, MNF-Iraq and Certain Missions and Personnel in Iraq) § 2 CPA/MEM/26 June 2004/17.

82. *Id.* at Annex A § 2.

83. Sarah Percy, *Morality and Regulation, in* FROM MERCENARIES TO MARKET: THE RISE AND REGULATION OF PRIVATE MILITARY COMPANIES 13, 14–18 (Simon Chesterman & Chia Lehnhardt eds., 2007).

84. The Agreement Between the United States of America and the Republic of Iraq on the Withdrawal of United States Forces from Iraq and the Organization of Their Activities During Their Temporary Presence in Iraq of Nov. 17, 2008, restored Iraq's sovereignty over private military companies.

This vulnerability to private wielders of violence was demonstrated by the Sierra Leone Truth and Reconciliation Commission's observation that the United Nations abandoned Sierra Leone at its hour of need in the thick of war in the early 1990s.[85] Although the Commission made no excuses for the governance failures of the Sierra Leonean State or the use of mercenaries in conflicts, the Commission concluded that Sierra Leone's decision to procure the services of Executive Outcomes was necessitated by a "desperate state of affairs."[86]

This resulting asymmetry between militarily weak and poor States, on the one hand, and private military security firms from the first world, on the other, gives these firms inordinately unequal power over these weak States—a primary theme in my discussion of international investment law in Chapter 5.

VI. EMERGING RULES AND NORMS TO REGULATE PRIVATE SECURITY COMPANIES

Regulation in the home countries where private military, security firms, mercenary groups, and individuals originate is an important part of the available governance options. These options include bans on groups and individuals engaging in mercenary activity abroad that engage in the overthrow of governments and combat for pay; registration of all firms and individuals serving in private military and security roles abroad; and the licensing of individual security and military contracts on a case-by-case basis. Registration could be preconditioned on the commitment of legitimate defense firms not to recruit employees who have been engaged in violations of international human rights or humanitarian law before or those who have been mercenaries. Regulation would also ideally include monitoring and evaluation systems, as well as a complaints mechanism, all ideally paid for by the defense and security industry or jointly funded with the government in question. Such national regulation would be an important tier in the movements toward heightened

---

85. Sierra Leone TRC, *supra* note 4, at ¶¶ 367, 406.
86. *Id.* at ¶ 404. *See also* Mark Malan, *Treading Firmly on the Layered Response Ladder: From Peace Enforcement to Conflict Termination Operations in Africa*, 6 AFR. SECURITY REV. (1997).

international regulation. Such international regulation would be required because not every country is likely to have such legislation, and as such companies are likely to incorporate in those countries with no regulation of private security or military firms.[87]

South Africa, which is a primary source of private military and security companies, has already passed an antimercenary law.[88] It bans direct or indirect participation, initiation or furthering of combat for private gain in an armed conflict. This includes the training, financing, recruiting, and using of combatants for private gain not only in an armed conflict, but also in a coup d'état, uprising, or rebellion against any government. Participation in an armed conflict by a South African must be licensed. South Africans are prohibited from enlisting in the armed forces of a foreign State or any armed force, unless authorized to do so. Unlike the current international conventions on mercenarism, the South African law is broader in scope. For example, in addition to the foregoing prohibitions, Section 3(10) of the Act prohibits the provision of "any other act" that furthers the interest of any party to armed conflict. By focusing on conduct that furthers conflict as opposed to specific prohibited mercenary activities, the Act addresses the definitional shortcomings of the United Nations and Organization of African Union Conventions on Mercenarism.

The United States also has a regulatory framework for private military companies which, in part, gives the President the power to "control the import and export of defense articles and defense services and to provide foreign policy guidance to person of the United States involved in the export and import of such articles and

---

87. For an excellent proposal on regulatory control, see BENEDICT SHEEHY, JACKSON MAOGOTO & VIRGINIA NEWELL, LEGAL CONTROL OF THE PRIVATE MILITARY CORPORATION (2009).

88. The Prohibition of Mercenary Activities and Regulation of Certain Activities in Country of armed Conflict Act 27 of 2007. (exploring a range of national—including corporate law reform—international, legal, and other proposals for control and concluding that no single approach will resolve the problems, but rather that in most cases "a combination of overlapping regulatory regimes is the more realistic and preferable option, and hence, various forms of regulation will likely have to coexist, cognizant of each other, working in conjunction, and in a complementary manner," *id.* at 174).

services."[89] The International Traffic in Arms Regulations in turn specifies the kind of services and articles that may be provided by U.S. firms. Firms providing military or security services abroad are required to be registered and a license for every contract is required. The United Kingdom's House of Commons in 2002 recommended a licensing system like that of the United States.[90] Although the United States and South Africa have been important source countries for mercenaries and their legislation is welcome, having rules of international law that would be apply to countries with no similar national regulation would close the gap in source countries and potentially protect weak States that would by themselves be incapable of regulating rogue private military and security firms or mercenaries that can mobilize more military power than these States can.

One important initiative to provide guidance on the operation of private military and security companies is the Swiss Initiative sponsored by the Swiss government, the International Committee of the Red Cross and Military and Security Companies. It was drafted collaboratively with government and nongovernmental organization representatives. This initiative resulted in the Montreux Document in September 2008, which, at the end of the drafting process was approved by all 17 countries that drafted it including Sierra Leone, Germany, Iraq, South Africa, and the United Kingdom.[91] The Montreux Document provides an exhaustive list of international legal obligations and good practices for private military and security companies as well

---

89. Arms Export Control Act, 22 U.S.C. § 2778 (2002). The Anti-Pinkerton Act of 1893 prohibits the U.S. government from using Pinkerton National Detective agency, or similar private police companies. 5 U.S.C. § 3108 (1893).

90. SELECT COMMITTEE ON FOREIGN AFFAIRS, PRIVATE MILITARY COMPANIES: NINTH REPORT (Oct. 2002). The UK's Foreign Enlistment act makes it illegal for British subjects to join the armed forces of any state warring with another state at peace with Great Britain.

91. MONTREUX, DOCUMENT ON PERTINENT INTERNATIONAL LEGAL OBLIGATIONS AND GOOD PRACTICES FOR STATES RELATED TO OPERATIONS OF PRIVATE MILITARY AND SECURITY COMPANIES (Sept. 17, 2008) [hereinafter MONTREAUX DOCUMENT].

as for their contracting,[92] home,[93] and territorial States.[94] The Montreux Document is perhaps the most comprehensive compilation of the obligations of all these States under international humanitarian and human rights agreements, as well as under customary international law. The Document does not therefore create legal obligations, and it makes clear that the duty to comply with the obligations they have undertaken is upon the States. The Document notes the mirror obligation of territorial, home, and contracting States to ensure respect for international humanitarian law and its implementation, including the enactment of legislation providing sanctions of its violation. In addition, the Document notes the obligation of these States to investigate, prosecute, extradite, or surrender persons who have committed international law crimes, such as torture or hostage takings.[95] The Document further notes that private military and security companies and their personnel, regardless of their status,[96] are obliged to comply with both international humanitarian and human rights law, as well as relevant national laws including those relating to labor, immigration, and tax. In Part Two, the Document then proceeds to provide a lengthy description of good practices relating to private military and security companies for contracting, territorial, and home

---

92. Contracting States are defined as "States that directly contract for the services of PMSCs [private military and security companies], including as appropriate, where such a PMSC subcontracts with another PMSC." *Id.* at ¶ 9(c) of the Preface.

93. Home States are defined as "States of the nationality of a PMSC i.e. where a PMSC is registered or incorporated; if the State where the PMSC is incorporated is not the one where it has its principal place of management, then the State where the PMSC has its principle place of management is the 'Home State.'" *Id.* at ¶ 9(e) of the Preface.

94. Territorial States are simply defined as the "States on whose territory PMSC's operate." *Id.* at ¶ 9(d) of the Preface.

95. The Document also notes the obligation of "all other States" to ensure compliance with international humanitarian law and to refrain from encouraging or assisting its violation by any party to an armed conflict.

96. The Document notes that superior responsibility attaches to governmental officials whether military or not, as well as directors and managers, if PMSC personnel are "under their effective authority and control" and that "superior responsibility is not engaged solely by virtue of conduct." *Id.* at ¶ 27(a) and (b) (Superior Responsibility).

States, including the factors that a contracting State ought to take into account in determining whether or not to procure the services of private military or security companies. These practices include some of those examined in the first paragraph of this section, and its aim is to harmonize these practices on a regional and international level. Amnesty International USA has supported the Montreux Document, but has also noted that its references to international law are inadequate insofar as they do not precisely detail the due diligence obligation and responsibility of States to protect and respect human rights including protection from abuse by transnational corporations.[97] Amnesty International also noted the absence of a reference to international human rights, the United Nations Draft Norms on the Responsibilities of Transnational Corporations and Other Business Enterprises With Regard to Human Rights in the Montreux Document.[98] These Draft Norms were adopted by consensus by the United Nations Human Rights Council in June 2008.[99] The IPOA welcomed the Montreux Document as providing private military and security companies guidance on how to engage in "ethical operations in conflict, post-conflict and disaster relief operations."[100] Clearly, IPOA did not understand, at least based on its Statement, the Montreux Document as requiring private military and security companies to conform their conduct to norms of international human rights. In fact, the Montreux Document does not have any binding legal commitments or any enforcement mechanism, an issue that arises with reference to the Codes of Conduct of private military and security companies.

Clearly, the Montreux Document fills an important gap by providing a comprehensive list of international legal rules and good practices

---

97. AMNESTY INTERNATIONAL, PUBLIC STATEMENT ON THE MONTREUX DOCUMENT ON PERTINENT INTERNATIONAL LEGAL OBLIGATIONS AND GOOD PRACTICES FOR STATES RELATED TO THE OPERATIONS OF PRIVATE MILITARY AND SECURITY COMPANIES DURING ARMED CONFLICT (Oct. 14, 2008).

98. E/CN.4/Sub.2/2003/12/Rev. 2 (2003) (approved by the Sub-Commission on the Promotion and Protection of Human Rights).

99. UN Human Rights Committee General Comment No. 31 CCPR/C/21/Rev.1/Add.13.

100. Press Release, Int'l Peace Operations Ass'n, IPOA Welcomes Agreement on Private Sec. Companies, (Sept. 17, 2008).

relating to the operations of military and security companies. However, it is important to note that efforts to bring the operations of multinational corporations, to conform to the best interests of the countries where they operate now date back more than a few decades.[101] The challenges being posed by military and security companies can therefore be regarded as yet another iteration in the relations between poor countries and investors from richer countries.

VII. CONCLUSIONS

The commercialization of war through contracts between private military and security companies, on the one hand, and governments, on the other, has been shrouded in secrecy and the lack of an effective international legal framework for curbing mercenary activity. States claim to have a right to engage in defense and security contracting without public, parliamentary, or other oversight because matters of national security are necessarily nonpublic. Yet, many States express strong outrage in opposition to mercenary groups and corporations providing military and security services, such as combat, running prisoner of war camps and other functions traditionally understood to be under the command of national military and security services. Sarah V. Percy referred to this state of affairs as constituting a strong norm against mercenarism, which has paradoxically produced a weak and ineffective law against mercenarism.[102]

This chapter shows the growing involvement of foreign and private military, defense, and security firms and mercenaries, particularly in the countries with the least effective control of their often remote and dangerous resource-rich territories. The reliance on private security firms and contractors to maintain order and effective control over the territory of weak and poor States is comparable to the kind of control that rogue non-State actors, such as the Revolutionary United Front, had in Sierra Leone in the early 1990s. Sierra Leone hired a private military company to help it restore order as the country

---

101. *See, e.g.*, Jeffrey Leonard, *Multinational Corporations and Politics in Developing Countries*, 32 WORLD POL. 454 (1980).

102. Sarah V. Percy, *Mercenaries: Strong Norm, Weak Law*, 61 INT'L ORG. 367 (2007).

became enveloped in chaos, and with no regional or multilateral intervention to avert it. Although the hiring of Executive Outcomes was roundly condemned by Western and non-Western States, this chapter has shown that, notwithstanding these strong objections to mercenarism, particularly by poor and weak States, these States are nevertheless more likely to rely on the private providers of force and other military and security firms in the absence of effective regional and multilateral responses to State failure. Precisely because of the lack of effective preventive multilateral and regional solutions, the underlying causes of fragility and weakness of poor States provide an ideal atmosphere within which the private use of force and violence can thrive. Private military and security companies, as shown in this chapter, pride themselves as responses to the failure of these structures of national, regional, and international public governance to play effective roles in maintaining peace and security.

However, although rich countries have effective domestic legal regimes containing the operations of both mercenary groups as well as military and security firms within their territories, it is in their operations in weak and poor States that raise the most concern; especially for purposes of ensuring compliance with international legal obligations, such as the nonuse of force as well as international human rights and humanitarian law. In addition, the natural mineral resources of these countries are vulnerable to mercenary groups and security and military firms.

This chapter has also shown that international law on regulating the use of violence of non-State actors, such as terrorism, is divided between those cases where the state responsibility has been laid down in mandatory terms by the Security Council. By contrast, the regulation of private military and security companies has not attracted the same kind of categorical obligations on the part of States. What is seen then is how the commercialization of violence has created differing responses in international law and institutions to the violence meted out by non-State actors—between those defined as terrorists and currently stringently regulated, on the one hand, and those that define themselves as providing security, order and other ancillary services, who are currently not as stringently regulated under international law.

In addition, this chapter has shown a divide between vigorously pursuing individuals responsible for commission of crimes against bodily integrity in the international criminal context, and much less of a focus on the economic actors who are often complicit as accessories to those crimes. Yet, as we saw above, such a policy that largely leaves out corporate actors who may be held individually liable is not inevitable. Individuals were charged and held responsible for war crimes in the Nuremberg Trials as well as in the recent Van Anraat trial under Dutch law. International and national criminal justice systems could do well to close the artificial gap between those responsible for directly engaging in war crimes, and those indirectly involved in so doing by providing access to arms, finance and markets for violently extracted resources that cause crimes to bodily integrity in the first place.[103]

Although an argument may be made for legitimate private military and security companies to help weak States, private military and security companies ought not be a substitute for having national militaries under civilian control.[104] After all, private military operators are profit-driven and may not afford the kind of outlays necessary to sustain a well-functioning, disciplined and equipped military. By contrast, well-functioning governments may and have often done so even in poor countries. As such, the market for military and security functions should not be a substitute for national militaries. Indeed, countries with such militaries under civilian control are less likely to fall into the kind of chaos and disorder that necessitates hiring of private providers of military services, including combat. Further, as private military companies are for-profit entities and unlike national armies that are paid even during peacetime, private military companies do not have the same incentive to end wars without which they have no business.

Finally, for countries unable to provide security and military services to ward off threats to their population and resources, regional and multilateral solutions operating with the consent of the governments of such countries and under international law is a much more

---

103. Dickinson, *supra* note 62, at 709 (noting that there are few ideal venues to hold non-state actors for violations of international law accountable).

104. Civilian control over military and police functions has been crucial in African states that have experienced coups and other kinds of political turmoil. *See* Samuel Decalo, *Modalities of Civil Military Stability in Africa*, 27 J. MOD. AFR. STUD. 547 (1998); Samuel Decalo, *Towards Understanding the Sources of Stable Civilian Rule in Africa: 1960–1990*, 10 J. CONTEMP. AFR. STUD. 66 (1990).

COMMERCIALIZING WAR 255

preferable alternative than the provision of private military force.[105] Indeed, the often cited instances of restoration of order by Executive Outcomes in places such as Sierra Leone were short-lived. Such brief restorations of order that hardly deal with the underlying political, social, and economic causes of the crises that are best addressed, not by profit-motivated private companies, but through a combination of national, regional, and multilateral initiatives over a sustained period of time.[106]

Ultimately, tougher regulatory controls through a new international legal framework and national standards, although important, will be ineffective without a concurrent multilateral commitment to dealing with mercenaries as decisively as with other non-State actors who wield violence.

---

105. It is difficult to draw the line between the provision of legitimate noncombat security or military services such as training, advice, intelligence gathering, or logistical support as these may quickly merge into combat and operational support for ongoing conflicts.

106. Perhaps in this context, these corporations can have a role. *But see* David Francis, *Mercenary Intervention in Sierra Leone: Providing National Security or International Exploitation,* 20 THIRD WORLD Q. 319 (1999).

INDEX

AAPL case, 168–77, 169*n*77, 170*n*82, 172*n*98, 173*n*101
Abbott, Hanger v. (1867), 21, 21*n*84
Abdjian Peace Agreement (1996), 226
Absolute immunity. *See* Drago doctrine
Absolutist rule, xvii–xviii, 2–3, 2*n*3
Acquired rights doctrine, 159
Adams, John
  on Barbary pirates, 56*n*49
  lifting of ban on armed merchant ships, 110
  relations with France, 109–11
Afghanistan war (2001-), 56*n*47, 74–75, 75*n*13
Africa. *See also specific countries*
  challenges to economic law, 158–68
  acquired rights doctrine and, 159
  clean slate theory, 158
  NIEO and, 160–62
  rejection of market-led development, 162–68
  State succession doctrine and, 158–59
  colonial mercantile companies in, 201–7
  constraints on development, 153*n*25, 190
  inherited colonial governance of, 221
  UN Security Council and, 6
  World Bank on mining and, 199
African Union, 231–32
Air Force, U.S., 82

Alexander the Great, 30–31
Alien Tort Act (1879), 93
Al Qaeda, 7
Alvarez, Jose, 6*n*21, 7*n*27, 52*n*31, 58*n*54, 89*n*78, 166*n*70, 236*n*48
Amelia (ship), 127–28
American exceptionalism, 101, 101*n*122, 102*n*127
American hegemony. *See* United States
American Insurance Co. v. 356 Bales of Cotton (1828), 3–4
American Manufacturing & Trading, Inc. v. Republic of Zaire (1997), 175–76
American Revolution, 16–17
Amity, Economic Relations, and Consular Rights Treaty, 183–84, 184*n*144
Amnesty International USA 251
Amodu Tijani v. Sec'y of S. Nig. (1921), 68, 68*n*87
Ando, Nisuke, 92
Anghie, Antony, 32, 141*n*207, 158
Anglo-Boer War (1899), 209
Antidepredation rules, xix
Anti-Federalists, 116–17
Arab countries, UN Security Council and, 6
Arab stereotypes, 100–101
Arbitral forums, 153–56
Argentina, 178, 178*nn*120–21, 181–83
Arms Export Control Act (2002), 249*n*89
Arthur, Chester A., 203

258 INDEX

Asia. *See also specific countries*
  challenges to economic law, 158–68
    acquired rights doctrine and, 159
    clean slate theory, 158
    NIEO and, 160–62
    rejection of market-led development, 162–68
    State succession doctrine and, 158–59
Asian Agricultural Products Limited v. Democratic Socialist Republic of Sri Lanka (1991). *See AAPL* case
AUC (United Self Defense Forces of Colombia), 228–29
Azerbaijan, oil resources in, 75*n*13

Baath Party (Iraq). *See also* De-Baathification
  confiscation of property, 8–10, 8*n*31, 9*nn*34–35
  racism and, xx
  prohibition against, 10, 10*n*39, 95–96
Baker, Nireaha Tamaki v. (1901), 68–69
Banco Sabbatino de Cuba v. Sabbatino (1964), 164–65
Banovic case, 56, 56*n*46
Barreme, Little v. (1804), 131–32, 132*n*155
Battles, Custer, 40*n*180
Beale, Joseph, 153*n*26
Belgium
  CERDS and, 163–64
  colonial mercantile companies, 201–7, 202*n*34
  diamond imports and, 214
Belligerent rights vs. commercial freedom, 105–44. *See also* Marshall, John; Native Americans
  overview, 105–7, 143–44
  Native American economic relations, 137–43

U.S. military, historical weakness and, 107–14
  international legal responses to, 115–37, 121*n*88
Benton, Laura, 33, 143
Berman, Nathaniel, ix, 48*n*14, 54*n*35, 55*n*40, 76*n*13, 145*n*1
Berlin Conference (1875), xvi
Berlin Conference (1884), 202–3
Bilateral investment agreements (BITs)
  in developing countries, 162
  inefficiency of, 190*n*156
  overprotection of investor rights, 166–68, 166*nn*69–70
  security escape clauses in, 179–82
  strict or absolute liability under, 169, 169*n*76
Bin Laden, Osama, 7
Black, Jeremy, 222
Blacklisting, human rights law and, 7–8
Blackwater USA, 228, 228*n*15, 244, 244*nn*75–76, 245–46
Blair, Tony
  on British values as universal, 96
  on justification for Iraq War, 34
Blood diamonds, 198
Bolivia, 166
Botswana, 214
Bremer, Paul, 36–37, 36*n*161
Bretton Woods, xvi, 145
British Association of Private Security Companies (BAPSC), 243–44
Brown v. United States (1814), 15, 15*n*62, 133
Burma, 229, 229*n*23
Bush, George W.
  Iraq War and
    disregard for international law and, 72–73, 89
    Executive Order 13303, 92–93, 92*n*91, 245

justification for, 34–36, 40, 40n179
private contractors and, 40n180, 92–93
torture violations and, 40, 40n179
on use of force with state or non-state enemies, 73n7

Caltex, United States v. (1952), 5
Calvin's Case (1602), 30–35, 140n198
Calvo doctrine
  CERDS and, 160
  origins of, 146–47, 155
  scope of, 157–58
Cambodia, 238
Canada, 112
Capital-exporting vs. capital-importing States. See also specific States
  acquired rights doctrine and, 159
  NIEO and, 160
  retaliatory threats and, 167–68, 168n74
  rules of economic governance and, 153–56
  State succession doctrine and, 158–59
  structural power and, 188, 188n153
Capitulation treaties, 157–58
Captured and Abandoned Property Act (1863), 22
Certain Norwegian Loans case (1957), 149–50
Charter of Economic Rights and Duties of States (CERDS), 160, 163–64, 164n62
Chase, Samuel, 2n3
Cheney, Dick, 75n13
Cherokee Nation v. Georgia (1831), 67n83, 140–41
Chesapeake (ship), 113–14
Chimni, ix
Chiquita Brands International, Inc., 228–29

Christian religion, prejudice against non-believers by, 30–34, 31n134, 140n198, 142–43
Civil War period
  confiscation cases, 3–5, 4n11, 10
  suspension doctrine and, 21, 21n84
Clean slate theory, 158
CMS Gas Transmission Co. v. Argentine Republic (2005), 181–83
Coalition Provisional Authority (CPA)
  Bush administration distancing from, 40n180
  de-Baathification and, 8–9, 8n31, 9nn34–35, 95–97, 95n101, 95n105
  on equal rights for women, 83–84, 84n51, 84n53
  on foreign investment profits, 36–39, 36n161
  free market model and, 91–93
  on private military and security companies, 245–46, 246n78
  UN Security Council and, 89, 89n75
Coke, Edward
  on European supremacy over non-Europeans, 140n198
  on sovereign confiscatory rights, 30, 32–34
Colombia, 228–29
Colonial disempowerment, xiv–xv, xxi
Colonial mercantile companies, 200–207
Coltan, 214
Commercial freedom vs. belligerent rights, 105–44. See also Marshall, John; Native Americans
  overview, 105–7, 143–44
  Native American economic relations, 137–43
  U.S. military, historical weakness and, 107–14
  international legal responses to, 115–37, 121n88

Confiscation, during wartime
  balancing commerce and, 20–28
  classical customary international
    law prohibition of, 46–58
  exemption of property/contract
    rights from extinction,
    47–51, 47n12
  inconsistent extinction of
    private property/contract
    rights, 51–58
  commerce and, 14–20
  exceptional circumstances
    doctrine and, 28–40
  of financial assets
    under antiterrorism initiatives,
    5–10, 5n21, 7n29, 58n54,
    235–36
  justification for, 2–14
  executive orders, 3, 3n6
  sovereignty, 2–3, 2n3
  war power vs. municipal
    power, 3–5, 3n4
  U.S. Supreme Court on, xviii, 3–4,
    14, 14n58, 21–22, 22n89
Confiscation Acts, 4–5
Congressional Act (1798), 24–25,
  25n103
Congressional Act (1799), 24–25,
  25n103, 124–26, 125nn106–7
Conquest, exceptional
  circumstances doctrine
  and, 28–40
Conquest, private property/contract
  rights and, 43–70
  overview, 43–45, 69–70
  hegemony and non-European
    property, 58–69
  Native American land claims,
    61–69
  prerogative of the Crown over
    corporate private property,
    59–61, 60n58
  prohibition of confiscation, 43n3,
    46–58

exemption of property/contract
  rights from extinction,
  47–51, 47n12
inconsistent extinction of
  private property/contract
  rights, 51–58
Constitution (Iraq, 2005), 10, 10n39,
  95–96
Constitution, U.S, 17, 17nn70–71.
  See also specific Amendments
Contract rights
  conquest and
    overview, 43–45, 69–70
    civil vs. military aspects of war
      and, 47–48, 50, 50n23
    considerations of humanity,
      50–51, 55–56, 55n45
    continuity of commerce
      and, 49–50
    Rousseau-Portalis doctrine
      and, 48–49, 49n19
    State succession and, 49n21
  conquest and inconsistent
    extinction of, 51–58
    civil vs. military aspects of war
      and, 54–56
    hegemonic militaries
      and, 51–54
    war against terrorism
      and, 56–58
  in occupied Iraq, 71–103
    overview, 71–75, 100–103
    applicable law and remedies,
      77–80, 77nn14–18, 78n19,
      79n28
    claims of Iraqis, 81–82, 81n38
    claims of Iraqi women, 82–85,
      82n45
    private and economic rights,
      comparative review, 93–99
    transforming of, 85–87, 85–93
Corruption, private contractors in
  Iraq and, 40, 40n180
Cote d'Ivoire, 215

INDEX 261

Counter-Terrorism Committee (UN)
  Iraq War and, 6, 57n50
  mandate of, 6n22
  U.S. anti-terrorism and, 57–58, 58n54
Crowe, S.E., 205, 205n51
Cuellar, Mariano-Florentino, 101
Cultural artifacts, looting of, 81, 81n41, 90

De-Baathification (Iraq)
  comparative review of, 93–99, 95n101
  confiscation of property, 8–10, 8n31, 9nn34–35
  racism and, xx
  CPA and, 8–9, 8n31, 9nn34–35, 95–97, 95n101, 95n105
  2005 Constitution and, 10, 10n39, 95–96
De-Baathification Council (Iraq), 9–10
Declaration of Rights of Man and Citizen, 17n68
De-Fascistization, comparative review of, 93–99
Democratic-Republican party. See Republican Party
Democratic Republic of Congo v. Uganda (2005), 19, 19n79, 177–78, 191–92, 192n4, 219–20, 230n27
Democratic Republic of the Congo (DRC)
  Coltan and, 214
  conflict diamonds and, 215
  corporate exploitation of, 239–40
  looting of natural resources from, 19, 19n79
  rebel groups in, 218–19, 221n112
De-Nazification, comparative review of, 93–99
Dependency theories, 161
Diamond trade. See Resource-extraction wars

Disu Raphael, Sunmonu v. (1927), 68
Drago, Luis M., 147–56
Drago doctrine, xviii–xix, 147–58, 147n2, 148n7
Dred Scott viewpoint, racism in, 5
Dupuy, Rene-Jean, 163–64, 164n62
Dutch East India Company, 201

East African Court of Appeal, 67–68, 210
East India Company, 200, 201n32, 202n34
Economic Community of West African States Æ Military Observer Group (ECOMOG), 227
Economic relations. See Investment law, war and
Educational, Scientific and Cultural Organization (UN), 83
Egypt, 175–76
El Shifa v. United States (2003), 5, 5n20
Emancipatory universalism, 50–51
Embargo Act (1807), 105n1, 113–14
Enlightenment, 16–17
Equality, international law guarantees of, xxi
Eritrea, State of, 1n2, 19
Eritrea-Ethiopia Claims Commission, 1n2, 19
Ethiopia, 1n2, 19
Eurocentrism, 222
European Convention on Human Rights, 98–99, 98n114, 99n116
European Court of Human Rights, 56, 56n46
European Court of Justice (ECJ), 7n29
European Union, 215n88
Exceptional circumstances doctrine, 28–40
Executive Branch, U.S., 44, 44nn5–6
Executive Orders
  13303, 92–93, 92n91, 245
  confiscation and, 3, 3n6

Executive Outcomes, 223–24, 224n3, 225–27, 227n13, 231–32, 247

Federal Democratic Republic of Ethiopia, 1n2
Federalists, 117, 120
Fifth Amendment, 3n4, 5
Findlay v. The William (1793), 22–23, 22n91, 122n94
Flick case, 240–41
Force, use of. *See also specific treaties*
   Bush on, 73n7
   Charter on use of force, 182n136
   ICJ on, 149–50
   prohibition on, xvi
   UN Charter on, 150–52, 150n18, 182
   UN Security Council lack of consent for in Iraq, 36
   U.S. National Security Strategy on, 73n7, 74n11
Foreign Assets Control Office, U.S., 3
Foreign Claims Act (1942), 82, 84–85, 85nn54–55
Foreign investment, in Iraq, 36–37, 36n161
Foreign investors, war damage settlements, xix
Fourth Geneva Convention. *See* Geneva Conventions
Framers intent, 17, 17nn70–71
France
   CERDS and, 163–64
   confiscation of American cargo, 23–26, 23n93, 109, 124, 124n100
   U.S. embargo against, 26–27, 26nn115–16
   early superiority of, xviii, 105
   French Revolution, 16–17, 16n66, 17n68
   opposition to U.S. Iraq occupation, 36n159
   seizure decrees, 26–27, 26n112
   size of army, 109

   U.S. early economic dependence on, 107–14
   war with Britain (1793), 119–20
Freedom Support Act (1992), 75n13
Free market model
   foreign investment and, 162
   in Iraq
   assumption of superiority, 36–40
   multinational corporations and, 75
   privatization and, 91–93, 103
   women and, 84, 84n53
   rejection of, 162–68
French Revolution, 16–17, 16n66, 17n68

Gaza Strip, 51, 53nn34–35
General Agreement on Tariffs and Trade (GATT), 144, 179–85, 180n124
Geneva Conventions
   Article 33, protection of civilians, 17–18
   Article 35, protection of private property, 18
   Article 46, protection of civilians during war or occupation, 53–54, 78–79, 89, 99
   Article 47, mercenaries, 18, 230–32
   Fourth Convention
   Article 46, protection of civilians during war or occupation, 78–79
   CPA and, 89
   Inter-American Commission of Human Rights and, 99
   Irsael opposition to, 53–54
   on Israel and Gaza Strip, 51, 53nn34–35
Germany
   CERDS and, 163–64
   de-Nazification, comparative review of, 93–99, 94nn98–99

INDEX 263

funding of restitution for Holocaust victims, 241
Montreux Document and, 249–52
Nazi confiscation of Jewish property, xx
Nuremberg trials and industrialists, 196n18, 237–38, 240–41
private property in, xx
recognition of International Association of the Congo, 205
Venezuela and, 147, 147n2, 155–56
Gerry, Elbridge, 110, 110n21
Ghana, 215
Global Witness, 214
Gordon, Thomas, 1
Gray, Horace, 49n19
Great Britain
  acquisition of Swazi Territory, 207–11, 209n66
  BIT with Sri Lanka, 169, 169n76, 172–75, 172n98, 173n101
  confiscation of American cargo, 23–26, 23n93
  U.S. embargo against, 26–27, 26nn115–16
  Hague Regulations and, 152, 152n22
  Imperial British East Africa Company and, 206–7
Iraq War and
  confiscation of Baathist property, xx
  economic reforms and, 91n86
  lack of UN Security Council consent for, 36
  recognition of International Association of the Congo, 205
  U.S. early economic dependence on, 107–14
  Venezuela and, 147, 147n2, 155–56
  Virginia debtors and, 115–37
Green Paper on Private Military Companies (Great Britain), 230
Griffin, Cyrus, 118

Grotius, Hugo, xvi, 11–13, 12n49
Group of, 77, 160–62
Grovogui, Siba, 63n63, 201n30
Gulf War (1991), 83
Gurkha Security Guards, 226n10, 227

Habeas relief, for U.S. detainees, 41n182, 44n5
Hague Conference (1906), 149–52, 151n20
Hague Convention Regulations (1907)
  overview, xvi, 115
  Article 23(g), on necessities of war, 46–47, 48n15
  Article, 43
    on looting of natural resources, 19, 19n79
    on scope of occupier, 86–87
    U.S expansion of occupying powers and, 76–77, 92
  Article 46, prohibition of confiscation, 18
  Article, 53
    on military use of objects, 86
    on reparations for violations of, 97–98, 97n112, 98n113
  Article 55, on safeguarding of public property by occupier, 85–86, 85n56
  Article 56, on cultural artifacts as private property, 81n41
  debate on private property rights of occupying forces, 78–80
  domestic law vs., 79–80, 80n31
  Drago doctrine and, xviii–xix
  Iraqi conquest/occupation and, 88–93, 103
  Jay's Treaty and, 1n2
  on mercenaries, 232
  on prohibition of destruction or seizure of enemy property, 17
Hall, W.E., 148, 148n9
Halliburton, Cheney and, 75n13

Hamilton, Alexander
　on commerce and peace, 16, 16n64
　on Jay's Treaty, 16
　on trade with British, 107–8
Hanger v. Abbott (1867), 21, 21n84
Harlan, John Marshall, 165n67
Haycraft v. United States (1874), 21–22
Hegemonic militaries, 51–54.
　See also Military, U.S.
Hegemony, 87. *See also specific countries*
Hegemony and non-European property
　conquest of Native American lands, 61–69
　prerogative of the Crown over corporate private property, 59–61, 60n58
High Commission for De-Baathification, 10
High-tech warfare, 54–56
Hochschild, Adam, 205, 205n52
Holland, 23n93
Humanitarian law, international
　ban on mercenarism and, 234–35
　IPOA and, 242–44
　military necessity and, 54n39, 55, 55n40, 55n43
　Montreux Document and, 250, 250n95
　non-State actors and, 217–19, 253
　Nuremberg trials and industrialists, 241–42
　property ownership and, 17–18
　U.S. occupation of Iraq and, 89–90
Humanity, considerations of
　high-tech militarization and, 55–56
　laws of war and, 80, 80n35
　Moore on, 50–51
　unintended consequences of war, 55n45
Human rights. *See also specific organizations*

mercenaries and, 234
prohibition of destruction or seizure of enemy property and, 17
protection of as guise for hegemony, 87
torture violations in Iraq and, 40, 40n179
Human Rights Council (UN), 251
Human rights law
　blacklisting and terrorism initiatives and, 7–8
　IPOA and, 242–44
　Montreux Document and, 250
　non-State actors and, 225, 241
Hussein, Saddam, 8–10, 34, 83, 88, 240. *See also* Baath Party (Iraq)
Hylton, Daniel, 118
Hylton, Ware v. (1796), 118–19, 134

Ideology, mercenarism and, xxi–xxii
Imperial British East Africa Company, 200, 206–7
Individualism, in Enlightenment, 16–17
Inter-American Commission of Human Rights, 99, 99n117
Inter-American Court of Human Rights, 99
International African Association, 201–7
International Association of the Congo, 203–7
International Center for the Settlement of Investment Disputes (ICSID), 162–63, 163n57, 166–68, 176n114. *See also specific cases*
International Committee of the Red Cross and Military and Security companies, 249
International Convention Against the Recruitment, Use, Financing and Training of Mercenaries (UN), 232

INDEX 265

International Court of Justice (ICJ).
See also specific cases
  on customary rules, 79n28
  on force and debt contracts, 149–50
  on Uganda's looting of natural
    resources, 19, 19n79, 239–40
International Criminal Court (ICC),
  19, 238–40
International Economic Emergency
  Powers Act, U.S. (1977), 3, 3n7
International Monetary Fund, 226
International Peace Operations
  Association (IPOA), 242–44,
  243n71, 251
International Traffic in Arms
  Regulations, 249
Investment law, war and, 145–90.
  See also specifc cases
  overview, 145–46, 188–90
  bilateral investment agreements,
    162, 166–68, 166nn69–70,
    169, 169n76, 179–82, 190n156
  Calvo clause influences, 146–47,
    157–58
  challenges to economic law, 158–68
  acquired rights doctrine and, 159
  clean slate theory, 158
  NIEO and, 160–62
  rejection of market-led
    development, 162–68
  State succession doctrine and,
    158–59
  forcible intervention/coercion
    and, 185–88, 188n152
  privatized investment dispute
    forums, 167–68
  rules of economic governance
    and, 146–56
  capital-exporting vs. capital-
    importing States, 153–56
  coercion and, 153–56, 154n31
  Drago doctrine and, 147–56
  Latin America and, 146–47,
    157–58

socialist approach to, 159n47
State responsibility for war
  destruction, 168–85
  due diligence and, 177–78,
    177n118
  national security issues and,
    171–85, 174n102, 176n114,
    177n118, 182n136
  potential commerce and, 183–85
  strict or absolute liability
    and, 169–77, 169n77
Iran, 183–85
Iraq. See also De-Baathification;
  Occupation of Iraq
  Arab stereotypes and, 100–101
  economy
    foreign investment
      and, 36–37, 36n161
    free market model in, 36–40,
      75, 84, 84n53, 91–93, 103
    U.S. intervention in, 36n161
    as militarily weaker State, 34
    Montreux Document and, 249–52
  oil resources in
    Cheney on, 75n13
    Executive Order 13303
      and, 92–93, 92n91
    lack of profit-repatriation in,
      36–37
    protection of multinational
      corporations and, 36–37,
      71–72, 71n2, 229–30
  Status of Forces Agreement and,
    246, 246n84
  UN sanctions on, 83
  U.S. Justice Department on legal
    reforms in, 96n107
Iraq Development Fund, 92–93
Iraqi De-Baathification Council,
  95–96
Iraqi Governing Council
  on citizen's rights, 72n3
  on equality, 83
  religious laws and, 83, 83n50, 84n51

Iraqi Liberation Act (1998), 88*n*74
Iraq War (2003-)
  Bush, G.W. and
    disregard for international law
      and, 72–73, 89
    Executive Order 13303, 92–93,
      92*n*91, 245
    justification for, 34–36, 40,
      40*n*179
    private contractors and,
      40*n*180, 92–93
    torture violations and, 40,
      40*n*179
  comparative review of, 33–40
  corruption among private
    contractors, 40, 40*n*180
  French opposition to, 36*n*159
  Great Britain and, 34, 36, 91*n*86
  Hague Regulations and, 88–93, 103
  humanitarian law and, 89–90
  looting in, 81, 81*n*41, 90
  oil resources in, 36–37
  racism and confiscation in, xx
  UN Security Council and, 6, 36,
    57*n*50, 88–89, 89*n*75
  U.S. justification for, 34–36
  U.S. torture violations and, 40,
    40*n*179
Iredell, James, 118
Irregular groups. *See* Non-State actors
*Islamic Republic of Iran v. United
  States*, 183–85
Israel
  Gaza Strip/West Bank territories
    and, 51, 53*nn*34–35
  occupation of Gulf of Suez, 18*n*76
Italy
  de-Fascistization, comparative
    review of, 93–99
  private property in, xx
  Venezuela and, 147, 147*n*2, 155–56

Japan
  post-war liquidation of Zaibatsu,
    93–99, 94*nn*99–100

private property in, xx
U.S. compliance with Hague
  Regulations in, 79
Jay, John, 118
Jay's Treaty (1794)
  Hague Convention Regulations
    and, 1*n*2
  Hamilton on, 16
  Marshall on, 136
  provisions of, 24*n*96, 108–9
Jefferson, Thomas
  on Barbary pirates, 56*n*49
  on behalf of merchants, 112
  on confiscation of private
    property, 22
  on embargo, 26, 26*nn*115–16,
    105, 105*n*1
  on lifting of ban on armed
    merchant ships, 110
  on property ownership, 17*n*68,
    17*n*70
Jeffersonians. *See* Republican
  Party
Jews, Nazi confiscation of
  property, xx
Johnson, Thomas, 129–31,
  134*n*169, 141
Johnson v. M'Intosh (1823), 29*n*121,
  30, 62–63, 63*nn*63–64, 80*n*37,
  138–40, 138*nn*184–85, 210–11
Jones v. Walker (1791), 118
Judge Advocate General's Corps
  (U.S. Air Force), 82
Judiciary Act (1789), 117
Juno, The (ship), 132–33
Jus ad bellum rules, 191*n*2, 196,
  196*n*18
Jus cogens norm, xxi–xxii, 7*n*29,
  150*n*18, 233
Jus gentium. See Law of nations
Jus in bellum rules, 191*n*2, 194,
  194*n*14
Justice Department, U.S.
  Chiquita Brands International,
    Inc. and, 228–29

INDEX 267

on Iraqi legal reforms, 96n107
private contractor corruption and, 40, 40n180

Kasson, John A., 202, 202n36
Kennedy, David, ix, xvii n7, 13n55, 48n14, 55n40, 135n172, 191n1
Kennedy, Duncan, 39n178, 154n31, 155n34, 199n26
Kimberley Process Certification Scheme, 198, 214–17, 215n86, 215n88, 216nn90–91
Klein v. United States (1869), 22, 22n89
Knox, Sands v. (1806), 132–33
Koh, Harold Hongju, 101
Kooijmans, Peter, 191–92, 219–20
Kuwait, 98n113

Latin America
 Calvo doctrine, 146–47, 157–58
 Drago doctrine, 147–49, 147n2
 UN Security Council and, 6
Lauterpacht, Hersch, 149–50
Law of nations. *See also* Marshall, John; *specific cases*
 Executive Orders and, 93
 Gray on, 49n19
 Grotius on, 12–13, 12n49
 history of, xvi
 Native Americans and, 32, 141n207
Leopard (ship), 113–14
Leopold II, King, 201–7, 205n52, 206n55
LG&E Energy Corp. v. Argentine Republic, 178, 178nn120–21
Liberia, 204, 204n46
Libya, 163
Lincoln, Abraham, 4
Little v. Barreme (1804), 131–32, 132n155
Locke, John, 17, 17n70
Looting
 in Iraq, 81, 81n41, 90
 in Uganda, 19, 19n79, 239–40
Lotus case, 232–33, 233n33
Lucas, Strother v. (1838), 61–69, 62n62

Madison, James
 on overreach of Executive power by Adams, 110
 on War of, 1812, 27, 111–12
Maley, William, 131
Maley v. Shattuck (1806), 131
Maori (New Zealand), 67
Marshall, John. *See also specific case*
 on commercial rights of non-belligerents and neutrals during wartime, 121–37
 on Jay's Treaty, 136
 on lack of fixed rule in law of nations, 125n109
 on liberal commerce, 128–31
 on right of limited hostilities, 127–28, 127n121, 129n137
 on rights of neutrals, 131–32, 132n155
 on suspension and restoration, 133, 133n164
 on international legal jurisprudence and neutrality, 119–21
 mission to France and, 110, 120–21, 121n87
 on Native Americans
  discovery and conquest of, 29–33, 29n121, 29n125, 137–43, 138nn184–85, 139nn196–97, 142n208, 210–11
  inability to trade with, 141–42
  nonrecognition of land rights, 63, 63n64, 66
  on rights of Cherokee nation, 67n83, 140–41
  as savages, 29–30, 139
  on U.S. as guardian of, 141–42
 on sovereign confiscatory rights, 25–26, 25n107, 28, 28n120
 on sovereignty and property rights, 14–16, 14n59, 15n62, 20n83
 on Virginian debtors vs. British creditors, 115–19, 116n59, 117–19

Marshall Court, overview, xviii, 105–7
Masai tribe (East Africa), 67–68, 67n82, 210
Mercenarism. *See also* Wars, commercialization of
 overview, xvi–xvii, xxi–xxii
 mercenary, definitions of, 230–32
Metropolitan authority
 incorporation of separate legal entities and, 33, 143
 non-Christian peoples and, xx–xxi, 142–43
Milan Decree (1807), 113
Militarized humanitarianism doctrine, 55
Military, U.S.
 formation of Navy and Marine Corps, 111
 historical weakness of, 107–14
 international legal responses to, 115–37
 Middle East bases, 75, 75n12
 outsourcing by, 227
 Pearl Harbor attack and, 5
 role of strength of, 74n11
 size of army, 109
 war veterans and, 227
Military necessity doctrine
 determination of, 46–48
 hegemonic objectives and, 70–77
 international humanitarian law and, 54n39, 55, 55n40, 55n43
 as justification for confiscation, 3
 Pearl Harbor and, 5
 principle of humanity vs., 80
 war crimes and, 18–19
Miller, *Sobhuza II v.* (1926), 207–11, 209n66
Miller v. United States (1870), 3n4, 4, 5, 21, 53n33
M'Intosh, Johnson v. (1823), 29n121, 30, 62–63, 63nn63–64, 80n37, 138–40, 138nn184–85, 210–11
Monroe, James, 112

Montesquieu, 16
Montreux Document (2008), 249–52, 250nn92–96
Moore, John Bassett, 50–51, 135
Morgan, John Tyler, 204
"Moving the Iraq Economy from Recovery to Sustainable Growth" (Treasury Department, U.S.), 37–38
Multinational corporations. *See also* Wars, commercialization of; *specific corporations*
 dependency theories and, 161
 Iraq occupation by U.S. and, 38, 71–72, 71n2, 75
 privatization and, 91–93, 103
 petroleum corporations, 229–30
Muslim stereotypes, 100–101
Mutua, Wa Makau, ix, 35n153, 193n6

Namibia, 214
Napoleon, 113
National security
 disregard of international law and, 72–75
 poor States and, xix
 restrictions on commerce and, xix–xx
 State responsibility for war destruction and, 171–85, 174n102, 176n114, 177n118, 182n136
National Security Strategy, U.S.
 preemption doctrine, 52n31, 74n11
 on use of force with state or non-state enemies, 73n7, 74n11
 on U.S. military bases in Middle East, 75n12
 on War Against Terrorism, 57
 in Muslim world, 74n8
 Obama administration and, 57n51

Native Americans
  discovery and conquest of, xv–xvi,
    xix, 31n134, 32n140
  Marshall on, 29–30, 29n121,
    29n125, 137–43,
    138nn184–85, 139nn196–97,
    142n208
  economic relations
    with U.S., 137–43
  hegemony and non-European
    property
  nonrecognition of land rights
    of, 61–69, 63n64, 64n70,
    66n76
  prejudice against based on
    religion, 30–34, 31n134,
    140n198, 142–43
  rights of Cherokee nation,
    Marshall on, 67n83, 140–41
  as savages, Marshall on, 29–30, 139
Natural law
  international ascendance of, xvi
  morality and
  prisoners of war as slaves and,
    11–13, 11n42
Natural resources/minerals, xxii. See
  also Resource-extraction wars
Nazi Germany
  confiscation of Jewish property, xx
  de-Nazification, comparative
    review of, 93–99, 94nn98–99
Nereide case, 25–26, 25n108,
  125n109, 128–31
Netherlands, 105, 240
Neumann, Franz, 20, 20n83
Neutrality Act (1794), 108
Neutrality doctrine
  history of, 22–28
  Marshall on, 110, 119–21, 121n87
  Supreme Court on, xviii, 122
New International Economic Order
  (NIEO), 160–62
New Zealand, 67. See also *specific
  cases*

Nicaragua
  opposition to ICSID, 166
  U.S. and, 180–82, 180n125,
    180n128, 183, 184
Nigeria, 68, 68n87, 229n25
Nireaha Tamaki v. Baker (1901),
  68–69
Non-Christian peoples
  metropolitan authority and,
    xx–xxi, 142–43
  prejudice against
    as justification for confiscation,
      30–34, 31n134, 140n198
  Vitoria's justification for killing
    of, 142
Non-European peoples. See
  Hegemony and non-European
  property; Non-Western societies
Nonintercourse doctrine, 49–50,
  50n22, 132–35, 134n169
Non-State actors. See also Wars,
  commercialization of
  humanitarian law and, 217–19, 253
  human rights law and, 225, 241
  pirates, 56, 56n49
  resource conflicts and, 192–200,
    193n8, 194, 194n13, 211–20,
    213n80
  terrorism and, 56–58, 236
Non-Western societies. See also
  Native Americans
  absolutist rule and, xvii–xviii
  definition of war and, 222,
    222n115
  hegemony and non-European
    property
  American exceptionalism
    and, 101–3
  prerogative of the Crown over
    corporate private property,
    59–61, 60n58, 67–69
  metropolitan authority and,
    xx–xxi
  racism and confiscation in, xx

North American Free Trade
   Agreement (NAFTA),
   166nn69–70, 167n72
Northern Ireland, 169
Nyerere doctrine, 158, 158n42

Obama, Barack
   anti-terrorism and, 57n51
   on international relations, 105n3
O'Connell, Mary, ix, 90n82,
   197n18, 228n16
Occupation of Iraq, private
   property/contract rights and,
   71–103. *See also* Hague
   Convention Regulations;
   Iraq War
   overview, 71–75, 100–103
   applicable law and remedies,
      77–80, 77nn14–18, 78n19,
      79n28
   claims of Iraqis, 81–82, 81n38
   claims of Iraqi women, 82–85,
      82n45
   multinational corporations and,
      38, 71–72, 71n2, 75, 91–93, 103
   private and economic rights,
      comparative review
   de-Baathification vs., 93–99,
      95n101
   de-Fascistization vs., 93–99
   de-Nazification vs., 93–99,
      94nn98–99
   liquidation of Japanese
      Zaibatsu vs., 93–99,
      94nn99–100
   transforming occupied Iraq
      applicable rules, 85–87, 85n56
      reforms in, 88–93
Oil Platforms case, 183–85
Oil resources, in Iraq
   Cheney on, 75n13
   Executive Order 13303 and,
      92–93, 92n91
   lack of profit-repatriation in, 36–37

protection of multinational
   corporations and, 36–37,
   71–72, 71n2, 229–30
Okafor, Obiora, ix, 41n181, 220n108
Ol le Njogo v. The Attorney General
   (1913), 67–68, 67nn82–83, 210
Orford, Anne, 55
Organization of African
   Union Conventions on
   Mercenarism, 248
Organization of African Unity
   (OAU). *See now* African Union
Organization of African Unity's
   Convention for the Elimination
   of Mercenarism in Africa, 231

Pacific settlement of disputes
   principle, 149–51
Pacta sunt servanda, 159
Paris Peace Treaty (1783), 54n36,
   116, 117–19
Partnership Africa Canada, 214
Pennsylvania District Court, 122
Percheman, United States v. (1833),
   14, 14n59, 28n119, 43, 60,
   135–37, 136n174
Percy, Sarah V., 252
Permanent Courts of International
   Justice (PCIJ), 232–33
Petroleum corporations, 229–30
Pinckney, Charles Cotesworth, 110
Pirates, 56, 56n49
Pothier, Robert Joseph, 137
Powell, Colin, 34
Power order, 154
Preemption doctrine, 52n31
Presidency, U.S. *See also specific*
   presidents
   designation of war-making
      property by, 5, 5n20
   executive orders, in conduct
      of war, 3, 3n6
Prisoners of war, as slaves, 11–13,
   11n42, 12n49

INDEX 271

Private contractors, in Iraq, 40,
  40n180, 92–93
Private military companies
  limits of self-regulation, 242–47,
    243n73
  exemption from suit
    by U.S., 245–46
  IPOA and, 242–44, 243n71
  State weakness and, 245–47
Private property rights
  conquest and, 43–46, 47–51
  overview, 43–45, 69–70
  civil vs. military aspects of war
    and, 47–48, 50, 50n23
  considerations of humanity,
    50–51, 55–56, 55n45
  continuity of commerce
    and, 49–50
  Rousseau-Portalis doctrine
    and, 48–49, 49n19
  conquest and inconsistent
    extinction of, 51–58
  civil vs. military aspects of war
    and, 54–56
  hegemonic militaries and, 51–54
  war against terrorism and,
    56–58
  in occupied Iraq, 71–103
  overview, 71–75, 100–103
  applicable law and remedies,
    77–80, 77nn14–18, 78n19,
    79n28
  claims of Iraqis, 81–82, 81n38
  claims of Iraqi women, 82–85,
    82n45
  private and economic rights,
    comparative review, 93–99
  transforming of, 85–93
Private security companies
  emerging regulatory rules and
    norms, 247–52
  limits of self-regulation, 242–47
  exemption from suit
    by U.S., 245–46

IPOA and, 242–44, 243n71
State weakness and, 245–47
Private Security Company
  Association of Iraq, 243
Privatization of warfare, overview,
  xvi–xvii
Privatized investment dispute
  forums, 167–68
Prize law, xx
Proclamation of Neutrality, U.S.
  (1793), 108, 120
Promotion and Protection of
  Investments Agreement
  (UK-Egypt), 175–76
Property Claims Commission
  (Iraq), 9–10, 9n35,
  95–96, 95n105
PSNR (Resolution on the
  Permanent Sovereignty over
  Natural Resource) (UN, 1962),
  164, 164n63

Racism
  disregard of private property
    rights and, xx
  Dred Scott viewpoint and, 5
Reciprocity
  fairness and, 154–55, 154n33
  lack of for developing economies,
    144, 154–55
  between Western industrialized
    countries, 144
Rehnquist, William, 3n7
Religion, xxi–xxii. *See also*
  Christian religion
Reno, Richard, 213, 213n80
Reno, William, 195, 195n15
Republican Party, 120
Republic of South Africa, 59–61
Resolution 1267 (UN), 7–8, 7n29
Resolution 1373 (UN), 5–6, 235–36
Resolution 1483 (UN), 89, 89n75, 91
Resolution 1735 (UN), 235–36
Resolution 1803 (UN), 39n176

Resolution on the Permanent
  Sovereignty over Natural
  Resources (UN-PSNR, 1962),
  164, 164n63
Resource-extraction wars
  overview, xiv, xvii, 191–200,
    220–22
  history of, 200–211
    Belgium's African colonies,
      200–207
    British acquisition of Swazi
      Territory, 207–11, 209n66
    colonial mercantile
      companies, 200–207,
      202n34
    Great Britain's African
      colonies, 200–207
    International African
      Association and, 201–7
    taxation and, 198–99
  non-State actors and, 192–200,
    193n8
  smuggling and, 194, 194n13
  public vs. private distinction,
    211–20
    Kimberley Process and, 198,
      214–17, 215n86, 215n88,
      216nn90–91
    monopolization of violence
      and, 191–211, 197n19
    sham States and, 192–200
Responsibilities of Transnational
  Corporations and Other
  Business Enterprises With
  Regard to Human Rights (UN
  Draft Norms), 251
Revolutionary United Front (RUF),
  212, 212n76, 225–26
Richardson, Henry III, 52n31
Rome Statute of the International
  Criminal Court, 238
Roosevelt, Franklin D., 150
Root, Elihu, 148–49
Rousseau, Jean-Jacques, 71

Rousseau-Portalis doctrine, 48–49,
  49n19
Rudko, Frances Howell, 132–33
Rules of law as politics, 154–55
Rumsfeld, Donald, 90
Rwanda, 238

Sabbatino, Banco Sabbatino
  de Cuba v. (1964), 164–65
Said, Edward, 100–101
Sanctions Committee (UN), 7–8
Sands v. Knox (1806), 132–33
Sanford, Henry S., 202–5, 202n35
Schabas, William, 239
Scott, William, 136–37
Second Confiscation Act
  (1862), 5, 5n15
Security companies. *See* Private
  security companies
Seeman, Talbot v. (1801), 25, 124–28
Sequestration law, 117–19
Serendib Seafoods
  Limited, 168–77
Shadow States, 192–200,
  195n15, 219
Sham States, 192–200, 195n15, 219
Shattuck, Jared, 131
Shattuck, Maley v. (1806), 131
Sierra Leone
  Montreux Document and, 249–52
  resource conflicts and, 211
    Executive Outcomes and,
      223–24, 224n3, 225–27,
      227n13
    Gurkha Security Guards
      and, 226n10
    RUF and, 212, 225, 226n10
  United Nations and, 247
  war crime tribunals and, 238
Sierra Leone Truth and
  Reconciliation
  Commission, 224, 247
Singer, Joseph, 19
Sixth Amendment, 3n4

Slaughter, Anne Marie, 101
Slaves
  prisoners of war as, 11–13, 11n42, 12n49
  as property, 4–5, 5n15
Smuggling, 194, 194n13
Sobhuza II v. Miller (1926), 207–11, 209n66
Somalia, 84–85, 195, 195n15
South Africa, 214, 248–49, 248n88
South Korea, 162
Sovereignty, absolutist rule and, 2–3, 2n3
Spain
  CERDS and, 163–64
  early superiority of, 23n93, 105
  land grants and, 61n61
  Native Americans and, 61–69, 142
  rights of neutrals and, 129
  treaty with U.S., 45n7
Spanish Constitution (1812), 16–17, 16n67
Sri Lanka
  AAPL case and, 168–77, 169n77, 170n82, 172n98, 173n101
  BIT with UK and N. Ireland, 169n76, 172–75, 172n98, 173n101
  ICSID and, 163
  Tamil Tigers and, xix, 168–77
Stanley, Henry M., 202, 202n34, 202n37, 205–6, 206n55
State Department, U.S.
  on Hague Regulations, 90
  on Israel occupation of Gulf of Suez, 18n76, 45n8
  on trade in Congo basin, 203
State succession doctrine, 49n21, 158–59
Status of Forces Agreement (2008), 246, 246n84
Story, Joseph, 129–31
Strange, Susan, 188n153

Strong, William, 4
Strong vs. weak States. See also specific States
  overview, ix–x, 144
  absolutist rule and, xvii–xviii
  rule of law and, 101–3
  rules of belligerent occupation and, 73
Strother v. Lucas (1838), 61–69, 62n62
Structural power, 188, 188n153
Sudan, 229, 229n24
Sunmonu v. Disu Raphael (1927), 68
Supreme Court, U.S. See also specific cases and justices
  on confiscation of cotton, xviii 3–4, 14, 14n58, 21–22, 22n89
  on doctrine of suspension, 21, 21n84, 133, 133n164
  on habeas for detainees, 41n182
  on international investment rules, 161–62
  on international law, 165n67
  on rights of British creditors, 119
  on rules of neutrality, xx, 122
  on sovereign confiscatory rights, 25, 28
  on Spanish land grants, 61n61
  nonrecognition of Native American land rights and, 61–69, 63n64, 64n70, 66n76
Supreme Court of Nigeria, 68, 68n87
Suspension and restoration doctrine, 21–22, 133, 133n164
Swaziland, 207–11, 209n66
Switzerland, 249

Talbot v. Seeman (1801), 25, 124–28
Taliban regime, 7
Tamil Tigers, xix, 168–77

Terrorism, war against. *See also specific countries and organizations*
  Arab stereotypes and, 100–101
  confiscation of financial assets, 5–10, 5n21, 7n29, 58n54, 235–36
  conquest and inconsistent extinction of private property/ contract rights, 56–58
  Counter-Terrorism Committee and, 6, 6n22, 57–58, 57n50, 58n54
  non-State actors and, 56–58, 236
  Obama administration on, 57n51
  U.S. National Security Strategy on, 57, 57n51, 74n8
  as war, 48n15
Thompson, Janice, 201, 201n32
Thompson, Smith, 141
Thorburn and Watkin company, 207–11
356 Bales of Cotton, American Insurance Co. v. (1828), 3–4
Trade, reciprocity and, 144, 154–55, 154n33
Trade Promotion Authority Act (2001), 166–67
Trail of Tears, 141
Treasury Department, U.S., 37–38
Treaties. *See also specific treaties*
  native tribes and, 67–68, 67nn82–83
  post-World War I, 53–54
  State succession doctrine and, 158–59
Treaty of Ghent (1814), 114
Trenchard, John, 1

Uganda, 19, 19n79, 177–78
Uniform Code of Military Justice, U.S., 90
Unintended consequences of war, 55n45
United Kingdom. *See also specific cases and countries*
  BIT with Egypt, 175–76
  CERDS and, 163–64
  diamond imports and, 214
  early superiority of, xx, 105
  European Convention on Human Rights and, 98–99, 98n114, 99n116
  hegemony and non-European property
  prerogative of the Crown over corporate private property, 59–61, 60n58
  licenses for trading with enemies, 50
  Maori land tenure and, 67
  Montreux Document and, 249–52
  post-World War II property confiscation, 54
  private military and security companies and, 236–37, 243n73, 249, 249n90
  on sovereignty and property rights, 15, 15n60
United Nations. *See also specific divisions and Resolutions*
  Charter on use of force, 150–52, 150n18, 182, 182n136
  endorsement of War Against Terrorism, 57–58
  establishment of, xvi, 145
  Group of 77 and, 160–62
  mercenarism and, xxi–xxii
  peacekeeping forces, 227
  sanctions on Iraq, 83
  sham States as members, 195, 195n15
  Sierra Leone and, 247
United Self Defense Forces of Colombia (AUC), 228–29
United States. *See also Military, U.S.; Native Americans; specific cases and presidents*
  American exceptionalism, 101, 101n122, 102n127
  BIT with Zaire, 175–76, 176n111
  Central Asian objectives, 75, 75n13

CERDS and, 163–64
diamond imports and, 214
as early weak State, xx, 23–28,
    23n94, 105–7
economic relations with Native
    Americans, 137–43
Executive Orders
    13303, 92–93, 92n91, 245
confiscation and, 3, 3n6
foreign investors in, 166–67,
    167n72
France and
    confiscation of American cargo,
        23–26, 23n93, 124, 124n100
    early economic dependence
        on, 107–14
    embargo against, 26–27,
        26nn115–16
    opposition to Iraq occupation,
        36n159
funding of restitution for
    Holocaust victims, 241
GATT security escape clause
    and, 180–82
Great Britain and
    confiscation of American
        cargo, 23–26, 23n93
    early economic dependence
        on, 107–14
    embargo against, 26–27,
        26nn115–16
Hague Regulations and
    compliance with in Japan, 79
    on force and debt contracts, 152
Iraq occupation
    confiscation of Baathist property,
        xx, 8–10, 8n31, 9nn34–35
    economic intervention
        by, 36–40
    UN Security Council and, 36,
        88–89, 89n75
    licenses for trading with
        enemies, 50
neutrality and, xx, 22–28, 108,
    119–21, 122

Nicaragua and, 180–82, 180n125,
    180n128, 183, 184
preemption doctrine, 52n31, 74n11
private military and security
    companies and, 236–37, 248–49
quasi-war, first, 124–28
recognition of International
    Association of the Congo, 203,
    203n42
Saddam Hussein regime
    change and, 88
Status of Forces Agreement
    and, 246, 246n84
as superpower
    hegemonic military of, 51–54
    international law and, 51–52,
        51n29, 52nn31–32
treaty with Spain, 45n7
war and separation of powers,
    79n30, 80–81
United States Trade Representative
    (USTR), 168n74
Universal values, western
    values as, 96
UN Security Council
    authorization of war, ix
    Counter-Terrorism Committee
        Iraq War and, 6, 57n50
    mandate of, 6n22
    on non-State actors, 236
    U.S. anti-terrorism and, 57–58,
        58n54
    CPA and, 89, 89n75
    Iraq War and, 6, 36, 57n50,
        88–89, 89n75
    Israel and, 53nn34–35
    refusal of consent to use of
        force in Iraq, 36
    Resolution 1267, 7–8, 7n29
    Resolution 1373, 5–6, 235–36
    Resolution 1483, 89, 89n75, 91
    Resolution 1735, 235–36
    Resolution 1803, 39n176
    Sanctions Committee, 7–8
UN World Summit (2005), 6, 6n22

van Anraat, Frank Cornelis
  Adrianus, 240
van Bynkershoek, Cornelius, 12, 137
Vattel, Emer de, 46, 46nn10–11, 121
Venezuela
  blockade of, 147, 147n2
  Drago doctrine and, xx–xxi, 155–56
  opposition to ICSID, 166, 166n71
Venus, The case (1814), 136–37
Versailles Treaty, 54nn36–37
Vienna Convention of the Law of
  Treaties, 80n31
Violence, monopolization of, xvii,
  191–211, 197n19
Virginia, 117
Vitoria, Francisco de
  on Native Americans, 141n207, 142
  justification for killing of, 142
  on sovereign confiscatory
    rights, 31–36
Voting rights, 27, 27n118

Wai, Robert, ix, 148n7, 154n28,
  187n149, 218n97
Walker, Jones v. (1791), 118
Walker, Thomas, 118
War
  antiterrorism as, 48n15
  civil vs. military aspects of,
    47–48, 50n23, 54–56
  contract rights vs. commerce
    in, 49–50
  high-tech, 54–56
  necessities of, 46–47, 48n15
  Rousseau-Portalis doctrine,
    48–49, 49n19
  State monopolization
    of, 191–93, 191n1
War and commerce, 1–42
  overview, 1–2, 40–42
  confiscation and
    balance between, 20–28
    commerce during wartime,
      14–20

exceptional circumstances
  doctrine, 28–40
  justification for, 2–14
War crimes. *See* International
  Criminal Court
War destruction, state responsibility
  for, 185–88
Ware, John Tyndale, 118
Ware v. Hylton (1796), 118–19, 134
War of 1812, 27–28, 111–12
War powers, as justification for
  confiscation, 3–5, 3n4
Wars, commercialization
  of, 223–55
  overview, 223–25, 252–55
  accountability of economic
    actors, 237–42
  banking system and, 239–40
  incorporation and, 237–38,
    238n51
  deferring accountability
    and, 225–30
  mercenaries and international
    law, 230–37
  mercenary, definitions
    of, 230–32
  payment with natural
    resources, 233–34
  terrorism and, 235–37
  private military companies and
    limits of self-regulation, 242–47
  private security companies and
    emerging regulatory rules and
      norms, 247–52
    limits of self-regulation, 242–47
Washington, George
  ban on armed merchant
    ships, 110
  as leader of Army, 111
  Neutrality Proclamation, 108, 120
  use of ports by British and, 109
Watson, Alan, 11–13, 11n42
*Wena Hotels Ltd. v. Arab Republic
  of Egypt* (2000), 176–77

INDEX 277

West Bank, 51, 53nn34-35
Western universalism, 35-36, 35n154
West Rand Central Gold Mining Company v. The King (1905), 59-61, 68n89, 69
Williams, Robert A., 31n134, 32n140, 142n210
Women, Iraqi occupation and, 82-85, 82n45
Worcester v. Georgia (1832), 139n197, 141-42
World Bank, 199
World Diamond Council, 214-15
World Trade Organization (WTO), 182, 215n87
World War I, 53-54, 54n36
World War II. See also Military, U.S. occupation and private property rights during, xx
post-war institutions, 145
post-war occupations
  comparative review, 93-99
  justification for, 86-87
  treaties and confiscation, 53-54, 54nn36-37

Young v. United States (1877), 14, 14n58
Yugoslavia, former, 238

Zaibatsu, Japanese, 93-99, 94nn99-100
Zaire, 175-76, 176n111